AS Level and A Level
Economics

CAMBRIDGE International Examinations

AS Level and A Level

Economics

Colin Bamford
Keith Brunskill
Gordon Cain
Sue Grant
Stephen Munday
Stephen Walton

CAMBRIDGE
UNIVERSITY PRESS

PUBLISHED BY THE PRESS SYNDICATE OF THE UNIVERSITY OF CAMBRIDGE
The Pitt Building, Trumpington Street, Cambridge, United Kingdom

CAMBRIDGE UNIVERSITY PRESS
The Edinburgh Building, Cambridge CB2 2RU, UK
40 West 20th Street, New York, NY 10011-4211, USA
477 Williamstown Road, Port Melbourne, VIC 3207, Australia
Ruiz de Alarcón 13, 28014 Madrid, Spain
Dock House, The Waterfront, Cape Town 8001, South Africa

http://www.cambridge.org

First published 2002
Third printing 2003

Printed in the United Kingdom at the University Press, Cambridge

Typeface Minion   *System* Apple Macintosh Quark® 4.04

A catalogue record for this book is available from the British Library

ISBN   0521 00781 X   paperback

Cover photo © Randy Faris/Corbis

The question on page 57 is reproduced with the kind permission of OCR.
The specimen papers and the questions on pages 60 and 69 are reproduced by permission of the University of Cambridge Local Examinations Syndicate.

Unless otherwise stated photographs courtesy of SA Picture Research.

The answers to selected self-assessment tasks are wholly the responsibility of the authors.

Every effort has been made to reach copyright holders of material in this book previously published elsewhere. The publisher would be pleased to hear from anyone whose rights they have unwittingly infringed.

The publisher has used its best endeavours to ensure that the URLs for external websites referred to in this book are correct and active at the time of going to press. However, the publisher has no responsiblity for the websites and can make no guarantee that a site will remain live or that the content will remain appropriate.

Contents

(handwritten notes)
- Inflation
- Economic growth
- price elasticity
- cost
- Demand/Supply

Contributors

Colin Bamford is Professor and Head of the Department of Logistics and Hospitality Management at the University of Huddersfield. He has written various applied Economics textbooks and published widely in his specialist field of transport economics. He is currently Chief Examiner in Economics with OCR and has over 30 years experience of examining Cambridge International and UK A Levels.

Keith Brunskill was formerly Head of Economics at Greenhead College, Huddersfield. He is currently a part-time member of staff at Huddersfield University Business School. An experienced A Level examiner with various examination boards, he has written a wide range of articles on topical areas of Economics.

Gordon Cain is a Sector Manager in Administration, Management and Business at Bury College. He has taught A Level Economics in a range of schools and colleges and has over 20 years experience of examining at A Level for the Cambridge board. He is a senior examiner with CIE and OCR, specialising in development economics.

Sue Grant is a Lecturer in Economics at West Oxfordshire College. She is an experienced A Level examiner and has written various text books and articles on Economics. She is a Principal Examiner with OCR and has a specialist area of interest in macroeconomic policies.

Stephen Munday is a Head Teacher at a school in Cambridge. An experienced A Level teacher, he has produced various textbooks on Economics. He is a Principal Examiner with OCR, with a specialist interest in the Economics of market failures.

Stephen Walton is Head of Economics at the Kings School Chester, having previously taught in Surrey. He is Principal Examiner with OCR and is a specialist in aspects of the Economics of Europe.

All authors have also contributed to the companion UK text, *Economics for AS*, published by CUP in 2000.

Preface

This book has been specifically produced for the new Cambridge International Examination (CIE) in Economics which has been introduced for examination for the first time in 2001 (AS) and 2002 (A Level).

The text is divided into two main units, Core (AS Level) and Extension (A Level), both of which represent a self-contained programme of study for students taking the CIE examinations. The Core unit provides for the new AS Level as well as an underpinning for students who wish to complete the A Level.

The book has been produced by six authors, all of whom have substantial teaching experience and who currently have senior examining roles with CIE or OCR, the UK awarding body for AS Level and A Level examinations.

The book has various important distinctive features:

◆ It is endorsed by CIE for use in its examinations.
◆ The subject content is arranged into two units, each of which is fully compatible with the CIE syllabus.
◆ The 'Introduction' provides students with the skills they will need to succeed in the AS Level and A Level examinations; a section on 'Preparing for examinations' provides specific advice on how these skills and concepts will be examined by the CIE and includes specimen CIE question papers.
◆ Self-assessment tasks are included in each chapter. These are designed for student-centred activity and for use by teachers in class situations. A small number of answers to these tasks have been provided for guidance.
◆ Each chapter contains key economic terms and concepts, which are all compatible with those provided by the CIE in Appendix C of the syllabus. The most important of these have been defined alphabetically in a glossary at the end of the book. The terms are deliberately set out for the Core and Extension sections of the syllabus to help students in their work and to assist teachers in the delivery of the syllabus.

Although the book has been specifically produced for the CIE's new Economics examination, it will also be of value to students and teachers of other CIE A Level Economics syllabuses. In particular, where possible, examples have been drawn from developing and newly industrialised economies. Some of the self-assessment tasks require students to draw upon their own economy. The book, therefore, has a wider appeal as a core text for international students.

Finally, could I record my thanks to the various people who have made the production of this text possible. In particular to: my fellow contributors who have responded positively to produce this book; my colleague, Tony Emery, Principal Examiner at CIE, for his comments on the draft text; Anne Rix for her prodding, prompting and dedication in managing the project; Karen Brooke for word processing the text; my wife Elisabeth and daughters Emily and Alice for their understanding and patience during the many hours I spent working on the manuscript.

My sincere hope is that this book will be well-received by students and teachers of the Cambridge International Examinations in Economics, in particular to help students achieve examination success and a long-lasting interest in the fascinating subject of Economics.

Colin G. Bamford
September 2001

Introduction
The economist's 'tool kit' and the Cambridge international examinations

On completion of this introduction you should:

➤ have a broad idea of what is meant by Economics
➤ know how economists seek to explain economic phenomena
➤ be aware of the 'tool kit' of skills required at AS Level and A Level
➤ be aware of the structure of the CIE AS/A Level Economics syllabus

What is Economics?

There are almost as many definitions of Economics as there are economists! Although a definition of the subject is to be expected, it is probably more useful at this stage to set out a few examples of the sort of issues which concern professional economists. These topics occur in an introductory form in the CIE AS syllabus and are developed further at A Level.

Let us take yourself first of all. Most teenagers find that they want to lead an exciting and full life but unfortunately do not always have the money necessary to do everything they would like to do. So, choices have to be made or, as an economist would say, individuals have to decide:

how to allocate scarce resources in the most effective way.

A body of economic principles and concepts has been developed to explain how people and also businesses react in this situation. This is a typical example of what an economist would refer to as '**microeconomics**'.

It is not only individuals and firms who are faced with having to make choices. Governments face many such problems. For example, how does your government decide how much to spend on the health service and how much should go into providing social security benefits? This is the same type of problem facing all of us in our daily lives but on a different scale.

The UK government for example has extensive responsibilities in looking after the well-being of the national economy. The Chancellor of the Exchequer prepares an annual budget for the economy, in which taxation and government expenditure plans are reviewed. It is also an opportunity to 'manage the economy', by seeking to ensure that policy objectives are being met. As the economist would say, the Chancellor has to decide:

'how to keep the rate of change of prices under control' or, alternatively, 'how to reflate the economy to increase the number of jobs which are available'.

These are typical topics which come under the broad heading of '**macroeconomics**' since they relate to the economy as a whole.

As you progress through this text you will come across many other economic problems and issues of both a micro and macro nature. You may now find it useful to complete the following self-assessment tasks.

Self-assessment tasks

1 Make a list, in your own words, of some of the economic decisions that:
   ◆ you are facing;
   ◆ your family has to take;
   ◆ your country has to take.
2 Pick up any quality newspaper. Look through it systematically and make a note of the various:
   ◆ microeconomic,
   ◆ macroeconomic,
   problems and issues you find.
   Have you found it easy to classify problems in this way?

The 'haves' and 'have nots' – Rocinha Slum, Rio de Janeiro, Brazil, with the prosperous city in the background
Source: Mark Edwards, Still Pictures.

The last part of the task is designed to get you to appreciate that many economic problems and issues cannot be satisfactorily classified as micro or macro. In other words, such problems encompass both of the main branches of Economics. For example, an increase in health prescription charges may reduce the demand for prescriptions from patients – depending on the extent of this there is an effect on the income of individuals and the government, and, in turn, this affects the economy as a whole. So, there can be complex inter-relationships coming into play. In many respects this makes Economics an interesting subject to study.

As you progress through this text, you will be introduced to concepts, theories and models which are used by economists to explain the many economic problems and issues which come within the scope of Economics. In time, you will build up a portfolio of such techniques, from both micro- and macroeconomic perspectives. Virtually all have their origin in some sort of empirical investigation, that is to say a study of real economic phenomena. Some concepts have their origin 200 years ago, others are much more contemporary or may have been refined and revised in the light of the growing complexity of the present-day global economy. Again, this serves to enhance the interesting nature of the subject.

Regardless of what you may think about Economics and economists at this stage of your studies, few would deny that Economics is a logical subject and that the advice provided by economists is derived from a set of well-established principles relating to the operation of the market economy. Figure 1 shows in simple terms how economists think and how they seek to explain real problems and issues like those you will have come across in the Self-assessment task above.

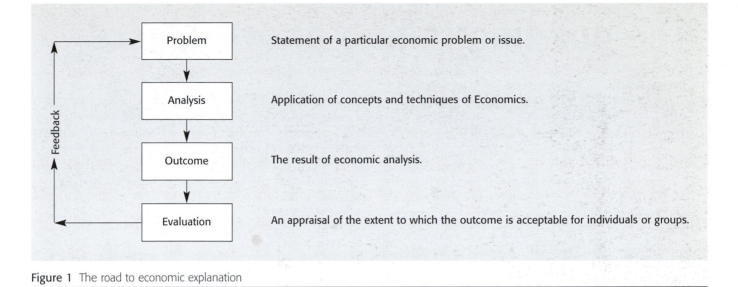

Figure 1 The road to economic explanation

At this stage, bear the process shown in figure 1 in mind and return to it whenever you are learning new concepts as it will help you understand how economists think and operate.

Economists cannot always be certain about what they say or the advice they might provide. Much of the content of this book though consists of **positive statements** which are descriptive and usually acceptable to all economists. For example:

◆ the inflation rate in 1999 was 2.5 per cent;
◆ the inflation rate of 2.5 per cent in 1999 provided an improvement in business confidence;
◆ the Quantity Theory of Money can be used to explain why inflation occurs in an economy.

On other occasions, economists make **normative statements** involving value judgements. For example:

◆ the government should cut fuel tax to reduce the rate of inflation,
◆ public sector workers should reduce their demands for higher wages.

These latter statements are expressing an opinion as to what ought to happen. Unlike positive statements, where economists can use data and empirical evidence, normative statements involve value judgements which are often drawn from the economist's personal views, political beliefs and ethics. As you study the context of the units, keep this important distinction in mind. You will also need to think about it when answering some of the more demanding CIE examination questions.

To conclude, therefore, it is appropriate to give a clear definition of 'What is Economics?' For a start,

Economics is a social science – it adopts a scientific framework but is particularly concerned with studying human behaviour, as consumers, in business or in taking decisions about the economy as a whole. More specifically:

Economics is the study of how scarce resources are or should be allocated.

All of the problems and issues you will come across fit into this broad definition.

Self-assessment task

Think again about what you have found out in completing the first self-assessment tasks. Now read the article from *The Economist* on the so-called puzzling failure of Economics. Do you agree at this early stage of your studies with what the author is saying? Why might you not yet be in a position to make a proper evaluation?

The economist's 'tool kit'

The economist has a varied 'tool kit', the term that can be used to describe the skills and techniques available for the analysis of economic problems. Two of particular relevance are:

◆ the ability to interpret and use data;
◆ the ability to write in a clear and effective way.

Each of these will now be considered. *You may find it helpful to return to these pages when you are undertaking some of the self-assessment tasks in the main units of the book. You should also refer back to these pages before you take any of the CIE examinations.*

The puzzling failure of economics

If the world were run by economists, would it be a better place? You might expect economists, not to mention a newspaper called *The Economist*, to think so. After all, many of the policies that people fight over have economics at their core – jobs, wages, investment, growth. Economists, professional and otherwise, are forever criticising those who do run the world for making such a mess of it, and are keen to change the way people think so that things will be run more to their liking. As one Nobel laureate put it, 'I don't care who writes a nation's laws ... if I can write its economics textbooks.'

Paul Samuelson, the author of that remark, has seen his wish fulfilled. His 'Economics', first published in 1948, has sold millions of copies and is still, with its 16th edition in preparation, doing well. Down the editions, the book's views on policy have changed, as have those of the profession at large. These shifting ideas have in turn influenced policy, and to a degree that would make other social scientists drool. Lately the results have been good. During the past decade, some of the worst economic incompetence has ended: central planning has given way to 'transition economics' in Eastern Europe and the former Soviet Union; many developing countries have opened their economies to the outside world; every week another state-run company is put up for sale. Textbook wisdom seems to prevail.

The message and the messenger

But don't praise the dismal scientists too much. Who designed those earlier policies, which failed so disastrously? Economists. Where were those theories of planning, of demand management, of industrial dirigisme and public ownership that did such harm in the third world so persuasively set out? In economics textbooks.

These days, it is true, the advice is better – but it often gets dangerously garbled in transmission. Trade is the best example. By pitting exporters against importers, successive rounds of trade negotiations have encouraged politicians in many countries to lower trade barriers. Yet this effort is based on a false premise: that freeing trade is good for you only if other countries do the same. This basic misunderstanding, left unattended, may one day lead governments to turn back the clock on liberal trade.

Other good policies have likewise been founded on bad economics. Privatisation, for instance, has more often been seen as a way to raise revenue than as a way to promote competition; and deregulation is often portrayed by governments as something that global markets have forced upon them, rather than as a way of raising living standards. As for bad policies based on bad economics, these remain too numerous to mention, despite Mr Samuelson's prodigious efforts.

Why has economics not done better? Economists tend to blame others for being too lazy or too stupid to understand their textbooks. There is doubtless something in this. Economics is hard to teach well. To the uninitiated, its basic principles often seem surprising or odd. And whereas most people will admit their ignorance of physics or biology, the armchair economist is convinced that he knows exactly what he is talking about.

But the economics profession itself also deserves much of the blame. Crucial ideas about the role of prices and markets, the basic principles of microeconomics, are uncontroversial among economists. These are the first ideas that politicians and the public need to grasp if they are to think intelligently about public policy, and the fact is that they are not widely understood. Yet because economists take these essential ideas for granted, they spend their time arguing about much more contentious notions, developed in one disputed way or another from those common underlying principles. The public and their politicians are treated to perpetual squabbles about the exact effects of raising interest rates or of cutting the capital-gains tax or whatever – and conclude that economists disagree about everything and understand nothing. As long as economists choose to talk loudest about the things they understand least well and to remain silent about the underlying ideas that unite them, this is unlikely to change.

And economists must shoulder a further portion of the blame for quite another reason. The biggest economic-policy mistake of the past 50 years, in rich and poor countries alike, has been and still is to expect too much of government. Statism has always found all the support it needs among mainstream economists. They are unfailingly quick to point out various species of market failure; they are usually much slower to ask whether the supposed remedy of government intervention might not, in practice, be worse.

This is not a failure of economics, in fact, but of modern (one might say Samuelsonian) economics. The classical economists viewed the market economy with a kind of awe. Amazing, it truly is, that all these workers, firms and households, acting without visible co-ordination and guided mainly by self-interest, manage to produce such extraordinarily beneficial results. Smith's 'Wealth of Nations' conveyed this sense that the market, for all its 'failures', is a marvel. Today precious few textbooks even try to guide their readers to any such inspiration. Implicitly, at least, their message is too often quite the opposite: that markets aren't perfect and governments (advised by economists) can be. Dismal is the word.

Source: *The Economist*, 23 August 1997.

Data skills

Five main skills are required in the AS specification – they will be further examined at the A level stage. These skills are:

◆ the ability to pick out the main trends and features in economic data;

◆ a knowledge of fractions, percentages, proportions and the rate of change in a set of time-series data;

◆ a working knowledge of index numbers;

◆ how to calculate a simple average and know what it means;

◆ how to understand economic information produced in visual form.

In addition, you will find it useful to know:

◆ what is meant by a forecast.

Each of the above will now be looked at. It is important that you feel confident in handling data – these simple skills will help you. You will also gain confidence as you become more familiar with economic data and complete the various self-assessment tasks in each section.

Economic data generally are of two main types. These are:

Time-series data – as the name suggests, the same information is recorded over a period of time, namely a period of years, for months in a year, days in a week and so on.

Cross-sectional data – the easiest way to imagine this type of data is in terms of a 'snapshot', that is a picture taken at a given time.

Another important introductory point concerns the nature of the data itself. Again two types can be recognised, namely:

Discrete data – the simplest way to imagine these is in terms of values which are shown as whole numbers, for example the number of people or number of cars.

Continuous data – such values can usually be measured in a precise way and are not confined to whole numbers, for example income, hours of work or economic growth.

So, when you are confronted with economic data for the first time, ask yourself:

◆ Is the data shown time-series or cross-sectional data?

◆ Are the values of the data discrete or continuous?

Data skill 1 – How to pick out the main trends and features in economic data

Look more carefully at the data in table 1. (You will find specific reference to unemployment statistics in section 5.)

The very first skill you need to develop is what is known as 'eyeballing'. All this means is looking down a column of data or going across rows of data very quickly. In examinations you should do this before you start answering the questions. For time-series data, like those in table 1, you might find it useful to very quickly write a '+' or a '–' between each year so you can see how the data changes over time. This is shown in the final column of the table. You can now tell from this that broadly speaking:

◆ unemployment fell at the beginning of the time period;

◆ it then increased for three years;

◆ it then fell consistently for the remaining years.

You can also get an overview of the data by comparing the end points in a time series, in this case 1989 and 1998. What is useful is to know how much the variable (in this case unemployment) fell over the period. To do this, you need to compare the total fall with the original level. The best way to do this is to calculate the *percentage change*. Using a calculator, this is

$$\frac{(2075 - 1766)}{2075} = 14.9\% \text{ (fall)}$$

Year	Number (in '000's)	Rate[2]	Annual charge
1989	2,075	7.2	
1990	1,974	6.8	–
1991	2,414	8.4	+
1992	2,769	9.7	+
1993	2,936	10.3	+
1994	2,736	9.6	–
1995	2,454	8.6	–
1996	2,334	8.2	–
1997	2,034	7.1	–
1998	1,766	6.1	–

Table 1 UK Unemployment 1989–1998[1]
Notes:
[1] Measured in Spring of each year.
[2] Total unemployment as a percentage of all economically active persons.
Source: Annual Abstract of Statistics, 1999, Office for National Statistics.

In other words, there has been a fall in unemployment of around 15 per cent over the period shown.

Looking at the cross-sectional data in table 2, you might find it useful to stand back and pick out the main patterns in these data. For example, you could look at the highest and lowest values and the difference between them. This is sometimes called the range. You could also see how each observation compares with the average. When you do this, you will find that:

- there is a difference of 3.9 per cent between the highest and the lowest;
- the average has relatively little regional significance – it is clear though that some regions, for example the South East and the East Midlands, are doing better than others;
- the peripheral regions in the UK, for example Scotland and the North West, have the highest unemployment rates;
- the rate for London is very high, particularly when compared with the South East.

Both of these techniques are simple to apply – between them they give you a very useful insight into cross-sectional economic data.

Region	%	
North East	6.1	
North West	8.2	
Yorkshire and Humberside	7.0	
East Midlands	4.9	
West Midlands	6.3	UK average 6.1%
Eastern	5.0	
London	8.1	
South East	4.3	
South West	4.5	
Scotland	7.4	
Wales	6.7	
Northern Ireland	7.3	

Table 2 UK regional unemployment rates 1998[1]
Note: [1] Seasonally adjusted.
Sources: As table 1.

Data skill 2 – Fractions, percentages, proportions and the rate of change

The simple calculations required to work with fractions, percentages and proportions should be well known to students with a knowledge of mathematics. (The use of percentage change over a period of time has already been referred to earlier.) Fractions, percentages and proportions are not far removed from each other – they are the same thing but with different names.

Let us stay with unemployment. Suppose a town has an economically active population of 50,000 and of these 5,000 are unemployed. The unemployment rate is therefore 1 in 10 or 1/10 as a fraction, 0.10 as a proportion and 10 per cent as a percentage. The mathematical relationship is that a fraction can be converted into a proportion by dividing the bottom number or denominator into the upper number or numerator. By multiplying this by 100, a percentage can be obtained. Knowing these relatively straightforward links helps in understanding economic data.

The idea of *rate of change* is rather more difficult to grasp. It is a very relevant mathematical tool widely used and applied in Economics. Referring back to table 1, if we look at the period 1993–8, unemployment has fallen from 2.936m to 1.766m. In other words, it has fallen by 1.170m or 1,170,000 people over a period of five years. In turn, this represents a percentage fall of $1.17/2.936 \times 100\%$, that is approximately 40 per cent over this time. Averaged out, this is an 8 per cent fall per year or a rate of change of 8 per cent per annum.

Looking at table 1, we can also see that the rate of change varied over the years in question. For example, there was a particularly steep fall between 1996 and 1997 (12.9 per cent) and a modest fall from 1995 to 1996 (4.9 per cent). The figures in brackets, which are rates of change per annum, when looked at over a shorter period of time, do vary from the 8 per cent over a five year period. So, when using a rate of change, be very careful to always specify the time period you are working with.

A final word of warning. Often with economic data absolute totals for a variable might increase, but this increase might be at a slower rate of change than in the past. Going back to table 1, if we look at the period 1990–1993, then unemployment increased from 1.974m to 2.936m. It increased in absolute terms for each year within this time window. However, the rate of change or increase varied quite dramatically from just over 22 per cent between 1990 and 1991 to 6 per cent between 1992 and 1993. If you are faced with these rates of change in isolation, you might be led to conclude that unemployment fell between 1992 and 1993, which is clearly not the case. Unemployment continued to increase – it was, though, growing at a slower rate during the period. So, once again, be careful when looking at data where rates of change are being used.

Data skill 3 – A working knowledge of index numbers

Table 3 contains a very familiar and useful set of data for economists (see section 5 for more details). Very simply, the 'Index of Retail Prices' attempts to measure the underlying inflation rate, that is the annual price change for a wide basket of goods and services which are purchased by consumers. Not only is this series an index in itself, it is usual to represent it in terms of a *base year or date*. So, 1985 is the base year and it is given an index of 100. What this means is that the value for 1985 acts as the base value. Subsequent values are calculated in terms of the percentage change from this initial figure. For example, between 1985 and 1986, the Index of Retail Prices rose 3.4 per cent. If the typical basket of shopping in 1985 had cost £20, in 1986 it would have cost £20.68. Although this is a gross simplification it illustrates how index numbers can be compiled.

So to construct an index number:

- choose a base value or a value for a base date and assign this an index of 100;
- divide it by 100;
- divide every subsequent value by this amount to calculate the index number for that value or year.

A crude 'eyeballing' of these data indicates that:

- retail prices have persistently increased on a year-on-year basis over the whole period;
- the annual rate of change has been more variable – it was particularly high between 1989 and 1990;
- there has been some relative slowing down in the rate of increase towards the end of the period.

Data skill 4 – How to calculate a simple average and know what it means

The *average* is a measure which is often used to summarise a particular set of data. Most of you will have come across it in mathematics, more specifically through being able to calculate various measures of average, such as the mean, median and mode. These different measures have their strengths and weaknesses from a mathematical standpoint. For the

1986	103.4
1987	107.7
1988	113.0
1989	121.8
1990	133.3
1991	141.8
1992	146.4
1993	148.7
1994	152.4
1995	157.1
1996	161.0
1997	165.9
1998	171.0

Table 3 'Index of Retail Prices' in the UK, 1986–1998 (1985 = 100)
Source: *Economic Trends*, 1999, Office for National Statistics.

economist, usually through an arithmetic mean or weighted average, individual comparisons can be made in relation to the average for the population group as a whole. A good illustration of this is shown in table 4 where the living standards in 12 of the economies of East and Southern Africa are compared with the average for a larger part of the continent. Section 11 of this book explains why the first indicator shown in table 4, GDP per head, is a good measure of living standards. It should also be recognised that for developing economies like those in table 4, the purchasing power parity measure shown in the second column of the table is an even better measure. It is therefore clear that all data should be looked at carefully before drawing any conclusions.

	$	PPP[1]
Botswana	3,240	6032
Ethiopia	100	599
Kenya	360	975
Lesotho	550	2,058
Malawi	190	581
Mozambique	230	797
Namibia	1,890	5,369
Rwanda	250	n.a[2]
South Africa	3,160	8,318
Uganda	320	1136
Zambia	320	686
Zimbabwe	520	2,470
Average for Sub-Saharan Africa	500	1,450

Table 4 GDP per head in selected countries of East and Southern Africa in 1999 ($US)
Notes: [1] Purchasing power parity. [2] n.a. – not available.

Self-assessment task

Study the data in table 4.

(a) What can you deduce about relative living standards in these African countries?

(b) What relevance might these data have for an economist employed by the World Bank?

Averages are also used by economists in the compilation of statistics. For example, the average weekly earnings of employed people in an economy would need to be calculated using a structured sample of all types of employee, that is male/female, professional/manual, salaried/hourly paid and so on. This would give the economist a sound estimate in order to be able to make comparisons and possibly point to areas of potential poverty. Some estimate might also have to be made for the earnings from the subsistence and informal sectors in the economy in order to provide a true picture.

Data skills 5 – How to understand economic information produced in visual form

So far in this section all of the data used have been presented in tabular format. This might give a false impression because economists do use a much wider variety of visual means to present economic information. Charts of one form or another are a very good way of showing the main trends in data or emphasising a particular economic issue. Also, when economists produce business reports or write newspaper articles, various forms of data presentation are often used.

Figures 2 and 3 are typical examples of two such forms, namely a *bar chart* and a *pie chart*. Both represent the rather tedious data of table 5 in a more effective manner. In particular, it is relatively easy to see:

- the rank order of importance of government spending;
- how government expenditure in one area compares with that in another.

The basic principle behind the bar chart is that the particular economic variables (in this case social security, defence and so on) are represented by a series of bars or blocks, each of equal width. The bars though are of variable height, indicating their relative importance as measured on the vertical scale.

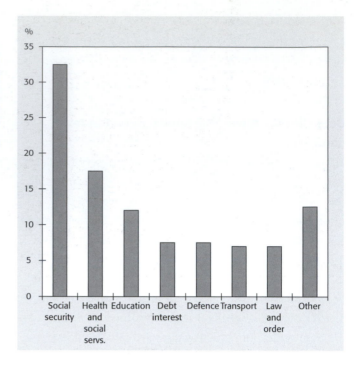

Figure 2 UK government spending in 1996/1997

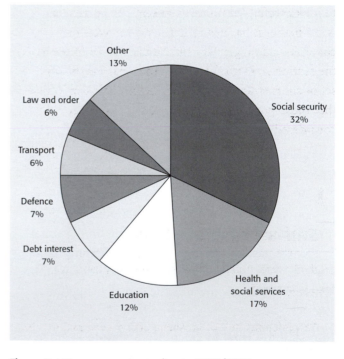

Figure 3 UK government spending in 1996/1997

In the pie chart, each slice of pie indicates the proportion or percentage of the total taken up by any one of the items. On figure 3, the respective percentages are indicated – but this is not always the case. Students

	% of total
Defence	7
Health and social services	17
Transport	6
Debt interest	7
Social security	32
Education	12
Law and order	6
Other	13
	100

Table 5 UK government spending in 1996/1997

familiar with spreadsheets, such as Excel, will know that a very wide range of bar charts and pie charts can be easily produced from this software.

When confronted with any chart, it is very important to look carefully at the vertical scale. In particular, see whether it has been modified to make small changes look bigger. You should also check to see if the section immediately above the origin is shown as a set of short straight cross lines. Again, this can indicate that the degree of change shown should be carefully considered.

Increasingly in newspapers and magazines, economic information is being represented in highly attractive ways, in the form of inter-related graphs, charts, pictures and diagrams.

Two excellent examples are shown in figure 4 (see page 10). These contain a lot more economic information than might seem to be the case at first sight.

The top pictograph shows how the Japanese economy has recovered from a period of downturn in the middle to late 1990s and how it is forecast to grow in strength in the early years of the twenty-first century. The lower diagrams show how some of its newly industrialising neighbours in South East Asia are expected to fare over the same period. Between them, these seemingly simple pictures contain a lot of valuable economic data and information.

How to plan an investigation into economic problems

So far in this introduction it has been assumed that the data being used by the economist are readily available and meet the particular need in hand. This is often the case – economists often use published data to support their views and theories. There are, though, many occasions where this is not possible and the economist has to carry out a specific investigation in order to obtain the data needed to make meaningful conclusions. This process in practice can be costly and time consuming.

Self-assessment tasks

Study the information in figure 4 and then tackle the following exercises.

1 With reference to the Japanese economy, describe the trend in:
   ◆ direct investment (that is investment from the rest of the world);
   ◆ forecasted GDP growth from 2000 to 2004.

2 Use **all** of the information to comment upon the likely economic prospects and problems facing the Japanese economy to 2004.

3 With reference to the newly industrialising countries of South East Asia:
   ◆ Which country is most likely to have a deficit on its balance of trade between 2001 and 2004? Explain your answer.
   ◆ Which country is likely to have the largest average annual income in 2004? Explain your answer.

4 Comment upon the likely threats that these newly industrialising countries could pose in the future for the Japanese economy.

Here comes a new Japan

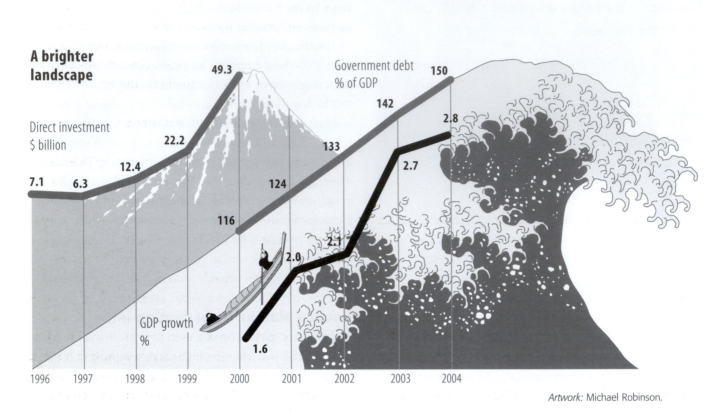

A brighter landscape

Direct investment $ billion

7.1 6.3 12.4 22.2 49.3

Government debt % of GDP

116 124 133 142 150

GDP growth %

1.6 2.0 2.1 2.7 2.8

1996 1997 1998 1999 2000 2001 2002 2003 2004

Artwork: Michael Robinson.

Two-speed Asia, one big problem

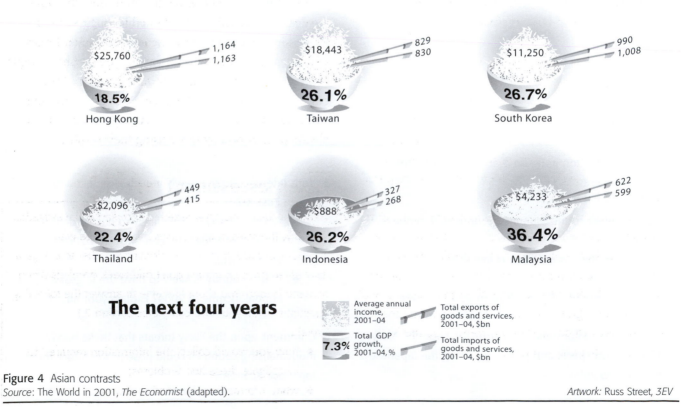

$25,760 1,164 1,163 **18.5%** Hong Kong

$18,443 829 830 **26.1%** Taiwan

$11,250 990 1,008 **26.7%** South Korea

$2,096 449 415 **22.4%** Thailand

$888 327 268 **26.2%** Indonesia

$4,233 622 599 **36.4%** Malaysia

The next four years

Average annual income, 2001–04

Total exports of goods and services, 2001–04, $bn

7.3% Total GDP growth, 2001–04, %

Total imports of goods and services, 2001–04, $bn

Figure 4 Asian contrasts
Source: The World in 2001, *The Economist* (adapted).

Artwork: Russ Street, *3EV*

Some basic knowledge of 'how to plan an investigation into economic problems' can help you understand the concepts concerned. This skill covers two main aspects:

1 The design of an economic investigation, that is how it might be carried out and how the information might be collected.
2 The information to be collected in order to investigate a particular economic issue, that is what data are needed in order to be able to make some conclusions or calculations.

Understanding this skill is not easy for students. It fits more into place once the economic concepts involved have been studied and understood. Some typical examples are:

◆ how to plan an investigation into the price, income or cross elasticity of demand for the product or products of a business (see section 2);
◆ how to plan an investigation into the benefits of economies of scale for a particular firm (see section 9);
◆ how to plan an investigation into the respective costs and benefits of a particular project (see section 3).

There are others which can be added to this list, not least as most economic concepts have developed as a consequence of economists undertaking investigations.

In general, there are two main sources of original data. These are:

1 *The internal information or records of a business or organisation.* For example, data on fixed and variable costs could be compiled in this way as might information on the benefits gained from economies of scale. Often, though, in practice data are not always available in the specific form required by economists.
2 *A particular investigation to obtain information.* Often in such cases the data required are not available or have never been collected. For example, this is likely to be the case with most cost–benefit studies or for businesses looking to estimate their price elasticity of demand for a given product or service. Some sort of survey needs to be carried out to provide the first-hand data that are required.

Many investigations require a *sample survey* to be undertaken. This is intended to be representative of the population from which it is drawn and, if properly carried out, permits the economist to make statements about the population's characteristics. Various types of survey methodology (for example, random, stratified or quota) are used in practice to obtain the information that is required.

Each has its strengths and weaknesses:

1 A *simple random sample* is one where respondents have the same chance of being selected. To be able to achieve this it is usual for the population to be listed on some sort of sampling frame, such as a listing of customers or households.
2 A *stratified sample* can produce more accurate and robust estimates, mainly because the population to be sampled is split into strata on the basis of variables such as income level, sex or occupation.
3 A *quota sample* is widely used by commercial market research businesses. In such cases, a sampling frame is unlikely to be available. The quota is intended to be a 'footprint' of the population, normally in terms of some fundamental characteristic such as age, car availability and similar variables.

It is also interesting and relevant to note that most government statistics are obtained through sample surveys. A good example is the Index of Retail Prices which was referred to earlier (see table 3). Other sample surveys are the *Family Expenditure Survey* and the *National Travel Survey*. All in all, these often provide valuable information – their accuracy, though, is not always understood by those using their results.

Self-assessment task

Your local 'take-away' has asked you to plan an investigation into how the sales of its products might change with variations in price. It is also considering whether to charge a discounted price on certain quiet mid-week evenings when demand is low. (You should be able to answer the following questions when you have completed section 2.)
Explain:
◆ how you would collect the information required to investigate these two problems;
◆ what information you need to collect.

How and why economists make forecasts

One of the most important tasks of the professional economist, whether in government or private sector employment, is to be able to forecast future economic phenomena. As figure 4 has shown, many economic variables are heavily dependent upon the state of the economy. Forecasts of economic growth in particular are widely used by economists for all sorts of reasons related to economic policy and business well-being.

Economists use various types of forecasting method. The three main ones are:

◆ statistical forecasts based on simple or complex future extrapolation techniques;

◆ using models to produce a range of forecasts – this is particularly true of models of the economy;

◆ forecasts based on intuition, experience or even guesswork – that is, not involving statistical methods.

Two examples of forecasts are:

Macroeconomic forecasts – the Chancellor of the Exchequer and other government departments in the UK find it essential to have estimates of projected variables, such as the unemployment rate, inflation rate, balance of payments position and economic growth rate (see figures 5 and 6 for typical examples). These are required on a short-term basis (1 year or less) or over a longer period of time. Take the case of the unemployment rate – the importance of forecasting is shown below in figure 7. This seems quite simple. In practice, though, the process is much more difficult to set out and at stages 3 and 4 requires further assumptions to be made with regard to other sources of revenue and taxation.

Microeconomic forecasts – these are not quite as obvious, but one example which develops out of sections 2 and 3 is the need to be able to forecast tax revenue from petrol consumption, which has a positive income elasticity of demand. This process is shown in a simplified way in figure 8.

How to write in a clear and effective way

It is really beyond the scope of this book to include a lot of material on this part of the 'tool kit'. But having said this, much of the work of economists is communicated

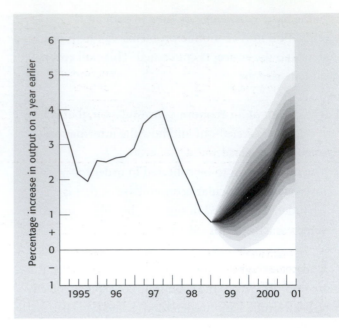

Figure 5 Current GDP projection based on constant nominal interest rates

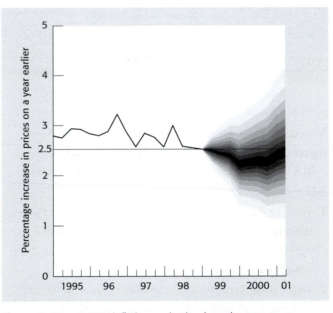

Figure 6 Current RPIX inflation projection based on constant nominal interest rates

in a written manner, in books and newspaper articles especially. For students, examinations in Economics (CIE included) require you to communicate your ideas in a written form. The section on Examination skills later in the book gives you very specific advice on how to impress examiners.

From a more general standpoint, you must always think about what you are writing and how you might improve your writing skills. You can enhance these skills

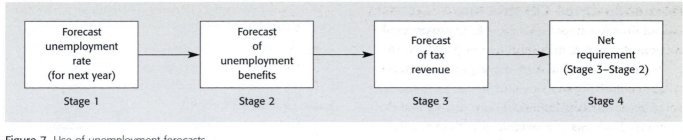

Figure 7 Use of unemployment forecasts

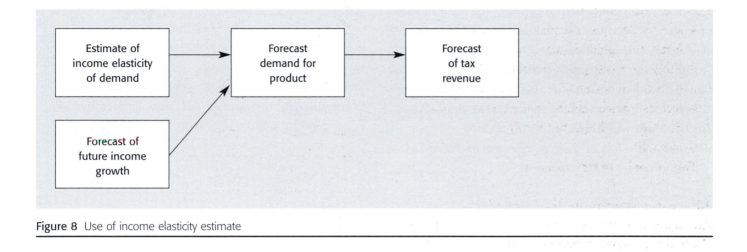

Figure 8 Use of income elasticity estimate

by reading a good newspaper, particularly if you read material which supports your AS/A level studies.

For the time being, you might like to think about the following 'Ten tips for budding writers':

1 *Be clear and precise in your writing* – use words you understand and when using technical terms be specific, not least because Economics has many terms which are very similar.

2 *Remember to match your writing to your audience* – in most cases this will be your teacher or a CIE examiner. They are likely to be older than yourself and will be looking to read material from you which is written in a relevant way.

3 *Write impersonally* – in other words, do not use 'I' or 'we' in your written essays and examination answers. This particularly applies when you are asked to make an evaluation of an economic issue or argument.

4 *Think carefully about what tense you are writing in* – try and be consistent.

5 *Take care with sentences and punctuation* – in general, try to write short sentences, to the point and which contain words you understand and know how to use.

6 *Use one idea per paragraph and develop your ideas* – this makes it relatively easy for someone reading your work to know what your answer is about and to see how your idea has been developed.

7 *Support your arguments* – in other words, never make rash statements you cannot back up. Always try to elaborate or develop your statements and arguments.

8 *Avoid humour* – if in any doubt, leave humour and wit out of your written answers. Many economists do have a sense of humour – examinations and essays are not the place for it to be demonstrated.

9 *Be professional* – do not insult or offend even if you do not agree with what you might have read or with the examination question. There are other ways in which you can make your opinions known.

10 *Keep working at your writing* – never be satisfied and keep thinking about how you can write in a clear, relevant, authoritative and positive way.

An outline of the CIE structure

It is useful from the outset for you to know the structure of the CIE syllabus. This is shown in figure 9.

Overall, it is what is called staged qualification. The syllabus consists of two so-called stages: an Advanced Subsidiary (AS) stage, which has two papers, and a further stage of two papers leading to the Advanced (A) level qualification. In terms of subject content, the AS stage draws upon the 'Core' (unit 1 of this book) and the A level stage draws upon the 'Extension' (unit 2).

What is probably new to you is that the AS is in itself a recognised international qualification. Some students may well decide to take this and terminate their studies on completion of this stage. Others will then need to take the two Extension papers in order to complete the A level. The important thing to note is the flexibility of this structure, which means you can:

◆ take the whole of the A level award at the end of your course (four papers);

◆ take the AS papers in order to obtain an AS award (two papers);

◆ take the AS qualification first, followed by the remaining two papers for the A level award.

Don't worry too much about this; your teachers will know what is best for you.

The last section of the book provides some important advice on how to prepare for examinations. It also contains some examples of the sort of questions you can expect in CIE examinations. Please study this section carefully before you take any of the papers.

As you systematically work through the sections in the two main units of the book, and undertake the various Self-assessment tasks, you will become increasingly familiar with the subject content of Economics and the assesssment methods used by CIE.

So, good luck and welcome to CIE Economics!

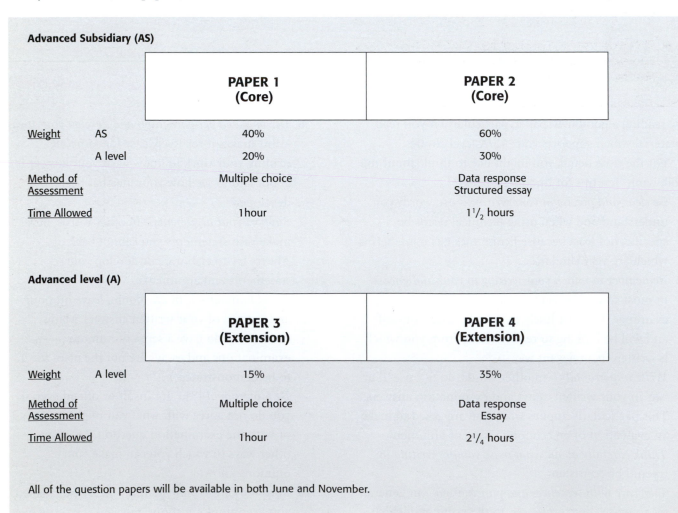

Advanced Subsidiary (AS)

		PAPER 1 (Core)	PAPER 2 (Core)
Weight	AS	40%	60%
	A level	20%	30%
Method of Assessment		Multiple choice	Data response Structured essay
Time Allowed		1 hour	1¹/₂ hours

Advanced level (A)

		PAPER 3 (Extension)	PAPER 4 (Extension)
Weight	A level	15%	35%
Method of Assessment		Multiple choice	Data response Essay
Time Allowed		1 hour	2¹/₄ hours

All of the question papers will be available in both June and November.

Figure 9 CIE's Economics syllabus

Summary

In this introduction we have established that:

- Economics is a social science concerned with how scarce resources are or should be allocated – it is often split into principles and concepts of microeconomics and macroeconomics.

- Economists have a varied 'tool-kit' to enable them to analyse economic problems and issues. Interpreting data and using data are particularly important – economists use many of the basic statistical skills for this purpose.

- There are occasions when economists need to make forecasts.

- Economists must be able to express their ideas in a clear, relevant manner so that they can be easily understood.

- The above skills will be assessed in CIE's Economics examinations at AS and at A Level.

- CIE's examination consists of two Core and two Extension papers which can be taken in various possible ways to best suit individual needs.

Unit 1
Core (AS Level)

1 Basic economic ideas

One economic problem or many?

Economists have to deal with a whole range of **economic problems**. You may have seen TV programmes about the misery of unemployment and poverty; you may have read about the difficulties caused by inflation or heard politicians discuss exchange rate crises on the evening news. You may also be aware of debates surrounding issues such as the UK's future relationship with the European Union, the problems of global warming and the population explosion in the Third World. Despite this extensive range of issues, which economists are trained to consider, they often talk about *the* economic problem. This is the fundamental problem from which all others arise. This is the fact that we have scarce **resources** to satisfy our unlimited **wants**. As a result of this problem, which is sometimes called the problem of **scarcity**, we have to make **choices**, and it is the task of the economist to explain and analyse the nature of choice facing economic agents, such as consumers, producers and governments.

The economic problem is

SCARCE RESOURCES IN RELATION
TO UNLIMITED WANTS

Because the basic economic problem exists, societies need to confront three interrelated questions. These are:

1 *What to produce*
   Because we cannot produce everything, we need to decide what to produce and in what quantities. We have to choose, for example, whether to produce lots of goods and services, such as food, clothing and vehicles, to improve our standard of living, or whether we need to produce lots of military hardware to improve our defences.

2 *How to produce*
   This question arises from the basic economic problem that, since resources are scarce in relation to unlimited wants, we need to consider how resources are used so that the best outcome arises. We need to consider how we can get the **maximum use** out of the resources available to us. It should be noted, however, that other issues besides purely economic concerns should be considered when deciding how to produce. It may be true, for example, that through slavery or forced labour we could produce more goods and services in an economy, but there is a moral objection to such arrangements. Similarly, crop yields could well be increased through the introduction of genetically modified plants but this may lead to damage to the ecosystem. The decision to maximise output and satisfy more wants would need to consider the full impact on the environment and any potential long-term health risks.

3 *For whom to produce*

Because we cannot satisfy all the wants of all the population, decisions have to be taken concerning how many of each person's wants are to be satisfied. On a broad level we need to decide whether everyone is going to have more or less an equal share of what is produced or whether some will have more than others. In some economies there are deliberate attempts to create a more egalitarian society through policies that re-distribute wealth and income from the rich to the poor. This could be through the adoption of progressive taxation systems. In other economies there are no such policies and inequalities of wealth and income, usually based upon inheritance, remain extreme. In answering this question, moral aspects of decision making again become important.

Self-assessment tasks

Read the article below and then tackle the exercises that follow.

Survey on the economics of ageing: The luxury of longer life

In the world's rich countries, when you retire at 65 you can expect to live, on average, for another 15 or 20 years. A hundred years ago you would, on average, have been already dead. The late 20th century has brought to many the ultimate gift: the luxury of ageing. But like any luxury, ageing is expensive. Governments are fretting about the cost already, but they also know that far worse is to come. Over the next 30 or 40 years, the demographic changes of longer lives and fewer births will force most countries to rethink in fundamental ways their arrangements for paying for and looking after older people.

In 1990 18% of people in OECD countries were aged over 60. By 2030 that figure will have risen to over 30%. The share of the 'oldest old' (those over 80), now around 3%, is set to double. The vast majority of these older people will be consumers, not producers. Thanks to state transfers, being old in developed countries mostly no longer means being poor. The old people will expect decent pensions to live on; they will make heavy demands on medical services; and some will need expensive nursing care. Yet while their numbers are expanding fast, numbers of people at work – who will have to foot the bill – will stay much the same, so each worker will have to carry a much heavier burden.

Mass survival to a ripe old age will not be confined to rich countries. Most developing countries, whose populations are now much younger than the developed world's, are starting to age fast. In Latin America and most of Asia, the share of over-60s is set to double between now and 2030, to 14%. In China, it will increase from less than 10% now to around 22% in 2030, thanks partly to the government's stringent population-control measures. Only Africa is likely to remain exuberantly young right through to the middle of the next century, though disease may reduce population growth in some countries.

Already the numbers of old people in poor countries are beginning to dwarf those in the rich world. By 2000, there will be 400m people over 60 in developing countries, twice as many as in the developed. In many places, the ageing process is being compressed from the four or five generations that it took in rich countries to just one or two.

A new twist to getting old

This will produce a historical first: countries with big old populations that are also poor. All the other permutations are familiar: old and rich (most of the industrial world), young and poor (most of the developing world for now) and, less common, young and rich (Australia, New Zealand, Ireland; up to a point, America, though not for much longer). Eastern Europe is something of an odd case out, being old but, thanks to its communist past, not as rich as it should be; and in

Russia life expectancy for men, against the trend elsewhere, is falling rather than rising.

The new combination of age and poverty in several countries in Latin America and Asia will create many problems that are already familiar to industrial countries, but with far fewer resources to tackle them. Ethical dilemmas over the use of scarce resources will be magnified. Financing of health care and pensions could be a nightmare.

When demographers first started drawing attention to the coming age bulge, the discovery was hailed as that rare thing in the affairs of nations, a foreseeable problem. Forewarned would, surely, mean forearmed. Even the tag invented for it, 'the demographic time-bomb', seemed to imply that the bomb could be defused. The demographic facts were inescapable because the people concerned had already been born. The same baby boomers who crowded the nurseries after 1945 would be packing the nursing homes of the 2030s. Yet so far there has been more talk than action.

The trouble has been that the demographic problems ahead, however predictable, are still not imminent enough to create any real sense of urgency. Modern democracies with electoral cycles of four or five years are not designed to solve problems that impose short-term costs to reap long-term benefits.

In many countries, older people are still too few in number, and for the most part too politically passive, to act as an effective pressure group for long-term policies to further their own interests (perhaps to the detriment of other groups). But that is changing as their numbers increase, and they learn to flex their political muscles. By 2030, it would be a bold politician who neglected one voter in three – especially as older people in general turn out to vote in much bigger numbers than others.

Source: Barbara Beck, *The Economist*, 27 January 1996.

1 Summarise the trends in world population structure identified in the article.

2 Discuss the significance of the changes for decisions concerning:
- ◆ what to produce;
- ◆ how to produce;
- ◆ for whom to produce.

Limited resources

In Economics we categorise the resources available to us into four types. These are known as **factors of production**:

1 Land This is the natural resource. It includes the surface of the earth, lakes, rivers and forests. It also includes mineral deposits below the earth and the climate above.

2 Labour This is the human resource, the basic determinant of which is the nation's population. Not all of the population are available to work however, because some are above or below the working population age and some choose not to work.

3 Capital goods These are any man-made aids to production. In this category we would include a simple spade and a complex car assembly plant. Capital goods help land and labour produce more units of output. They improve the output from land and labour.

These three factors are organised into units of production by firms.

4 Enterprise *(or entrepreneurship)* This factor carries out two functions. Firstly, the factor enterprise organises the other three factors of production. Secondly, enterprise involves taking the **risk** of production, which exists in a free enterprise economy. Some firms are small with few resources. The functions of enterprise are undertaken by a single individual. In larger, more complex firms the functions are divided, with salaried managers organising the other factors and shareholders taking the risk.

Some economies have a large quantity of high-quality factors of production at their disposal. They can create lots of goods and services to satisfy the wants of their population. They are said to have a good **factor endowment**. Some economies lack sufficient quantities of one or more of the factors. Developing countries, for example, might have large quantities of land and labour but lack sufficient capital and enterprise. The former planned economies of Eastern Europe, such as Poland, have found it difficult to develop because they have few people with entrepreneurial experience.

Production and consumption

Resources are combined in the process of **production** to create goods and services. Goods and services have the capacity to satisfy wants. The process through which individuals use up goods and services to satisfy wants is known as **consumption**. Some goods, such as a chocolate bar, are quickly used up to satisfy our wants. Others satisfy wants over a longer period of time. These are called consumer durables. Examples of consumer durables include television sets, refrigerators and vehicles.

Unlimited wants

If we were asked, we could all identify certain basic wants which must be satisfied if we are to stay alive. These include the obvious essentials of food, shelter and clothing. We might also identify those wants which are clearly less essential but which we think improve our quality of life. Some might include television sets, cars, trips to the cinema and so on. These are sometimes called luxuries but it is important to remember that what might be a luxury for one individual may be considered an essential for others. This is because we all have a **scale of preference** with our more urgent wants at the top and the less urgent ones at the bottom. Each individual's scale of preference is a product of a complex set of influences, involving our culture,

upbringing and life experiences. These together influence our likes and dislikes. Unsurprisingly, since we all have different experiences, there is bound to be great variation between any two individuals' scales of preferences. You may find it interesting to conduct a class exercise in which everyone makes a list of ten wants in descending order of priority. When you compare results you may be surprised to find that, although there may be broad agreement on the first few choices, there is likely to be considerable variation as you compare people's choices over the full list. You may also consider how your list would compare to lists compiled by others with very different life experiences, such as your teacher, your grandparents or even a student of Economics in another country, such as in the UK. A further point to consider is whether you could imagine any end to your list if you were not limited to ten choices. It is important to remember that our wants are continually expanding, developing and changing.

Some wants expand as we grow up, marry and raise a family. Imagine how our housing needs change as we go through this process or how we change from wanting a small car with two doors to wanting a large family saloon with four doors. Some of our wants develop and expand when we see others around us enjoying goods and services and we feel the need to keep up. Sometimes our wants change as we have new experiences, for example we might become vegetarian because we have seen a TV programme on the health risks of eating meat.

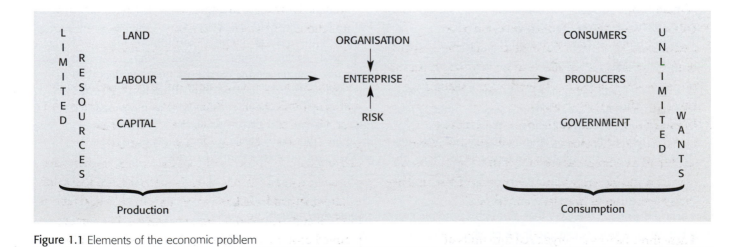

Figure 1.1 Elements of the economic problem

All of this points to the fact that we can never imagine a time when all our wants are satisfied. Our wants are continually expanding and changing. Despite the fact that we are continually finding new, more efficient ways to produce more and more goods and services with the resources available to us, we are still faced with the basic economic problem that we have limited resources and unlimited wants. This is sometimes called the problem of **scarcity**. As a result we have to make choices.

Specialisation and exchange

One of the ways in which more goods and services can be produced in the economy is through the process of **specialisation**. This refers to a situation where individuals and firms, regions and nations concentrate upon producing some goods and services rather than others. This can be clearly illustrated at the individual level. Within the family there may be some specialisation in the performance of household tasks, with one person doing the ironing and gardening while

Self-assessment tasks

Read the case study below and answer the questions that follow.

Rich and miserable … or poor and happy?

It's often said that those who say that money can't buy you happiness simply don't know where to shop. So when you've finished leafing through the Guardian, the odds are that you'll be off to the mall, armed with your plastic for a bit of conspicuous consumption.

After all, Christmas is only five weeks away and spending money makes you happy, right? Wrong. According to economists it's a myth that the more we spend, the better we feel.

The evidence – to be published in this month's edition of The Economic Journal – that the link between happiness and income/consumption is tenuous – is quite compelling.

The West is much richer than it was 50 years ago but:
- in the USA, reported 'happiness' has gone up only fractionally over this period;
- in Europe, 'satisfaction with life' is actually lower than it was 20 years ago.

This is evidenced in a number of ways. For example:
- in rich countries, male suicide rates have gone up;
- unemployment rates have increased – unhappiness is far more prevalent amongst the jobless.

According to Professor Andrew Oswald of Warwick University, money is to blame for this state of affairs. He argues that it buys very little well-being, yet everyone wants more of it. He says it is akin to the spectator who stands up at a football match to get a better view; by the time all of his neighbours are standing up, everybody is no better off than before.

Other economists agree:
- Yew Kwang Ng, a Chinese economist, has argued that production and consumption, 'to keep up with the Joneses, continue to impose substantial environmental costs, making economic growth happiness decreasing.
- Robert Frank, an American economist, argues that we would be better off if we all agreed to consume less. We could work less, meet other people more regularly and cut down on workplace commuting.

But what can we do to change?
Frank's solution is a progressive consumption tax, levied on a family's income minus its savings. A large standard deduction would ease the burden on poor families with low levels of consumption. For everyone else, the resulting real increase in consumption would encourage greater savings and permit a transfer of resources into the things that really make us happy – better education, good health and a decent environment.

Source: *Guardian*, 22 November 1997 (adapted).

This article expresses the view that, through economic growth, people may actually be worse off.

1 What other examples can you think of which might support the views of these economists?

2 Do you see any conflict between these views and your understanding of the 'economic problem'?

another does the shopping and cooking. At the workplace, of course, the fact that some people are labourers or lorry drivers while others have office jobs is also a reflection of specialisation. At this level, specialisation allows individuals to concentrate upon what they are best at and thus more goods and services will be produced. With such specialisation, however, although more is produced no-one is self-sufficient. It becomes necessary to exchange goods and services. As an individual specialises they will produce a surplus beyond their needs, which they can exchange for the surpluses of others.

With the expansion of trade and the development of markets, the benefits of regional and national specialisation became apparent. Surpluses produced by regions and countries were bought and sold, allowing world living standards to rise. Just as individuals concentrated on what they were best at, so did regions and countries.

Specialisation has clearly resulted in a massive expansion in world living standards, but there are dangers in specialisation. Given the pace of technological change in modern society, there is always the possibility that the specialist skills and accumulated experience, which any individual has acquired, may become redundant as the economy develops. Individuals need to be flexible and multi-skilled and be able to move between occupations. At regional and national levels, changes in consumers' wants can sometimes mean that the goods and services produced in a region or country are no longer required in the same quantity and unemployment can result. Policies then have to be adopted to deal with the economic and social problems that will arise. This issue will be looked at in depth in section 13.

The division of labour

With the technical advances of the last few hundred years, production of goods and services has taken place on a much bigger scale. The concentration of large numbers of workers within very large production units allowed the process of production to be broken down into a series of tasks. This is called the **division of labour**. For example, Adam Smith, writing at the end of the eighteenth century, showed how the production of pins would benefit from the application of the division of labour in a factory. He suggested that pin-making could be divided into 18 distinct operations and that, if each employee undertook only one of the operations, production would rise to 5,000 pins per employee per day. This was compared to his estimate that each employee would be able to produce only a few dozen each day if they produced pins individually.

Although the division of labour raised output, it often created dissatisfaction in the work force, who became bored with the monotonous nature of their task. The process was taken a stage further in the 1920s when conveyor belt production was introduced in the United States car industry by Henry Ford. Ford's method of car production provided the model for much of manufacturing production in the twentieth century. In more recent times the de-humanising impact of production techniques, such as those using a conveyor belt, have been recognised and alternative methods of production have been introduced.

Money: its functions and characteristics

Money is something that virtually all of us take for granted in so far as we need it to carry out our daily lives. Riding on a bus, purchasing a soft drink or an ice cream are simple yet very frequent examples of when we hand over a few coins or a note to whoever is providing these things for us. The process is so simple in fact that we have no need to even think about it. Having said that, all of us (except possibly for Bill Gates of Microsoft!) would like more money, but that is a different matter as we saw earlier.

Bill Gates of Microsoft
Source: Photo by Popperfoto/Reuters.

The money we hand over for purchases is usually our national currency, such as dollars, pounds, euros, ringgits, rupees and so on. The coins and paper notes themselves have little or no intrinsic value – their value to us stems directly from the fact that sellers have complete confidence in the money we are giving to them and so exchange it for the goods and services we require. This confidence in turn enables them to buy supplies for their shop or petrol for their bus and so on. In the simple way described above, we have shown the functions of money.

The practice of using money is absolutely essential for the smooth operation of businesses and international transactions in the modern global economy. In the absence of the sort of money we know, people would have to rely on **barter**, the term used to mean the direct exchange of one good or service for another. Where this is the only way of exchange (as was the case in some former Russian republics quite recently) then the whole process of meeting ones needs is slow, cumbersome, time consuming and very impractical. There must be what is called **double coincidence of wants**, whereby two people have to have the appropriate goods or services which each other wants. Money therefore makes the whole process of exchange and trade so much easier and simpler.

Just what makes up the money supply is covered in section 11. For the time being, bearing in mind what has already been said, money is anything that is regularly used to buy goods and services. Normally, of course, this is coins, notes, cheques, credit cards and debit cards. It could though be a valuable commodity (such as gold and silver) or even chocolate and Levi jeans, both of which were scarce and widely accepted as payment in the former Soviet Union in the 1980s, when people were losing confidence in the Russian rouble. Implicit in the above are the characteristics of money; money is anything which is generally acceptable, durable, portable, scarce and divisible into small units.

From the economist's standpoint, money has three necessary functions. Let us look at each briefly.

First, money is a **medium of exchange**. The function was amplified earlier in recognising that money is the 'medium' that buyers use for purchases and that sellers are willing to accept in 'exchange' for these purchases.

By physically handing over money, there is a common and automatic acceptance of money fulfilling its function as a medium of exchange.

Money's second function is as a **unit of account**. As such, money is used as the 'unit' by which prices are established in dollars and cents, pounds and pence and so on. This function applies for both current and projected transactions, for example when banks agree to lend a certain sum of money to a borrower and also agree on how much interest has to be paid by the borrower to the bank for this service. The 'account' aspect stems from money units being accountable, in the sense that the value of the money can be recorded and summed. It is also a means by which the relationships between various units of a currency are established, for example 100 cents equalling $1.

The third function of money is that of a **store of value**. Here, it is recognised that money can be held or 'stored' for a period of time before it is used, or it can be accumulated (if you are fortunate enough) to provide a source of wealth. As with the medium of exchange function, the holder of the money is confident that money will retain its value compared to when it was received. Not only coins and notes but bank deposits, bonds, stocks and other forms of holding money can be used as the basis for storage over time. In all cases, this accumulation of money can be realised in monetary terms in the future.

These three functions of money are very important and necessary for the smooth working of all economies except for subsistence economies. If any of these functions break down and cannot be met, people lose confidence in money. When this occurs, economic collapse is the only outcome. There is therefore an important need for government economic policy to ensure that this does not happen. The most obvious sign when this is the case is that money fails to act as a store of value at times of hyperinflation and, in a short time, people can no longer have confidence in money as a medium of exchange (see section 6).

Choice and opportunity cost

Given limited resources and unlimited wants we have to choose which wants to satisfy. The true cost of any choice we make between alternatives is expressed by economists through the notion of **opportunity cost**. This looks at the cost of our choice in terms of the next best alternative forgone. For example, suppose you were given a $15.00 gift voucher for your birthday. You could either buy a new compact disc which costs $15.00 or two paperback books for $7.50 each. It is clear that you could not have the CD *and* the books. The opportunity cost of the CD, therefore, is the two paperback books. The value of the concept of opportunity cost is that it brings home to us the real cost of our choices. It can be applied in a variety of contexts in Economics and is helpful for economic decision makers, such as households, firms and governments.

Production possibility curves

How many goods and services an economy is capable of producing is determined by the quantity and quality of resources available to it, together with the state of technical knowledge. These factors determine an economy's production possibilities.

Example: An imaginary economy, given its available resources, can either produce military goods or consumer goods or a combination of each. The various possibilities are shown on the following production possibility schedule.

Military goods	Consumer goods
10,000	0
8,000	4,000
6,000	8,000
4,000	12,000
2,000	16,000
0	20,000

It is sometimes useful to illustrate the choices open to an economy by considering the production possibility curve. From the above schedule we can produce a production possibility curve with military goods plotted on the vertical axis and consumer goods on the horizontal axis.

Figure 1.2 shows all possible combinations of military goods and consumer goods which could be produced

Two books or one CD?

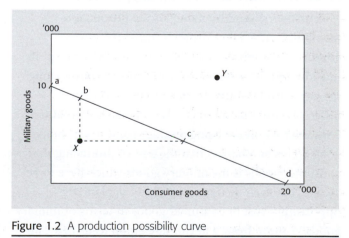

Figure 1.2 A production possibility curve

given the existing quantity and quality of resources in our imaginary economy and the existing state of technical knowledge. At point a, only military goods are produced, and, at point d, only consumer goods are produced, but between these two extremes lie all the other possibilities. The term production possibility curve emphasises that this shows what levels of output an economy can achieve with its existing resources. It can also be used to show what the economy is *not* able to achieve. Point Y on the graph represents a combination of military and consumer goods which it is not possible to achieve. It is beyond our production possibilities. Sometimes the curve is called a **production frontier** because it draws the boundary between what can and cannot be achieved.

This diagram is also useful in illustrating the real cost to society of unemployed resources. The point X on the diagram represents a production of 4,000 military goods and 2,500 consumer goods. This is possible to achieve because it is within the production frontier, but it represents a point where some resources are unemployed or not employed effectively. The economy is capable of moving to point b with more military goods and the same number of consumer goods or to point c, which would bring more consumer goods and the same quantity of military goods. Alternatively, at a point between b and c, the economy can have more of both types of goods. Looking at the diagram in this way illustrates the waste from unemployed resources. We are not satisfying as many of our wants as possible.

A further alternative name for the production possibility curve is the **product transformation curve**. This emphasises a further use for the concept in introductory Economics. As the economy moves along the curve from point a through to point d then a different combination of goods is being chosen. More consumer goods are being produced and fewer military goods. This emphasises that the cost of producing more consumer goods is the military goods which have to be sacrificed. Given the figures, we can calculate the opportunity cost of consumer goods in terms of military goods. A move from b to c on the graph leads to a gain of 4,000 consumer goods but we sacrifice 2,000 military goods. The opportunity cost of one consumer good is therefore half of a military good. This is equivalent to one military good having an opportunity cost of two consumer goods. As we move along the curve the

composition of our output is being transformed. We should also note that for this to happen we need to switch our resources from one use to another. Resources have to be switched from producing military goods to producing consumer goods and vice versa. This is known as the **reallocation of resources** and in the real world, as we decide to change the composition of our output, we need to consider the costs of reallocating resources between uses. These include the costs of re-training our work force in the skills required to produce different types of goods and services. This might take a considerable period of time and might only be possible as new entrants to the labour force are trained in new skills. The extent to which resources can be reallocated from one line of production to another is known as **factor mobility** and, if we want resources to be swiftly allocated to the use we choose, we have to ensure that factors are as mobile as possible.

It should be noted that, in our example, the opportunity cost of military goods in terms of consumer goods has not changed because we have chosen different combinations of the two goods. This is in fact quite unrealistic. A more likely outcome is that the production possibility curve will illustrate increasing costs. Consider the production possibility schedule in table 1.1, which shows the quantities of agricultural goods and manufactured goods that can be produced in an economy given existing resources and state of technology.

Assume that initially the economy is producing at point p with 660 agricultural products and 100 manufactured products (figure 1.3). Then assume that it is decided to move to point q to gain an extra 100 units of manufactured products. Clearly, resources need to be reallocated from agricultural use to manufacturing. At

Agricultural products	Manufactured products
700	0
660	100
600	200
500	300
300	400
0	500

Table 1.1 A production possibility schedule

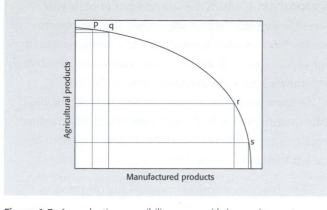

Figure 1.3 A production possibility curve with increasing costs

first the least fertile land will be reallocated and only 60 units of agricultural produce will be sacrificed. This means that each extra consumer good has cost 0.6 of an agricultural good. Now compare this with a movement from r to s, to gain an extra 100 manufactured goods we have to sacrifice 200 agricultural goods. This means that one extra manufactured good has cost 2 agricultural goods. The cost has increased as we have reallocated our resources. This is because at this stage we are switching the more fertile land into manufactured good production so that agricultural output is going to be affected to a much greater extent. This diagram illustrates a production possibility curve with increasing costs.

Shifts in production possibility curve

A production possibility curve is drawn on the assumption that the quantity and quality of resources and the state of technology are fixed. Through time, of course, economies can gain or lose resources; the quality of resources and the state of technical knowledge can change. Such changes will shift the production possibility curve to a new position. Figure 1.4 illustrates the outcomes of changes in the quantity and quality of resources and changes in technology.

Figure 1.4(a) shows a situation in which the production possibilities available to an economy have expanded. This is known as **economic growth**. This could be due to an increase in the quantity and/or the quality of resources available to the economy or an improvement in the state of technology. Here the changes have improved the economy's ability to produce both agricultural and manufactured products. In figure 1.4 (b), however, only our ability to produce agricultural products has been improved. This could perhaps be because there has been a technological breakthrough in producing agricultural products, which does not apply to the production of manufactured products. Nevertheless, this economy's production possibilities have improved and the curve has shifted outwards from the origin.

The production possibilities could also have declined. This could be because in some way the resources available to the economy have declined. Perhaps some of the economy's natural resources have become exhausted or the working population is falling. It might also be because the technology available to us has changed. An example might be the impact of controls on global emissions, which will affect our production possibilities as controls become more rigorous.

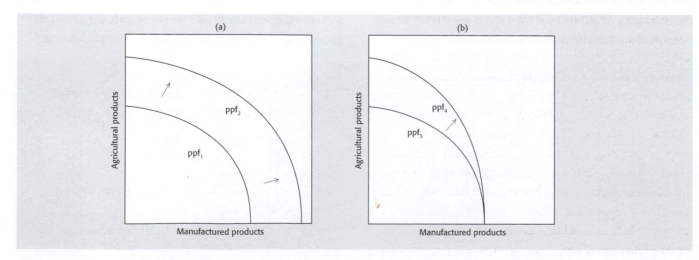

Figure 1.4 Shifts in production possibility curves

Applications of production possibility curves

We can use production possibility curves to illustrate some of the issues facing economic decision makers in the real world.

Jam today or more jam tomorrow? As stated previously, the production possibilities open to an economy are determined by the quantity and quality of resources available. In the process of production, resources are used up and they need to be replaced if production possibilities are to be maintained. The terms **capital consumption** or **depreciation** describe the using up of capital goods during the process of production. Some resources need to be devoted to the production of capital goods if production possibilities are to be maintained. The creation of capital goods in the process of production is known as **investment**.

This can be defined as *any production not for current consumption*. A choice has to be made therefore between producing consumer goods and services or producing capital goods through the process of investment. The more consumer goods and services produced, the higher the standard of living in the current time period, but the standard of living might fall in the future if there is a failure to produce enough capital goods to replace those worn out in the process of production. In addition, the quality of an economy's capital goods will not be improved and the full benefits of new technology will not be enjoyed if there is a failure to devote sufficient resources to investment.

Figure 1.5 shows the production possibilities between capital goods and consumer goods. These possibilities are determined by the quantity and quality of resources in the economy, which include the capital goods that have been produced in the past. If we assume that the quantity

of capital goods which are wearing out in each time period is shown at a, then we can see the consequences of our choices. If we fail to produce the quantity at a then our capital stock will decline. Our production possibilities will diminish and the curve will shift to the left.

We use the term 'gross investment' to describe the total quantity of capital goods produced. If we deduct from this the capital consumption allowance then we are left with net investment:

Gross investment minus capital consumption = Net investment

Self-assessment task

Use the terms gross investment, capital consumption and net investment to analyse the effect of economic decision makers choosing each of points p, q and r in figure 1.5. Explain the choices in terms of the present and future standard of living in the economy.

Hard choices for developing economies Developing **economies** are characterised by low standards of living. If they are to grow then they need to increase their capital stock. Like all economies they need to divert resources from current consumption to investment. Some resources must be devoted to consumption, however, to keep their expanding populations alive. We refer to this as the subsistence level of consumption. The difficulty they face is that in the poorest developing economies almost all their production possibilities need to be devoted to subsistence.

In figure 1.6, 0a represents the capital consumption in a developing economy and 0b represents the consumer goods required for the subsistence of the population.

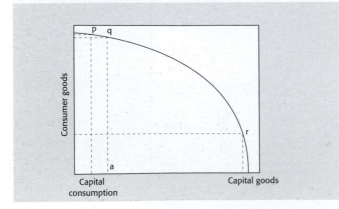

Figure 1.5 The choice between consumer goods and capital goods

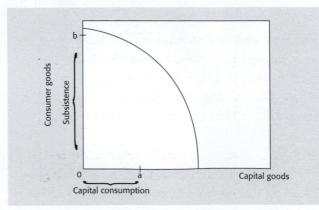

Figure 1.6 Capital consumption in a developing economy

Different allocative mechanisms

The problem of scarcity, which in turn requires choices to be made, is one that is common to all economies, rich and poor. The choices that are made and which can realistically be made in turn are determined by the **economic system** of a particular country. This is the term used to describe the means or allocative mechanism by which its people, businesses and government make choices. Traditionally, economists have recognised three distinct types of economic system – these are the **market economy**, the **command or planned economy** and the **mixed economy**. Let us briefly consider each in turn.

The market economy

In such an economy decisions on how resources are to be allocated are usually taken by millions of households and thousands of firms – the exact number will of course depend on the size of economy. The key point is that they interact as buyers and sellers in the market for goods and services. Prices and the operation of the price system underpin this interaction; in turn prices act to indicate the likely market value of particular resources. For example, a commodity in short supply but which has a high demand attached to it will have a high price. Alternatively, one which has a high supply and low demand will have a much lower price attached to it. Prices and the self-interest of people and businesses therefore act as a guide to the decisions that have to be taken.

The fundamental principles of the market mechanism and price system are analysed in the next section; in section 4, their applicability to international trade is explained. Elsewhere, further examples and the development and elaboration of the basic principles can be found.

Economics as a subject has its origin in the notion that prices and the market mechanism are the 'best' way of handling economic problems. This notion can be particularly attributed to the Scottish economist Adam Smith, who is remembered for his reference to an 'invisible hand' (the price system) that brings together private and social interests in an harmonious way. This is the fundamental philosophy underpinning the workings of the market economy.

The government has a very restricted part to play. For example, in Smith's view, it should control national defence, act against monopolies, issue money, raise taxes and so on whilst protecting the rights of the private sector. It certainly should not try to influence the dealings of individuals in the market or to regulate the workings of that market. Figure 1.7 is a simple representation of these functions.

Before moving on, it must be made clear that the market economy is an ideal which does not exist in today's complex, globalised economy. Arguably, its most important representation is the United States of America (USA), and it should be stressed that here federal and state governments play important roles in the economy and society, as well as in providing defence, law and order and other public services.

The command economy

Like the market economy, the command or centrally planned economy in its purest form exists only in theory. In this second type of economy, the government has a central role in all decisions that are made and unlike the market economy, the emphasis is on centralisation. Decision making is taken by central planning boards and organisations to enterprises that are state-owned or under state regulation and control. Whereas in a market economy consumer sovereignty

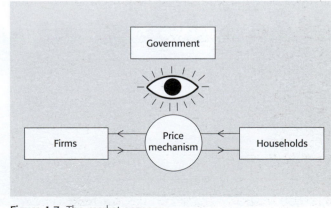

Figure 1.7 The market economy

influences resource allocation, in a command economy, it is central planners who have to determine the collective preferences of consumers and manufacturing enterprises.

The planned economies of the last fifty years or so have their economic logic in the Marxian criticism of the market economy. This particular objection was essentially one of class conflict between the wealthy owners of capital and the poor working classes who provided this wealth through the production process. Marx was also critical of the built in unemployment arising out of the market system. For example, he had observed the trend to replace labour with machines (capital) and the inability of labour to secure higher wages. Under a command economy, unemployment is not an issue. Marx was also very concerned about the way in which the market economy fostered the concentration of productive resources in the hands of large monopolistic industrial and commercial organisations. As such he maintained that they corrupted the workings of demand and supply and, if

powerful enough, could exert pressure on governments. Retrospectively, and in the light of empirical experience, economists have with some justification concluded that Marx's criticisms were excessive. Nevertheless, his general recognition that more centralisation should occur and that more emphasis should be placed on economic planning, have been applied by those countries which have pursued the notion of a planned economy.

So the key features of a command economy are that central government and its constituent organisations take responsibility for:

- the allocation of resources,
- the determination of production targets for all sectors of the economy,
- the distribution of income and the determination of wages,
- the ownership of most productive resources and property,
- planning the long-term growth of the economy.

Queuing for bread in the former Soviet Union
Source: Photo by Hjalte Tin, Still Pictures.

From a practical standpoint, some of these decisions have to be de-centralised, either geographically or sectorally, to other government organisations. In certain cases, these bodies have control over the workings of a limited market mechanism. A good example of this is where basic foodstuffs such as bread and meat are heavily subsidised to keep prices at a fixed level and so exempt consumers from the vagaries of price fluctuation which are so commonplace in the market economy. Artificially low prices result in excess demand relative to supply – queuing becomes a way of life (see photograph). Also from a practical standpoint it is very difficult for all enterprise to be state-owned – there has to be a limited opportunity for the private ownership of small businesses such as shops, restaurants and personal services like hairdressing and cleaning

The outcome of the command economy is that central planning tends to set goals for the economy that differ from those of the market economy. In particular they have a clear objective of achieving as high a rate of economic growth as possible in order to 'catch up' on the progress being made by much more advanced market economies. Popularly known as the 'guns and butter' argument, it is more correctly described as one of sacrificing current consumption and standards of living in order to achieve enhanced future well-being. This is the sacrifice that has to be made by the present generation for the benefit of future generations.

The last point can be illustrated by returning to the production possibility curve. Figure 1.8 indicates that the economy can choose between capital goods or consumer goods. The former represent an investment in machinery, equipment, infrastructure, technology and so on which will in time increase the productive capacity in the economy. Consumer goods like cars,

refridgerators and televisions are for current consumption. In making this choice, command economies have chosen to produce at point X on their production possibility curve rather than at point Y, where consumer needs are satisfied in full.

This is of course a highly simplified representation of what in reality is a very complex process of centralised decision making. The extent to which economies choose X rather than Y also varies, depending on the degree to which the economy sees growth first and foremost as its only economic objective.

The mixed economy

It is clear from the brief analysis of market and command economies that, in the 'pure' sense, these types of economic systems occur in theory and not in reality. In contrast, the mixed economy is undoubtedly the characteristic form of economic organisation within the global economy. As its name indicates, it involves both private and public sectors in the process of resource allocation. Consequently, decisions on most important economic issues involve some form of planning (by private as well as public enterprises) and interaction between government, businesses and labour through the market mechanism. Private ownership of productive resources operates alongside public ownership in many mixed economies, although, increasingly, the trend is towards the privatisation of certain activities that were once in public sector hands (see section 10).

The best example of this is undoubtedly the UK economy in the mid-1970s when the public and private sectors, broadly speaking, contributed equal proportions of the Gross Domestic Product (GDP) (see section 10). At this time the government was responsible for:

◆ substantial areas of public expenditure such as health, social services, education and defence;
◆ the direct operation of nationalised industries, such as coal, iron and steel, railways, gas, water, telephones and electricity;
◆ providing support for large areas of manufacturing, such as vehicle production, aerospace and electronics, in partnership with the private sector.

Since 1979, when Mrs Thatcher's Conservative government was elected, the strength of the public sector has been substantially reduced, not only through privatisation but also through a policy of non-intervention when private companies experience financial

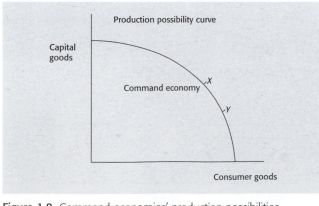

Figure 1.8 Command economies' production possibilities

difficulties in their markets. Controversially, in the last few years, governments have made little or no attempt to stem the virtual closure of car manufacturing in the UK as, one by one, former British-owned companies have been rationalised by their non-UK owners.

The modern view of UK governments, Conservative and Labour, is that their responsibilities are for the overall management of the macro-economy and for the funding of particular public and merit goods which overall would be underconsumed if left to the private sector alone to provide (see section 3). It is also the case that new forms of regulation and control have had to be introduced in order to protect consumers from possible exploitation by the private sector providers of essential services. A very popular outcome of the UK experience is that millions more people now hold shares in such businesses.

Elsewhere, there have been similar trends. One of the most dramatic has been the restructuring of the economy of the former Soviet Union (*perestroika* as it is sometimes called). Under President Gorbachev's reforms, small private businesses could be set up in the service sector (for example, cafés, retail shops, garages and taxi hire) and workers could form their own co-

operatives to market and sell surplus production from monolithic state manufacturing companies.

The US economy is also an example of a mixed economy, somewhat contrary to common perception. For example:

◆ the government at all levels is an important employer and provides basic services, such as education and various types of medical care;
◆ government agencies regulate and control the provision of some essential services, such as energy, telecommunications and transportation;
◆ indirect support is given to various strategically important companies.

These are over and above the expected provision of external defence and internal security services.

Just how important a role the government plays in any particular mixed economy is not easy to explain. About the only real explanation that can be given is that in most cases it is usually a consequence of differing political philosophies. Figure 1.9 provides a largely normative assessment of where particular economies fall in terms of the relative strengths of market and planned systems of resource allocation. In all cases, except

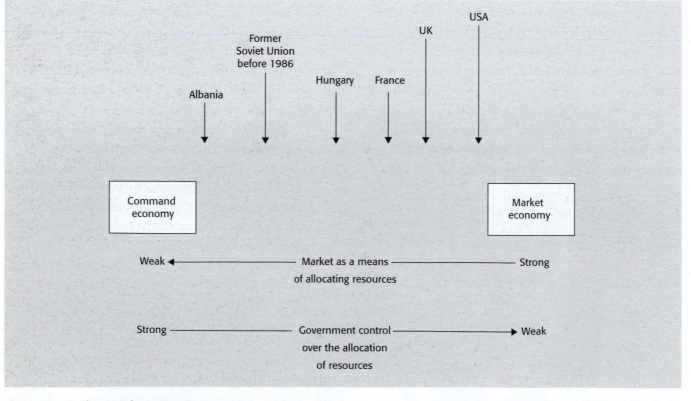

Figure 1.9 Mixed economic systems

arguably for Albania, the prevailing wind is to move their economic structures towards that of an ever-increasing role for the market mechanism.

In more recent times, the experience of the newly industrialising countries (NICs) is interesting. In terms of allocative mechanisms, some, such as Singapore and Hong Kong, opted for a strong focus on the market to allocate resources and through this have created an economic situation where enterprise can be encouraged and rewarded. Other South East Asian Tigers have placed more emphasis on central planning, whilst China's phenomenal growth over the last decade has been based on the controlled management of the economy within a global context.

The new **Tiger economies** of central Europe, particularly the Czech Republic, Hungary and Poland, have re-orientated their economies to foreign investors. In this way, they hope to achieve forecasted growth rates of around 5–7 per cent per annum. These are very much in line with those experienced by their Asian counterparts, yet significantly higher than those experienced in the past by more developed economies (see section 12).

Self-assessment tasks

1 Think carefully about the ways in which your own economy allocates resources. Make a few notes on the ways in which
   ◆ the government,
   ◆ the market mechanism,
   are responsible for decision making.

2 Use the above information to insert your own economy into the scale shown in figure 1.9. How has its relative position changed in recent years?

3 What information might an economist use to quantify the relative importance of the government and the market mechanism within an economy?

Hong Kong, the new jewel in China's crown

Summary

In this section we have recognised that:

- All economies face the so-called economic problem of limited resources and unlimited wants.

- Choice is necessary in order to decide what to produce, how to produce and for whom to produce.

- Factors of production (land, labour, capital and enterprise) are essential for the production process.

- Specialisation allows more goods and services to be produced. Money facilitates specialisation and exchange.

- The true cost of choices we have to make is known as opportunity cost.

- A production possibility curve is a representation of what can be produced in an economy and the trade-offs involved in making choices.

- There are various types of economic system for the allocation of resources.

Key words

Definitions of Key words can be found in the Glossary.

barter	mixed economy
capital consumption	money
capital goods	opportunity cost
choice	planned economy
command economy	production
consumption	production frontier
developing economy	production possibility
division of labour	curve
double coincidence of	product transformation
wants	curve
economic growth	resources
economic problem	reallocation of resources
enterprise	risk
factor endowment	scale of preference
factor mobility	scarcity
investment	specialisation
labour	store of value
land	Tiger economies
market economy	unit of account
maximisation	wants
medium of exchange	

2 The price system

On completion of this section you should know:

➤ what a demand curve is and how you can sketch one

➤ how individual demand curves can be aggregated into a market demand schedule

➤ what factors determine the demand for a particular product or service

➤ what is meant by consumer surplus

➤ what can cause a shift in a demand curve and why this is not the same as a movement along a demand curve

➤ what a supply curve is, both for the products of an individual firm and for the market as a whole

➤ what can cause a movement along a supply curve and a shift of a supply curve

➤ how equilibrium price and quantity are determined in a market

➤ how prices can signal changes in the allocation of resources and rationing in a market

➤ what is meant by price, income and cross elasticity of demand and how they can be calculated

➤ what is meant by price elasticity of supply

➤ the business relevance of the various demand and supply elasticity estimates

Markets

'Oil prices fall to $10 per barrel – consumers everywhere will rejoice at the prospect of cheap, plentiful oil for the foreseeable future' (*Economist*, 6 March 1999)

'Cheap mortgages fuel boom in house prices' (*Sunday Times*, 28 March 1999)

'Buy one, get one free on selected lines this week at McDonald's' (*The Daily Mirror*, 8 January 2001)

'Rent one of our new widescreen TVs and you can get a Nicam stereo video for only £5 per month extra' (Advert in *East Anglian Daily Times*, 11 March 1999)

'Fly with us to Singapore for £355 return and get quality accommodation from only £20 per night' (Advert in *Independent on Sunday*, 28 March 1999)

To many people a market is something that happens in the town or city centre once or twice a week. It is characterised by a large number of traders setting up stalls that sell a whole range of products: food – such as fruit, vegetables, fish – clothes and a wide selection of other items. Economists, however, take a broader view of the word 'market'. The essence of any market is trade – somebody has something to sell and somebody else wants to buy the product that is being offered. So, whenever people come together for the purposes of exchange or trade, we have a market.

For example, economists talk about the housing market, where people buy and sell houses; look in the newspapers or estate agents and you will see evidence of this market. They also refer to the labour market, where individuals' labour power is 'bought and sold' – if any of you have jobs part time or full time, then you have participated in the labour market as a seller of labour.

The television news often makes reference to the stock market, where shares are bought and sold, and the foreign exchange market, where currencies are bought and sold.

These examples indicate that to an economist a market does not have to have a clearly defined physical presence as the typical town or street market might

Self-assessment task

How do you participate in the following markets:

◆ the fast food market?

◆ the telecommunications market?

◆ the transport market?

have. It is simply a term used to describe the process through which products that are fairly similar are bought and sold.

Sub-markets

You might, however, begin to feel a bit uneasy at this point. Whilst it is clear that houses, labour, personal computers (PCs) and fast food may be fairly similar, it is also clear that there are significant differences within each market – the types of houses, PCs, transport services that are traded are not identical. So a good question to ask is: 'How valid is it to lump all the different types of computer together into one single market?'

Whenever we break an investigation down into smaller sections of the overall market, we are looking at **sub-markets**. So, if we want to look at the sub-markets of the computer industry, we might want to look at the various types of computer: memory, speed, features, PCs and laptops, the various brands and so on. We may need to consult (or become!) specialists in the economics of particular industries.

Demand

Let us first of all look at the buying side of the market – this is referred to as the demand side of the market. To an economist:

> **demand** refers to the *quantities* of a *product* that *purchasers* are *willing and able* to buy at *various prices* per *period of time, other things remaining the same.*

Definitions are of critical importance in Economics, so let us break this definition down to understand in some depth what this means.

- *Quantities* – economists often deal with numerical values and very often try to represent information in a quantitative way. This point is reinforced by the use of the term 'prices'.
- *Product* – this is a general term that simply refers to the item that is being traded. It can be used for goods or services. We could also stretch this to include tradable items like money or other financial assets such as shares.
- *Purchasers* – these are the buyers of the product and are often referred to as 'consumers', although they may simply be intermediaries in the

Self-assessment tasks

1 What are the various sub-markets that we could identify if we wanted to look in more detail at the following products:
   - soft drinks?
   - transport?
   - fast food?
   - personal computers?

2 Why do you think it is often important for companies to look more at sub-market issues? How could we break the market down even further to find out about an individual consumer's demand for a particular product?

3 Find out about the last big equipment order placed by your school or college – see if you can find out what factors influenced the decision of the person who made the choices.

production–consumption chain, for example Nestlé purchasing large amounts of cocoa to be used in the production of chocolate for sale to the final consumer. We could look at an individual purchaser's demand for a product or, more usefully, we can aggregate this to look at the demand of an overall market or sub-market.

- *Willing to buy* – clearly purchasers must want a product if they are going to enter into the market to buy it. Economists use the terms 'satisfaction' or 'utility' to describe the benefit or pleasure that the final consumer derives from the product.
- *Able to buy* – to an economist, the **notional demand** for a product, which emerges from wanting it, must be backed by purchasing power if the demand is to become **effective**. Companies are only willing to sell a product if the purchaser has monetary ability to pay for the product – the world is full of wishful thinkers who would love to own something they just cannot afford. It is, however, effective demand that is of real importance for economists.
- *Various prices* – prices are crucial to the functioning of a market. Although demand for a product is influenced by many things, it is at the moment of purchase, when we have to hand over our money and pay the price, that we really judge

whether the product is value for money, that is, whether we really are willing and able to buy it. As the price goes up, and provided no other changes have occurred, more and more people will judge the product to be less worthwhile.

◆ *Per period of time* – demand must be time related. It is of no use to say that the local McDonalds sold 20 Big Macs to consumers unless you specify the time period over which the sales occurred. If that was per minute then demand is probably quite high, but if that was per week then clearly there is little demand for Big Macs in this sub-market.

◆ *Other things being equal* – we will see shortly that there are numerous potential influences on the demand for a product. Analysing the connections between the various elements is very difficult if lots of these elements are changing simultaneously. The process is similar to that of a scientist who, when conducting an experiment, will control the general conditions except for the two elements that he/she wishes to investigate. So, for simplicity, we start with the assumption that all the other factors are constant and analyse the response of purchasers on

the basis that price alone changes. We will relax this assumption as we progress. Economists often use a Latin phrase, **ceteris paribus**, to indicate this assumption – this simply means '*other things being equal*'.

The demand curve

Let us now take the definition of demand and represent it diagrammatically to construct what is known as a **demand curve**. We will make up an example based on the overall market demand for PCs to illustrate the point. Let us make an assumption that we can identify a typical PC, that is one with a set of standard specifications. Remember we can break the analysis into sub-markets later if we want to become more detailed. Let us also assume that we have collected statistical data about people's preferences and that the quantity of PCs that people are willing and able to buy at various prices per period of time, ceteris paribus, can be represented by the data in table 2.1. This is known as a **demand schedule**. We can now plot the **market demand** schedule on a graph to see how the quantity demanded

McDonald's is now the world's largest fast food business, serving millions of people a day across five continents. This 'drive-in' restaurant is on Spain's Costa Brava
Source: McDonald's Corporation.

of PCs relates to variations in price. This demand curve therefore represents the aggregation of many individual demand curves. Figure 2.1 shows the market demand curve for the data in table 2.1.

Price of a 'standard' PC ($)	Quantity demanded per week – demand curve D_0
2,000	1,000
1,800	2,000
1,600	3,000
1,400	4,000
1,200	5,000
1,000	6,000
800	7,000

Table 2.1 Market demand schedule

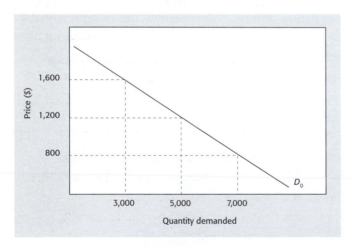

Figure 2.1 The market demand curve for PCs

Points to note:
- An inverse or negative quantitative relationship between price and quantity demanded.
  When price goes up, there is a **decrease** in *quantity demanded*.
  When price goes down, there is an **increase** in *quantity demanded*.
  Notice the language that is being used here – changes in price cause *changes in quantity demanded* and we illustrate this by movements up and down the demand curve.
- A causal relationship – we are saying that changes in price cause changes in quantity demanded.

- A linear relationship – this demand curve has been drawn, again for simplicity, as a straight line. However, it is perfectly acceptable for price and quantity demanded to be related in a non-linear manner.
- A continuous relationship – we could look at the diagram and find out at what price consumers would be willing and able to buy 1,259 PCs.
- A time-based relationship – the time period here is weekly.

Note that we are also assuming ceteris paribus – you should briefly review what this means.

Notice how important it is to label diagrams – the price axis, the quantity demanded axis, the demand curve and the P and Q_D reference points on each axis.

Self-assessment tasks

1 How many PCs per week are people willing and able to buy if the price is $1,100?

2 What price will persuade people to buy 1,350 PCs per week?

3 What assumptions are you making when you answer these questions?

A typical personal computer
Source: Hewlett Packard.

Self-assessment task

Explain how the area under the demand curve could be used to illustrate total consumer expenditure/total revenue of the firms selling PCs.

Figure 2.1 is a very useful diagram since it allows us to visualise a quite complex relationship – simple pictures are usually easier to understand and remember than a large number of words. It also allows us to estimate how much consumers may spend when buying PCs, or conversely how much revenue companies may receive from selling PCs. If the price of each PC is $1,800 and the above information is accurate then consumers will buy 2,000 units and their total spending will be equal to $3,600,000, which, of course, will be the revenue that companies receive from selling this quantity of the product. (Note that, since we do not know the firm's production and distribution costs, we are as yet unable to say anything about profit.)

Consumer surplus

The underlying principles behind the demand curve are relatively simple to understand. They are also ones which many of us follow in our daily lives. For instance, when a product is on 'special offer' in a local shop, and its price has been reduced, more will be demanded and purchased.

For any good or service, though, there are always some people who are prepared to pay above the given price to obtain it. Some of the best examples where this happens are in the cases of tickets to popular rock concerts or, in England, to watch Premier League football clubs, such as Manchester United, or to see a major Test cricket series where all tickets are sold out. The stated price of tickets may well be $40 per ticket, but there will always be some people who are willing to pay over $40 to obtain a ticket. Another example might be the case of a chocoholic who is prepared to pay over the odds to get a bar of his or her favourite chocolate. To the economist, such situations introduce the concept of **consumer surplus**.

Consumer surplus arises because consumers would be willing to pay more than the given price for all but the last unit they buy. This can be illustrated in figure 2.2(a) where consumer surplus is the shaded area under

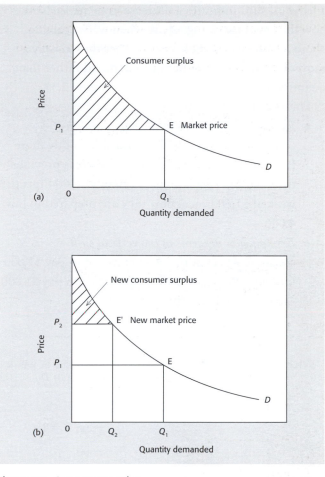

Figure 2.2 Consumer surplus

the demand curve and above the price line. More specifically, it is the difference between the total value consumers place on all the units consumed and the payments they need to make in order to actually purchase that commodity.

If the market price changes then so does consumer surplus. For example, if the price increases then consumer surplus is reduced as some consumers are unwilling to pay the higher price. This reduction is shown in figure 2.2(b). The loss of consumer surplus is shown by the area $P_1P_2E'E$.

Shifts in the demand curve

Whilst the above analysis is useful, it is clearly limited because the price of a PC is not the only, or in many cases not the most important, factor influencing demand for it – other things play a part and are not always constant. Changes in these 'ceteris paribus' factors can be illustrated by shifts in the demand curve. A rightward shift indicates an increase in demand;

a leftward shift indicates a decrease in demand. Notice how the language changes here when we are talking about a shift in the whole curve rather than simply a movement along it – a **change in demand** rather than quantity demanded (see table 2.2 and figure 2.3).

Points to note:

◆ *Explanation in terms of the horizontal shift –* consumers are now willing and able to buy more PCs at each and every price. So, whereas previously they had only been prepared to buy 3,000 units per week at $1,600 each, now they are prepared to buy 4,000.

◆ *Explanation in terms of the vertical shift –* consumers previously were prepared to pay $1,600 for 3,000 PCs, now they are prepared to pay $1,800 each for that quantity.

Price of a 'standard' PC ($)	Quantity demanded per week – demand curve D_2
2,000	2,000
1,800	3,000
1,600	4,000
1,400	5,000
1,200	6,000
1,000	7,000
800	8,000

Table 2.2 Shifts in the demand curve

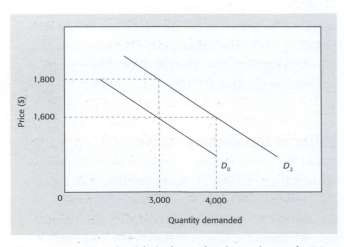

Figure 2.3 A shift to the right in the market demand curve for PCs

Self-assessment task

Use the information below to draw a demand curve and explain what has happened to that demand curve – you are showing a decrease in demand. Draw in demand curve D_0 from figure 2.3 as well so that you can use it as the basis for your comparison.

Price of a 'standard' PC ($)	Quantity demanded per week – demand curve D_1
2,000	0
1,800	1,000
1,600	2,000
1,400	3,000
1,200	4,000
1,000	5,000
800	6,000

Causes of shifts in the demand curve

Individuals may differ widely in their attitudes towards products. We could therefore spend a lot of time constructing a very long list of non-price influences. This might be useful in certain circumstances but not in all cases. Fortunately, economists have identified that there are three key non-price categories that can be used to describe and analyse the factors that influence the demand for most products. They are:

(a) the financial ability to pay for the product;

(b) our attitudes towards the product itself;

(c) the price, availability and attractiveness of related products.

Let us look at each in turn.

The financial ability to pay

We have already noted the importance of effective demand. So what influences someone's ability to pay for a product? The key factors are:

◆ the purchasing power of their income after taxation;

◆ the availability of loans/credit and the interest rate that must be paid on loans or credit card balances.

In general we would expect a positive relationship between the financial ability to pay and the demand for a product. So an increase in purchasers' financial ability to pay generally leads to an increase in demand, and this would be represented by a rightward shift in the demand curve from D_0 to D_2 in figure 2.3. A decrease in the ability to pay would lead to a decrease in demand, and this would be represented by a leftward shift in the demand curve from D_2 to D_0.

There is an important qualification to this general rule. The single most important influence on people's financial ability to pay for goods and services is generally considered to be income. In most cases there is a positive relationship between income and product demand – that is, as income rises, normally the demand for the majority of goods and services also increases; as income falls, so does the demand for most products. Products that are characterised by such a relationship are labelled **normal goods**.

However, there are some products that are characterised by a negative relationship between income and demand. As income rises the demand for dated types of PC, such as 386 and 486MHz speed PCs, will fall; as income rises people tend to choose better quality clothing. Products that are characterised by such a relationship are referred to as **inferior goods**.

Self-assessment task

Draw diagrams and briefly explain how you expect changes in the following to influence the position of the demand curve for PCs:
- an increase in interest rates;
- a large increase in unemployment;
- a sustained rise in earnings from work;
- a reduction in income tax.

Attitudes towards the products

We all buy products for a reason, that is our behaviour is purposefully motivated, at least at the time of purchase! Economists usually consider our behaviour to be a reflection of our tastes and preferences towards different types of goods and services. You may buy a particular type or brand of PC because of its reputation for reliability. You may buy a pair of brand-name trainers because you want to play sport and you genuinely believe them to be of better quality or you may buy them simply because they are fashionable and you want to look cool.

Detailed understanding of the psychological motives that determine our behaviour are beyond our scope here, but clearly we are influenced by our own

Self-assessment task

Would you classify the following products as normal goods or inferior goods? In each case draw a diagram to explain how a decrease in income will shift the demand curve. Explain your reasoning. What difficulties did you have in deciding? What information would you need to resolve these difficulties?

- Premium brand orange juice   Supermarket own label orange juice
- Holidays overseas   Holidays at home
- Black and white TV sets   Nicam stereo, digital TVs

individual likes and dislikes, by peer pressure and by advertising and the marketing images that surround us. Nowhere of course is this more evident than in markets for clothing and recorded music, where tastes and preferences can be extremely volatile.

Self-assessment tasks

1 What, at present, is the dominant brand of sports clothing? Why do you think it is dominant? Is it because it is of genuinely superior quality or is there another explanation?
2 Think of a successful advertising campaign that is running on the TV at present. Why is it successful and what impact would you expect it to have on sales over the next six months?

The price, availability and attractiveness of related products

Economists classify types of related products into two categories: **substitutes** and **complements**.

- *Substitute products* are alternatives – products that satisfy essentially the same wants or needs. The range of substitutability can be fairly narrow, for example in terms of different product brands: Hewlett Packard and Dell computers, Casio and Accurist watches and Ford and General Motors cars. Or the range of substitutability can be broad, in terms of product groups, for example different types of transport – rail, buses and cars; different types of soft drinks – lemonade, Pepsi Cola, or fruit juices. Changes in the price or attractiveness of one of these products will have an impact on the demand for all substitutes.

◆ *Complements* are products that enhance the satisfaction we derive from another product. Common examples are fish and rice, TVs and video recorders, airline flights and hotel accommodation, PCs and modems or software. In some cases, without the complement the main product would be useless. Examples here include: cars and fuel; video recorders and video tapes. Once again changes in price or attractiveness of one of these products will have an impact on the demand for the complementary product.

Self-assessment tasks

1 What would you expect to happen to the demand for Dell PCs if Hewlett Packard cut their prices?
2 What would you expect to happen to the demand for all PCs if the price of software and printers came down sharply?

Use a diagram to help explain your answers.

Other demand-influencing factors

Clearly this is not an exhaustive list of the factors that influence demand. Each product will have some factors that are peculiar to it, for example the weather may influence the demand for ice cream. Expectations of the future can be important in determining the demand for certain products. If house prices or share prices are expected to rise, this can be a major influence in boosting demand. If unemployment or interest rates are expected to go up, this can have a dampening effect on the demand for some products. The skill of the economist is to use the categories above and knowledge or intuition to identify the key influences on demand, in any particular market, to explain past behaviour or to try to predict future behaviour.

Supply

We now turn our attention to the other side of the market and consider the meaning of and influences on supply. To an economist:

> **supply** refers to the *quantities* of a *product* that *suppliers* are *willing and able* to *sell* at *various prices* per *period of time, other things remaining the same.*

Note the similarities below with the definition of demand:

◆ *'Quantities'* – once again we must emphasise that economists often deal with numerical values and very often try to represent information in a quantitative way.

◆ *Product* – as with demand we are using the term to refer to any item that is being traded. It can be used for goods or services. We could also stretch this to include tradable items like money or other financial assets such as shares.

◆ *Suppliers* – these are the sellers of the product and are often referred to as 'producers', although they may not be manufacturers of the product but again may simply be an intermediary in the production–consumption chain or they may be selling services. We could look at an individual company's supply of a product or, more usefully, we can aggregate to look at the supply for an overall market or sub-market.

◆ *Willing and able to sell at various prices* – clearly, in a market economy, companies must gain from selling their products. The ability to earn profits is likely to be a major (but probably not the only) influence on company behaviour – the higher the price, ceteris paribus, the more profit companies are likely to make. However, as companies produce more, they may find that **costs** start to go up (because of something called diminishing returns or capacity constraints), so they may need to sell at higher prices to convince them to produce more of the product.

◆ *Per period of time* – supply must also be time related. It is of no use to say that Hewlett Packard supplied 200 computers unless you specify the relevant time period. Clearly this needs to be consistent with the time period being used for demand.

◆ *Other things being equal* (ceteris paribus) – we will see shortly that there are numerous potential influences on the supply of a product. Analysing the connections between the various elements is very difficult if lots of these elements are changing simultaneously.

The supply curve

We need to take this definition and represent it diagrammatically to construct what is known as a **supply curve**. We could do this for an individual firm selling PCs or, by aggregating each separate company's supply curve, we could get the industry or market supply curve for PCs. Assume again that we have collected statistical data about companies' selling intentions and that these plans can be represented by table 2.3 (this is known as a market **supply schedule**). We can now plot this supply schedule to see how the quantity of PCs supplied relates to variations in price. Figure 2.4 shows the supply curve (S_0) for the data in the table.

Price of a 'standard' PC ($)	Quantity supplied per week – supply curve S_0
800	1,000
1,000	2,000
1,200	3,000
1,400	4,000
1,600	5,000
1,800	6,000
2,000	7,000

Table 2.3 Market supply schedule

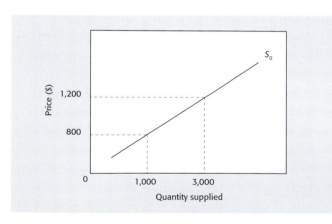

Figure 2.4 The market supply curve for PCs

Points to note:
- A positive or direct relationship between price and quantity supplied.
  When price goes up there is an *increase* in *quantity supplied*.
  When price goes down there is a *decrease* in *quantity supplied*.

- Again notice the language that is being used – changes in price cause changes in quantity supplied and we illustrate this by movements up and down the supply curve (again some economists prefer to use the terms 'extension of supply' for a movement up the supply curve and a 'contraction of supply' for a movement down the curve).
- A causal relationship – we are saying that price changes cause the change in quantity supplied.
- A linear relationship – the supply curve has been drawn for simplicity as a straight line, but of course there is no reason why the supply curve should not be represented in a non-linear way.
- A continuous relationship – we could look at the curve to find out how many PCs companies would plan to supply at a price of $1,150.
- A time-based relationship – the time period again is weekly.

Note we are also assuming ceteris paribus – any other factor influencing supply is assumed to be unchanged.

Self-assessment tasks

1 How many PCs per week are companies planning to supply if the price is $1,100?
2 What price would persuade companies to supply 1,350 PCs?
3 What assumptions are you making when you answer these questions?
4 What might be the advantages and disadvantages of using a diagrammatic form such as in figure 2.4 to represent supply?

Shifts in the market supply curve

Whilst the above is useful, one of the limitations is that companies' supply intentions are influenced by factors other than the price of the product (which, if you think about it, is the most tangible expression of consumers' buying intentions). Other things are most certainly not always equal. Changes in these 'ceteris paribus' factors can be illustrated by shifts in the supply curve. A rightward shift indicates an increase in supply; a leftward shift indicates a decrease in supply. Notice again how the language changes when we are talking about a shift in the whole curve rather than simply a

Price of a 'standard' PC ($)	Quantity supplied per week – supply curve S_2
800	2,000
1,000	3,000
1,200	4,000
1,400	5,000
1,600	6,000
1,800	7,000
2,000	8,000

Table 2.4 An increase in supply

movement along it – a change in supply rather than quantity supplied (see table 2.4 and figure 2.5).

Points to note:

◆ *Explanation of horizontal shift* – companies are now more willing and/or more able to supply PCs at each and every price. Previously they had only been prepared to supply 3,000 units per week at $1,200; now they are prepared to supply 4,000.

◆ *Explanation of vertical shift* – companies previously wanted $1,200 per unit to persuade them to supply 3,000 units per week; now they are prepared to accept $1,000.

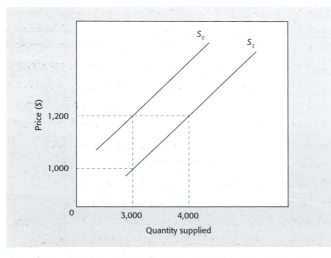

Figure 2.5 A shift to the right in the market supply curve for PCs

Causes of shifts in the supply curve

Companies clearly differ in their willingness and ability to supply products and, as with demand, we could spend a long time building a list of possible factors other than price that will affect supply. If we were required (and

Self-assessment task

Use the information below to draw a new supply curve (S_1) and explain what has happened to that supply curve – remember you are showing a decrease in supply. Draw in supply curve S_0 as well so that you can use it as the basis for your comparison.

Price of a 'standard' PC ($)	Quantity supplied per week – supply curve S_1
1,000	1,000
1,200	2,000
1,400	3,000
1,600	4,000
1,800	5,000
2,000	6,000

paid!) to conduct a detailed analysis of supply conditions in a particular industry, that might be justified. For our purposes we need to simplify and generalise about the factors that can influence supply in most industries. As with demand, we can focus on three main influences:

◆ the costs associated with supplying the product;
◆ the size, structure and nature of the industry;
◆ government policy.

Let us discuss each in turn.

Costs

In a market-based economy, no firm (in the absence of government support) can exist indefinitely if it makes losses, so companies will make supply decisions on the basis of the price they can get for selling the product in relation to the cost of supplying it. You will see in section 9 how costs may rise as a firm increases production with a given capacity – this will influence the shape of the supply curve. What we are interested in here, however, is what factors can influence the position of the supply curve – in other words, what factors can cause an increase or a decrease in the costs of supplying each and every unit, since it is likely that this will impact on the price that companies charge per unit. Below are listed some potentially influential factors – if the factor pushes up costs, there is likely to be a leftward shift in the supply curve or decrease in supply; if the factor lowers costs, there is likely to be an increase in supply:

- wage rates;
- worker productivity (output per worker);
- raw material and component prices;
- energy costs;
- equipment maintenance costs;
- transport costs;
- the state of technology.

Self-assessment task

Go through each of the above factors in turn and work out what sort of change in that factor will cause:
- an increase in supply,
- a decrease in supply.

The size and nature of the industry

If it is clear that there is substantial profit to be made by selling a product, firms inside and outside the industry are likely to react. Firms currently in the industry may invest in capital equipment in an attempt to grow bigger and take advantage of the situation. Firms outside the industry may try to enter this market and of course new firms may set up in business. The ease with which they can do so will depend on whether there are any **barriers to entry** into the industry and, if there are, how easy it is to overcome them (see section 9). Nonetheless if the size of the industry increases, because there are more firms or bigger firms, then it is likely that the supply of the industry will increase. Equally, if firms in the industry start to compete more intensively on price, it is likely that the supply curve will shift to the right as the effects of this price competition start to affect the price that all companies are willing to accept for their products. Of course if a fierce price war does break out, then consumers, at least temporarily, may enjoy very much lower prices for any given level of supply.

Self-assessment tasks

1 Why might firms choose to leave an industry?
2 What is likely to happen to the industry supply if the size of the industry shrinks?
3 What might happen to supply if all firms decide to try and increase the amount of profit they make on each unit they sell?

Government policy

Governments influence company decisions in many ways. Legislation designed to protect consumers or workers may impose additional costs on companies and this may affect the supply curve. Governments may also impose indirect taxes (excise duties or value added tax) on companies. These taxes can act like a cost increase because companies may seek to pass the tax on to the consumer in the form of higher prices. As such, indirect taxes often result in a decrease in supply. On the other hand, a relaxation of certain types of legislation or government subsidies can increase supply by encouraging firms to reduce prices for any given level of output.

Self-assessment task

Refer to the supply curve S_0 in figure 2.5. What would happen to this curve if the government introduced a tax of:
- $100 per computer?
- 10% on the pre-tax selling price?
- legislation that raised companies' costs by about 20 per cent on average?

Other supply-influencing factors

As with our treatment of demand, this is not intended to be a complete list of the factors that influence supply. Each industry will have some features that are relevant to it. For example, the supply of agricultural produce is particularly influenced by weather conditions. Some industries may be able to switch production from one product to another fairly easily and so the relative profitability of alternative product areas may be important. In financial markets, like the stock market or the foreign exchange market, supply may be significantly influenced by expectations of future prices. Once again the skill of the economist is to use theory, insight and observation to identify the key influences on supply in any situation to explain the past or to try to predict the future.

Putting supply and demand all together – markets in equilibrium and disequilibrium

We have now analysed each side of the market separately and it is time to put it all together. At any point in time, there will be a given set of conditions influencing demand and a given set of conditions influencing supply (see table 2.5). Let us say that those conditions are reflected in demand curve D_0 and supply curve S_0 from earlier on – these relationships have been drawn for you in figure 2.6.

Price of a standard PC ($)	Quantity supplied per week	Quantity demanded per week
800	1,000	7,000
1,000	2,000	6,000
1,200	3,000	5,000
1,400	4,000	4,000
1,600	5,000	3,000
1,800	6,000	2,000
2,000	7,000	1,000

Table 2.5 Market supply and demand schedules for PCs

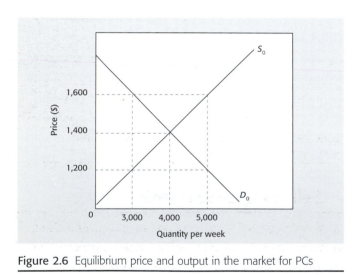

Figure 2.6 Equilibrium price and output in the market for PCs

The term **equilibrium** refers to a situation of balance where at least under present circumstances there is no tendency for change to occur. In this particular situation, equilibrium will exist when the plans of consumers (as represented by the demand curve) match the plans of suppliers (as represented by the supply curve).

The market equilibrium in this case will, therefore, be at a price of $1,400 with 4,000 units bought and sold. These are often referred to as **equilibrium price** and **equilibrium quantity**. Total consumer expenditure (and therefore industry revenue) will be $560,000 per week. Just think about what would happen if for some reason companies thought that consumers were prepared to pay $1,600 and supplied 5,000 units to the market. In this case the market would be in a disequilibrium (an imbalance where change will happen). At a price of $1,600, under present circumstances, consumers are only planning to buy 3,000 units. As such companies will build up excess stocks at the rate of 2,000 PCs per week. There is a **disequilibrium** of excess supply. Companies would be irrational to carry on with this unplanned stockbuilding. How might they react? Well for a start they could cut price; they would also probably start to reduce the quantity they supply to the market. Of course, as they cut price, some consumers who would not have been prepared to pay the higher price are now attracted back into the market – the disequilibrium starts to narrow. Provided there is no change to any of the conditions of supply or demand, and nothing prevented companies adjusting in this way, then eventually, perhaps through expert decision making or simply trial and error, the market price and quantity should move back to equilibrium.

Think now what would happen if the price was set at $1,000. Again we have a disequilibrium – this time of excess demand. Consumers are now keen to snap up what they consider to be a pretty good deal. However, given the low prices, supplies are fairly low and there are not enough PCs to meet demand – suppliers run out of stocks far quicker than they had expected, so there are unmet orders. Profit-oriented companies, if they are reasonably sharp, will recognise this and will start to raise price and increase the number of PCs available for sale. However, as prices rise, some consumers will decide that PCs are a bit too expensive at the moment and the quantity demanded will fall. Once again, as a result of trial and error and good management on the part of businesses, the market will adjust back to the equilibrium.

This process of market adjustment may not happen instantly; there will be time lags, perhaps quite lengthy ones if companies are managed badly. The point, however, is that there will always be a tendency for the market to move back to its equilibrium because that is where the underlying motives and plans of consumers and suppliers are driving it.

Self-assessment tasks

In the figure 2.7 below symbols, instead of numbers, are used to represent the same situation.

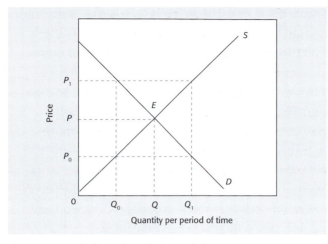

Figure 2.7 Typical supply and demand diagram

1 What is the market equilibrium price and quantity?
2 What area will show the total expenditure by consumers? This will be the same as the total revenue earned by companies.
3 What is the state of the market if the price is at P_1?
4 What is the state of the market if the price is at P_0?
5 Explain what will happen if the market is in a disequilibrium of:
   ◆ excess demand;
   ◆ excess supply.
6 What advantages/disadvantages are there in using symbols, such as P_s and Q_s, to analyse markets rather than actual numbers?

Changes in the equilibrium

The equilibrium will change if there is a disturbance to the present market conditions – this could come about through a change in the conditions of supply (the supply curve shifts) or a change in the conditions of demand (the demand curve shifts).

A change in demand

Look at figure 2.8 – notice we are using P and Q symbols again instead of actual numbers – if there is an increase in demand (D_0 to D_2), then, at the

Self-assessment tasks

1 Review the factors that can cause the demand curve to shift.
2 Review the factors that can cause the supply curve to shift.
3 Review how disequilibrium positions are eliminated in a market.

original price, there is now a disequilibrium of excess demand equal to $Q_1 - Q_0$. As suppliers begin to recognise this they will start to raise price and increase quantity supplied. The rise in price will lead some consumers to decide they do not want to buy the product at the higher price. Although the process may take some time, the market will move back towards the new equilibrium at $P^* Q^*$, where the market is once more in balance. Note that the new equilibrium is at a higher price with a larger quantity traded than in the original situation.

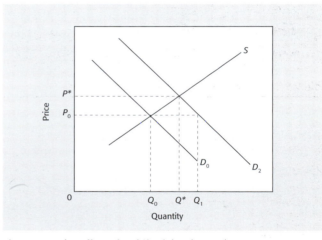

Figure 2.8 The effect of a shift of the demand curve on equilibrium price and quantity

Self-assessment task

What will happen if there is a decrease in demand? Use a properly labelled diagram to explain clearly how both the market equilibrium price and quantity traded will fall.

A change in supply

Look at figure 2.9 (see p. 48) – if there is an increase in supply (from S_0 to S_2) then, at the original price (P_0), there is now a disequilibrium of excess supply ($Q_1 - Q_0$). This would of course eventually be eliminated as price falls towards its new equilibrium level and the quantity traded in equilibrium rises from Q_0 to Q^* where the plans of consumers and companies once more coincide.

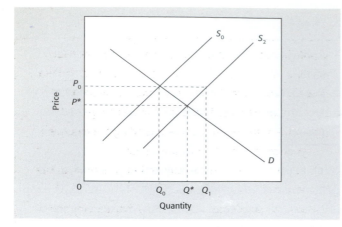

Figure 2.9 The effect of a shift in the supply curve on equilibrium price and quantity

A change in supply and demand

The above analysis is useful to deal with simple situations. However, in many situations the conditions of both supply and demand may change simultaneously. Look at figure 2.10. The initial equilibrium is at P and Q with the demand curve D_0 and the supply curve S_0. The increase in demand for the product (caused by, say, the increase in the price of a substitute) puts upward pressure on price. However, the simultaneous increase in supply (caused by, say, a fall in raw material and energy costs) puts downward pressure on price. The resulting effect is that the equilibrium price remains unchanged, although of course there is a fairly significant increase in the quantity traded (from Q to Q^*).

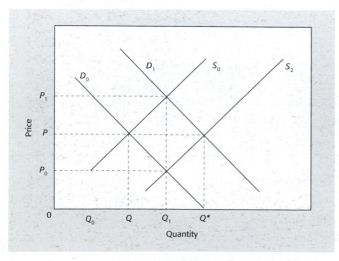

Figure 2.10 An unchanged equilibrium price and a changed equilibrium quantity

Self-assessment task

What would happen if there was a decrease in supply? Use a properly labelled diagram to explain clearly how the market equilibrium price would rise but the equilibrium amount traded would fall.

Prices as a rationing mechanism

It should be clear from the last part of this section that prices play a very important part in the allocation of resources in markets. The workings of the **price mechanism** as we have described it are in the main automatic; in other words, price variations act as a signal in response to changes in demand or supply or both. This self-regulating mechanism (referred to by Adam Smith as 'the invisible hand') is an important feature of the market economy. It is a means by which equilibrium indicates where consumers' demand and the producers' willingness to supply meet.

In certain situations, this mechanism can serve to also **ration** resources in a particular market. This process can be achieved with or without intervention on the part of the government. Let us consider a few examples.

♦ If a producer has limited capacity or wishes to restrict the supply of products, then,` if these products have a high price, the market mechanism will automatically result in a type of rationing occurring. A good example could be the ways in which exclusive car manufacturers or designer fashion companies charge very high prices for their products. Price therefore limits demand and in turn seeks to ensure that it is in line with the quantity that is supplied.

♦ Governments may also wish to use the price mechanism as a means of rationing. A good example could be the way in which some governments try to restrict sales of alcohol or tobacco products through imposing very high rates of taxation on their consumption (see also section 3). Another example could be the use of minimum price legislation, in this case to ration demand in relation to supply. In these cases, the government is interfering with the workings of the price mechanism in order to meet some other particular objective.

Self-assessment tasks

1 See if you can explain the following situations. Use a diagram to help you in each case – remember both the supply and demand curves are shifting now:

   (a) an increase in demand, but the equilibrium price falls;

   (b) a decrease in demand, but the equilibrium price goes up;

   (c) a decrease in supply, but the equilibrium quantity remains unchanged;

   (d) an increase in supply, but the equilibrium price increases.

2 (a) Explain the factors which might determine the demand for Caribbean holidays by households in the UK.

   (b) Discuss the impact of a reduction in air fares on the demand for holidays to the Caribbean and in the UK.

3 The opening of the Channel Tunnel increased the supply in the market for cross-Channel trips between England and France. With the aid of a diagram explain how this will affect travellers on cross-Channel trips.

4 Do some research to find out what has happened:

   (a) to the numbers of people attending the cinema in your country in the last ten years;

   (b) to house prices, nationally and in your area, in the last year.

   Use supply and demand analysis to explain why the changes may have occurred.

5 Analyse with the aid of diagrams:

   (a) the likely effect of a reduction in the price of pre-recorded compact discs (CDs) on the demand for visits to live music concerts;

   (b) the likely effect of a reduction in the entrance price to live music concerts on the demand for pre-recorded CDs.

The Channel tunnel shuttle train emerges from the tunnel opening on the French side at Sangatte on 28 April 1993 as tests continued prior to the official opening ceremony on 6 May.
Source: Popperfoto Reuters.

A change in price is unlikely to affect demand for high-performance sports cars
Source: Dick Barnard.

The importance of elasticity

So far our analysis of markets and sub-markets has concentrated on understanding the direction of any change in supply, demand, prices or output and sales. For example, we have looked at what can cause an increase or decrease in demand and whether this change will raise or lower prices or output. We now want to add more depth to our understanding by looking at the *extent* of demand changes and whether there is likely to be a large or a small impact on the equilibrium. In some cases, a small increase in income, for example, may have a really big impact on demand and this in turn may have a really significant impact on the equilibrium price. In other cases, the same increase in income may have little impact on demand and the market equilibrium. We need some tools or concepts to help us understand these changes more precisely. The concept that allows us to move forward in this way is **elasticity**.

Elasticity is simply a way of quantifying cause and effect relationships. It is defined generally as a numerical measure of *the responsiveness of one economic variable (the dependent variable) following a change in another influencing variable (the independent variable), ceteris paribus!* Where relationships are elastic (responsive), a small change in the cause or the independent variable has a big effect on the other dependent variable. Where relationships are inelastic, a large change in the cause has limited effects on the dependent variable. This

might seem a bit confusing, so let us look at specific examples of elasticity – this general definition will then start to become clearer.

Price elasticity of demand (PED)

Price elasticity of demand is a numerical measure of the responsiveness of demand for one product following a change in the price of that product alone. If demand is elastic, then a small change in price will result in a relatively large change in quantity demanded. On the other hand, if price goes up by a lot and quantity demanded only falls slightly, then demand would be price inelastic. A numerical example will help clarify this. First, however, we need a way of expressing PED in a numerical form – the formula we will use at this stage is

$$PED = \frac{\% \text{ change in quantity demanded of a product}}{\% \text{ change in price of that product}}$$

Let us take two specific examples of price changes for two general products that we will call product A and product B (see figure 2.11). Assume that both of these unrelated products currently are priced at $100 and demand for them is 1,000 units per month. Consider what is expected to happen to the demand for A and B if the price rises to $105. The quantity demanded of product A only falls from 1,000 to 990, whereas the quantity demanded of product B falls from 1,000 to 900. Now let us put these values into the PED equation to calculate the elasticity.

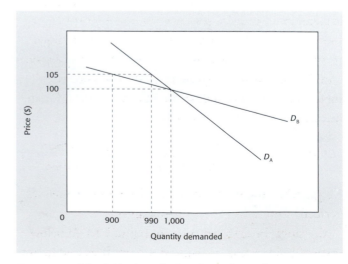

Figure 2.11 Price inelastic and price elastic demand curves

Product A $\dfrac{\text{\% change in quantity demanded of A}}{\text{\% change in price of A}} =$

$\dfrac{1\% \text{ fall}}{5\% \text{ increase}} = (-)0.2$

Product B $\dfrac{\text{\% change in quantity demanded of B}}{\text{\% change in price of B}} =$

$\dfrac{10\% \text{ fall}}{5\% \text{ increase}} = (-)2.0$

Notice that in both cases a negative figure is given. This is because of the negative (or inverse) relationship between price and quantity demanded, that is, as the price goes up, the quantity demanded goes down. Conventionally economists refer to PED in absolute terms by ignoring the negative sign.

Product A – because the numerical value (0.2) is less than one we say that the demand for this product is relatively inelastic or unresponsive to price changes. Over this particular range of prices, the 5 per cent increase has resulted in a much smaller change in quantity demanded.

Product B – because the numerical value (2.0) is greater than one, we say that the demand for this product is relatively elastic or responsive to price changes. Over this particular range of prices, the same 5 per cent price change has caused a much bigger change in quantity demanded.

Some special PED values

It is important to realise that mathematically PED values can range from 0 to infinity. These values need explanation. Consider, for example, the demand curve shown in figure 2.12. Irrespective of the price charged, consumers are willing and able to buy the same amount – in this case demand would be said to be **perfectly inelastic**. Let us just look at the PED calculation for an increase in price from $10 to $11

$$PED = \frac{\text{\% change in quantity demanded}}{\text{\% change in price}} = \frac{0\%}{+10\%} = 0$$

Hence, when the PED = 0, demand is perfectly inelastic, perfectly unresponsive to price changes.

Consider the demand curve in figure 2.13. At below a price of $10 per unit consumers are not prepared to buy any of this product; however, if price falls to $9, they

will buy all that is available. The relative change in quantity demanded here, of course, is infinite, since the original demand was zero

$$PED = \frac{\text{\% change in quantity demanded}}{\text{\% change in price}} = \frac{\infty}{-10\%} = (-)\infty$$

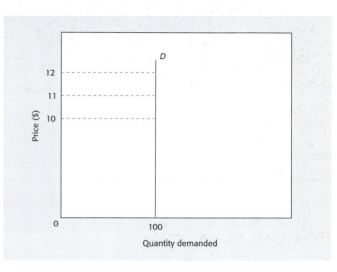

Figure 2.12 A perfectly inelastic demand curve

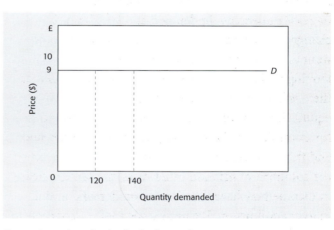

Figure 2.13 A perfectly elastic demand curve

Unitary elasticity

If the relative increase in price is exactly matched by the relative fall in quantity demanded, then the PED value will equal (–)1 and demand will be said to have **unitary elasticity** over that particular price range. So, for example, if the price of the product goes from $1,000 to $1,050 and quantity demanded decreases from 10,000 to 9,500, then the PED will equal (–)1 over this particular range of prices.

Self-assessment tasks

1 Calculate the PEDs in each of the following cases and explain whether demand would be considered price elastic or price inelastic.

Original price	New price	Original quantity demanded	New quantity demanded
(a) $100	$102	2,000 units per week	1,950 units per week
(b) $55.50	$54.95	5,000 units per week	6,000 units per week

2 With the aid of a numerical example of your choice explain the meaning of these PED values:

  (a) PED = (−)1.5,   (b) PED = (−)0.6.

Factors that influence price elasticity of demand

There are three key factors that influence whether, over a particular price range, demand for a product is likely to be price elastic or inelastic.

◆ *The range and attractiveness of substitutes* – the greater the number of substitute (alternative) products and the more closely substitutable those products are, the more we would expect consumers to switch away from a particular product when its price goes up (or towards that product if its price falls).

It is important, however, to distinguish between the substitutability of products within the same group of products and substitutability with goods from other product groupings. For example, different types of orange juice are a group of products in their own right; they are also part of a larger group of fruit juices and part of the even bigger category of products that we could label as 'drinks'. If we are concerned with the price elasticity of demand for a particular type of orange juice produced by a specific manufacturer, then it will have a fairly high PED (probably) because of the range of substitutes. As we aggregate products into groupings, such as 'fruit juices', or 'all soft drinks', demand will start to become more price inelastic.

Other substitutability issues to consider include:
  – the quality and accessibility of information that consumers have about products that are available to satisfy particular wants and needs;
  – the degree to which people consider the product to be a necessity;
  – the addictive properties of the product, that is, whether the product is habit forming;
  – the brand image of the product.

Self-assessment tasks

1 Classify the following products into whether, in your opinion, the PED is likely to be relatively high (elastic) or relatively low (inelastic):

◆ Coca Cola
◆ Pepsi Cola
◆ soft drinks in general

◆ Nike trainers
◆ Cadbury chocolates
◆ all sweet products

◆ a particular brand of petrol
◆ all forms of car fuel

Justify your classification.

2 A manufacturer has received a market research estimate of PED values for their shirts that are currently sold in three markets: to independent retailers, to prestige fashion stores and via mail order.

Market	Current price	Current sales	PED value
Independent retailers	$8	40,000 p.a.	−1.0
Fashion stores	$15	10,000 p.a.	−0.2
Mail order	$10	3,000 p.a.	−3.0

Explain and comment upon the PED values shown above.

◆ *The relative expense of the product* – a rise in price will reduce the purchasing power of a person's income (real income). The larger the proportion of income that the price represents, the larger will be the impact on the consumer's real income level of a change in the product's price. For example, a 10 per cent increase in the price of a flight to Malaysia will have a bigger impact than a 10 per cent rise in the price of a bus trip into town. The greater the relative proportion of income accounted for by the product, the higher the PED, ceteris paribus!

◆ *Time* – in the short term, perhaps weeks or months, people may find it hard to change their spending patterns. However, if the price of a product goes up and stays up, then over time people will find ways of adapting and adjusting, so the PED is likely to increase over time.

PED and a downward-sloping linear demand curve

So far the impression may have been created that PED and the slope of a demand curve are the same – this, however, is incorrect. Table 2.6 and the associated self-assessment task will help you see the difference.

Income elasticity of demand

Income elasticity of demand (YED) is defined as a numerical measure of the responsiveness of demand following a change in income alone. Once again if demand is responsive, then it is classified as elastic; if unresponsive, it is inelastic.

The formula used in this case is

$$YED = \frac{\% \text{ change in quantity demanded}}{\% \text{ change in income}}$$

Price of product R ($/unit)	Quantity demanded of product R (units per week)
10	0
9	1,000
8	2,000
7	3,000
6	4,000
5	5,000
4	6,000
3	7,000
2	8,000
1	9,000
0	10,000

Table 2.6 Demand schedule for product R

Self-assessment task

Use the information in table 2.6 to calculate the PED values as price falls from $10 to $9, from $9 to $8, from $8 to $7 and so on. You should see that the PED value falls as you move down the demand curve in figure 2.14. In the top half of the demand curve, PED > 1; in the bottom half of the demand curve, PED < 1. We could show that for very small changes in price, PED = 1 at the mid point of the demand curve. That is why, in theory, a demand curve with unitary price elasticity throughout can be drawn – it is called a **rectangular hyperbola**. Total expenditure (the area beneath this curve) for any price quantity combination is constant.

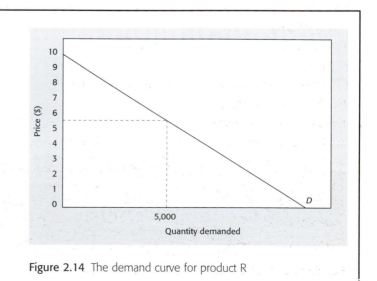

Figure 2.14 The demand curve for product R

It is important to recognise that the relationship between income and demand changes may not always be positive. If an increase in income leads to an increase in demand (or a decrease in income leads to a decrease in demand), then there is a positive relationship and the product is classified as normal, and the YED has a positive value. However, there are some products (inferior goods) that exhibit a negative relationship between income and demand. Here an increase in income would cause a decrease in demand (a decrease in income would cause an increase in demand) and the YED has a negative value. So the sign that precedes the YED tells you the nature of the relationship between income and demand; the numerical value tells you the strength of that relationship.

For example, there has been a 2 per cent increase in consumer income and that has led to the following changes in demand.

	Original demand (per period of time)	New demand
Product A	100 units at the current price ($10)	103 units at the same price ($10)
Product B	100 units at the current price ($10)	99 units at the same price ($10)
Product C	100 units at the current price ($10)	101 units at the same price ($10)

The YED of A $= \dfrac{3\% \text{ increase in demand}}{2\% \text{ increase in income}}$

$= +1.5$ (normal good – elastic response)

The YED of B $= \dfrac{1\% \text{ decrease in demand}}{2\% \text{ increase in income}}$

$= -0.5$ (inferior good – inelastic response)

The YED of C $= \dfrac{1\% \text{ increase in demand}}{2\% \text{ increase in income}}$

$= +0.5$ (normal good – inelastic response)

Self-assessment task

Use figure 2.15 to explain the YED calculations for the three products A, B and C. Note: the sign indicates the direction in which the demand curve shifts, the numerical value indicates how far the curve shifts at the original price.

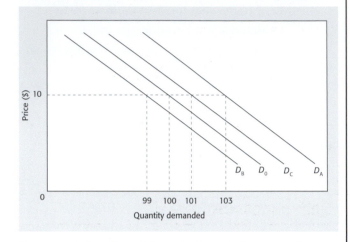

Figure 2.15 The effect of alternative income changes on the demand curve

Cross elasticity of demand

Cross elasticity of demand (XED) is a numerical measure of the responsiveness of demand for one product following a change in the price of a *related* product alone. Note the causal relationship that is being measured; and, since this has altered the conditions of demand, we would illustrate the impact of this change in the price of a related product by a shift in the demand curve (similar to YED above).

The formula used is

$$XED = \frac{\% \text{ change in quantity demanded of product A}}{\% \text{ change in the price of product B}}$$

Products that are substitutes for each other (for example, different types of laptop computer) will have positive values for the XED. If the price of B goes up, then people will begin to turn to product A because of its more favourable relative price. If the price of B falls, then consumers will start to buy B instead of A. Products that are complements (for example, computers and printers or software) will have negative values of XED. If the price of B goes up, the quantity demanded of B will drop and so will the complementary demand for A.

A numerical and diagrammatic illustration Assume the current average market price of a standard type of personal computer is $1,000 and current sales are 100 units per day (figure 2.16). Consider what might happen if, following a 2 per cent decrease in the price of laptop computers (a substitute product), demand for PCs falls from 100 units to 98 units per day at the original price (D_0 to D_1). Our calculation becomes

$$\text{XED} = \frac{2\% \text{ fall in demand for PCs}}{2\% \text{ decrease in price of laptops}}$$
$$= +1$$

The positive sign indicates that the products are substitutes.

Self-assessment task

What would have happened to the demand for PCs if, following the same change in the price of laptops, the XED had been +2. Redraw figure 2.16 to illustrate this.

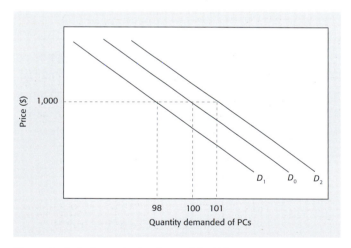

Figure 2.16 A change in the demand for PCs

Now consider that the average price of software (a complement) falls by 5% – this encourages extra sales of PCs so that demand for PCs rises to 101 per day at the original price and the demand curve shifts from D_0 to D_2.

The elasticity calculation is

$$\text{XED} = \frac{1\% \text{ increase in sales of PCs}}{5\% \text{ fall in price of software}} = -0.2$$

Note again that the sign indicates the nature of the relationship (a negative one between complements), and the numerical value indicates the strength of that relationship.

Self-assessment tasks

1 What would happen if demand for PCs had risen to 110 units per day? Calculate the XED and redraw the diagram to illustrate what has happened.

2 The owner of a local golf course loans out equipment to non-members who want to play occasional rounds. She estimates that in June and July, if she lowers the hire price of clubs by 10 per cent, the number of non-members playing will increase by 25 per cent. Calculate and comment on the XED. What other factors should the owner consider?

Price elasticity of supply

Price elasticity of supply (PES) is a numerical measure of the responsiveness of supply to a change in the price of the product alone. The supply could be that of an individual firm or group of firms; it could of course refer to the supply of the overall industry. It is expressed as

$$\text{PES} = \frac{\% \text{ change in quantity supplied}}{\% \text{ change in price}}$$

Since the relationship between the price and quantity supplied is normally a direct one, the PES will tend to take on a positive value. If the numerical value of PES is greater than 1, then we say that supply is relatively price elastic, that is supply is responsive. If the numerical value of PES is less than 1, then supply is relatively price inelastic, that is supply is unresponsive.

Figure 2.17 shows five supply curves each with different PES values.

Factors influencing PES

The key words in understanding PES are supply flexibility – if firms and industries are more flexible in the way they behave, then supply tends to be more elastic. The main influences on PES are:

♦ *The ease with which firms can accumulate or reduce stocks of goods.* Stocks allow companies to meet variations in demand through output changes rather than price changes – so the more easily manufacturing firms can do this, the higher the

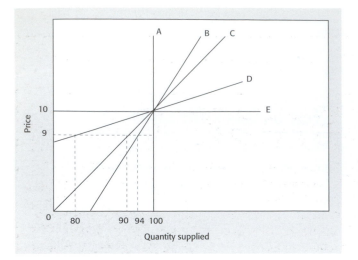

Supply curve	% change in quantity supplied	/ % change in price	= PES	Description
A	0%	/ 10% decrease	= 0	Perfectly inelastic
B	6% decrease	/ 10% decrease	= +0.6	Relatively inelastic
C	10% decrease	/ 10% decrease	= +1.0	Unitary elasticity
D	20% increase	/ 10% increase	= +2.0	Relatively elastic
E	Firms are not prepared to supply any at a price below \$10 but will supply as much as they can at \$10 (or above!)		= + ∞	Perfectly elastic

Figure 2.17 Five different supply curves

PES. Companies that provide services are, of course, unable to build up stocks.

◆ *The ease with which they can increase production.* In the short run firms and industries with spare productive capacity will tend to have a higher PES. However, shortages of critical factor inputs (skilled workers, components, fuel) will often lead to inelastic PES. This is particularly the case with agricultural products.

◆ Over time, of course, companies can increase their productive capacity by investing in more capital equipment, often taking advantage of technological

advances. Equally, over time, more firms can enter or leave an industry and this will increase the flexibility of supply.

Business relevance of elasticity
Price elasticity of demand

An understanding of PED is useful to help understand price variations in a market, the impact of changing prices on consumer expenditure, corporate revenues and government indirect tax receipts.

In figure 2.18 you can see how variations in PED can lead to price volatility following a change in the conditions of supply. D_e represents a demand curve with PED > 1 over the relevant price range. D_i represents a demand curve with PED < 1 over the relevant price range. In both cases, however, the current market equilibrium is at $P_e Q_e$. Now, a decrease in supply resulting from an increase in, say, production costs, would result in a leftward shift in the supply curve, from S_0 to S_1. Whilst we can see in both cases that the change in equilibrium leads to higher prices and a reduction in the quantity traded, the extent of the changes varies according to the PED. For D_e, as producers try to raise prices (to pass on the higher costs to their customers), consumer reaction is to stop buying this product. This reaction constrains the extent to which prices rise only from P_e to P_1 – quantity, therefore, takes the strain here and falls considerably from Q_e to Q_1. On the other hand, when demand is relatively price inelastic, producers have the scope to raise prices considerably (P_e to P_2) without suffering from a significant drop in sales (Q_e to Q_2).

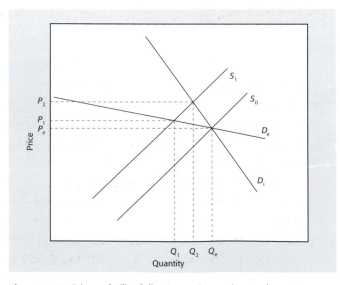

Figure 2.18 Price volatility following a change in supply

Self-assessment tasks

This question has been adapted from one set by OCR in June 2001. Read the case study and then tackle the exercises that follow.

Coffee Break

Recent research has shown that 93% of UK households have bought instant coffee in the last year. Moreover, coffee as a drink continues to increase in popularity, as consumers try variations such as cappuccino, espresso, mocha and latte. This expansion in demand has also led to an increase in the types of manufactured coffee available, although instant coffee remains the largest seller.

Raw coffee, when it leaves the plantation, is pale green, hence the name 'green coffee' when it is traded. It is bought and sold on world commodity markets in London and New York. At any one time, the amount to be sold and the quantity that manufacturers and processors wish to purchase are key factors determining its price. Like any product, therefore, the price of raw coffee is determined where market supply and demand are equated.

The final price of raw coffee is very important for the economic well-being of millions of people living in countries such as Costa Rica, Kenya and Colombia which are heavily dependent on this crop. Typically, farmers in such countries practise small-scale production – their plots of land might be no more than 1 or 2 hectares. It is therefore unrealistic for them to sell their product direct to the world market. So what usually happens is that they sell their crop to a government-controlled agency which in turn releases stocks onto the world market, depending on market conditions.

An alternative approach, practised by major manufacturers such as Nestlé, is for coffee to be bought direct from local farmers. This happens only in countries where Nestlé manufactures locally and also for export. In such circumstances, Nestlé offers a 'fair price' to farmers to ensure a regular supply of green coffee. This price is widely advertised as the minimum price that will be paid for supplies. It also follows that the higher the quality, the higher the price. This arrangement ensures that farmers continue to grow coffee, whilst providing Nestlé with regular supplies outside the uncertainties of the occasionally volatile world commodity market.

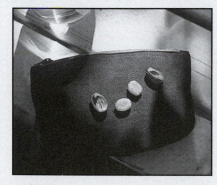
Coffee bean

Coffee beans on bush

1 (a) How is the market price of raw coffee determined on the world commodity markets?

(b) Excluding price, state and explain two other determinants of the demand for raw coffee in world markets.

(c) Suppose a major coffee producing country decides to reduce supplies to the world market. Assuming no change in demand, use a diagram to explain how this action would affect the world raw coffee price.

2 (a) Define elasticity of supply.

(b) Would you expect the price elasticity of supply for raw coffee to be relatively elastic or inelastic? Justify your answer.

(c) Would you expect the price elasticity of supply for instant coffee to be relatively elastic or inelastic? Justify your answer.

3 (a) The 'fair price' of raw coffee paid to small farmers by Nestlé in a particular developing country is usually fixed above the normal equilibrium price. With the aid of a diagram, explain how this affects the market for raw coffee in that country.

(b) Briefly describe the benefits of a 'fair price' for the producers of the raw coffee in this developing country.

PED and total expenditure/total revenue

PED can help us understand how total spending by consumers will change as price rises or falls assuming the price change is caused by a shift in the supply curve.

$$\text{Total expenditure} = P \times Q = \text{Total revenue of a firm or industry}$$

In figure 2.19, assume there are two products each with the same equilibrium price ($10) and quantity traded (100 units per day). Total expenditure by consumers per day = $10 × 100 = $1,000 – this is of course equal to the revenue received by companies. Now, if the price rises to $11, the differences in PED indicate that consumers respond in different ways, and the total expenditure will change:

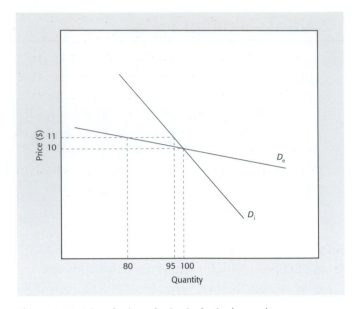

Figure 2.19 Price elastic and price inelastic demand curves

Self-assessment tasks

1 You used this demand schedule when we looked at PED on a linear demand curve at the beginning of this section. Figure 2.20 shows the resulting demand curve.

Refer back to how PED varies along a linear demand curve – note, in the top half of the demand curve PED > 1 whereas in the lower half PED < 1.

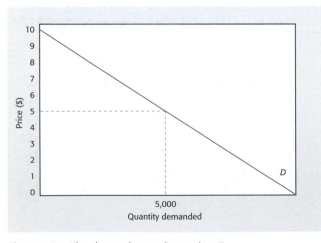

Figure 2.20 The demand curve for product R

Calculate the total expenditure (TE)/total revenue (TR) figures and graph the resulting values underneath the demand curve in figure 2.20 (put TE on the vertical axis and quantity on the horizontal axis – it will help if you use the same scale on the horizontal axis).

Price of product R ($/unit)	Quantity demanded of product R (units per week)	Total expenditure $ per week
10	0	
9	1,000	
8	2,000	
7	3,000	
6	4,000	
5	5,000	
4	6,000	
3	7,000	
2	8,000	
1	9,000	
0	10,000	

- ◆ What do you notice about TE/TR figures as price is cut from $10 towards $5 per unit?
- ◆ Why does this happen?
- ◆ What do you notice about the TE/TR figures as price is raised from $0 to $5?
- ◆ Why does this happen?
- ◆ Where is TE/TR maximised?

2 If a government is interested in raising more revenue from indirect taxes, such as VAT or excise duties, should it tax products that are price elastic or price inelastic? Explain and illustrate your answer with diagrams and examples.

◆ D_e is relatively price elastic over the relevant price range, and quantity falls considerably to 80 units (PED = –2). Total expenditure is now down to $880 per day – the reason, of course, is that the relative fall in sales is greater than the relative increase in price.

◆ D_i is relatively price inelastic over the relevant price range and the quantity traded only falls slightly to 95 units (PED = –0.5). Total expenditure actually rises even though less is traded! The reason is that the increase in price exerts a more powerful influence in this case.

Income elasticity of demand

Since YED provides information about how demand varies as income changes, the concept is potentially of great importance to planners in business organisations and government.

If the YED for a normal good exceeds unity, then demand for that product will grow more rapidly than consumer incomes during normal periods of economic growth – hence considerably greater productive capacity may be required. However, during a recession, when incomes fall, firms producing this sort of product will be extremely vulnerable, given the large reduction in demand that might be expected.

If the YED is negative then firms producing such inferior goods will see their sales decline steadily over time as the economy grows – however, they may be the sort of business to benefit from the hard times of recession.

Self-assessment tasks

1 What will happen to sales of a product whose YED = + 0.6?
2 How could you use YED values to advise a company on how to produce a mix of goods and services that would reduce the risk often associated with only producing a very narrow range of products?
3 Why might government planners be interested in the YED values of different products?

Cross elasticity of demand

Many companies are concerned with the impact that rival pricing strategies will have, ceteris paribus, on the demand for their own product. Remember that substitutes are characterised by a positive XED: the higher the numerical value, the greater the degree of substitutability between these alternatives in the eyes of the consumer. In such cases there is a high degree of interdependence between suppliers, and the dangers of a rival cutting price are likely to be very significant indeed.

Companies are increasingly concerned with trying to get consumers to buy not just one of their products but a whole range of complementary ones, for example computer printers and print cartridges. XED will identify those products that are most complementary and help a company introduce a pricing structure that generates more revenue. For instance, market research may indicate that families spend most money at the cinema when special deals are offered on ticket prices, even though the PED for ticket prices is low. In this case, for example, the high negative cross elasticity between ticket prices and the demand for food, such as ice cream and popcorn, means that, although the revenue from ticket sales may fall, this may be compensated for by increased sales of food. This points to the need for a more sophisticated pricing structure within the cinema looking at the relationships between the demand for all products and services offered.

Price elasticity of supply

You have already seen how variations in PED will influence the nature of a change in the equilibrium following a given shift in the supply curve. Figure 2.21 also confirms that the PES will influence the nature of a

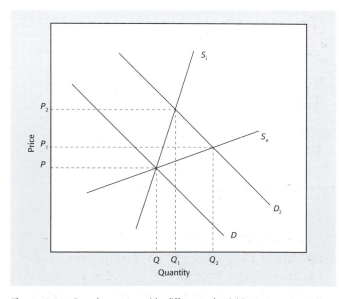

Figure 2.21 Supply curves with different elasticities

change in the equilibrium following a given shift in the demand curve. The diagram illustrates two alternative supply curves with different elasticities over the relevant price range. S_e is relatively price elastic, S_i is relatively price inelastic.

If the initial equilibrium is at PQ and then demand for a normal good increases, perhaps because of an increase in income, in both cases the new equilibrium price and quantity are higher. However, in the case of S_e, the greater flexibility in supply allows companies to respond to this increased demand without raising prices so much. In the case of S_i, the inflexible nature of supply means that companies raise prices more sharply in response to the surge in demand.

Cautionary note

We have assumed that calculating elasticity values is straightforward. In fact there are enormous statistical problems. As an example consider the difficulties of calculating PED values from historical data. Have the price changes only been caused by supply variations? Have there been any non-price demand influences at work? Remember, if we are to calculate the PED value accurately, we need to separate out all the other influences and just measure the impact of the price change alone on

Self-assessment task

Redraw figure 2.21 to consider what will happen if there is a decrease in demand, perhaps because of a change in tastes and preferences away from this product. Remember you are analysing the impact of variations in PES on the new equilibrium.

◆ Under what conditions will prices fall most? Why is this?

◆ Under what conditions will there be the greatest decrease in sales? Why is this?

You will note that as with PED, prices tend to be more volatile when supply is inelastic, and quantity is more changeable when supply is price elastic.

quantity demanded – the difficulty encountered here is referred to as the identification problem. Collecting data from other sources, such as market testing, or surveys (using questionnaires and/or interviews), is costly in terms of time and money and may not be particularly valid or reliable. As such, many companies may prefer to make rough 'guesstimates' of elasticity values or to work with incomplete data, particularly if they are operating in markets where rapid change means past data cease to be a good indicator of the future.

Self-assessment tasks

1 (a) Explain the difference between price elasticity of demand, cross elasticity of demand and income elasticity of demand.

   (b) Discuss how an understanding of these concepts might be useful to a professional football club in deciding the price of tickets for its matches.

2 A market research company has recently published estimates about UK consumers' demand for holidays in certain countries. A summary of the main findings is given below:

Holiday destination	Price elasticity of demand	Income elasticity of demand
Spain	−1.8	−0.1
USA	−1.2	+1.3
Caribbean	−0.5	+2.0

Price refers to the average combined price of a direct flight (economy class) and seven days' accommodation, half board in a standard hotel.

With reference to the above data:

(a) Explain the difference between normal and inferior goods.

(b) Explain how an increase in consumers' income might affect the demand for each of the holiday destinations shown.

(c) Use the figures to discuss the possible effects that a 10 per cent increase in the 'average price' of each of the holiday destinations shown might have on demand.

3 The directors of a small travel agency in the east of England have got hold of this research. Why would you advise them to treat the findings cautiously – what extra research might they need to undertake themselves before using elasticity figures as the basis for company policy?

Source: UCLES, Paper 4381, November 1996 (adapted).

Summary

In this section we have recognised that:

- A market exists whenever people come together for the trade or exchange of goods and services; it is also possible to identify sub-markets.

- The buying side of the market is referred to by economists as the demand side. It is possible to derive a demand curve for any market – this shows how the quantity which is demanded varies with the price of a product or service.

- Consumer surplus arises because some consumers are willing to pay more than the given price for what they buy.

- The demand curve shifts to the left or right when, 'other things being equal', the assumption is changed. Three important causes of this are a change in income, a change in consumer tastes or attitudes and a change in the price of related products.

- The selling side of the market is known as the supply side. It is possible to derive a supply curve for any market – this shows how the quantity which is supplied varies with the price of the product or service.

- The supply curve shifts to the left or right when, 'other things being equal', the assumption is changed. Three important causes of this are a change in the costs of supply, a change in the characteristics of the industry and changes in government policy.

- Equilibrium occurs in the market where there is no tendency for change, when the plans of consumers match the plans of suppliers. A change to the equilibrium position will produce a new equilibrium price and quantity.

- Elasticity is a very important concept in markets; it is the responsiveness of one economic variable following a change in another variable.

- Price, income and cross elasticity of demand are relevant numerical measures which have considerable value and use in enhancing our understanding of how markets operate. The price elasticity of supply is relevant in understanding how producers can react in markets.

Key words

Definitions of Key words can be found in the Glossary.

ceteris paribus	market
change in demand	market demand
change in quantity	normal goods
complements	notional demand
consumer surplus	perfectly elastic
costs	perfectly inelastic
cross elasticity of demand	price elasticity of demand
demand	price elasticity of supply
demand curve	price mechanism
demand schedule	rationing
disequilibrium	rectangular hyperbola
effective demand	sub-market
elasticity	substitutes
equilibrium	supply
equilibrium price	supply curve
equilibrium quantity	supply schedule
income elasticity of demand	total revenue
inferior goods	unitary elasticity

3 Government intervention in the price system

On completion of this section you should know:

➤ why governments may find it necessary to intervene in the workings of the price mechanism

➤ why therefore such situations are seen by economists as cases of market failure

➤ what is meant by an externality and why situations where there are negative and positive externalities signal market failure

➤ the meaning and significance of private costs, external costs and social costs; the meaning and significance of private benefits, external benefits and social benefits

➤ what is meant by a cost–benefit approach and how a cost–benefit analysis can be used as an aid for decision making

➤ what is meant by public goods and merit goods and why these have to be provided by governments

➤ how various forms of government intervention can be used to correct market failure

Market failure

As analysed in the last section, when left to its own devices and totally free from any form of government intervention, the 'invisible hand' of the market mechanism works to provide an effective allocation of resources in an economy. Demand and supply interact to determine prices, which in turn vary with changes in the conditions of demand and supply. This self-regulating mechanism is central to the operation of the market economy. For many types of market, this process works well. In other circumstances though the market 'fails'. By this we mean that the self-regulating mechanism does not lead to the best allocation of resources. Far from it, the market fails to deliver what is expected. This in turn is the signal for possible government intervention.

A few examples will illustrate this point:

◆ Why should people be required to have an inoculation to reduce the risk of an infectious disease?

◆ Why do governments, central and local, provide defence, police and fire services?

◆ Why are firms not investing in pollution control when they know they can be prosecuted if they pollute the environment?

◆ Why are some types of education and health care provided by public authorities?

In all cases the answer is the same – *these actions are necessary to combat the common problem of* **market failure**.

As economies develop, then increasingly they are faced with problems of market failure (reference to a good newspaper can often provide relevant examples). If unchecked, these market failures can distort the processes of resource allocation.

Three examples of market failure will be looked at:

◆ where there are **externalities** present in a market;

◆ where **merit goods** have to be provided because the market will fail to provide them;

◆ where **public goods** are provided by the government, again because the free market will fail to do so.

In all cases, alternative forms of government intervention will be identified.

Externalities
Defining externality

If the market system is to work well, it is important that the people who make economic decisions are those who are affected by those decisions. A transaction between a supplier and a consumer for a product needs only to affect the supplier and consumer involved. As long as this is the case, then both sides will act only so long as both feel that they will benefit from any action – all is well in the market. However, a problem could clearly arise if someone else, not party to the economic decision, is affected by that decision. This is the economic concept known as externality.

An externality is said to arise if a third party (someone not directly involved) is affected by the decisions and actions of others. If you decide to shout loudly to your friend in public, then others (third parties) not involved in making that decision are affected by the assault on their ear drums.

Private and social costs

Another way of understanding the same concept is to define an externality as any divergence between private and social costs or benefits. The **social costs** of any action are all of the related costs associated with that action. The **private costs** are those costs involved in an action that accrue to the decision maker.

Negative externalities

It is quite possible that these private and social costs are the same: all of the costs of an action accrue to the decision maker and there are no further costs. If this is the case, then there are no externalities. However, it is possible that there will be a difference: private and social costs may not be equal to each other. For example, if you make a decision to take a journey in your car, you consider the costs of the petrol and the time taken. However, you do not consider the further costs that you may be imposing on others in terms of your contribution to road congestion, to environmental damage and to possible car accidents. In this situation, a **negative externality**, or an **external cost**, is said to exist. The situation is illustrated in figure 3.1. Here, private

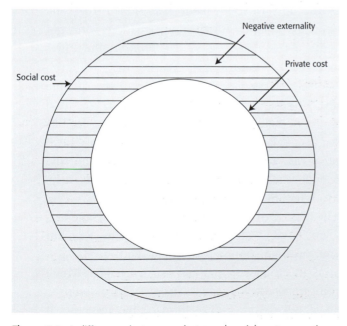

Figure 3.1 A difference between private and social costs: negative externalities

costs are part of the social costs involved in a decision. However, they do not represent all of the social costs. The difference between the two is the negative externality.

Private and social benefits

A similar situation can also exist with benefits rather than costs. The **social benefits** of a decision are all of the benefits that accrue from that decision. The **private benefits** are those that accrue solely to the decision maker. Again, these may or may not be the same.

Positive externalities

It is possible that the social benefits of a decision may exceed the private benefits. If this is the case, then a **positive externality**, or **external benefit**, is said to exist. For example, if you make a decision to go to the doctor to be inoculated against a particular disease, then clearly you receive the private benefit of not catching that particular disease against which you have been inoculated. However, you may not be the only one to benefit. The fact that you do not get the disease has some possible benefit to all others with whom you come into contact, who will now not catch the disease from you.

The problem created by externalities

The essence of the problem created by externalities is that they will lead to an inappropriate amount of the product involved being produced: the free market will lead either to too much or too little production.

Consider a firm that produces a chemical. There are costs that the firm will have to meet in producing a certain quantity of this chemical. These would include such things as:

- raw material costs;
- labour costs;
- energy costs.

All such costs would be termed 'private': they have to be paid for by the decision maker (the firm). These costs form part of social costs. However, there are further social costs likely to be involved as well. These might include any dumping of chemical waste, perhaps in a local river, which creates clean-up costs, any atmospheric pollution that creates clean-up costs and ill

Self-assessment tasks

1 Identify and explain whether each of the following involves a positive or a negative externality:

- ◆ a next-door neighbour playing his/her music loudly;
- ◆ a person being educated beyond the compulsory school leaving age;
- ◆ the dropping of litter;
- ◆ smoking in a public place;
- ◆ a new, well-designed and pleasant public building;
- ◆ the use of pesticides.

2 Read the adaptation of a newspaper article below and then tackle the exercises that follow:

Cheap food – at a huge price

Why do the British shop in supermarkets? Easy. Price, convenience, quality and choice: the mantra of the market economy. But is perception matched by reality?

Supermarkets are very cheap for some goods, but what you save on the loss-leading swings, you lose on the marked-up roundabouts. Take fruit and vegetables. Last summer we compared prices between supermarkets and street markets of the old-fashioned endangered variety. Like for like, the markets won on almost every count.

If they're not such paragons on price, at least supermarkets are safe, convenient and accessible by car. Or are they? If, like a third of the population, you don't have the use of a car, they are not. But even getting to the store by car may be far from convenient. Over the past 20 years, the number of shopping trips has increased by a third, and driver shopping mileage has more than doubled. Given Britain's congestion, more journeys of increasing length doesn't sound very convenient. Nor is it: in the Sixties, according to Professor Jonathan Gershuny of Essex University, consumers spent on average 41 minutes per day shopping and in related travel. In the Eighties this has risen to 70 minutes, with studies showing that food shopping accounts for more than three-quarters of total shopping time. According to Professor Gershuny, 'the increase in shopping time reflects the growth of "self servicing" and the growth in the size of supermarkets ... the larger the supermarket the more walking for the shopper and the greater the average distance from

the shopper's home ... The retail industry in effect externalises a large part of its costs.'

On quality and choice, supermarket products may be varied and consistent – but is what you see what you really get, and are you paying the real costs? Supermarkets' huge buying power and demand for absolute consistency means that fruit and vegetable production are now industrialised processes. Multiples have 60 per cent of the market and suppliers who cannot supply 52 weeks a year need not supply. Your Brussels sprouts may be perfectly formed, but at what costs to the countryside? Biodiversity on the shelf is increasingly at the cost of biodiversity in the field.

While it has long been recognised that the perceived benefits of the supermarkets are not evenly spread between social groups (the chief executive of the supermarkets' own research organisation acknowledges that old and poor people will have serious problems over where to buy food because of the growth of superstores and the lack of town centre stores), our research leads us to believe that, even for the better-off and mobile, the advantages of supermarkets are beginning to be outweighed by the drawbacks.

The decline of the town centre is well documented and attributable, at least in part, to the development of out-of-town shopping centres. The big retailers' claims to efficiency in transport are bogus. Much freight transport is unnecessary – produce could be sold locally. More than a third of the increase in freight transport since the late Seventies has been food, drink and tobacco – which together account for less than one tenth of the economy. Next time you use a motorway, count the supermarket trucks. No wonder the big retailers are such lavish supporters of the British Road Federation.

It's the same story with packaging. According to the government, 'the stocking policies of supermarkets ... largely contributed to non-returnable [packaging] attaining [its] present share of the market', while MEPs reported that an EU directive to reduce packaging was 'the most lobbied issue in the (EU) Parliament's history'. The supermarkets are used to getting their way; the directive was duly changed.

Britain's retailing policies need a radical shake-up. We need more smaller shops, buying locally, and revitalised street and covered markets. We still need tougher rules on out-of-town development, and freight companies could pay the real cost of their operations.

Source: Hugh Raven and Tim Lang, *The Independent*, 10 January 1995 (adapted).

(a) Explain what is meant by Professor Gershuny's phrase, 'The retail industry in effect externalises a large part of its costs.'

(b) Identify and explain the different negative externalities arising from the development of out-of-town supermarkets that are mentioned in this article.

health, and possible road congestion that results from the transportation of the chemicals. These are negative externalities. The problem is that only the private costs of producing the chemical will be taken into account by the firm when making the pricing decision about its chemical. The further external costs, which are real costs to society, will *not* be taken into account. This will mean that the price will be lower than if all social costs were taken into account. In turn, demand and production will be higher than if the full social costs had been considered. Thus, a negative externality will lead to too much of a product being produced. The situation can be seen in figure 3.2.

The price that will occur in the market will be P_1 where the supply schedule that takes account of the private costs, S_1, is equal to demand. This price is associated with production of Q_1. However, if the supply schedule took into account all of the social costs, S_2, which are greater than just the private costs, then this would result in a price of P_2. This price is associated with a lower production of Q_2. Thus, the negative externality has led to $Q_1 - Q_2$ too much production. Too many scarce resources are being devoted to the production of this product. The market has failed.

The opposite problem is true of a positive externality. Here, the problem is that too little of the product will be produced. If only the private benefits, and not the full

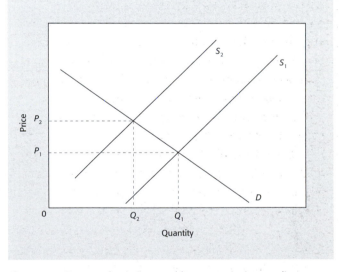

Figure 3.2 Over-production caused by a negative externality

social benefits, are considered, then there will be under-production. This is illustrated in figure 3.3.

This time, the problem is with demand. If only the private benefits are registered, then demand is represented by the demand schedule D_1. This leads to a price of P_1 and an associated production of Q_1. However, if the further extra benefits to society were registered (which they will not be by the private decision maker involved), then demand would be greater at D_2. This would lead to a price of P_2 and a

Various forms of environmental pollution arising from the exploitation of crude oil – but who pays for the clean-up costs?
Source: Gil Moti, Still Pictures.

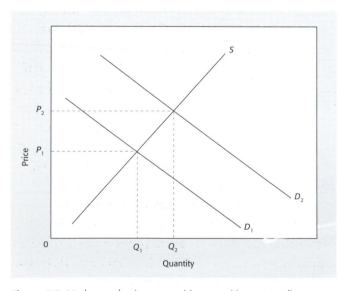

Figure 3.3 Under-production caused by a positive externality

production of Q_2. Thus there is an under-production of $Q_1 - Q_2$ associated with the positive externality. Insufficient scarce resources are being devoted to the production of this good or service. The market has failed.

We must, therefore, suggest that externalities are likely to be a source of market failure as they will mean that resources are not allocated in the ideal way: too few or too many resources are likely to be directed to the production of certain products.

The cost–benefit approach

We have identified various causes and consequences of market failure, that is where there is a divergence between private and social benefits and costs.

It is in such circumstances that a cost–benefit approach has been used by economists as a means of decision making, not least to ensure that the right choice of action is being made. Here we will be concerned with situations where major projects produce important and often controversial side effects, in particular where there are substantial costs and benefits which fall upon people and communities who have no direct connection with the particular project, either as consumers or suppliers.

A particularly relevant and widespread case of this occurring in the UK is where a new retail development is planned. In all types of economy there are many examples of where environmental pollution results in external costs being imposed on the local community. The so-called *spillover effects* upon third parties (those not involved in the particular project) can be far-reaching and substantial. **Cost–benefit analysis** (CBA) genuinely attempts to quantify the opportunity cost to society of the various possible outcomes or sources of action. It is therefore a procedure for making long-run decisions where present actions have implications far into the future.

The cost–benefit approach differs from private sector methods of appraisal in two main respects. These are:

◆ It seeks to include all of the costs and benefits, not just private ones.

◆ It often has to impute **shadow prices** on costs and benefits where no market price is available. Very relevant examples here would be how to value the degradation of scenic beauty or the loss of agricultural land in the case (say) of building new houses on an attractive area. Other examples might be how to value the benefit of cleaner air or being able to live in a less noisy environment.

A new housing development on former agricultural land in the UK

The framework of cost–benefit analysis

Whatever the problem under investigation, there are four main stages in the development of a cost–benefit analysis. These are shown in figure 3.4.

The first stage is to identify all of the relevant costs and benefits arising out of any particular project. Systematically, this involves establishing what are the private costs, the private benefits, the external costs and the external benefits. On the surface this may seem a relatively simple task. In reality, and with a little more thought, it is not so. There are particular problems when it comes to establishing external costs and benefits. These are often controversial, not easy to define in a discrete way and have the added difficulty that it is not always possible to draw the line in terms of a physical or geographical cut-off. The spillover effects of a new retail development, for example, are wide-reaching and often affect people and communities way beyond the immediate vicinity of the proposed development (see self-assessment task, question 1).

The second stage involves putting a monetary value on the various costs and benefits. This is relatively straightforward where market prices are available. For example, in the case of a new retail development, a monetary value can be put on the jobs created or the increased profits arising from the development. For other variables, though, a monetary value must be inputed for costs and benefits where no market prices are available. This particular measurement difficulty has occupied economists for thousands of hours over the years. It has also been a very controversial matter in situations where cost–benefit analysis has come under close public scrutiny. A particularly good example of this is the issue of valuation of time, especially travel time and savings in travel time. Another relevant example is how to put a monetary value on the cost of accidents, particularly where serious injuries or a loss of life is involved.

The third stage of the cost–benefit analysis applies in situations where projects have longer-term implications which stretch well into the future. Here, economists have to employ statistical forecasting techniques, sometimes of a very crude nature, to estimate costs and benefits over many years. This particularly applies to proposed projects where massive capital expenditure is involved. In other cases, this stage may actually not be needed, particularly if two alternatives are being considered (see self-assessment task, question 2).

The final stage is where the results of the earlier stages are drawn together so that the outcome can be presented in a clear manner in order to aid decision making. The important principle to recognise is that if the value of benefits exceeds the value of the costs, then

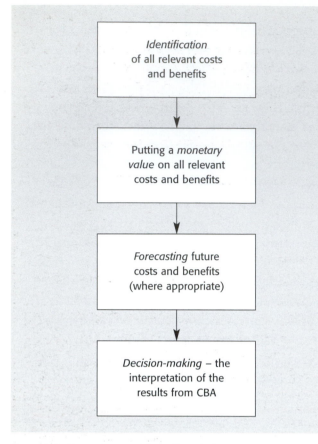

Figure 3.4 Stages in a cost–benefit analysis

the particular project is worthwhile since it provides an overall net benefit to the community (see self-assessment task, question 2 for a simple example of such a situation).

The four stages in a cost–benefit analysis provide a coherent framework by which decisions can be made in situations of market failure. Students should therefore see any cost–benefit study or application in these terms.

Finally, to conclude, it is relevant to recognise that in practice cost–benefit analysis is fraught with many difficulties. Some have already been stated such as:

◆ which costs and benefits should be included;

◆ how to put monetary values on them.

Additionally, there are others, particularly when it comes to the acceptance of the outcome by the community as a whole. For example:

◆ CBA does not always satisfactorily reflect the distributional consequences of certain decisions, particularly where public sector investment is involved. In the case of a new retail development, external costs are likely to be highly localised whilst external benefits, in terms of employment creation for instance, are likely to be more widely spread.

◆ Many public sector projects (for example that analysed in self-assessment task, question 3) are very controversial and subject to much local aggravation from pressure groups. It may be the case that the outcome of the CBA is rejected for local political reasons, with the consequence that the most expedient decision may not be the one recommended by economists. Where this happens, it is easy to dismiss the technique of CBA as irrelevant. This is not a fair conclusion, not least as CBA has at least brought out the issues involved so that a decision can be taken on the basis of all of the information available. CBA is an aid and not a replacement for decision making.

Self-assessment tasks

1 Read the case study below on traffic problems in Bangkok and then tackle the exercises which follow.

Traffic problems in Bangkok

Bangkok, the capital of Thailand, is one of Asia's megacities. For its citizens, and those who visit as tourists or for business reasons, one thing that no-one can get away from is its horrendous problem of traffic congestion. The population is increasing at a massive 2 per cent per annum and as in all parts of Asia, vehicle ownership levels are increasing at a substantial rate as a consequence of economic advancement. This situation means increasing stress levels, a deterioration in the quality of life and increasing health problems for its teeming population.

A recent government report has estimated that
● the typical resident spends 44 working days a year stuck in traffic
● peak vehicle speeds have fallen to 6km per hour
● lost production due to congestion is estimated to be 10 per cent of Thailand's GDP
● much of the energy used to move vehicles is wasted because of the congestion
● 1 million people a year suffer from diagnosed respiratory diseases linked to the air pollution quality which has 18

- times more CO_2 emissions than the WHO maximum guideline
- there is a high incidence of lung cancer amongst the adult population and children have unacceptable levels of lead in their blood
- thousands of people a year suffer strain and stress-related illness directly accountable to the severe congestion

- school children leave home for school at 5am to beat the congestion

Unlike its 'neighbours' such as Kuala Lumpur, Singapore and Hong Kong, Bangkok does not have a rapid transit system, although one has been planned for at least 30 years. The time has surely come when this has to be authorised.

Suppose you have been asked by the authorities in Bangkok to produce a cost–benefit analysis for a new rapid transit system for the city.

(a) Using the above information as a guide, what costs and benefits would you include in your analysis?

(b) On what theoretical basis might you:

◆ recommend that a new rapid transit system be constructed,

◆ recommend that there is no case for a new rapid transit system.

In each case, comment upon how confident you might be of your recommendations.

2 The following case study is an adaptation of an A level question set by UCLES in June 1997. Read it and then tackle the exercises that follow.

Cavalier Pet Products

Cavalier Pet Products is a large privately owned manufacturer of canned pet foods based in Bolton, Lancashire. The company, which employs 300 people, is long-established and has been on its present site since it was founded by its owners, the Fazackerley family, in 1906. It is a market leader, producing own-branded products, which are widely advertised and well known.

Through the nature of its manufacturing processes, the company is a polluter of the local environment. The nauseating smells from the factory, particularly in hot weather, are the main source of complaint; the firm also creates noise disturbance and quite recently was successfully prosecuted for discharging effluent into a local stream running alongside the factory. There is increasing local pressure from residents for something to be done about the whole question of the firm and its operations.

The obvious answer is for the firm to move to another location. The Managing Director of Cavalier Pet Products, Basil Fazackerley, favours such a move but is quite adamant that, 'We shall not pay the full cost. If the local council want us to move, then they will have to help us to do so.'

The decision to relocate the factory has long-term implications both for its owners and for the community. In particular, new jobs will be created as the firm increases output and the local environment within the vicinity of the present site will experience environmental gain.

The local authority have agreed to contribute to the relocation, as they can see a benefit to the community. Cavalier Pet Products remain concerned that they should pay a realistic contribution to the cost of relocation.

In order to sort out these difficulties, a local university was asked to carry out a cost–benefit analysis of the proposed relocation. A summary of their findings is given in the table below

Costs		Benefits	
Private costs of the relocation	1,300	Private benefits	1,500
Contribution from local authority	300	External benefits	1,200
External costs	400		
Total costs	**2,000**	**Total benefits**	**2,700**

Estimated discounted[1] costs and benefits of the relocation of Cavalier Pet Products (£000)

Note: [1] Discounting is a procedure whereby a present value is given to costs and benefits that will occur some time in the future.

(a) What is the specific purpose of the cost–benefit analysis in this case?

(b) With reference to the proposed relocation, give an example of:

◆ a private benefit,

◆ an external benefit,

arising from the proposed relocation. Explain your choice.

(c) Use the information in the table to state what conclusions you could draw from the cost–benefit analysis.

(d) You are asked to plan an investigation to estimate the various external costs and benefits of the proposed relocation. Explain how you might do this and comment upon some of the problems you might face.

3 Read the newspaper article on the next page and then answer the following questions.

Bush defies Europe over pollution

US rejects Kyoto as 'it makes no sense'

President Bush's decision to abandon the Kyoto Protocol on reducing greenhouse gases provoked almost universal outrage among European leaders yesterday.

A senior environmental activist said Mr Bush had 'put two fingers up to the rest of the world'.

Chancellor Gerhard Schröder of Germany told the President in Washington that America, as the biggest economy and energy consumer in the world, must accept responsibility for the planet's climate.

They met in the Oval Office a day after Christine Todd Whitman, head of the United States Environmental Protection Agency, said that Kyoto was 'dead' because Congress would not ratify it and Mr Bush thought that it would damage the economy.

Some observers saw the timing of the announcement as a calculated insult to Mr Schröder, who is in coalition with the Green Party.

Mr Schröder said the talks had been 'frank'.

Mr Bush said: 'The idea that somehow we are supposed to get enormous amounts of natural gas on line immediately to be able to conform to a treaty that our own Senate sent a very overwhelming message against, and that many other countries haven't signed, makes no economic sense. It makes no common sense.'

Michael Meacher, the environment minister, said that Mr Bush's decision was 'exceptionally serious'.

The EU, France, Ireland and Italy quickly joined the chorus of indignation.

Dominique Voynet, The French environment minister, said: 'Mr Bush's unilateral attitude is entirely provocative and irresponsible'.

Japan and Australia expressed dismay and one of the smallest nations, the Micronesian islands of Kiribati, said it would 'drown' in the rising Pacific unless global warming was stopped.

America, with four per cent of the world's population, produces 25 per cent of the greenhouse gases, believed to be responsible for the warming.

The Kyoto treaty aimed to reduce major industrialised nation's emissions by an average of 5.2 per cent below 1990 levels by 2012 to avoid disastrous weather changes.

Mr Bush defended his decision, which had been widely signalled during his election.

'We'll be working with Germany; we'll be working with our allies to reduce greenhouse gases, ' he said.

'But I will not accept anything that will harm our economy and hurt our workers. We have an energy shortage.'

Before Al Gore, as vice president, signed the treaty in 1997, the Senate voted 95-0 against backing any deal that did not include developing countries such as India and China. The Kyoto agreement has never been presented to the Senate for ratification.

Britain clung to the hope that Europeans would still be able to influence the 'debate' in Washington and bring the administration around in climate talks later in the year.

'The fact is that we do have a lot of leverage', Mr Meacher told Radio 4's Today programme. 'I certainly don't think we should despair or try to ostracise the US.

'This is not the end of the story. There is clearly a power struggle going on in Washington and we have to keep hammering on.

British officials fear that Mr Bush's decision will make it harder to convince developing countries, especially India and China, to accept pollutant limits.

The EU will send a high-level delegation to Washington next week to urge him to change his mind

A follow-up meeting on Kyoto last November collapsed when the EU and America failed to agree on mechanisms to reduce carbon dioxide emissions.

Fresh talks were originally set for Bonn in May, but were postponed until July.

Charles Secrett, of Friends of the Earth International, said of Mr Bush: 'This ignorant, short-sighted and selfish politician, long since firmly jammed into the pockets of the oil lobby, clearly could not care less.'

Source: Anton La Guardia and Toby Harnden, *The Daily Telegraph*, 30 March 2001.

Smog, smog and more smog – the reality of life in US cities where tall buildings exaggerate the effects of vehicle emissions
Source: Ray Pfortner, Still Pictures.

(a) Why has President Bush decided to abandon the Kyoto protocol?

(b) Why is it difficult to get developing economies to accept pollution limits?

(c) Why will the President's decision make it even more difficult for developing economies to cut their emission levels of greenhouse gases?

4 Look in local newspapers for examples of situations where there are problems of environmental pollution.
See if you can put these problems in a cost–benefit framework.

Merit goods, de-merit goods and information failures

Defining merit and de-merit goods

Another way in which markets may fail is due to the existence of what are termed **merit** and **de-merit goods**.

Sometimes, merit and de-merit goods are simply seen as an extension of the idea of externalities, as discussed above. A merit good may be described as a good that has positive externalities associated with it. Thus, an inoculation might be seen as a merit good because others who may not catch the disease from the inoculated person also benefit. A de-merit good is seen as any product that has negative externalities associated with it. Thus, cigarettes can be seen as a de-merit good in so far as secondary smoking can be viewed as a possible cause of ill health (a clear negative externality). If this is all there is to merit and de-merit goods, then they cannot be seen as a separate category of market failure from externalities.

However, merit and de-merit goods can (and indeed should) be defined in a different way, which does make them clearly different from externalities. The essence of merit and de-merit goods in this definition is to do with a **failure of information** to the consumer. Consumers do not perceive, it is suggested, quite how good or bad a particular product is for them: either they do not have the right information or they simply lack some relevant information.

Merit goods

With this idea of a failure of information, a merit good is defined as a good that is better for a person than the person who may consume the good realises. Under this definition, education is often defined as a merit good. The individuals who make decisions about how much education to receive (or how much to allow their children to receive) do not fully appreciate quite how much benefit will be received through being educated. We do not appreciate how good education is for us. We do not perceive its full benefits at the time of making the decision about how much education to receive.

De-merit goods

De-merit goods, on the other hand, are those products that are worse for the individual consumer than the individual realises. Cigarettes are taken to be a typical example here. It is suggested that when a person makes a decision to smoke a cigarette, he or she is not fully in possession of the information concerning the harmful effects of smoking. If he or she were in possession of such information, then there would be a greater reluctance to smoke.

It is interesting to note that the example of a de-merit good given here, namely smoking, is the same as the example of a product that can be seen as having negative externalities associated with it. However, the reason for identifying the product is different. Here, it is not due to the damage done to others that the issue arises, but rather due to the unperceived damage done to the person through consuming the product.

Merit goods, de-merit goods and value judgements

It may have been noticed in the above definitions that a significant question poses itself with regard to merit and de-merit goods. Who is to say what is 'good' or 'bad' for a person? If an individual consumer makes a

presumably rational decision to consume a product, what right has the rest of society to say that he or she is making a 'wrong' decision. It seems clear that if this is what is going on, we have entered the area of **value judgements** and thus normative economics. If society is able to say to consumers that they do not fully realise what is good or bad for them, then we are accepting that 'society knows best' and has some right to make such a judgement. In effect we are allowing **paternalism** to be a legitimate part of Economics. It is acceptable for us to say that society can judge what is, or is not, good for a person, regardless of what that person believes. In this area, then, we may have gone beyond our allegedly 'value-free' positive economics (see section 1).

The problems caused by merit and de-merit goods

Why, then, might merit and de-merit goods be identified as a failure of the market? The problem is that their existence will cause an inappropriate amount of the products concerned to be produced.

Merit goods will be under-produced in a free market situation. Insufficient scarce resources will be devoted to their production. The problem is that the lack of information about how good the product is for individuals will result in insufficient demand being registered for the product in the market. This is illustrated in figure 3.5. Here, the 'correct' level of demand, if consumers appreciated the true value of the product to themselves, would be D_1. This would lead to a

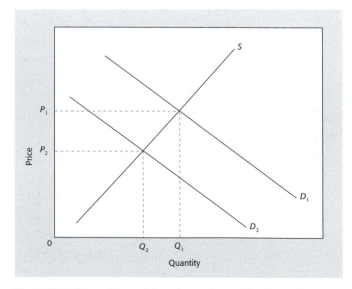

Figure 3.5 The under-provision of a merit good by the market

market price of P_1, where D_1 is equal to the supply of product, S. This price would be associated with a level of production and consumption of Q_1, the ideal quantity of the good. However, because consumers under-value the product, demand is only registered as D_2. This leads to a market price of P_2 (where D_2 is equal to supply S), which is associated with production and consumption of Q_2. This is below the optimum level: the market has failed.

Figure 3.6 illustrates the problem of a de-merit good. Here, the 'correct' demand should be at D_1, which will lead to a price of P_1 and a production and consumption of Q_1. As consumers over-value the product, demand is registered at the higher level of D_2. This leads to a market price of P_2 and a production and consumption of Q_2. Too many scarce resources are devoted to the production of this de-merit good: the market has failed.

It is worth noting that there is another important example of market failure, as we have defined it, that can arise due to failures of information.

The health care market Why does anyone go to the doctor? The most usual answer to that question is presumably because we are not sure what ailment we may have and/or are unsure what can be done about our ailment. To put it another way, we lack appropriate information. Thus we go the doctor to try to gain the necessary information. On the basis of the advice that we are given, we then make a decision about what to do. This system may be satisfactory as long as the doctor

does not inadvertently or deliberately give us the wrong information. Our problem is that we have no way of knowing the veracity of the information that we are given. If it happens to be wrong, we may well make an undesirable choice about possible treatment. In economic terms, there will be a misallocation of resources. There is a market failure.

Public goods
Defining public goods
A different type of good from a merit or de-merit that may cause the market to fail is referred to as a **public good**. Here, it is not a matter of too much or little provision of the good in question, but rather whether the product will be provided at all.

There are two specific characteristics that a good must possess if it is to be classified as a public good:
1 It must be **non-excludable**. This means that once the good has been provided for one consumer, it is impossible to stop other consumers from benefiting from the good.
2 It must be **non-rival**. As more and more people consume the product, the benefit to those already consuming the product is not diminished.

Once one begins to think about these characteristics, there are a number of goods that can be seen as public goods. Take the example of a lighthouse. Once a lighthouse is built to warn one ship at sea away from a dangerous area of rocks, then, by its very nature, this service will automatically be provided to all ships that sail within a certain distance of the lighthouse. It is non-excludable. Equally, the fact that other ships see the light given by the lighthouse and are warned away from the dangerous rocks does not reduce the benefit that any one particular ship receives from that warning. It is non-rival.

The problem caused by public goods
The problem that may be caused in a free market by the existence of public goods is a serious one: the market may fail to produce them at all. There may be a consumer demand for such products (consumers are willing and able, in principle, to pay for the product's services), but the free market may not have a mechanism for guaranteeing their production.

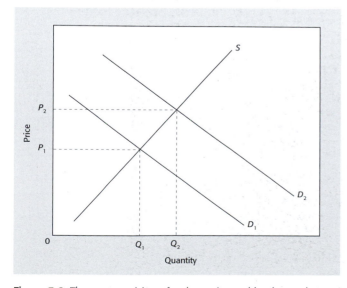

Figure 3.6 The over-provision of a de-merit good by the market

Self-assessment tasks

1 Discuss whether each of the following may be considered to be either a merit or a de-merit good:

   ◆ wearing a seatbelt;
   ◆ visiting a museum;
   ◆ children eating sweets;
   ◆ listening to very loud music;
   ◆ the provision of health care.

2 Read the short newspaper extract below and then tackle the exercises that follow.

Museum charges will always be too high a price to pay

'If you wish to continue to look at this painting, please insert another compulsory donation token.' Can the day be far off when our museums and art galleries are cordoned off from the rest of public space and charges introduced across the board? That will be a shame. Either this country continues to glory in a series of great national art and cultural collections into which citizens can walk on a whim, in their lunch breaks or in between shopping. Or it slips and slides into a state of affairs in which 'culture' is seen as a segmented economic activity, marked off, labelled as elite, and paid for.

Yes, of course this is an elitist issue. Many cultural institutions already charge. The Science and Natural History Museums in London are not cheap. You have to pay to go to a theatre or listen to a concert. Why are the fine arts and provincial museums different? Well, they are different because as communities we recognise that we all gained from them, even if we personally never understood why a photograph would not be a better likeness, or why we could not read about the Rosetta stone in a book.

Natural History Museum, London

Source: Leader article, *The Independent*, 1 December 1997 (adapted).

(a) In what way does this article suggest that fine art and certain museums might be viewed as merit goods?

(b) Discuss whether it can be justified to provide admissions to certain museums free while consumers have to pay for virtually all other services.

The essence of the problem is summed up in the phrase free riding. Consumers attempt to gain a 'free ride' on the back of other consumers' purchases of the public good. It is entirely reasonable that they may attempt to do this. One of the key characteristics of public goods as stated above is that they are non-excludable. This implies that once one consumer has purchased the product, all other consumers cannot be prevented from benefiting from that product. Take the example of the lighthouse. Once one particular fisherman has provided a lighthouse close to some dangerous rocks for his benefit, then all other fishermen in the area will benefit equally from the lighthouse. Their advantage, however, is that they do not have to pay for

Pendeen Lighthouse, Cornwall – a classic example of a public good
Source: Turid Nyhamar and Roy Valentine photographers.

this lighthouse: they have received a free ride on the back of someone else's purchase. The logical thing to do, then, would seem to be for all fishermen to sit back and to wait for one fisherman to be foolish enough to provide a lighthouse so that those not purchasing can benefit without paying. Unfortunately, the implication of this is that the lighthouse is never provided: everyone waits for someone else to provide it, and nothing happens.

It could be argued that a more likely scenario to the one described above is that all fishermen in an area might agree to club together in order to make the purchase and thus the lighthouse would be provided. However, there is still a problem here as it is in the interest of any one fisherman to conceal his desire for the lighthouse, refuse to pay but still to gain the final benefit once it is provided. Again, if all fishermen behave thus, the lighthouse is not provided.

The existence of public goods may thus mean that scarce resources are not used in a way that would be desirable. People may wish for the provision of such goods (they yield utility), but the demand may never be registered in the market.

Self-assessment tasks

1 Explain whether each of the following may be described as a private, or as a public good:
- ◆ a nuclear defence system;
- ◆ a chocolate bar;
- ◆ a public park;
- ◆ a firework display;
- ◆ street lighting;
- ◆ traffic police.

2 Read the short case study below and then tackle the exercises that follow.

The prisoners and their dilemma

The two prisoners lay in their cells as night descended. Tomorrow morning they would both have to give their respective pleas: 'Guilty' or 'Not guilty'. Both had been arrested for the same crime. The judge and jury knew that at least one of these prisoners was guilty, but were unsure whether both were. If both prisoners were to plead guilty, then both would be assumed to be guilty and would receive five years each in prison for their crime. If one were to plead guilty and the other not guilty, then the one pleading guilty would receive eight years in prison and the other would be assumed to be innocent and would be set free. However, if both prisoners pleaded not guilty, then both would be assumed to have committed the crime and would receive seven years each in prison. The dilemma of each prisoner is thus whether to plead 'Guilty' or 'Not guilty' in the morning.

(a) Assuming that the prisoners make their decisions separately and that all they are interested in is minimising the length of time they spend in prison, explain why they are both likely to plead 'Not guilty'.

(b) Explain how the prisoners could do better if they managed to agree to make the same plea of 'Guilty'.

(c) Discuss how this illustration can help to explain the principle of attempted 'free-riding' that can lead to the free market failing to provide public goods, even though many people might in principle want them and be prepared to pay for them.

Government intervention

You have only to glance at a newspaper or listen to the news or a political debate for a few minutes to realise that one of the more controversial areas of Economics is concerned with the extent and reasons for government intervention in markets. All governments in the world intervene to a greater or lesser extent and the reasons for intervention vary enormously between them. However, the justification for intervention is usually given under two broad headings:

> *market failure* and the desire to achieve a *fair or equitable distribution of resources* in economy.

The first intervention occurs when markets do not allocate resources efficiently and the second is concerned with ensuring that all members of society have fair access to goods and services. The role of the government is to intervene in markets that are not seen to be allocating resources in the most efficient or the most equitable manner. When governments attempt to achieve this aim it must be recognised that there is also the possibility that they will fail and create rather than remove distortions.

Methods of government intervention

Government policy and methods of intervention can be summarised under four broad headings: regulation, financial intervention, production and transfer payments. The method chosen will depend to a large extent on whether the reason for intervention is concerned with market failure or with the desire to achieve equity.

Regulation

The government uses a large number of methods of **regulation** as a means of controlling a market. Legal and other methods are used to control the quality and quantity of goods and services that are produced and consumed. For example, the government may regulate the sale of certain drugs by making them only available on prescription from a qualified doctor. Hygiene laws set standards for the production of foods. There may be *controls* on shop opening hours or the setting of a minimum age at which a person can buy certain products, such as alcohol, cigarettes and lottery tickets. Other forms of regulation may include the requirement for an individual to purchase an insurance policy before

being legally permitted to drive a car, the age at which people are required to attend school and the payment of social insurance contributions.

Regulation may not only apply to the quantity and quality of goods and services sold but may also refer to prices. Examples of price controls include minimum wage legislation, maximum price and rent controls.

Financial intervention

Financial tools, such as **taxes** and **subsidies**, are also frequently used by governments to influence production, prices of commodities, incomes or the distribution of wealth in an economy. Price subsidies may vary. They might be in the form of a partial subsidy, as in the case of public transport, or total, as in the case of free eye tests for children in full-time education.

Tax instruments may also vary. For example consider two different forms of taxation that are currently applied to the use of vehicles in the UK. Vehicle Excise Duty is paid once every six months or year, unless the vehicle is more than 25 years old. The same amount is paid whether the car is used daily or only once a month. In addition vehicle users pay a tax on petrol. In this case the amount of tax paid rises with the number of miles driven. The first type of tax may deter ownership of a vehicle whilst the second deters use of the vehicle.

Governments also provide the finance that is needed to produce a good or service. It is very important to note at this early stage that just because the government provides the finance for a product, it does not necessarily mean it has to produce the product too. For example, the government could finance education but all schools, colleges and universities could be privately owned and run. Health care may be provided free (financial intervention) but the drugs used in prevention and cure of illness could be privately produced.

State production

In addition to providing the finance it is also possible for a government to take over the production of a good or service, either in whole or in part. State-owned industries are often referred to as **nationalised industries**. Industries such as the electricity, coal mining and railway industries are entirely owned and managed by the state in many countries. This is no longer the case in the UK following the major shift towards privatisation that took place in the 1980s and

1990s. It is also very common to find some goods and services being produced by both the state and the private sectors. Education and health care are particularly good examples of these types of service industries. NHS hospitals function alongside private hospitals and independent schools operate alongside state schools.

Income and other transfers

Income transfers are used by governments as a means of redistributing income or transferring income from one group in society to another group, for example from people in work to those who are retired or from relatively rich people to those who are in poverty. The justification for these transfers is to achieve fairness or equity in an economy. These transfers of income may be in the form of a cash benefit paid by the government to someone with a low income. Income transfers may also be used to cover the unexpected loss of income when a person is not working due to illness or unemployment. These cash transfers include social security benefits, such as income support, a job seeker's allowance or a state pension. These will be discussed later in section 10.

Self-assessment task

Identify and explain the method of government intervention referred to in each of the following:

- the part of an annual vehicle test that limits the amount of carbon particles that can be emitted from a vehicle's exhaust pipe;
- the setting of a minimum wage rate;
- higher tax rate charged on lead substitute rather than unleaded petrol;
- free eye tests for pensioners;
- driving tests;
- age limits on individuals being able to purchase lottery tickets;
- the building and staffing of schools.

The impact of government intervention on markets

The impact of these different methods of government intervention will vary according to both the reasons for market failure and the conditions facing the markets.

Public goods

Public goods, such as defence, need to be financed by the government but they do not necessarily need to be produced by the government. The government will decide upon the optimal amount of defence expenditure and raise revenue through taxation to fund it. The problem facing the government is deciding on the best or fairest method of raising the tax revenue required. One approach is to tax individuals according their ability to pay tax. Thus those who have the highest incomes (or wealth) will pay most in taxation. Many governments use the 'ability to pay' principle as a basis for the tax system and it has a wide acceptance amongst the electorate as being the fairest means of raising tax revenue. In most countries the government takes a larger percentage of income in tax from the rich than the poor. This is called a **progressive tax** system.

Externalities

Setting standards and regulation Governments frequently use regulation to overcome market failures caused by externalities. Let us consider the case of an electricity company that pollutes the surrounding countryside. The government might intervene by setting standards which restrict the amount of pollution that can be legally dumped. The government would then need to regulate and inspect the company to make sure that these restrictions are enforced. It can do this in several ways, for example by imposing large fines on any company that contravenes the law.

Exhaust fumes from cars pollute the atmosphere and to reduce this problem the government can set legal limits on the amount of carbon particles that are emitted from a car's exhaust pipe. This can be tested in the annual MOT test, although it also possible to conduct random on-the-spot tests. Regulations of this type are particularly effective when there are a large number of potential sources of the external cost. There are 17 million vehicles using Britain's roads and it is not possible to individually test every vehicle every day.

Financial intervention – taxes Financial intervention will take the form of taxes or subsidies; these can also be used in the case of externalities. A tax would normally be imposed on the individual or firm that causes the externality. If this happens then economists say that external costs are internalised.

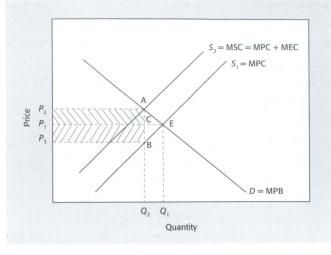

Figure 3.7 External cost and use of taxation

In figure 3.7, in the case where there is no government intervention, the equilibrium occurs at point E, where supply, S_1, which is given by MPC or marginal private cost, equals demand, D, which is given by MPB or marginal private benefit. However, if external costs are included in this diagram, then the supply curve becomes S_2 or MSC, marginal social cost. The vertical distance between these two supply curves is marginal external cost, MEC. The socially optimal level of output is therefore equal to Q_2, where S_2 cuts the demand curve. At this socially optimal level of output, the marginal external cost is equal to the vertical distance AB.

The government intervenes in this market and imposes a tax which is equal to the marginal external cost. This tax is added to the cost of producing the product and thus the supply curve S_2 is also equal to the MPC plus tax. Looking at the diagram, you can see that the price at which the product is sold has increased from P_1 to P_2. This is less than the tax applied by the government. At first sight this may appear a little strange, but the producer has accepted a cut in the price received from P_1 to P_3. The producer has borne the burden of part of the tax. The total tax paid is equal to the area P_2ABP_3, of which the consumer's share of the burden is P_2ACP_1 and the producer's share is P_1CBP_3.

Financial intervention – subsidies Financial intervention to overcome market failure caused by external benefits or positive externalities will take the form of a subsidy. This is shown in figure 3.8. The

equilibrium without government intervention is at point F where MPC = MPB or $D = S_1$. In this case, marginal external benefit is added to the MPB curve to give the MSB or marginal social benefit curve. The MSB represents society's demand curve for the product.

If the government subsidises production of this product then the supply curve moves to the right from S_1, which equals MPC, to S_2, which equals MPC minus the subsidy. The marginal cost of supplying the good is reduced by the amount of subsidy and the vertical distance GH is equal to the value of the subsidy. Thus the equilibrium after the subsidy is given by point H, which is where D_1 crosses S_2 and the optimal amount of goods Q_2 is sold by the market.

As you might expect, there is considerable debate over which is the best method of government intervention when externalities are present in a market. If we accept the argument that education provides external benefits, then one solution would be to provide a subsidy to education. This can be seen in the UK where the government subsidises university education. Students still have to pay towards their education in the form of a fee, which can be represented by P_3 in figure 6.3. The government provides the difference between P_2 and P_3 by providing a subsidy.

Maximum price controls and price stabilisation
We will conclude this section by considering how governments impose maximum price controls in markets and how in agricultural markets price stabilisation policies can be applied.

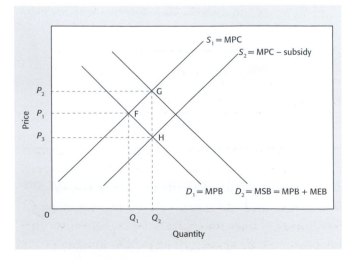

Figure 3.8 External benefits and use of a subsidy

Maximum price controls are only valid in markets where the maximum price that is imposed is *below* the normal equilibrium price as determined in a free market. Governments use legislation to enforce maximum prices for:

◆ staple foodstuffs, such as bread, rice and cooking oil;

◆ rents in certain types of housing;

◆ services provided by utilities, such as water, gas and electricity companies;

◆ transport fares where a subsidy is being paid.

Figure 3.9 indicates that at the price ceiling of P_1, production is not sufficient to satisfy everyone who wishes to buy the product. Consequently, as price cannot rise, the available supply has to be allocated on some other basis. The most likely way is by means of queuing, a much evidenced form of control in the former planned economies of Central and Eastern Europe (see section 1). Rationing is another means of restricting demand – it inevitably leads to a black market for the products involved, with consumers then having to pay inflated prices well above the ceiling price.

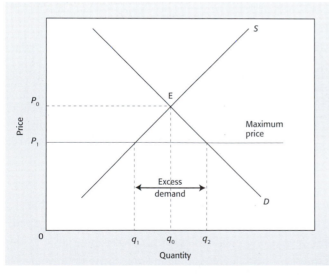

Figure 3.9 The effects of maximum price control

Price stabilisation policies, especially in agricultural markets, are designed to lessen the effects of unplanned fluctuations in supply. A producers' association or a government-backed marketing board regulates supply by releasing stocks on to the market in order to stabilise farm incomes. By releasing buffer stocks at times of shortage or by purchasing excess stocks at times of surplus production, price can be stabilised at a predetermined level. Although theoretically simple in terms of their economic logic, such policies are often criticised as they do not promote efficiency and tend to protect farmers from the full force of competition in world markets.

Summary

In this section we have recognised that:

● Markets do not always operate as suggested by economic theory. There are various reasons why markets fail.

● Where negative and positive externalities exist in a market, the outcome is an inappropriate level of production.

● Using cost–benefit analysis can be an important aid to decision making.

● Merit and de-merit goods will not be provided in the right quantities by the maket.

● Public goods will not necessarily be provided by the market.

● Government intervention can take various forms including regulation, financial intervention and direct provision of goods.

● Financial intervention in the form of taxes and subsidies has been widely advocated for use in markets where there are negative and positive externalities.

Key words

Definitions of Key words can be found in the Glossary.

cost–benefit analysis	private benefits
de-merit goods	private costs
external benefit	progressive tax
external cost	public goods
externalities	regulation
income transfer	shadow price
information failure	social benefits
market failure	social costs
merit goods	spillover effects
nationalised industry	state production
negative externality	subsidies
non-excludable	taxes
non-rival	value judgement
paternalism	

4 International trade

On completion of this section you should know:

➤ what is meant by the principles of absolute and comparative advantage

➤ the extent to which these principles can be used to explain international trade flows in the international economy

➤ the arguments put forward for free trade and why protectionist measures may be applied to limit international trade

➤ what types of protection are used in international trade and what are their likely effects

➤ what is meant by economic integration and the principal characteristics of free trade areas, customs unions and economic unions

➤ what is meant by the terms of trade and how it can be estimated

➤ the main components of the balance of payments of an economy

The global economy of the twenty-first century

International trade is the lifeblood of virtually all modern developed and developing economies. As such, it involves the buying and selling of goods and services across national frontiers. At a personal level this is clearly seen through the many imported items that can be found in supermarkets and other retail stores. Products such as Coca Cola, Fuji film, Nike trainers and Nescafé coffee are global brands and are widely available throughout the world.

Coca Cola: a much traded product of the global economy

Increasingly, through international trade, economies have become more and more economically dependent upon each other. For example, the well-being of the US economy affects the well-being of many other economies in Central and South America, Europe, Asia and Africa. Similarly, the South East Asian currency crisis of 1996 had knock-on effects throughout the world (see section 6). This dependency can crudely be shown by the respective contributions of **exports** and **imports** to a country's Gross Domestic Product (GDP) (see section 11). For the UK, in 2000, these were approximately 29 per cent and 32 per cent respectively. In other economies, this percentage was even greater.

Trade provides an important link between developed and developing economies. From a very general standpoint, the developed economies provide a range of consumer goods, capital equipment and financial services in exchange for raw materials, certain types of agricultural products and, increasingly, for a range of manufactured goods from the developing economies. Also included in international trade are the ever-increasing global receipts from international tourism. These are of very substantial importance, both domestically and as a source of foreign exchange, for many developing economies in the Caribbean, East Africa and Asia.

On the surface, it may seem best if we 'buy local'. After all this promotes sales of home-produced goods and restricts the drain on foreign currency reserves caused by the need to pay for imports. But if all countries followed this strategy, there would be very little international trade except for certain essentials that could not be produced in the home market. As we shall see below, this state of affairs is very wasteful and the world economy as a whole would be poorer as a consequence.

Trade permits countries to specialise in products and commodities which they can produce relatively efficiently. The reasons for this **specialisation** are many and include the availability of particular factors of production. Economies which have naturally occurring resources, such as oil or copper, can exploit these and trade them on the world market. Alternatively, the climate or soils of a country may make it a good source of certain types of food product or a good destination for international tourists. Other economies may have a highly skilled workforce or have unit labour costs below that of others so enabling them to competitively produce clothing, electrical goods or vehicles. These examples are a very clear link to the factors of production identified in section 1.

From an accounting standpoint, the **balance of payments** in an economy is a financial record of all such international transactions. In principle, receipts from exports of goods and services can be used to pay for imports which cannot be produced as efficiently or which cannot be produced at all. The nature of the global economy though is that this is not as simple an exchange process as might be indicated. Some economies, such as Germany, Japan and China, have traditionally had export surpluses. In contrast, others, such as the UK, the US and many developing economies, have spent more on imports than exports. Although by definition the world economy's trade flows balance, for individual countries this may not happen. If the imbalance is other than marginal, corrective action has to take place (see section 7).

Self-assessment task

Think about the main types of goods
- imported into your country,
- exported by your country.

Make a list of these and see if you can come up with a simple explanation as to why this is so. Make reference to the factors of production in your explanation.

The principles of international trade

The economic logic which has underpinned the development of international trade has its origins over 200 years ago in the writings of classical economists who firmly advocated what we now refer to as **multilateral free trade**. Their principles of absolute and, particularly, of comparative advantage have modern relevance in the objectives of the World Trade Organisation (WTO), which exists to promote free trade amongst all countries in the world economy.

The simple economic principles involved are summarised below. These show that trade will take place when countries have a clear-cut or **absolute advantage** over other countries. If we look at the UK's position for example:
- India has a clear-cut advantage over the UK in the production of tea;
- the Windward Islands can produce bananas, which the UK cannot produce;
- France has an obvious advantage in producing wine for export to the UK.

A list like this can be quite extensive; we could also compile a similar list of items for the trade of any economy.

What is obvious is that, under certain circumstances, trade can also be beneficial where a country may not have such clear-cut advantage. Provided it has a relative or **comparative advantage** in the production of a particular good over another country, trade can produce gains for both partners.

Summary of the principles of absolute and comparative advantage

The following assumptions are made:
- there are just two countries involved in trade;
- each can produce just two products (say, cloth and cheese);
- productivity differs between them, so varying quantities of each are produced;
- production costs and opportunity costs are constant for each product.

The production possibilities are shown in figure 4.1.

If each country was self-sufficient and devoted half of its resources to each product then the situation would be as shown at points A and B on these production possibility frontiers.

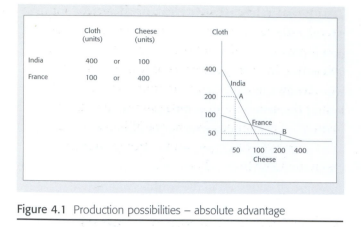

Figure 4.1 Production possibilities – absolute advantage

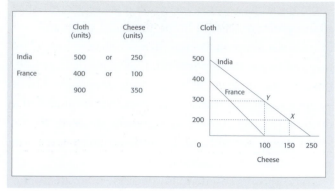

Figure 4.2 Production possibilities with one country having absolute advantage in both products

	Before trade (half of all resources to each industry)		After trade (all resources to chosen industry)	
	Cloth (units)	Cheese (units)	Cloth (units)	Cheese (units)
India	200	50	400	0
France	50	200	0	400
Total world production	250	250	400	400

Table 4.1 The gains from trade under absolute advantage

India is clearly better at cloth production, France is better at producing cheese. India is said to have an **absolute advantage** in cloth, France in cheese. If, however, they subsequently specialised, concentrating on those products where they had absolute advantage, each country would actually be better off as a result of trade taking place (see table 4.1).

India could now import 200 units of cheese from France, an overall gain of 150 units, without losing any cloth production. France can similarly benefit from buying cloth from India.

The above situation, sometimes called reciprocal absolute advantage, means that one country is better at producing one product, the other is superior in the production of the other. This rather obvious situation can be developed a stage further through the principle of **comparative advantage** – this states that trade between two countries should still take place and be mutually beneficial provided the domestic opportunity costs of production differ.

Going back to our earlier example, let us assume that India has a clear-cut advantage over France in the production of both cloth and cheese (somewhat unlikely, but remember this is no more than a simple model!). Factor endowments, including more advanced machinery, good pasture land and a more productive workforce, could provide this advantage. On the surface, there may seem little point in the two countries trading because India has the edge in producing both cloth and cheese. This situation is shown in figure 4.2.

If India decided not to trade at all, opting for self-sufficiency, each time it wanted more cloth, say, it would have to divert resources from cheese production. This trade-off, applying the concept of opportunity cost, can be illustrated by a movement on the production possibility frontier from X to Y. As India gained 100 units of cloth, it had to sacrifice fifty units of cheese production – the opportunity cost being that each unit of cloth gained resulted in a loss of half a unit of cheese. A reverse movement would produce a gain of one unit of cheese for every two units of cloth sacrificed. In the case of France, to gain an extra unit of cheese, there would be an opportunity cost of four units of cloth whereas each additional unit of cloth produced would result in a loss of a quarter of a unit of cheese.

The outcome of this principle is that countries should specialise in those goods in which they have the greatest relative efficiency over their trading partners. So, using the data above, India should concentrate on producing cheese, France on cloth. If this were to happen, and all resources were re-allocated in this way, total production would increase. This is shown in table 4.2.

	Cloth (units)	Cheese (units)	
India	0	500	Total production
France	800	0	has increased by
	800	500	50 units

Table 4.2 The gains from trade under comparative advantage

The simple principles explained above are based on several assumptions. These are:

- The production possibility frontiers are linear.
- The exchange rate operating for international transactions must be between the respective domestic opportunity cost ratios. Otherwise trade will not be mutually beneficial. Indeed, where the differences between these opportunity costs are widest, then the potential for trade is greatest.
- No transport costs are charged. In today's global economy, this is very unrealistic, but it does reinforce the point made immediately above. There will be a gain from trade if the production benefit is greater than the transport costs.
- The two-country, two-product assumption is again a long way from reality in the twenty-first century. Countries might specialise in narrowly defined product areas, for example, high-quality woollen cloth, not cloth in general, and there are many potential trading partners in the global economy.
- Production costs are most unlikely to be constant. As countries specialise, for example, then they are likely to benefit from economies of scale as specialisation proceeds. They may also experience diseconomies of scale if specialisation goes too far.
- There are no restrictions on free trade between those countries which possess absolute and comparative advantage. This is clearly a very unrealistic assumption that has to be made.

Notwithstanding these assumptions, there are clear gains from international trade as the principles of absolute and comparative advantage indicate. These principles are extendable of course to any number of countries and any number of products – the more of each, the greater the total gains from trade, as long as the principle of comparative advantage is followed.

Multi-lateral free trade is therefore beneficial for the overall well-being of the world economy. It ensures that goods are produced in those countries that are most efficient, minimising the waste of scarce resources. Conversely, it is clear that restrictions on trade will reduce the gains that free trade can produce. In the interests of economic efficiency tariff barriers and any other measures which protect the free movement of goods are to be frowned on.

Types of protection and their effects

Since free trade leads to a rise in world economic welfare, why should any country adopt policies which prevent free trade? Sometimes policies are adopted which distort market forces in order to give a competitive advantage to the domestic industry of an economy. Such policies are called **protectionist** policies because they provide some degree of protection from foreign competition. There are various methods of protecting domestic industry.

Tariffs

A **tariff** is a tax on imports. It can be either specific, that is so much per unit, or *ad valorem*, which is a percentage of the price. Like all indirect taxes, tariffs have the impact of reducing the supply and raising the equilibrium price of the import. This gives a competitive advantage to home-produced goods and services, which become more attractive to consumers, resulting in a fall in imports.

A modern UK-registered container vessel
Source: Bibby Line Group.

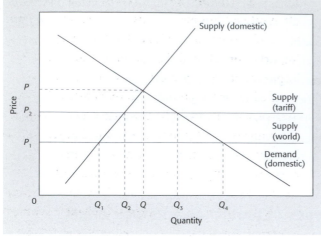

Figure 4.3 The effects of a tariff

Consider the economy in figure 4.3. If it did not engage in world trade, consumers would pay price P and consume quantity Q. This would be determined by the domestic supply and demand for the commodity. If the economy engaged in international trade, then consumers would benefit from international specialisation. World supply is shown as supply (world). Under these circumstances prices would fall to P_1. Consumption of the good would rise from Q to Q_4. At this price, however, only Q_1 would be supplied by the domestic producers. This means that domestic production has fallen from Q to Q_1. Lower-cost overseas producers have free access to the market, which has benefited consumers, but domestic producers have suffered, leading to a fall in employment in the industry. The imposition of a tariff, like all indirect taxes, would shift the supply curve upwards. This would increase the price to domestic consumers from P_1 to P_2. Production by domestic producers would increase from Q_1 to Q_2. Some jobs in the domestic economy would be saved.

Clearly, tariffs distort market forces and prevent consumers from benefiting from all the advantages of international specialisation and trade.

Quotas

Quotas are restrictions on the maximum quantity of imports. Their effect is to reduce the supply of imports on the domestic market. This will lead to a higher equilibrium price than would occur in a free market. Just as with tariffs the impact is to prevent the domestic consumer from benefiting from all the advantages of

international trade. One difference is that whereas the government gains revenue as a result of tariffs, with quotas the increased price paid by consumers results in the foreign firm which supplied the imports earning higher profits. One answer might be for the government to sell licences to foreign firms to allow them to sell some allocation of the quota on the domestic market. The prospect of raised profits would ensure a market for the import licences.

Exchange control

One way of preventing excessive spending on imports is to set legal limits on the dealings in foreign currency that a country's citizens can make. If importers are limited in their access to foreign currency, they cannot pay for imports to the full extent of the domestic demand that exists. Imports will fall to a level below that which will occur in a free market. Again the consumer would suffer. **Exchange controls** existed in the UK before 1979 and there have been periods when there was a limit to the amount of foreign exchange that British citizens could take on overseas holidays. In 1979, all exchange controls were abandoned by the newly elected Conservative government. All member states of the European Union abandoned exchange controls in 1993.

Export subsidies

We have defined 'protectionism' in terms of any policy that distorts market forces to give competitive advantage to domestic industry. Sometimes, this is achieved through direct subsidies on exports. The impact of an export subsidy is to increase the supply of an industry's exports on the world market, which will have the impact of reducing price below that determined in a free market. Foreign consumers will enjoy an increase in their economic welfare as the price of the good falls. Those employed in the domestic market might also benefit as production increases to match demand for the lower-priced goods. They might enjoy higher wages and their jobs might be more secure but only as long as the subsidy lasts. Those who lose are the taxpayers who have to pay for the subsidy. In addition, as firms divert output to the overseas market, the supply of goods may fall in the domestic market, leading to rising prices and reduced welfare for domestic consumers.

The methods of protectionism described so far are all quite clear and obvious ways in which domestic industries can be given a competitive advantage over foreign industry in order to reduce imports and/or boost exports. Because these methods so obviously distort international market forces in pursuit of the more narrow national interest, they are all generally forbidden, except under very limiting circumstances, under the terms of international trading agreements such as the former General Agreement on Tariffs and Trade (GATT).

Protectionist policies are sometimes called *expenditure switching* policies because their aim is clearly to switch expenditure, both domestic and foreign, to the output of goods and services of the domestic economy (see section 7 also).

An assessment of the arguments in favour of protectionism

International specialisation and free trade are justified because they lead to an optimal allocation of resources on a world scale and to a rise in the economic welfare of consumers. Any arguments advanced in justification of protectionist policies can only be assessed if the impact on world resource allocation and consumer welfare is considered.

It is often argued that protectionism is justified:

◆ *To safeguard employment in the home economy.*
An examination of the UK's trade accounts over the last few years will reveal the extent to which imports of manufactured goods have increased. The import penetration ratio is the proportion of the domestic sales of a product which is taken up by imports. For example, in 1968 the import penetration ratio in textiles was 16 per cent. This means that out of every £100 spent on textiles in Britain, £16 was spent on imported textiles. By 1997 the figure had risen to 53 per cent. In the category radio, television and communications equipment, the import penetration ratio was as high as 98% in 1997. As import penetration rises, domestic firms come under increasing pressure to maintain sales and the less successful will have to lay off workers and some may close down completely. This can result in considerable structural unemployment and can lead to calls for

some degree of protection from imports. Very often interest groups, such as trade unions, will call for tariffs when faced with a flood of cheap imports from abroad. Any argument in favour of import controls to protect jobs can only be justified on social grounds. To maximise economic welfare, labour should be considered as a resource that must be swiftly allocated and reallocated to its best use. This process can be aided by any measures to improve the occupational and geographical mobility of labour. Looked at in this way 'a flood of cheap imports' should be welcomed as a benefit to the consumer rather than seen as a threat to jobs.

◆ *To correct balance of payments disequilibria.*
Typical policies include raising income taxes and interest rates to prevent consumers purchasing imports. These policies were sometimes known as *expenditure dampening policies.* In addition to preventing imports, such policies also reduce consumer spending on the output of domestic industry, so the side effect is a rise in unemployment. This results in a call for expenditure switching policies as an alternative way of protecting the balance of payments and the exchange rate. These policies will be analysed in detail in section 7.

◆ *To prevent the exploitation of labour in developing economies.*
Very often when cheap goods are imported into a market there are claims that the goods are cheap because labour in the exporting countries is paid a very low wage. It is claimed that the labour is exploited and as a result imports should be prevented. This results in a call for import controls on moral grounds but also often on the grounds that firms in the importing country cannot compete with the cheap imports because they have to pay higher wages. This argument in favour of import controls is often combined with the argument that they are required in order to protect jobs. Such arguments in favour of import controls have no economic justification whatsoever. If labour is cheap in an economy this is a reflection of that economy's factor endowment. A large supply of unskilled labour will lead to low wages

and usually low priced products. The law of comparative advantage suggests that this will lead to increased economic welfare as those economies with cheap labour specialise in those products in which they have the lowest opportunity costs. This will be in those products which are highly labour intensive. It should be noted that there may well be moral arguments to justify protectionism in this case, but it should also be considered that any measures which reduce imports from such countries are likely to make the problem of low wages worse. This is because any fall in demand for imports from such economies will reduce the

demand for labour further and make wage rates fall even lower.

◆ *To prevent dumping.*

Dumping is a term in economics which describes the process of selling goods in an overseas market at a price below the cost of production. This is a form of price discrimination because consumers in the home market will pay a higher price than those in the overseas market. The purpose of dumping might be to destroy existing competition in the overseas market or to prevent new firms in the overseas market from becoming established. Dumping can be achieved through

Self-assessment tasks

Read the newspaper editorial below and then tackle the exercises that follow.

Free trade is fair

'Fair trade, not free trade' is the banner carried by protestors outside the World Trade Organisation conference. It is code for quotas, tariffs and prohibitions. So when Britain's man in Seattle blathers approvingly about 'fair trade', it matters. By adopting the language of the protectionists, Stephen Byers, the DTI Secretary, advertised before the hard bargaining had even started that this Government will not exert leadership to defeat obscurantism. Nor will President Clinton, who is backing away from America's commitment to free trade in order to appease the rioters and their friends in the media. If the two powers that built the world's open trading system – and are still seen as its custodians, even if Britain has surrendered trade policy to the EU – do not have the gumption to face down Dyke Action and the Raging Grannies, God help us.

Free trade does not happen of its own accord. The natural condition of the world is protectionist: the gains of increased commerce are spread widely, and to some degree invisibly, while the losses are concentrated heavily in sectors that mobilise quickly for political action – as French farmers and Detroit's motor industry have shown in their time. Trade barriers are rarely

reduced without a Herculean effort by far-sighted leaders, acting in concert, at grand summits like this one in Seattle. So far, it looks as if the current generation of leaders is incapable of making such an effort.

The European Union is seeking to do little more than protect its ruinous system of farm subsidies, while suggesting otherwise with disingenuous demands for a comprehensive agenda. President Clinton – already electioneering for Al Gore – has abruptly changed US trade policy in a sop to the trade unions, calling for the WTO to extend its power into the area of labour rights. Mr Clinton is making emotive noises about 'child labour', but the real issue is cheap labour, which is the one competitive advantage left to poor countries. The gambit is rightly regarded as an invidious form of rich world protectionism by most of the WTO's 134 members. If pressed, it will wreck the meeting.

It is lamentable that the governments of the world's richest countries cannot find the political will – in the easiest of conditions, at the height of a long economic boom – to uphold the system that made them so rich. The best that can now be expected from this miserable summit is a fudge that does no damage.

Source: Daily Telegraph, 3 December 1999.

1 What is meant by 'fair trade'?

2 Discuss why the EU is reluctant to reduce its quotas, tariffs and prohibitions on trade with developing economies.

export subsidies provided by the home government or through ensuring that consumers in the home market pay a sufficiently high price to cover total costs. Alternatively, firms might be prepared to suffer losses in the short term if this allows them to destroy competition and create a monopoly, increasing excess profits in the long term. Clearly, if dumping leads to anti-competitive behaviour in the long run and prevents the emergence of comparative advantage, then import controls on products dumped in a market can be justified. It should be noted, however, that firms which face competition through cheap imports will often claim that goods are being dumped, when in reality the low prices of such goods are merely a reflection of the greater efficiency of the exporting firm. Whether a good is truly being dumped on a market needs careful investigation before import controls can be justified.

◆ *To safeguard infant industries.*
As shifts in comparative advantage occur, conditions for the location of industries in particular economies can become favourable. Establishing a fledgling industry can be quite difficult in the early years, however, especially if the new industry faces competition from a long-established company. The **infant industry** with only a small part of the market will not be able to benefit from all potential economies of scale and will be unable to compete in the market. It will be in the interests of the established firm to try to drive the new industry out of business and it might cut prices fiercely to retain its market. If the infant industry does have the potential to develop into an efficient producer in line with comparative advantage, then import controls may well be justified in this case. It should be noted, however, that many industries call for protection in their fledgling state but they then develop a vested interest in maintaining this protection once they have become established. Interest groups develop to lobby politicians to prevent import controls from being removed.

From theory to reality: trade and globalisation

Over the last 20 years or so, international trade in the world economy has grown more quickly than GDP growth. This trend is expected to persist, as the various economies of the world become more dependent upon each other through **globalisation**. Markets across the world are becoming more integrated, with developed and developing economies becoming much more economically dependent upon each other. For developing economies, trade is the main way in which they can realise the benefits of globalisation.

Figure 4.4 shows in aggregate terms how over the 1990s an ever-increasing percentage of the GDP of developing countries is being generated through international trade. Consistent with the simple economic principles referred to earlier:

◆ Consumers in developing countries have an increasing variety of products to choose from as **multi-national corporations**, such as Nestlé, Kelloggs, Sony, Microsoft, Coca Cola, Toyota and so on, import goods into these countries and companies such as Exel provide the logistic support for this to take place smoothly.

◆ Imports provide additional competition for domestic producers of food and drink products especially. It also exposes them to the best practices of such corporations.

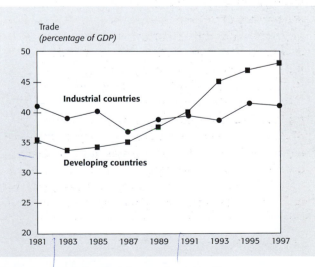

Figure 4.4 International trade growth, 1981–97
Note: Trade is the sum of exports and imports of goods and services.
Source: World Bank, *World Development Indicators*, 1999.

◆ In turn, exports enlarge the markets for the products of developing countries, benefiting producers and their employees.

◆ Trade gives firms in developing countries access to improved capital inputs, such as machine tools, so improving their own productivity.

◆ There has been a substantial re-allocation of resources in the world economy. This is particularly evidenced through the on-going shift in manufacturing activity from industrial countries to developing economies. International tourism growth has also benefited many developing economies.

The World Trade Organisation (WTO), set up in 1995, has sought to create an environment in the world economy conducive to multi-lateral free trade. The most sensitive task it has faced to date has been to reduce trade barriers on international trade in agricultural products. These products provide genuine opportunities for many developing economies to trade in world markets. Unfortunately, some of the wealthy countries (the USA especially) have blocked moves to reduce tariffs and quotas on such trade, fearing competition from lower-priced imports. Notwithstanding, more developing countries have joined the WTO, recognising its importance in promoting their interests in the continued liberalisation of world trade (see figure 4.5).

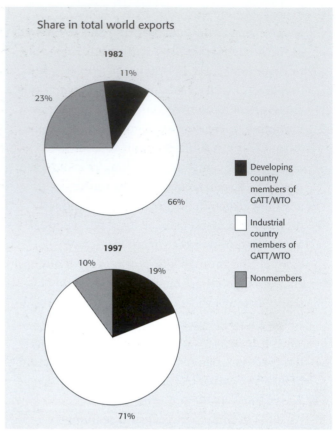

Share in total world exports

1982

11%
23%
66%

1997

10%
19%
71%

Developing country members of GATT/WTO

Industrial country members of GATT/WTO

Nonmembers

Figure 4.5 The WTO in international trade, 1982 and 1997
Source: WTO, *Annual Report*, 1997.

Nestlé tomato ketchup factory in Malaysia
Source: Mark Edwards, Still Pictures.

Transport combination finds that the time is right at last

As NFC and Ocean merge to form Exel, Juliette Jowit assesses the sector

Consolidation within the European logistics industry has long been planned but until yesterday there had been little movement.

Only Deutsche Post, the acquisitive German post office, which has spent $5bn (£3.1bn) in the past two years, had done very much.

NFC and Ocean Group admitted yesterday that they have been thinking about a deal for four years. Their time came at last.

Now investors expect the same cocktail of globalisation, outsourcing growth and e-commerce to precipitate more action, triggered by the need to compete with the new Exel.

'They [Exel] have set the agenda and the others will have to react,'

said Peter Magill, head of European transport at KPMG.

Economic growth, more outsourcing and the need to deliver e-commerce purchases is fuelling logistics businesses everywhere.

Data Monitor, the market research group, forecasts growth of 3–5 per cent in mature markets such as Germany, France and the UK, rising to 10 per cent in less developed industries in Europe and North America.

Also, as customers outsource more work, they want one or two logistics providers to offer the full range of services and cover all their markets.

Exel meets all these demands: it has geographic fit – with only a few gaps in Italy, parts of Germany and Japan; it has the resources to invest in new technology and distribution systems; and it has a large customer base to generate more business.

It also has the skills mix to meet increasing demand not just for traditional functions, such as warehousing and transport, but managing inventories and optimising supply chains.

Many customers are now outsourcing their whole logistics strategy – which explains why the once unglamorous business is now often a board-level priority.

This is another area where Exel's rivals will have to catch up, says Mr Magill.

To trust an outsider with such a vital part of the business, customers will want to know they are buying expertise.

For this reason, industry specialisation and not just size should be the driver for the coming consolidation, he says. 'Size is of course important, but so are

competencies. The potential for them comes in focusing on specific industries such as automotive, electronics, pharmaceuticals, food retailing.'

Such talk inevitably focuses attention on the likely predators and targets.

Industry insiders see Exel's focus as being on south-east Asia and the US. But in the very fragmented European industry there is still a lot to be done.

Most vulnerable could be traditional ground-based logistics providers, which have not benefited from the high growth and exciting ratings enjoyed by air freight forwarders and parcel carriers.

The most obvious predators are big US parcel carriers, UPS and Federal Express, thought to be keen to buy into a more secure income stream.

DHL, their UK rival, might also be interested.

Among existing logistics companies, Deutsche Post is still

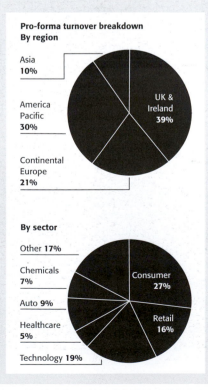

**Pro-forma turnover breakdown
By region**

Asia 10%

America Pacific 30%

Continental Europe 21%

UK & Ireland 39%

By sector

Other 17%

Chemicals 7%

Auto 9%

Healthcare 5%

Technology 19%

Consumer 27%

Retail 16%

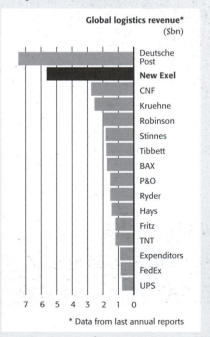

Global logistics revenue*
($bn)

Deutsche Post
New Exel
CNF
Kruehne
Robinson
Stinnes
Tibbett
BAX
P&O
Ryder
Hays
Fritz
TNT
Expenditors
FedEx
UPS

7 6 5 4 3 2 1 0

* Data from last annual reports

89

seen as aggressive, but could be tied up with competition lawyers for some time.

Tibbett & Britten and possibly Hays Logistics in the UK, and Frans Maas in the Netherlands are other contenders.

However, some of these are also on the likely target lists.

Tibbett & Britten, whose shares surged in the second half of last year, is considered the most attractive UK prize. It has the best penetration into the US of the remaining UK companies, some of the best regarded in-house technology and the highly rated John Harvey as its chairman.

Christian Salvesen, itself hoping to spend £300m–£450m on a rival in Benelux, Italy or France; and Transport Development Group, its smaller UK rival, could also be attractive to European companies wanting to buy into the UK.

Unfortunately for remaining participants, there are few big prizes left in the industry: after Deutsche Post and Exel, Consolidated National Freightways of the US and Kuehne & Nagel in Switzerland are the only two companies with logistics revenues over $2bn.

Then there is the problem that many European targets are protected by legal restrictions on takeovers or reluctant private owners.

And if, as many in the industry hope, ratings do now rise – Tibbett & Britten is already on a prospective price/earnings ratio of 16 – the multiples demanded may become another obstacle.

Source: Financial Times, 22 February 2000.

Economic integration

Despite the work of the WTO, the structure of international trade in the twenty-first century is such that the benefits are being realised, not so much on a global scale, but through the increasing role of 'regional' trading blocs. Much of world trade takes place within these blocs, although the WTO continues to press for greater exchange between the blocs and developing countries.

There are four main organisations. These are:

- the European Union (EU) – 15 member states in Western Europe, soon to be enlarged through the accession of countries in Central and Eastern Europe (see figure 4.6);
- the North American Free Trade Agreement (NAFTA) – this includes the USA, Canada and Mexico;
- the Free Trade Area of the Americas (FTAA) – various members in Central and South America plus NAFTA members;

- the Asian-Pacific Economic Co-operation (APEC) – principally Australia, New Zealand, China, Hong Kong, Japan, Taiwan and South Korea plus NAFTA members.

Geographically, the most recent development has been the participation of the powerful NAFTA countries in the FTAA and APEC organisations. The latter especially provides a substantial counterveiling force to the EU, the world's largest trading bloc.

The process by which these trading blocs have been established is referred to as **economic integration**. It refers to deliberate ways in which national economies agree to merge their economic affairs into a single economic organisation. Consequently, there is a 'blurring' of their boundaries as their economies become more closely linked to each other.

Table 4.3 shows the three main forms of organisation. These are:

Type of organisation	Characteristics	Comments
Free trade area	Removal of tariffs and quotas on internal trade	Members are free to determine their own external trade policy towards non-members. NAFTA, FTAA and APEC are still at this stage
Customs union	As above but with the agreement of a common external tariff on trade with non-members	Results in some trade being deflected from outside the union to within. Applied to the EC before moves to EMU
Economic union	As above but with more harmonisation and centralisation of economic policies	EU has moved beyond this with single currency and European Central Bank

Table 4.3 Main forms of economic integration

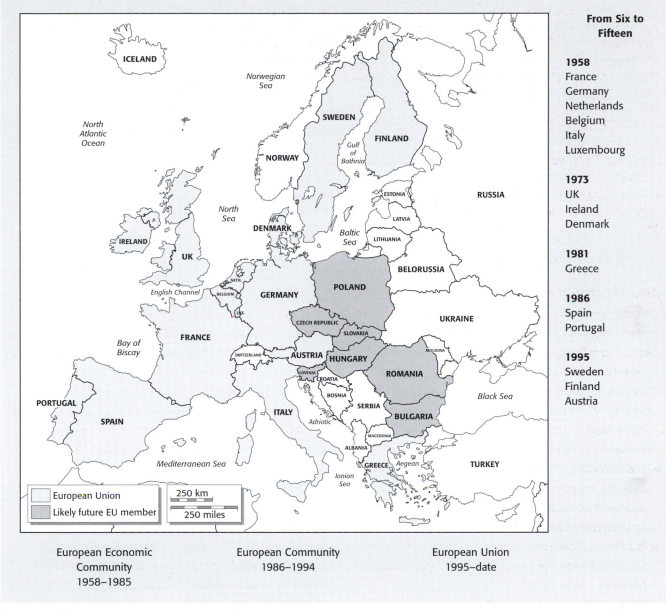

From Six to Fifteen

1958
France
Germany
Netherlands
Belgium
Italy
Luxembourg

1973
UK
Ireland
Denmark

1981
Greece

1986
Spain
Portugal

1995
Sweden
Finland
Austria

European Economic
Community
1958–1985

European Community
1986–1994

European Union
1995–date

Figure 4.6 The New Europe

◆ **Free trade area** – the loosest form of organisation involving the systematic removal of trade restrictions between members. In practice, this may be for just a selected range of commodity types, such as manufactured goods. The sensitive nature of trade in agricultural goods has meant that they have been either excluded or partially excluded from all groups except for EU internal trade.

◆ **Customs union** – the crucial feature is that members agree to erect a common external tariff on trade with non-members. This tariff may be on all trade or, as is the case with the EU, mainly on imported goods which member states are able to adequately produce themselves. Agriculture has always been a very sensitive issue in the EU, with policy being to very clearly protect the interest of EU member states. Consequently, developing countries are highly critical of this policy, despite preferential access for the agricultural products of some developing countries.

◆ **Economic union** – this involves the removal of restrictions on the movement of factors of production (labour, capital and enterprise) between members. In the case of the EU, it has also meant the development of various common policies in areas such as agriculture, transport, regional and social affairs. There has also been the deliberate harmonisation of other aspects of economic affairs in order to ensure a highly competitive environment. Controversially for some member states like the UK, the EU is now progressing towards an objective of Economic and Monetary Union (EMU), with a singly currency and centralised economic policies.

Within the context of this section, the most important issue is whether these regional trading blocs actually enhance, or detract from, global economic welfare. This is a very difficult question to answer. Economists do though point to two main effects. These are:

◆ **Trade creation** – consistent with absolute and comparative advantage, trade is generated between members over and above what might otherwise have happened. Greater specialisation occurs and less-efficient producers lose markets as imports from within the group replace their production. Resources are therefore more efficiently allocated. All of the organisations referred to in table 4.3 aim to gain these benefits.

◆ **Trade diversion** – more difficult to explain and only occurs when external trade restrictions are imposed. Trade from outside the group is replaced by trade from within; this is not consistent with an efficient allocation of resources as the prices paid for such goods will be higher than if purchased on the open world market.

Table 4.4 shows an analysis of intra-EU imports of goods for selected member states. In particular, it indicates how, through increasing economic integration, trade creation has taken place, bringing the economies much closer to each other. In some respects, the UK remains the 'odd European out', with a lower percentage of exports to its trading partners than any other member state; in contrast, the higher import volume accounts for its similar overall position to France and Germany.

In the case of the UK's membership of the EU, former Commonwealth countries especially have had a decreasing share of imports to the UK. This is crude evidence of trade diversion. For many poor countries in Africa and Asia, this diversion has had a particularly negative impact on their economies through reduced

Intra-EU trade in goods (% GDP)				
	1973[1]	1983	1993[2]	2000
UK	9.2	11.7	11.4	12.0
Belgium	34.5	45.5	37.2	45.0
Germany[3]	9.5	13.4	9.8	12.8
France	8.6	10.9	9.7	12.3
Netherlands	23.0	25.3	21.6	25.0
Ireland	29.8	32.7	25.5	28.7
Sweden	12.7	16.5	13.9	20.0

Table 4.4 Development of intra-EU trade, 1973–2000
Notes:
[1] Date the UK joined the former European Economic Community.
[2] Completion of the Single European Market.
[3] West Germany to 1990.

employment and a destabilising of their balance of payments. This aspect of international trade globalisation has most certainly *not* enhanced their economic well-being.

The terms of trade

A very important assumption of the simple principles of international trade explained above was that 'the exchange rate operating for international transactions must be between the respective domestic opportunity cost ratios'. This exchange rate is more specifically known as the **terms of trade**. It measures the rate at which the goods of one country exchange for the goods of another. Referring back to figure 4.2, trade will only be mutually beneficial if the terms of trade lie somewhere in the area between the two production possibility frontiers.

From a practical standpoint, the terms of trade are represented as an index of the ratio of export prices and import prices

$$\text{Terms of trade index} = \frac{\text{Index of export prices}}{\text{Index of import prices}} \times 100$$

The ratio is calculated from the average prices of the many thousands of goods which are traded in world markets. In turn, these prices are weighted by the relative importance of each good which is traded. It is therefore a very complex calculation to work out for any type of economy.

Official statistics show the terms of trade as a single index in relation to a given base year. For example, if year 0 has a base year index of 100, then

Year 1   Terms of trade index   =   102.4

This means that on average a country is receiving relatively better prices for its exports than it is having to pay other countries for its imports. So, in this case, the *terms of trade have improved.*

In contrast

Year 1   Terms of trade index   =   98.4

This means that on average a country is having to pay a relatively higher price for its imports than it is receiving for its own exports. In this case, *the terms of trade have deteriorated.*

Relatively minor changes on a year-by-year basis have only limited economic significance. On a longer-term basis though, the time trend in the terms of trade can have a very marked impact on an economy. The reality of the global trade market is that in general:

- The terms of trade for most developing economies have been deteriorating. This means that year by year they have to export more and more goods (especially primary agricultural products) to support a given volume of imports.
- Fuel-exporting developing economies have been in a much stronger position, although in recent years,

	Ten year averages	
	1982–91	**1992–2001**
Sub-Saharan Africa	−0.4	0.4
Asia	−0.8	0.6
Middle East	−7.6	0.2
Southern Hemisphere	−3.1	−0.7
Primary products	−0.4	−0.5
Fuel	−7.5	−0.4
Manufactures	−1.7	0.3
Services, inc. tourism	0.6	0.4

Table 4.6 Terms of trade for developing countries (annual % change)
Source: International Monetary Fund.

there has been considerable volatility in their terms of trade as the world price of crude oil has fluctuated widely. This hardly makes for sensible long-term economic planning.

- The terms of trade for most developed economies have experienced longer-term improvement. This means that they have continued to receive increased real prices, especially for their exports of manufactured consumer goods.

These trends are shown in an aggregated way in table 4.5 and for selected geographical groups of developing economies and commodities in table 4.6.

Self-assessment tasks

1 Study the data in table 4.5. With a base year of 1992 = 100, use a calculator to work out the terms of trade index for 2000 for
  - advanced economies,
  - fuel-exporting developing economies,
  - non-fuel-exporting developing economies.

  Make a few notes on the economic implications for each grouping of the changes you have observed

2 Study the data in table 4.6. From 1982, which geographical group and which product group has experienced
  - most relative deterioration,
  - most relative improvement in the terms of trade?

  Make a few notes on the economic implications in each case.

	Advanced economies	Developing economies	
		Fuel exporters	**Non-fuel exporters**
1982–91 (average)	1.1	−7.5	−1.1
1992	1.4	2.8	−1.6
1993	2.0	−6.2	−0.1
1994	0.4	−5.9	2.6
1995	0.4	−2.1	3.1
1996	−0.8	10.2	−1.2
1997	−0.8	−0.4	−0.5
1998	1.7	−22.9	−1.1
1999	0.9	17.3	−1.0
2000	−2.3	20.1	1.1

Table 4.5 Terms of trade in world trade, 1982–2000 (annual % change)
Source: International Monetary Fund.

The balance of payments

It is important that governments have an accurate record of all the transactions which take place between residents of their country and all other countries in the rest of the world. These transactions are recorded in the **balance of payments.** In practice this record is a very complex financial statement – though there is an internationally agreed method for its presentation. This has been recommended by the International Monetary Fund (IMF) and permits economists to make international comparisons. The basics of this method are outlined below.

The balance of payments consists of the **current account**, the **capital account**, the **financial account** and the **international investment position**. We can use the UK accounts to explain the various components of the accounts.

It should be noted that the balance of payments accounts are simply a record of flows of money between residents of the UK and non-residents. Following basic accounting principles this means that every credit (+) entry is matched by a debit (–) entry. For example, if a UK resident exports goods abroad, this is recorded as a credit entry (+) in the accounts. We also have to record how foreign residents paid for these exports. Perhaps the foreign resident had a bank account in the UK which was used to pay the exporter. This would be shown in the accounts as a debit entry as a decrease in UK liabilities abroad (–). This means that the foreign resident has less of a claim on a UK bank account. The important point is that we have accounted for the spending and recorded both sides of the transaction. Since every credit item is matched by a debit item in the accounts, it follows that in an accounting sense, the balance of payments must always balance. In practice however, we cannot have fully accurate information. As a result, a section of the accounts is entitled net errors and omissions to allow for discrepancies in the calculations.

The current account

The current account consists of four main headings:

- ◆ trade in goods,
- ◆ trade in services,
- ◆ income,
- ◆ current transfers.

Trade in goods

The goods account covers items that can be touched, weighed or counted as they are traded. For this reason, they are sometimes known as visibles. For example, the import of cars from Germany is a debit item in the current account of the UK, whereas the export of cashmere sweaters to Japan is a credit item. The difference between visible exports and imports is sometimes referred to as the **balance of trade**.

Trade in services

The services account covers exports and imports of services. For example, if a UK resident purchases an airline ticket from a foreign airline, this has the same impact as the import of a good and is recorded as a debit item. However, if a merchant bank in the City of London raises a loan for a foreign firm, the fee charged by the bank is equivalent to an export and will be recorded as a credit item. The difference in trade in such items is known as the invisible balance.

Income

The income account is made up of payments made to employees, for example, those who work abroad and send money home, and income from investments abroad. The former is not very significant for the UK but investment income is very large. This covers any earnings from foreign investment and financial assets and liabilities. For example, any dividends paid on foreign shares held by UK residents are recorded as credits, whereas interest paid to foreign holders of deposits in UK financial institutions is recorded as a debit item.

Current transfers

Current transfers are made up of central government transfers (for example, payments and receipts from the EU) and other transfers by private individuals (such as gifts of cash).

Capital account

The capital account records transactions which involve the transfer of ownership of fixed assets and the acquisition or disposal of non-financial assets. An example of the former might be a government investment grant to undertake a large construction project, such as a water purification plant abroad. An example of the latter might be land purchased or sold by a foreign embassy.

Financial account

The financial account was formerly known as the capital account. This section of the accounts records the forms of investment overseas by UK residents and the inward flow of investment funds from foreign residents. It is this flow which gives rise to flows of investment income in the current account.

Balance of payments examples

Table 4.7 shows a summary of the balance of payments current accounts for selected countries in 1998. (For ease of comparison all of the data are shown in $US). It shows some interesting contrasts such as:

◆ The UK has traditionally experienced a deficit in its annual trade in goods and services. This is particularly the case for trade in goods.
◆ The USA has a massive deficit on trade in goods and services; in contrast, both Germany and Japan have substantial surpluses.

	Goods and services		Net income	$USm Net current transfers	Current account balance
	Exports	Imports			
Developed economies					
UK	372,594	386,579	23,589	−10,754	−1100
Germany	623,416	587,353	−9,203	−30,303	−3443
Japan	436,456	363,488	56,570	−8,842	120,696
USA	933,906	1,098,181	−12,269	−44,075	−220,559
Developing economies					
Hungary	25,657	27,101	−1,878	1,018	−2,304
Jamaica	3,383	3,970	−304	635	−255
Malaysia	71,900	60,200	0	−1,094	−4792
Singapore	128,706	113,698	3,783	−1,177	17,614
Zimbabwe	2,535	2,742	−346	n.a	n.a

Table 4.7 Balance of payments current accounts, 1998

	£m Credits	Debits	Balances
Current account			
Trade in goods	164,132	184,897	−20,765
Trade in services	60,070	47,817	12,253
Income	111,365	96,191	15,174
Current transfers	15,596	22,122	−6,526
Total current balance			136
Capital account	1269	848	411
Financial account	105,304	114,329	−9025
Total current, capital and financial accounts	457,736	466,204	(−8468)
(Net errors and omissions)	(−8,468)		

Table 4.8 The UK balance of payments in 1998
Source: Office of National Statistics, 2000.

◆ Developing economies invariably have a deficit in their trade in goods and services; Malaysia and Singapore have substantial export earnings from manufactured goods and financial services.
◆ Net income from investments abroad is very high for Japan; its multinationals have widespread interests across the world.
◆ A persistent deficit on the current account is a cause for concern (see section 7).

Table 4.8 gives a summary of the UK balance of payments in full for 1998. This table represents a great simplification of what is a very complex set of accounts.

Self-assessment task

Obtain an outline of the balance of payments account for your own economy. Summarise this in terms of the main headings used above and write a few sentences on what the data show.

Looking at this particular year in isolation we can see that:

◆ Surprisingly, the current account was virtually in balance, indicating that broadly equal sums of money flowed into and out of the UK.

◆ As noted from table 4.7, the main deficit balance item was in the UK's trade in visible goods with the rest of the world. This has been a persistent feature of the UK's balance of payments. The credit for trade in services has though served to reduce the scale of this important part of the current account.

◆ There was a healthy inflow of income from UK investments abroad to offset deficit balances elsewhere, including central government transfers.

◆ Relatively, the remodelled capital account is a small item on the balance of payments; the financial account in 1998 was in deficit, indicating a net outflow of investment funds.

Looking at the balance of payments over time is in many respects more relevant to the economist than the information for just one year, as given in tables 4.7 and 4.8. In this way, medium- and longer-term trends can be identified and analysed and appropriate policies put in place to deal with any problems that are identified. These policies will be analysed in section 7.

Summary

In this section we have recognised that:

● International trade is an essential and beneficial feature of the global economy of the twenty-first century.

● The principles of absolute and comparative advantage can be used to show the benefits of free trade.

● Tariffs, quotas, exchange control and export subsidies distort the benefits of multi-lateral free trade for the world economy; in certain circumstances, protection may be relevant especially for developing economies.

● Increasingly, economic integration through the setting up of free trade areas and the European Union can bring benefits to the members of such organisations.

● The terms of trade index measures the rate at which the goods of one country exchange for those of another.

● The balance of payments is an important financial record of the international trading transactions of a country.

Key words

Definitions of Key words can be found in the Glossary.

absolute advantage
balance of payments
balance of trade
capital account
comparative advantage
current account
customs union
dumping
economic integration
economic union
exports
financial account
free trade (multi-lateral)
free trade area

globalisation
imports
infant industry
international investment position
invisible balance
multi-national corporations
protectionism
quotas
specialisation
tariff
trade creation
trade diversion

5 Measurement in the macro-economy

On completion of this section you should know:

➤ what constitutes the main components of the labour force in an economy

➤ what is meant by labour productivity and how it can be measured

➤ how to measure unemployment in a general way

➤ how to calculate the general level of prices in an economy

The labour force

The **labour force** in an economy is defined as the total number of workers who are available for work. It therefore refers to all males and females, normally 16 years and over in most developed countries, who can contribute to the production of goods and services. As well as those actually in employment, it also includes those who are unemployed as these people are available for work. The size of the labour force depends upon a wide range of demographic, economic, social and cultural factors, such as:

♦ the total size of the population of working age,

♦ the number of people who remain in full-time education after leaving secondary school,

♦ the normal retirement age for males and females,

♦ the number of women who join the labour force on a full- or part-time basis.

Table 5.1 shows the size of the labour force for selected economies in 1999. In themselves the aggregate statistics have little meaning – they really need to be seen in relation to the productive potential of these economies. They do though give a very crude indication of the relative strength of these countries from an economic standpoint. In virtually all developed economies, the labour force has increased at a steady rate over the past generation, but with some slowing down in more recent years, largely as a consequence of workers retiring before the statutory retirement age and an increase in the number of school leavers remaining in higher education. The rate of change for Japan has been negative in recent years, indicative of that country's troubled economy.

	Labour force (millions)	Estimated % of change per annum to 2005
UK	29.42	0.5
Germany	41.37	0.4
France	26.21	0.6
European Union	168.20	0.8
USA	138.06	1.0
Japan	67.81	0.1

Table 5.1 The labour force in selected economies, 1999

A second complementary measure is the **labour force participation rate**. This refers to the percentage of the total population of working age who are actually classified as being part of the labour force. Table 5.2 shows these rates for the economies included in the previous table. A lower participation rate usually indicates that an economy has a high participation rate in higher education and a relatively large number of people opting for early retirement. In the case of the UK, government policy in recent years has been to increase the higher education participation rates; this is one of the lowest amongst EU member states and seen as a possible deterrent to enhancing competitiveness.

Comparable statistics for developing economies are unreliable for various reasons including:

♦ the existence of a large subsistence sector,

♦ differences in the official secondary school leaving age,

♦ differences in attitudes towards married women seeking paid employment,

♦ practical problems of data collection.

	%
UK	76.0
Germany	73.9
France	68.0
European Union	69.1
USA	67.1
Japan	78.1

Table 5.2 Labour force participation rates, 1999

From a general perspective certain demographic trends are having an important influence on the size of the labour force in most developing economies.

- Unlike in developed economies **birth rates** exceed **death rates**. Consequently, the total population and hence the labour force in these countries is increasing.

- Dependency ratios in most developing economies are high as a consequence of high birth rates and an increasing life expectancy. Consequently, there is an increase in the number of economically inactive people relative to those who constitute the labour force.

- Many developing economies have experienced a rapid growth in their urban populations, as there has been significant **migration** from rural areas. This ever-increasing **urbanisation** has made it very difficult for these economies to provide enough jobs to meet the needs and aspirations of its labour force. Rural dwellers unfortunately are often unaware of the realities of life in grossly over-populated cities.

These important issues will be elaborated in section 12.

Labour productivity

Productivity refers to the quantity of goods and services that a worker is able to produce in a particular period of time. (It should not be confused with production which is an aggregate measure, not directly related to a particular input.)

In looking at measurement in the macroeconomy, it is invariably true that variations in living standards between economies can often be explained in terms of variations in the productivity of the main factors of production (see section 12). Labour is *not* a uniform resource, hence there are variations in the productivity of labour depending on the education, training, experience and skills of the workforce in an economy. Clearly, when a skilled workforce is equipped with large stocks of capital and technological know-how, productivity is invariably higher than when this is not the case. The formal relationship between all inputs and outputs is represented in the production function (see section 9).

At this stage the importance of productivity is in recognising that, although the labour force in an economy is a key resource, the output it is able to produce is to a large extent directly related to the skills, technical knowledge and motivation of its workforce. This key point is clearly shown in the newspaper article on raising productivity in the UK economy.

The teaming urban population of Hong Kong
Source: Ingrid Moorjohn, Still Pictures.

Raising productivity

I f Britain's workforce can increase its productivity there will be long-term benefits for the economy. Improved education and training are the key…

Whichever way you measure it, Britain's productivity growth is poor by comparison with its major competitors and Mr Brown, the UK Chancellor of the Exchequer, is determined to do everything in his power to close the gap…

Optimists believe the hi-tech boom means the UK is on the verge of a sharp acceleration of productivity growth, mirroring the success of the US…

But Mr Brown still believes the state has an important role to play, firstly by delivering a stable macro-economic climate, and secondly by improving the economy's supply-side potential through reform of capital gains tax and encouraging entrepreneurship and extra investment in basic scientific research to ensure technological transfer from the laboratory to the marketplace…

The UK's economic and, therefore, interest rate cycle has traditionally been much more volatile than in other countries, making it hard for businesses to plan for the long term. In theory, a more stable climate should encourage firms to increase investment in physical and human capital, boosting productive capacity…

Mr Brown claims to have laid the foundations by giving control of interest rates to the Bank of England, a move which prevents politicians interfering with monetary policy for electoral gain, and establishing a new framework for fiscal policy, which binds the Treasury by strict rules about borrowing and debt. There is no hard evidence linking economic stability and productivity but economists are prepared to give the Chancellor the benefit of the doubt…

The Chancellor's biggest potential contribution will probably be in the field of education and training. Mary O'Mahoney, research fellow at the National Institute of Economic and Social Research, who produced an exhaustive study of UK productivity last year, says the underlying cause of poor productivity performance is low skills…

No amount of investment in physical capital can make up for a poorly trained and educated workforce because without it new machinery is of questionable value…

Unfortunately, improving skills levels takes many years if not decades, requiring sustained investment in education, from the basic level right up to the top. The Republic of Ireland is a case in point… In the 70s and 80s the Irish government invested an enormous amount in education, running up large deficits in the process. At the time, people said the money was wasted. But with hindsight it can be seen to have been a smart move, laying the foundations for the current hi-tech boom, fuelled by the dozens of computer firms which have been flocking to Dublin to take advantage of the availability of highly educated but relatively cheap labour…

If the UK wants to achieve similar success it will have to invest the same proportions of time and money in schools and colleges.

Source: Extracts from Mark Atkinson, *Guardian*, 14 April 2000.

Employment and unemployment

Countries measure the numbers in employment and the numbers of those unemployed. The sum total of these is the labour force as described above.

$$\text{Labour force} = \begin{matrix}\text{Total number} \\ \text{of workers in} \\ \text{employment}\end{matrix} + \begin{matrix}\text{Total number} \\ \text{of workers who} \\ \text{are unemployed}\end{matrix}$$

Data on the UK's labour force and population in 1999, are shown in figure 5.1.

The specific way in which employment and unemployment are measured will be analysed in detail in section 12.

The measurement of employment and unemployment is very important from the standpoint of the macro-economy. For example, if there is unemployment in an economy:

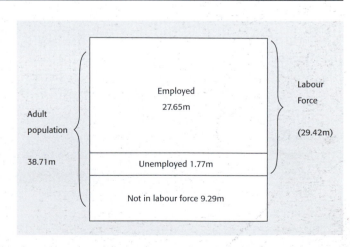

Figure 5.1 The adult population of the UK in 1999

◆ Output will be below its potential level. The economy will be operating inside its production possibility curve (see section 1). Resources are not being used to the full, but, as the number

Urban decay – Leeds, UK
Source: Mark Edwards, Still Pictures.

employed increases towards full employment, the economy will reach its production possibility frontier.

◆ The tax revenue received by the government will be lower than with a higher level of employment; if applicable, the amount of money paid out in the form of state benefits for the unemployed will in turn be lower (see section 12).

◆ A high level of unemployment may result in civil unrest, increased crime rates and substantial personal problems for those unemployed and their families. The gap in economic well-being between those in work and those who are unemployed can be substantial, particularly in developing economies where the degree of state support is limited.

The level of unemployment though should be distinguished from the rate of unemployment. The level refers to the total number of people who are unemployed (for example, 4.3 million) whereas the rate of unemployment is the number of unemployed people divided by the labour force. So, in an economy with a labour force of 50m people, 4.3m of whom are unemployed, the rate of unemployment is 8.6 per cent.

There is no universal measure of employment, but the term does cover some or all of the following:

◆ those in full-time paid employment,
◆ those on recognised training schemes,
◆ those working for a minimum number of hours per week.

Normally, those working in subsistence non-monetarised situations would be excluded, as would unpaid volunteers.

Self-assessment tasks

1 For your own country, see what information you can obtain on:
   ◆ the number of people in employment,
   ◆ the number of people who are unemployed.
2 Can you identify any trends in these important variables over the past ten years?
3 Make a few comments on the likely accuracy of any data you may obtain.

The general price level and price indices

A further important macroeconomic variable which is measured by governments in all types of economy is that of the general price level. This is a recognised measure of the cost of living in an economy at any one point in time. Changes in the general price level on a year-by-year basis in turn are a measure of the rate of inflation in an economy (see next section for more details).

In its simplest form, the general price level in an economy is calculated periodically using some form of **price index**. In the UK, the Retail Prices Index (RPI) is a measure of changes in the prices of consumer goods bought by people in the UK. Much attention is paid to this index by the media, politicians, business people and consumers (see Introduction also).

weighted price index.

The RPI is a weighted price index. Its calculation is a major statistical task, involving three main stages. These are:

◆ a survey to find out what families buy and how much they spend on particular items – this provides the **weights**;

◆ recording how much the prices of some 600 selected items have changed – this information is collected from all main types of retail outlet, as well as from gas, water, electricity and transport suppliers;

◆ the percentage change in price for each item is then multiplied by its weight – from this the average change in the RPI is determined.

Bottoms fall out of the shoppers' price index

Strappy tops have replaced women's ski pants. Jars of salad cream have given way to mayonnaise. And streaky bacon, that traditional breakfast fare, is out of favour in the nation's 'shopping basket'.

All have fallen foul of Britain's changing consumer tastes to such an extent that they have been dropped from the list of goods in a monthly shopping basket used to calculate inflation.

In their place are a number of must-have goods and services that reflect the growing fascination with diet, leisure and technology.

The list of 650 items, the cost of which are used to calculate the Retail Price Index, now includes organic food, mayonnaise, mini-disc players and health club membership.

Their price will be used today for the first time to calculate the change in the cost of living.

A spokesman for the Office for National Statistics, which compiles the data, said: 'Changes in consumer tastes mean that prices for a number of goods and services will no longer to sampled every month.

'A simple way to understand the nature of the index is to think of it as a very large shopping basket made up of all the different kinds of goods and services bought by a typical household in the course of a year.

'To keep the index basket representative of spending patterns, it is important to keep under review the actual items priced.

'All these changes form part of the annual review of the "basket" of 650 goods and services that are sampled every month to see how prices are changing.

'Fresh items are added to the basket to represent new or increasing spending while other items are deleted as spending on them falls.

'We put a lot of effort into ensuring the index is up to date and representative of consumer spending patterns.' Britain's increasing obsession with do-it-yourself is reflected by the inclusion of laminate flooring and home removal costs. Gardening is covered by inclusion of the lawn edge strimmer.

Home entertainment has been subject to a revolution too. Jigsaw puzzles have been ousted by mini-disc players, DVDs and personal computers, although the soft toy remains a favourite.

The ever-increasing desire to travel is reflected by the appearance of sunscreen lotion and foreign exchange commission for the first time in the list's 54-year history.

As well as membership of the gym, health consciousness is demonstrated by inclusion of fizzy energy drinks, organic fruit and vegetables, cereal snacks and herbal tea bags.

Rainbow trout is rejected in favour of salmon fillets while a Continental touch comes from the baguette.

Changes in fashion which saw the demise of ski pants have seen the inclusion of women's vests and strappy tops as well as more expensive evening dresses.

But all this change in consumer costs has come at a cost… bank overdraft charges are counted for the first time as part of household costs.

For more than half a century, the index has been calculated from post-war rationing to the take-away.

During that time prices have risen more than 20-fold, although that has been more than offset by a 50-fold rise in average earnings.

In 1947, a typical shopping basket of bread, milk, beef, eggs, sugar and butter cost just 27p compared with more than £6 today.

In 1947, 200 items were included in the list, compared with 650 today.

Many items have come and gone during the years. The 1950s saw the introduction of canned fruit and motor cars, the swinging Sixties saw sliced bread, jeans and fish fingers for the first time.

It was not until the 1990s that satellite dishes, foreign holidays, computer games and replica football kits were included in calculations.

What's in and what's out of the RPI basket

Food and drink:
In: salmon fillets; organic fruit and veg; mayonnaise; french stick/baguette; chilled desserts; herbal/fruit tea bags; cereal snacks; soft drinks; large multipacks
Out: rainbow trout; leeks; salad cream; streaky bacon; delivered milk, sterilised milk

Household goods:
In: home office computer desks; cutlery sets; crockery sets; laminate flooring; greeting cards
Out: nest of tables; table knife; bread bin

Household services:
In: bank overdraft charges; home removals; catering for a function; foreign exchange commission
Out: bank custody of a sealed envelope

Clothing and footwear:
In: women's vest/strappy tops; women's evening dress; baseball caps
Out: women's ski pants

Price comparisons

	1947[1]	1997
Frock[2]	£15.10	£69
Women's suit[2]	£23.15	£203.99
Women's cardigan/jumper[2]	£4.16	£35
Cold cream	11p	£2.65
Bar of chocolate (1/2lb bar)	7p	79p
Road tax	£1.00	£145
Family saloon car[2]	£416.03 (Austin A40)	£12,280 (Ford Escort 1.4cl)
'Over to you' by Roald Dahl	38p	£5.99
Six bedroom house, Wimbledon	£7,250	£775,000
2 weeks in Lucerne	£57.75	£815
Headache tablets	7p	£1.85
Man's wristwatch	£6.40	£29.50
Copy of *The Observer*	1p	£1.00
Copy of *Daily Hansard*	3p	£5.00
Music recording	24p (12" classical)	£15.99 (Spice Girls' album)

Notes: [1] – equivalent decimal price   [2] – subject to rationing

Source: Daily Telegraph, 20 March 2001.

Although not all countries have such a comprehensive price index, the basic principles of construction remain the same irrespective of the level of sophistication.

$$\text{Cost of living index, year 1} = \sum_{i=1}^{n} \frac{W_{i1} \, P_{i1}}{W_{i0} \, P_{i0}} \times 100$$

where W = weight of item in family expenditure
   P = price of item
   n = total number of items in index

If the index is calculated to be over 100 in year 1, then the cost of living has increased compared with the base date, year 0. For example, if the index is 105, then the cost of living has increased by 5 per cent since the base year. An index of below 100 in year 1 would indicate a fall in the cost of living.

The change in the cost of living index is usually measured in **nominal** terms, that is in terms of the prices operating in the year in which the goods are produced.

Self-assessment tasks

1 Thinking of your own country, briefly describe how you might construct an appropriate cost of living index.

2 If such an index exists, how does it compare with your own ideas on how it might be constructed?

Summary

In this section we have recognised that:

● The measurement of certain macroeconomic variables is important for economists to understand differences between various types of economy.

● The labour force is an important economic resource; variations in both its size and participation rate can be measured across different types of economies.

● The productivity of labour has an important bearing on the living standards in an economy.

● Unemployed labour is a resource which can be used to help an economy achieve its productive potential.

● The cost of living in an economy can be measured by means of a weighted price index.

Key words

Definitions of Key words can be found in the Glossary.

birth rate
cost of living
death rate
labour force
labour force participation
  rate
migration

nominal
productivity (of labour)
Retail Prices Index
unemployment
urbanisation
weights

6 Macroeconomic problems

On completion of this section you should know:

➤ how to define inflation and what it means

➤ the main causes of inflation

➤ how inflation affects the domestic and international economic well-being of a country

➤ why a low rate of inflation gives less concern than a high rate of inflation over a longer period

➤ what is meant by equilibrium and disequilibrium in the balance of payments

➤ the main causes of such disequilibrium

➤ the consequences of balance of payments disequilibrium for the domestic and international economic well-being of a country

➤ what is meant by a foreign exchange rate and the ways in which it can be measured

➤ how various types of exchange rate are determined

➤ why exchange rates fluctuate on world markets

➤ the effects on an economy of a changing exchange rate

Introduction

Every day stories appear in the newspapers and on the television news about how the economy is performing. Some recent ones have been:

'3100 Motorola jobs go'
Daily Telegraph, 25 April 2001

'Inflation drops to its lowest level for 25 years'
Financial Times, 19 April 2000

'Thai interest rates to rise after radical policy reversal'
South China Morning Post, 5 June 2001

'Tourism fears spells doom for the Balance of Payments'
Mail on Sunday, 15 April 2001

'Fears of down-turn hit the Dow'
USA Today, 28 May 2001

These stories appear in the media because, in all cases, the events affect our lives. For example, Motorola is an important employer at Bathgate in Scotland and, from a wider perspective, provides many more thousands of jobs in firms which supply it with electronic

components and other supplies. A problem such as this will be analysed in detail in sections 11 and 12.

The rate of inflation was referred to in the last section. Where the rate is low then on the surface there are fewer problems for the government than when it is, say, 10 per cent, 25 per cent or even higher. People are interested in inflation because it affects the prices of all goods and services we buy in shops, markets and other places. Indirectly, it determines how much or how little we can buy with our weekly wages or monthly salaries.

On the surface, problems in the balance of payments may seem to be of little concern to individuals. Even so, many people in the UK depend upon tourism for their livelihoods and, from a broader perspective, a fall in international tourism can have a detrimental effect on the trade in services earnings (see section 4).

So, how the economy is performing can have a major impact on people's lives. In this section we shall look at problems which arise from:

◆ a persistent increase in the general price level in the economy,

◆ disequilibrium in the balance of payments,

◆ fluctuations in the foreign exchange rate.

Each has particular significance for the economic well-being of developing countries as well as for developed economies.

Inflation

Inflation refers to a situation in the economy where there is a general and sustained increase in prices, measured in terms of the indices described in section 5. In the UK and most other economies over the last twenty years or so, the control of inflation has been the main priority of government economic policy. Price stability is crucial for governments to achieve all of their macroeconomic objectives.

A few important points should be made:

1 An increase in a small number of prices does not constitute inflation. The key thing is for the increase to be measured across a wide range of items that affect the spending of consumers. One of the few exceptions to this is the price of fuel, which, when increasing, can have a substantial effect across the economy as a whole.

2 The increase in prices is inflationary if it is sustained over a period of time. Experience in the UK economy over the last 40 years or so is that the general price level has increased at variable rates in the broad range 2–26 per cent per year.

3 A low and steady rate of inflation may not be a bad thing for an economy as it allows businesses to plan ahead with confidence (see below).

Virtually all developed economies have managed to contain inflation to less than 5 per cent per annum over

the last decade. This has not been true of the developing countries as table 6.1 shows. It is therefore clear that the degree of inflation, sustained over a period of time, is important. There is no hard and fast rule but the classification shown in table 6.2 may be useful in determining the relative severity of inflation as a macroeconomic problem.

It is clear from table 6.1 that most of the countries shown have experienced some form of inflation problem over the period since 1982. In most the tendency has been for inflation to be more under control by 1999 than at any other recent time. The most spectacular turnaround has been the case of Brazil, where inflation is now seemingly under control. From a wider perspective, the table shows a very clear relationship between inflation and political upheaval in countries such as Angola, Belarus and Russia.

	Average 1982–91	1994	1999
Africa			
Angola	8.1	949.8	248.2
Kenya	12.3	28.8	3.5
Mauritius	8.0	9.4	5.6
Zimbabwe	14.9	22.2	58.2
Caribbean			
Barbados	4.9	1.3	1.5
Jamaica	22.7	33.2	6.3
Trinidad and Tobago	10.1	3.7	3.4
Asia			
Malaysia	2.7	3.7	2.8
Philippines	13.6	8.4	6.7
Vietnam	132.6	9.5	4.2
South America			
Argentina	452.7	4.2	−1.2
Brazil	384.7	2075.8	4.9
Paraguay	22.8	26.5	6.0
Central Europe			
Belarus	n.a.	2434.1	293.7
Hungary	13.5	18.8	10.0
Poland	77.7	32.2	7.3
Russia	n.a.	307.4	85.9

Table 6.1 Inflation rates in selected developing economies (annual percentage change in consumer prices)
Source: World Development Report, World Bank, 2001.

Discounts everywhere

A general decline in retail and wholesale prices in Japan has led to a mushrooming of budget shops. Products with their prices slashed include:

◆ Half-price burgers at fast-food outlets
◆ Cut-price gyudon (beef bowl) at food stalls
◆ Marked-down lunch boxes at 24-hour convenience stores
◆ Low-priced garments at discount stores
◆ Factory over-runs going at fire-sale prices at American-style malls.

But lower prices have not necessarily led to smaller profits for many companies.

When the Matsuya chain slashed the price of its gyudon to 290 yen (US$4.35) last September, it enjoyed a 30-per-cent jump in customers.

McDonald's Japan, which sparked off the country's fast-food price war last year with its half-price basic hamburgers, has also seen its earnings go up.

Source: Kwan Weng Kin, Singapore, 3 June 2001.

% change per annum over a period of time	Outcome
<4	Very mild inflation which can actually aid competitiveness
4–10	Mild inflation, which must be kept under control to avoid future difficulties
10–20	Inflationary pressures build up with increased wage demands and high interest rates; savings begin to be affected. Strict policies essential if problem is to be resolved
20–50	Serious inflation. Economic relationships in real danger of breaking down. Confidence in money is seriously eroded
50 and above	Signs of hyperinflation. Depending on severity, domestic economic structures collapse and currency becomes worthless on foreign exchange markets and also internally

Table 6.2 Degrees of inflation

Causes of inflation

The high levels of inflation that have been recorded by some countries over the time period shown in table 6.1 have led to considerable interest amongst economists as to the causes of inflation. Section 11 will analyse some of the main theories; for the time being, let us identify in a simple way what these causes are.

A good starting point is to note what the well-known US economist Milton Friedman had to say about inflation. He said that 'inflation is always and everywhere a monetary phenomenon'. In other words, periods of inflation coincide with increases in the money supply. So

↑ money supply ⟶ ↑ rate of inflation

There is though an important qualification; namely, that this will only occur if the rate of growth of the money supply is greater than the increase in the level of output in the economy, so forcing up prices. This has been an obvious cause of inflation for some of the economies shown in table 6.1. It is in many respects an example in the macro-economy of supply being greater than demand. This can be shown diagrammatically in figure 6.1. This figure shows that:

◆ the demand curve for money is like any other demand curve – people want to hold a larger quantity of money when the value falls as they need more money to buy their particular purchases;
◆ the supply curve for money is vertical since it is fixed by the central bank;
◆ at the initial equilibrium (X), the demand for money and supply of money are balanced – the value of money is at *p* and the price level at 2*p*;

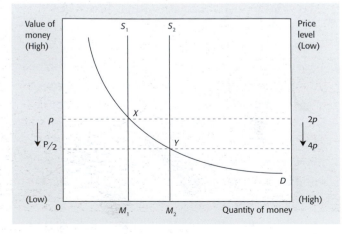

Figure 6.1 The effects of an increase in the money supply

- an increase in the supply of money (for example by printing more notes) shifts the supply of money from S_1 to S_2;
- the outcome is that there is a new equilibrium position at Y where the value of money has fallen and the price level increased pro-rata.

In taking the above line, monetarists such as Milton Friedman make use of the so-called **Quantity Theory of Money**. This theory is based on an interpretation of the equation

$$MV = PT$$

where M is the money supply, V is the number of times money changes hands, P is the price level and T is the output or transactions in the economy.

This equation (or Fisher equation as it sometimes known) has to be true since both sides represent total expenditure in the economy. By holding V and T constant, as they are unaffected by changes in the money supply, it follows that a change in the money supply causes an equal percentage change in the price level.

This is a highly simplified representation of what is a most complex situation, but it can be used to show quite clearly how the reckless printing of money can result in an increase in the general level of prices. This has clearly happened where governments have sought to get out of debt and finance their own spending by simply printing more money. It is by no means the only reason – where there is war, political upheaval and civil unrest, high inflation can result as people panic and lose confidence in the money supply, preferring to hold their assets in physical rather than monetary forms (see below).

There are two other recognised causes of inflation. Most developing economies rely heavily on imported oil. There have been times, such as 1973/74 and the early 1980s, when actions by the Organisation of Petroleum Exporting Countries (OPEC) have resulted in oil supplies being restricted for political motives. As demand is unaffected, it is again basic economics that prices will rise. So, in this case of what is known as **cost-push inflation**, prices are forced upwards. Higher oil prices quickly lead to a rise in domestic inflation across all oil-importing countries. Relatively, developing

Oil Rigs – an increase in the price of crude oil is a major cause of cost-push inflation
Source: BP AMOCO plc.

economies are more seriously affected than their developed counterparts and have to suffer:

- higher raw material costs (oil),
- higher prices for imported consumer goods,
- increased demands for higher wages to cover the increased cost of living,

so triggering a cost-induced inflation. Another cause of cost-push inflation, again of particular relevance for developing economies, is where there is a substantial fall in the foreign exchange rate. The Brazilian cruzeiro and the Thai baht are two recent examples of currencies which have been affected in this way. The fall means that the price of imports into their domestic economies increases rapidly, although export prices, in terms of other foreign currencies, are lower. A worrying consequence of a substantial fall over a short period is that people lose confidence in that currency, both at home and in the international market. In turn, this further fuels inflation.

The third main cause of inflation is **demand-pull inflation** which occurs when there is an increase in the total demand for goods and services in an economy. It is so called because this increase in demand 'pulls' prices upwards if the economy does not have spare capacity to meet these increased needs. This cause of inflation has been used to explain inflation in the UK economy at various periods over the past forty years, mainly when an increase in consumer spending (often government induced) at a time of low unemployment has pulled up the price level.

Finally, though, an important word of warning. Inflation in practice is a complex phenonomen. Its causes are often complex, not necessarily just one of the simple reasons stated above – so much so in fact that economists disagree about the actual line of causation.

Consequences of inflation

The effects of inflation depend on:

- the rate at which it is rising;
- whether the rate is accelerating or stable;
- whether the rate is the one which had been expected;
- how the rate compares with that in other countries.

The inflation rate

An inflation rate of 20 per cent is likely to cause more problems than an inflation rate of, say, 2 per cent

because money will be losing its purchasing power at a rapid rate. A very high rate of inflation is known as **hyperinflation**. When this occurs people will lose confidence in money and may even go back to barter.

In Germany between 1913 and 1923 the price level rose 755,700 million times and people switched from using cash to using cigarettes to buy goods. More recently in Georgia in 1994 when inflation reached 15,000 per cent, a wheelbarrow was needed to carry enough money to purchase a loaf of bread.

Hyperinflation can also cause political instability. People become dissatisfied with the government's failure to control the high rise in prices and may look to parties offering radical solutions to the problem. Even less dramatic inflation rates of, say, 10 per cent can cause problems. People who are on a fixed income or on an income which does not rise as fast as inflation will experience a fall in their purchasing power.

High rates of inflation also mean that people and companies may lose considerable purchasing power if they keep money lying idle and not earning interest. Economists refer to shoe leather costs. These are the costs involved in moving money from one financial asset to another in search of the highest rate of interest. The term can also be applied to firms and consumers spending more time searching out the lowest prices.

Inflation makes it more difficult to assess what is happening to the price of goods and services. A rise in the price of a good may now not mean that it has become more expensive relative to other goods – indeed it may have risen by less than inflation and so have become relatively cheaper. This tendency for inflation to confuse price signals is referred to as inflationary noise. It can result in consumers and producers making the wrong decisions. For example, producers seeing the price of their good rising may increase output when this higher price is the result of inflation rather than increased demand. This will result in the misallocation of resources.

Firms will also suffer from **menu costs**. These are the costs involved in changing prices. For example, catalogues, price tags, bar codes and advertisements have to be changed. This involves staff time and is unpopular with customers.

Whilst there are clear disadvantages of a high rate of inflation there can be advantages of a low, stable rate of inflation of, say, 2 per cent. If the rise in the general price level is caused by increasing aggregate demand, firms can feel optimistic about the future. They will also benefit if prices rise by more than costs since this will mean that profits will increase.

Inflation may also stimulate consumption. This is because real interest rates may be low or even negative as the nominal rate of interest does not tend to rise in line with inflation. So debt burdens may fall and people may be able and encouraged to spend more. For example, those who have borrowed money to buy a house may experience a fall in their mortgage interest payments in real terms. At the same time the price of their house is likely to rise by more than inflation, which may make them feel better off, and so they may spend more.

The existence of inflation may also help firms which need to reduce costs to survive. For most firms the major cost is wages. With zero inflation, firms may have to cut their labour force. However, inflation would enable them to reduce the real costs of labour by either keeping nominal (money) wages constant or not raising them in line with inflation. During inflation workers with strong bargaining power are more likely to be able to resist cuts in their real wages than workers who lack bargaining power.

Accelerating versus stable inflation

An accelerating inflation rate is likely to have more serious consequences than a stable rate. If, for example, inflation three years ago was 5 per cent, two years ago it was 8 per cent and last year it was 15 per cent, people and firms will be likely to expect a further rise in inflation. The way they react is likely to bring about what they fear. For example, workers may press for higher wages, firms may raise prices to cover expected higher costs and consumers may seek to purchase goods now before their prices rise further. Accelerating, or indeed fluctuating, inflation will also cause uncertainty and may discourage firms from undertaking investment. The need to devote more staff and effort to estimating future inflation will also increase administration costs. Whereas if inflation is stable it will be easier to predict future inflation and hence easier to plan and protect people from the harmful effects.

Self-assessment task

The rate of inflation in France was reported to have been 8 per cent in 1996. Explain what this figure means and how it might have been calculated.

Anticipated versus unanticipated inflation

Anticipated inflation is when the rise in the general price level is the one, or close to the one, expected. If firms, workers, consumers and the government have correctly predicted the inflation rate then, as mentioned above, they can take measures to avoid the harmful effects. For example, firms can adjust their prices, nominal interest rates can be changed to maintain real interest rates if considered desirable, consumers may be able to distinguish between changes in the general price level and relative prices, and the government can adjust tax thresholds and index-linked pensions, benefits and civil servants' pay (that is adjust them upwards in line with inflation).

In contrast, unanticipated inflation occurs when inflation either was not expected or is higher than had been expected.

Unanticipated inflation can bring with it a number of problems. As people and firms have been caught unawares they are likely to be uncertain about future inflation. This can result in a fall in consumption and investment.

There can also be an arbitrary redistribution of income. Borrowers tend to gain and lenders to lose. This is because nominal interest rates usually rise more slowly than the inflation rate. So real interest rates often fall with inflation. Indeed in some years they have been negative.

Income may also be transferred from the old to the young as the former tend to be net savers whilst the latter tend to be net borrowers. It is also because, state pensions are raised in line with inflation, so they fall behind wages, which usually rise at a faster rate than inflation.

International price competitiveness

Inflation may make a country's goods less price competitive. This may result in balance of payments problems. Consumers at home and abroad may switch away from buying the country's goods and services,

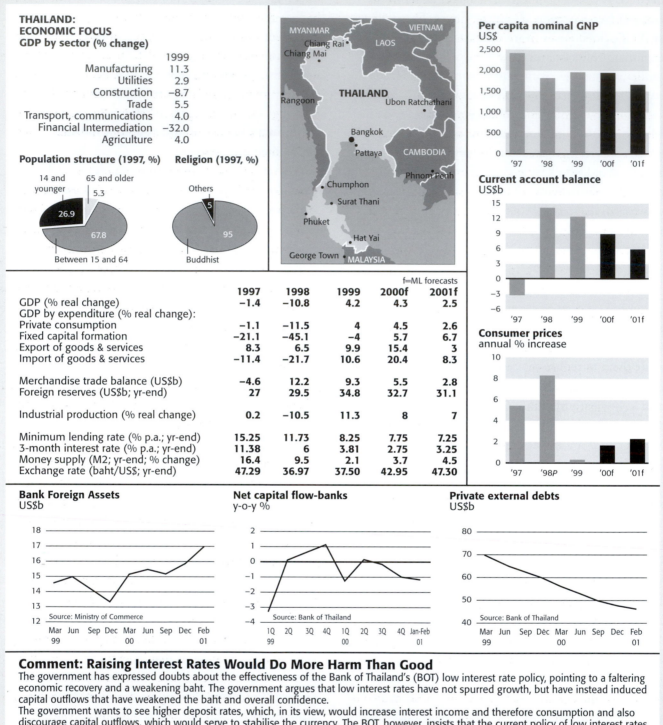

THAILAND:
ECONOMIC FOCUS
GDP by sector (% change)

	1999
Manufacturing	11.3
Utilities	2.9
Construction	−8.7
Trade	5.5
Transport, communications	4.0
Financial Intermediation	−32.0
Agriculture	4.0

Population structure (1997, %)

14 and younger: 26.9
65 and older: 5.3
Between 15 and 64: 67.8

Religion (1997, %)

Others: 5
Buddhist: 95

Per capita nominal GNP
US$

Current account balance
US$b

Consumer prices
annual % increase

	1997	1998	1999	2000f	2001f
					f=ML forecasts
GDP (% real change)	−1.4	−10.8	4.2	4.3	2.5
GDP by expenditure (% real change):					
Private consumption	−1.1	−11.5	4	4.5	2.6
Fixed capital formation	−21.1	−45.1	−4	5.7	6.7
Export of goods & services	8.3	6.5	9.9	15.4	3
Import of goods & services	−11.4	−21.7	10.6	20.4	8.3
Merchandise trade balance (US$b)	−4.6	12.2	9.3	5.5	2.8
Foreign reserves (US$b; yr-end)	27	29.5	34.8	32.7	31.1
Industrial production (% real change)	0.2	−10.5	11.3	8	7
Minimum lending rate (% p.a.; yr-end)	15.25	11.73	8.25	7.75	7.25
3-month interest rate (% p.a.; yr-end)	11.38	6	3.81	2.75	3.25
Money supply (M2; yr-end; % change)	16.4	9.5	2.1	3.7	4.5
Exchange rate (baht/US$; yr-end)	47.29	36.97	37.50	42.95	47.30

Bank Foreign Assets
US$b
Source: Ministry of Commerce

Net capital flow-banks
y-o-y %
Source: Bank of Thailand

Private external debts
US$b
Source: Bank of Thailand

Comment: Raising Interest Rates Would Do More Harm Than Good

The government has expressed doubts about the effectiveness of the Bank of Thailand's (BOT) low interest rate policy, pointing to a faltering economic recovery and a weakening baht. The government argues that low interest rates have not spurred growth, but have instead induced capital outflows that have weakened the baht and overall confidence.

The government wants to see higher deposit rates, which, in its view, would increase interest income and therefore consumption and also discourage capital outflows, which would serve to stabilise the currency. The BOT, however, insists that the current policy of low interest rates is supportive of economic recovery and that the capital outflows have been appropriate as they have been mainly debt repayment. The central bank also believes that further lowering of interest rates would not produce benefits given the impaired banking system.

Are capital outflows the result of corporate debt repayment or capital flight? Evidence shows that the bulk of capital outflows have been debt repayment, although this portion declined in the first two months this year. Only a small part of the outflows can be accounted for as capital flight, because the BOT strictly regulates foreign exchange transactions by residents. Evidence suggests that it is banks acquiring foreign assets that is sustaining capital outflows. The government's other argument is that added interest income from a rise in deposit rates would spur consumption. A 100-basis points rise in deposit rates would boost interest income by 42 billion baht (about HK$7.21 billion), 0.84 per cent of gross domestic product. However, 75 per cent of total bank deposits are concentrated in less than one million accounts, and the relatively wealthy who own these accounts do not have a high marginal propensity to consume. If lending rates rise by the same amount, interest expense on good loans would rise by about 30 billion baht. However, this does not account for the risk of increased non-performing loans and greater difficulty in debt restructuring, either of which would significantly erode confidence and dim the prospects for economic recovery.

Thanomsri Fongarun-Rung, senior economist

Source and comment: Merrill Lynch, Singapore.

which may cause a deficit to arise or get larger in the trade in goods and the trade in services sections. The uncertainty that arises from inflation may also discourage financial and capital investment in the country.

In a **floating exchange rate** system (see below), a fall in demand for a country's goods and services and a reduction in the inflow of investment from abroad will reduce the exchange rate. This in turn will lower export prices and, at least initially, restore price competitiveness. However, there is danger that a vicious cycle will develop with inflation causing a lower exchange rate which in turn results in higher import prices, cost-push inflation and then a fall in the exchange rate. Also, if the root cause of the inflation is not tackled, it will continue.

However, inflation will not necessarily have adverse effects on the country's international trade position. If the country's inflation rate is below that of its main competitors, its goods and services will become more price competitive. In addition, if a country's goods and services were originally cheaper than their rivals, even with a higher inflation rate they may still be at a lower price.

It also has to be remembered that, whilst price is an important influence on demand, it is not the only one. A country may be able to sustain its output and sales at home and abroad even with inflation if the quality of its goods and services is rising or if, for example, its marketing is improving.

Balance of payments problems
Introduction
The structure of the balance of payments was outlined in section 4. In principle, the overall deficits and surpluses for any economy should balance – this is a function of the way in which the accounts are drawn up and how the inclusion of a balancing item (net errors and omissions) produces an outcome which is seemingly in equilibrium. The same is true on an international scale. A surplus on the balance of payments for one country for example, is offset by a deficit or deficits elsewhere. So, if this is the case, why are economists concerned about balance of payments problems?

In order to answer this question it is necessary to distinguish between equilibrium and disequilibrium in

the balance of payments. In this context, equilibrium has a rather different meaning to the way the term was introduced in section 2. Here, equilibrium refers to a situation where manageable deficits are cancelled out by modest surpluses over a period of time. Under such circumstances there is no particular tendency for the exchange rate to change (see below). So, on a short-term basis it does *not* necessarily mean that a deficit is bad and a surplus is good.

Two situations of equilibrium might be:
1 *Where the imports of goods and services exceeds exports but where this is offset by an inflow of foreign direct investment.* In other words, a current account deficit is counterbalanced by a financial account surplus. The UK economy is a good example of this.
2 *Where the exports of goods and services exceed imports but where there is substantial investment abroad by companies and residents.* Here, a current account surplus is recorded, but matched by a deficit on the financial account.

It is difficult to put a time period on this – the crucial thing is not to look at the balance of payments of an economy on a one year only basis.

Disequilibrium occurs when, over a particular period of time, a country is recording persistent deficits or surpluses in its balance of payments. As a consequence, it has to be recognised that the exchange rate is either overvalued or undervalued on the foreign exchange market. In such situations, particularly in the case of a deficit, corrective action is required in order to prevent the economy draining its foreign currency reserves or ending hopelessly in debt (see figure 6.2 below).

The problem of debt will be analysed in section 13. The significance for the balance of payments of many developing economies is that large sums of capital were borrowed from commercial banks in the 1970s and early 1980s to fund development projects from which it was expected future income streams would be generated. Many such projects have turned out to be very poor investments; in other cases the money has been spent on other things or has been used corruptly by recipients. The legacy is one of chronic balance of payments deficits. The problem for many countries is that a very substantial part of their export earnings has to be paid annually in order to service this debt.

With this in mind, disequilibrium in the balance of payments can arise where:

1 The imports of goods and services exceed exports and the financial account is in deficit.

2 Exports of goods and services may just exceed imports but there is a persistent deficit on the financial account.

3 Exceptionally, there is a large surplus on the current account, generating an overall balance of payments surplus. A pertinent example of an economy in this situation for many years has been the case of Japan.

Current account contrasts in emerging economies

Some of the largest South East Asian economies are still running big trade surpluses. For example, in the year to May 2001, China's surplus was $21.1bn, South Korea's $15bn and Taiwan's $11.4bn. All had similar surpluses on the current account of their balance of payments (see table 6.3).

	Trade balance ($bn)	Current account ($bn)
China	+21.1	+20.5
Hong Kong	−11.9	+8.8
Indonesia	+26.1	+5.5
Malaysia	+15.6	+8.4
Philippines	+7.3	+9.5
Singapore	+4.2	+21.8
South Korea	+15.0	+14.0
Taiwan	+11.4	+12.0
Thailand	+3.1	+6.9

Table 6.3 Current account contrasts in SE Asia, 2000–2001

In contrast, emerging economies in central and South America and in cental Europe (Venezuela and Russia excepted) had worrying deficits on both (see table 6.4).

	Trade balance ($bn)	Current account ($bn)
Argentina	+1.6	−9.4
Brazil	+34.7	−26.6
Mexico	−9.5	−17.8
Venezuela	+17.5	+12.5
Czech Republic	−3.6	−2.7
Hungary	−2.4	−1.7
Poland	−10.0	−8.8
Russia	+60.7	+45.9

Table 6.4 Current account contrasts in emerging economies, 2000–2001

The particular case of Brazil (figure 6.2) clearly shows the economic problems that can result from persistent trade and current account deficits.

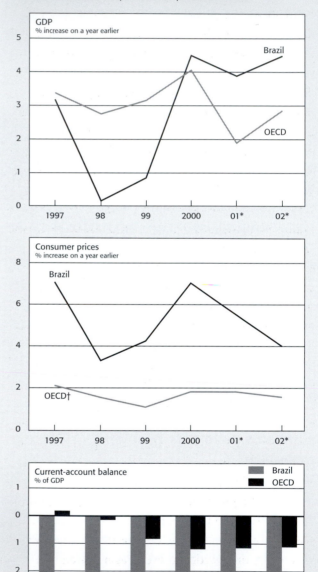

Brazil
Economic reforms have enhanced Brazil's growth prospects, argues the OECD in its first survey of the country. But a big current-account deficit means that the economy is vulnerable to external shocks. The OECD calls for more tax and public-pension reforms. It also recommends that the central bank be made independent to keep inflation in check.

Figure 6.2 *Forecast. †Private-consumption deflator, excluding Hungary, Mexico, Poland and Turkey.
Sources: OECD.
The Economist, 17 June 2001 (adapted).

Causes of balance of payments disequilibrium

Let us assume that the disequilibrium is that referred to above in the first two situations. This type of problem can be experienced by all types of economies. Three main causes of the disequilibrium can be identified. They are:

1 The economy has a high propensity to import goods. Consequently, substantial deficits are recorded annually on the trading account. The UK is typical – the balance of trade in goods for all recent years except for 1997 has been in deficit, particularly with respect to trade with the rest of the EU. UK citizens like to purchase imported cars, clothing, footwear, food, drink, electrical goods and so on, even though all of these items can be produced in the UK. The perception of many people is that 'British is not best'. There are similar problems in developing economies. The cause though is different – such countries have very limited domestic production and have to rely on imported goods for much of their consumer demand. As far as exports are concerned, developing economies often rely heavily for their export revenue on sales of primary products on world markets. As shown in section 4, the terms of trade are often unfavourable, meaning that they have to continually export a greater volume of goods for the same export revenue. It is therefore easy to see why many have trading deficits on their trading accounts.

2 There may be lack of confidence in a particular economy, resulting in few capital inflows. There may even be a situation of an exodus of capital from the economy. The determinants of the level of confidence are very difficult to explain in simple terms. It is a complex phenomonen related to the macroeconomic variables referred to in section 5, often set within a political context. Confidence may also be severely affected by one particular event, again often of a political rather than of an economic origin, and this may well deter foreign investors.

3 From a shorter-term standpoint, a period of expansion in the macro-economy, leading to increased consumer spending power, could produce a situation where much of this is spent on imported rather than locally produced goods. Imports are therefore 'sucked in' to the economy, with potentially serious problems for the overall balance of payments.

Cosmopolitan Singapore offers superb eating as well as world class shopping

Self-assessment task

Using the data collected for the task on page 95, decide whether the balance of payments of your country is in equilibrium or disequilibrium. Can you explain why this is so?

Consequences of balance of payments disequilibrium

There are consequences of disequilibrium in the balance of payments for

◆ the domestic economy,
◆ the external economy.

For the domestic economy, the consequence is that there will be a pressing need for corrective action (see section 7). This need will be evidenced through a domestic economy which is characterised as having a very narrow type of economic structure and still heavily dependent on agriculture in the case of developing countries. For the UK it is shown through the closure of many types of manufacturing firm (see quotes at the beginning of this section). Vast sectors of industry have suffered de-industrialisation, so increasing the demand for imported goods. Long-term unemployment therefore is an obvious consequence.

A second domestic consequence is that because of low business confidence, foreign investors are increasingly reluctant to invest in an economy with a balance of payments disequilibrium because of the risks that are involved. Economic prospects will be uncertain and there is a likely possibility that the currency may be devalued (see below). A situation like this hardly encourages new foreign investors to invest in an economy.

A third consequence is that for consumers there is likely to be fewer stocks of certain exotic imported consumer goods (for example, perfume, designer clothes) and the general range will be restricted, often to products not produced domestically. Imports are also likely to have a higher rate of tax imposed on them in order to restrict consumption.

For the external economy, it is often the case that disequilibrium in the balance of payments will put pressure on the government to introduce or upgrade some of the methods of protection described earlier in section 4.

A second consequence is shown in figure 6.3. Suppose the economy starts from the disequilibrium position shown in diagram (a) where at r_1 the total demand for foreign currency exceeds the supply of foreign currency by $0Q_1 - 0Q_2$. This is a consequence of imports of goods and services exceeding exports, but with a balanced capital inflow and outflow (see diagrams (b) and (c) respectively). As will be elaborated in section 7, the corrective action that is needed is for the exchange rate to be devalued. This results in overall equilibrium (at r_2, Q_3) in diagram (a), with a reduced current account deficit and a financial account surplus.

In turn though the consequences for the domestic economy should be recognised. For example:

◆ import prices will rise, in turn increasing the cost of living and fuelling cost-push inflation;

◆ export prices will fall – depending on the products involved, revenue may increase, as indeed will employment;

◆ confidence in the economy might be affected in the short term, possibly due to the fear of a further devaluation.

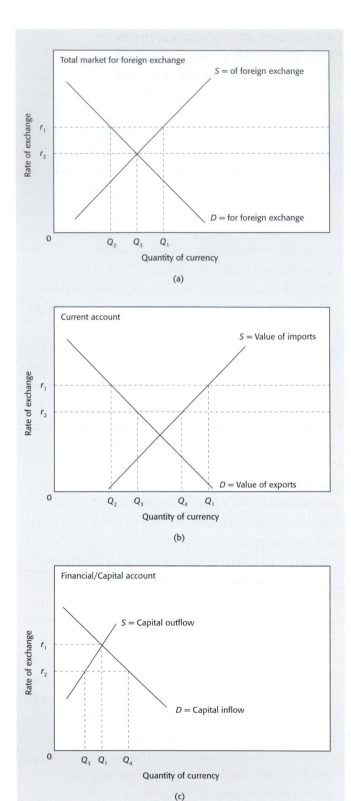

Figure 6.3 Disequilibrium and equilibrium in the balance of payments

The causes and consequences of fluctuations in foreign exchange rates

The measurement of exchange rates

When international rather than domestic trade takes place, there is a crucial difference. If a UK resident, for example, purchases a product made by UK factors of production in the UK, only one currency, the pound sterling, will be involved. If, however, a UK resident buys a good which has been produced abroad and imported into the UK, currency exchange must take place. This is because the UK resident will use sterling to buy the product in the shop but the foreign factors of production will require payment in their own currencies. If, for example, a UK consumer purchases a television set which has been produced in Malaysia he or she will use pounds sterling, because this is the currency which is used as the medium of exchange in the UK. In Malaysia, however, the pound sterling cannot be used to settle debt because the ringgit is the medium of exchange. This means that those who worked in the Malaysian television factory will not accept the pound in payment of their wages. They will insist that their wages are paid in ringgits. At some stage in the transaction, currency exchange must take place. At some stage pounds must be exchanged for ringitts. The exchange of one currency for another takes place in the **foreign exchange** market.

Nominal exchange rates

The nominal exchange rate is simply the price of one currency in terms of another, so that for example we might quote the price of the pound sterling in terms of the ringgit, or the price of the US dollar in terms of the yen. The prices of foreign currencies are usually quoted in the national newspapers. On the 23 December 2000, the pound/dollar rate was quoted in the British newspapers as 1.4765. This means that £1 would buy just less than $1.48. Similarly, on this day £1 would buy 5.27 Malaysian ringgits. Changes in the nominal exchange rate of one country's currency with that of another will affect the transaction price of goods and services bought and sold between these two countries. Because one country's currency is expressed in terms of that of one other country, nominal exchange rates are bilateral rates.

Trade weighted exchange rates

As explained, changes in the nominal exchange rate of one country's currency with that of another will alter the price of goods and services traded between these two countries. In the modern world, however, most countries trade with lots of other countries. A country's nominal exchange rate may be falling against the currency of some of its trading partners and rising against those of others. In 1999, for example, the US dollar fell against the Japanese yen, rose against most European currencies, and remained generally steady against the Canadian dollar. Given this information alone, it is hard to say whether the US dollar strengthened or weakened during the year. A far more useful measure of exchange rate changes is arrived at through what is known as a **trade weighted exchange rate**. This is a measurement in index form of changes in the value of a country's currency against a basket of other currencies. These are weighted according to the relative importance in trading terms for the country in question of each of the currencies in the basket. If, for example, the UK undertakes three times as much trade with the US as with Canada, the US dollar will be given three times as much weight in the calculation of the index as the Canadian dollar. Since the currencies of more than two countries are involved in the calculation of a trade weighted index, this is known as a multilateral exchange rate.

The real effective exchange rate

As stated earlier, changes in a country's exchange rate will affect the transaction prices of goods and services which that country imports and exports. These transaction prices are not only affected by changes in the exchange rate; they are also affected by differences in inflation rates between trading countries. As a result, changes in the real effective exchange rate are calculated which adjust changes in exchange rates to take into account relative rates of inflation. For example, if a country's exchange rate is depreciating this means that exported goods from this country have now become cheaper in foreign markets. This is because a given amount of that country's currency can now be purchased using less of the importing country's currency. Effectively the impact of the declining exchange rate is that the price of the good has fallen in the foreign market. It may be, however, that the exporting country has been suffering from inflation at a higher rate than the inflation rate in the overseas market. As a result, in *real* terms its export prices could actually be increasing. Whether the exported goods are actually cheaper in the importing country depends upon the exchange rate change, together with the effects of any price changes in both of the trading countries. The real effective exchange rate takes price changes *and* exchange rate changes into account. It is the most accurate way of measuring changes in the competitiveness of an economy's goods and services in international markets.

The determination of exchange rates

The buying and selling of foreign exchange takes place on the foreign exchange market. Importers of goods into the UK will use pounds to buy the currency of the country from which they are purchasing the goods. This act provides a supply of pounds on to the foreign exchange market. Similarly, those who have bought products from the UK will be using their own currencies to purchase pounds – this action creates a demand for pounds.

The foreign exchange market does not exist in a single location but is made up of banks and other financial intermediaries that buy and sell foreign currency on behalf of their private and business customers. There is a continuous flow of currency through the market on a particular day. The price of the currency or exchange rate is determined by the relative strength of the supply and demand for the currency.

So far we have considered the supply and demand for pounds which arises from the export and import of goods into the UK. There are, however, other sources of the demand for and supply of pounds on the foreign exchange market.

Figure 6.4 shows the flows of currency on to the market. These are indicative of the structure of the balance of payments (see section 4). These flows are generated through trade in both goods and services and in addition short- and long-term capital flows that move between economies in search of the highest returns.

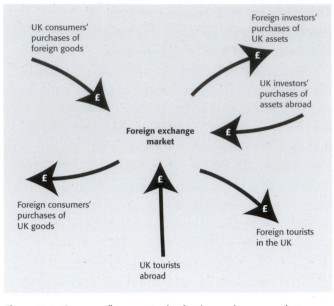

Figure 6.4 Currency flows on to the foreign exchange market

The determination of the equilibrium exchange rate in a free market

In a free market, the value of the exchange rate is determined solely by the forces of supply and demand. Figure 6.5 shows the supply and demand for pounds on the foreign exchange market. For simplicity we will illustrate this only with reference to the relationship between the pound and the dollar.

In this figure we see that the demand for pounds slopes down from left to right. This is because when the price of the pound in terms of dollars is high at P_3, then British goods and services are expensive to US consumers – they have to pay lots of dollars to gain

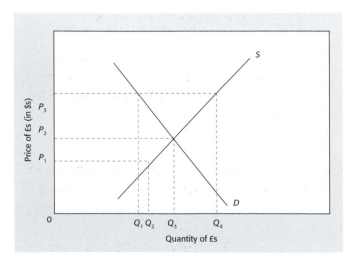

Figure 6.5 Exchange rate determination in a free market

pounds. As a result, the demand for British goods and services will be very low in the US and this means that few pounds are demanded on the foreign exchange market. As the value of the pound falls against the dollar however, US consumers can gain more pounds for their dollars and so more pounds are demanded on the foreign exchange market. The supply curve of pounds is shown to be upward sloping from left to right. This is because when the pound is very low against the dollar, for example, P_1, then US goods are very expensive in the UK. Few UK consumers will buy US goods and, as a result, few pounds will be supplied to the foreign exchange market. As the value of the pound against the dollar rises, US goods become more affordable to the UK consumers and more pounds are supplied to the market.

Now imagine that the price of the pound on the foreign exchange market is at P_3. Here the pound is overvalued because UK goods cannot sell in the US market. They are too expensive. The demand for pounds is very low but, because US goods are so cheap in the UK, British consumers are buying lots of US goods and services and supplying lots of pounds to the market. As we can see, at this exchange rate there is an excess of pounds on the market. Whenever there is an excess supply in a free market, market forces will result in a fall in price. The exchange rate of the pound will fall to an equilibrium rate at P_2 where supply equates to demand.

Self-assessment tasks

1 With reference to figure 6.5 explain what would happen to the value of the pound if the rate was at P_1.
2 The explanation of exchange rate determination provided considers only the demand and supply of goods and services. Discuss whether the analysis would be different if the impact of the financial account of the balance of payments was included.

Causes of changes in the equilibrium exchange rate

Any change in supply or demand for a currency will cause a **depreciation** or **appreciation** in the exchange rate.

For illustration we will now consider the market for US dollars in terms of all other currencies.

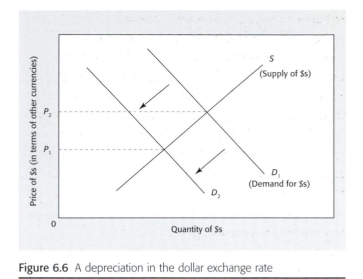

Figure 6.6 A depreciation in the dollar exchange rate

1 A depreciation in the exchange rate A depreciation in an exchange rate can occur, as shown in figure 6.6. Here there has been a fall in the demand for the dollar. This is represented by a shift of the demand curve to the left and could be caused, for example, by:

◆ *A reduction in the number of US goods and services sold abroad.* Importers of US goods and services are demanding fewer dollars to settle accounts with US firms. This could be caused, for example, by an increase in the price of US goods and services due to inflation or a longer-term decline in the quality of US goods and services.
◆ *A reduction in the number of international investors who wish to place their funds in the US economy.* This might be because interest rates in the US are lower than in other economies and, as a result, give a poorer return to investors.

2 An appreciation in the exchange rate An appreciation in the exchange rate can occur as shown in figure 6.7. Here there has been a decrease in the supply of the dollar. This is represented by a shift in the supply curve to the left and could be caused, for example, by:

◆ *A decrease in the number of foreign goods and services imported into the US.* US importers are using dollars to purchase foreign currency on the foreign exchange market. They provide a supply of dollars on to the market. The fall in the number of foreign goods purchased in the US could be caused by a rise in the price of foreign goods and services relative to those produced in the US, or perhaps there has been a decline in the quality of foreign goods and services.

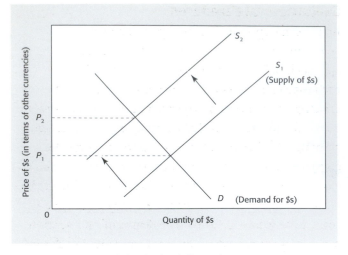

Figure 6.7 An appreciation in the dollar exchange rate

◆ A decrease in the number of US investors who want to place their funds in foreign economies. Again, if interest rates fall abroad, then US investors will want to place their funds in US banks rather than abroad. They will now choose not to exchange their dollars for foreign currencies and the supply of dollars on the foreign exchange market will decrease.

Self-assessment task

Consider the impact of the following changes upon the value of the dollar. Provide a sketch for each change.
◆ a rise in interest rates in the US;
◆ a substantial current account deficit on the US balance of payments.

Effects of changing exchange rates on the economy

As stated earlier, if there is a change in the value of a country's currency against that of others it will change the transaction price of any goods and services which that country buys or sells in international markets.

◆ A fall or depreciation in the value of the exchange rate will mean that the price of imports into the country will rise and the price of the country's exports will fall.
◆ A rise or appreciation in the country's currency will mean the opposite, that is the price of imported goods will fall and the price of the country's exports will rise.

The impact of a depreciation on the exchange rate

As we have seen above, a balance of payments deficit will cause a depreciation in a country's currency, which will mean that import prices will rise. This will have a number of consequences. Domestic manufacturers who sell in the home market will find that their goods are now more competitive compared to imported manufactures that have now become more expensive. They may find that there is an increase in demand for their products and they will try to expand production to meet this demand. There will be an increase in the demand for the factors of production, including labour. The impact of this will depend upon the level of employment in the economy. If there is a lot of spare capacity in the economy with lots of labour unemployed we would expect unemployment to fall. As full employment is approached however, labour becomes increasingly scarce and, as a result, we would expect labour to ask for higher wages. Because they are facing increased demand, manufacturers will be prepared to pay the higher wages and pass this on to the consumer in the form of higher prices. The extent to which cost increases can be passed on to consumers depends upon the price elasticity of demand for domestic manufactured goods. The higher the price elasticity of demand for domestically produced manufactured goods, the less domestic manufacturers will be able to raise prices. Nevertheless, we would expect some inflationary pressure because of increases in the demand for domestically produced goods when an economy's currency depreciates. Inflationary pressure will also arise from the supply side of production when a currency depreciates. This is because any imported raw materials will become more expensive when the exchange rate falls. If there are no domestic supplies of the raw material then manufacturers have no alternative but to pay the increased price if they wish to respond to the increase in domestic sales. Again they will try to pass the increase in cost on to the consumer so prices will tend to rise.

A depreciation of a country's exchange rate will also mean that its export prices will fall. This will mean that there will be an increase in the demand for that country's products in foreign markets. This in turn could be inflationary because exporting firms will be competing with other firms who are producing in a buoyant domestic market.

Despite the inflationary pressure we would expect the depreciation of the exchange rate to lead to a fall in imports and a rise in exports which will mean that the balance of payments deficit is replaced by a balance of payments surplus.

The impact of an appreciation in the exchange rate

When a country experiences a balance of payments surplus we have seen that this will cause a rise in that country's exchange rate. This will have a number of consequences. Import prices will fall and export prices will rise. Domestic consumers will switch to imported goods and services while foreign consumers will turn to their own country's products in preference to imports. As a result we would expect the volume of imports to rise and the volume of exports to fall. The extent of the volume change is determined by the price elasticity of demand for both imports and exports. There will be a decline in demand from both domestic and foreign purchasers of goods and services produced in the country with the appreciating currency, which may well lead to unemployment as producers face declining sales both at home and abroad.

The appreciation of the currency should have sufficient impact upon import and export spending that the balance of payments surplus is replaced by a balance of payments deficit.

Exchange rate systems

In deciding upon their exchange rate policy, governments can choose between a variety of approaches. They can decide to have a **floating exchange rate system**. This means that the rate of exchange of a currency is decided purely by the flows of demand and supply of that currency on to the foreign exchange market. An alternative approach is for the government to intervene in the foreign exchange market either directly or indirectly to influence the value of the currency in some way. Managed exchange rate systems come in a variety of forms. The degree of intervention can vary quite considerably. A government may choose to have a **managed float**. This describes an exchange rate policy in which the value of the currency is broadly decided by market forces but the government takes action to influence the rate of change of the currency's value. If the exchange rate is depreciating for example, the government might take action to slow down the rate of fall. A **pegged exchange rate system** however, involves far more intervention. The term describes a system in which the government declares a central value for its currency and then intervenes in the foreign exchange market to maintain this value. There are a number of ways in which this system might work. Sometimes, for example, the value of the currency is held at a constant rate. In other systems the rate is allowed to vary within a narrow band with upper and lower limits. Sometimes the currency is pegged against

Self-assessment tasks

Calculate the impact of the following exchange rate changes upon transaction prices in the following cases: Assume that the nominal exchange rate of pound sterling to US dollars is £1 = $1.5. A cashmere sweater made in the UK and which sold for £200 would cost a US importer $300. Similarly a US car which sold for $12,000 would cost a UK importer £8,000.

1 Assume that the nominal exchange rate changes to £1 = $2.0:
  (a) Calculate the cost of the cashmere sweater to the US importer.
  (b) Calculate the cost of the US car to the UK importer.
  (c) What would you expect to happen to the volume of UK exports of cashmere sweaters and imports of US cars as a result of the new exchange rate?

2 Assume that the nominal exchange rate now changes to £1 = $1.0:
  (a) Re-calculate the cost of the cashmere sweater to the US importer.
  (b) Re-calculate the cost of the car to the UK importer.
  (c) What would you expect to happen to the volume of UK exports of cashmere sweaters and imports of US cars as a result of the new exchange rate?
  (d) As the exchange rate has changed it has changed the transaction prices of the trade in cashmere sweaters in the UK and the US. As a result we will expect the volumes of imports and exports to change. Explain what further information would be required to assess the impact of these changes in sales upon total spending on exports and imports.

one other major currency, such as the US dollar; sometimes it is pegged against a 'basket of currencies'. We need to consider in more detail how each of these systems operates, and then consider the advantages and disadvantages of each.

Floating exchange rate systems

When the value of a currency depreciates or appreciates purely as a result of market forces, that is, changes in demand and/or the supply of a currency, then the exchange rate is said to be freely floating. Under this system the exchange rate is determined purely by market forces. The major advantage of this is that since the government has no exchange rate target it is free to pursue other policy objectives, such as full employment. This means that where freely floating exchange rates are adopted there is considerable independence in economic policy making.

This can be explained as follows. If a country suffers inflation at a higher rate than its competitors in world trade, then the likely outcome is that this country's goods and services become uncompetitive in world markets. Domestic consumers will turn to lower-priced imports, and consumers in overseas markets will purchase their goods and services from low inflation countries. This is likely to lead to a deficit on the current account of the country's balance of payments. As we have seen, this leads to a fall in the exchange rate of that country's currency as an excess supply of the currency occurs in the foreign exchange market. A fall in the exchange rate will restore competitiveness of the economy's goods and services, because domestic consumers will now find that they have to pay more to obtain imports. Also foreign consumers now find that they have to give up less of their own currency to buy the exports of the country with the depreciating currency. The subsequent fall in imports and rise in exports should correct the balance of payments deficit.

This adjustment process does depend upon certain assumptions however, including the responsiveness of consumers to the price changes that result from the depreciating currency. In addition we have seen that one of the consequences of a declining currency is that inflationary pressures are created in the economy. This means that, as the currency depreciates to offset the inflation which has made the country's goods and services uncompetitive, it may well create further inflationary pressures within the economy which will mean that the goods and services remain uncompetitive and the cycle goes on. The inflationary pressure can become so bad that there is a complete loss of confidence in the currency in both the domestic and in foreign exchange markets. Nevertheless, as explained it is usually expected that given sufficient time it is likely that demand for exports and imports is sufficiently price elastic to ensure that the deficit is removed, despite the inflationary pressures that are created. This tendency for deficits (and surpluses) in the balance of payments to be removed through changes in the exchange rate with no need for government action is known as an automatic adjustment mechanism.

Despite the advantages of the self-regulating nature of floating exchange rate, most governments tend to favour some degree of intervention in foreign exchange markets. This is because of a number of serious disadvantages which freely floating regimes bring. These can be summarised as follows:

1 The fact that exchange rates fluctuate discourages trade. When contracts are signed to finance international trade in goods and services entrepreneurs will assess the usual risks when considering whether a venture will result in profits being earned. They will consider their costs and revenue and this will allow them to estimate profit. In a floating exchange rate regime an extra risk is added to the transaction. A sudden fluctuation in the exchange rate might upset their calculations and wipe out estimated profit. It could, of course, result in severe losses if revenue falls below costs. There are several ways in which the risk of losses through currency fluctuation can be minimised, but the uncertainty which surrounds trade in floating exchange rate regimes remains a serious disadvantage of such a system.

2 It is suggested that the fact that a floating exchange rate system has a self-regulating mechanism to deal with balance of payments deficits means that governments do not face any pressure to exercise financial discipline in their policies. As we have seen, any inflation which results from lax economic policy-making is offset by a decline in the exchange rate. It is clear from the above analysis, however, that the decline in the exchange rate can itself cause prices to rise. As a result, it is claimed that floating exchange rates can be inflationary.

The disadvantages of floating exchange rates have encouraged governments to seek ways of intervening in the foreign exchange market to manage exchange rate change in order to provide stability and a favourable environment for growth in trade.

Managed exchange rate systems

If governments are to manage their exchange rates they need to intervene in the foreign exchange market. They can intervene directly by buying and selling currencies in order to offset upward or downward pressure on the exchange rate. This means that governments must have access to a large quantity of reserves of foreign exchange sufficient to influence the price in the market. They can also intervene indirectly through variations in the rate of interest. If, for example, there is downward pressure on the exchange rate because there is an excess supply of the currency on the foreign exchange market, a rise in domestic interest rates will attract inflows of capital in search of good returns. This will create an increase in the demand for the currency and offset the downward pressure. This means that the rate of interest is used as a tool to maintain the exchange rate.

Figure 6.7 shows the principles of a pegged exchange rate system, whereby the currency has a par value of $0P$, with an upper and a lower limit. If there is an increase in the supply of dollars, for example due to an increase in imports, then the supply curve shifts to S_1. This will reduce the value of the dollar in a free market to below its agreed lower limit. To maintain the currency at its lower limit, the demand for dollars has to shift to the right, an action requiring the use of foreign exchange

reserves by the government. If it wishes to return the dollar to its par value, then even greater reserves are needed to bring it back to $0P$. This is fine in theory but in practice can involve a massive drain on the foreign exchange reserves held by a country. (The UK's withdrawal from the Exchange Rate Mechanism in 1993 was a consequence of such actions failing to address the pound's fall in value).

The South East Asia currency crisis

In 1996 South East Asia was hit by a currency crisis which provides a vivid example of the difficulties associated with a pegged exchange rate regime. At this time most of the countries had exchange rates pegged to the value of the US dollar – the USA provided the main market for the goods and services produced and exported from here. These countries, which included Thailand, Indonesia, South Korea and Malaysia, found that pegging their rate against the US dollar would ensure that their goods and services would not lose competitiveness in the US market because of an exchange rate appreciation. This was seen as the key to export-led growth. The crisis started in Thailand. The Thai currency unit, the baht, was rigidly fixed to a basket of currencies which was dominated (85 per cent) by the US dollar. In 1995 the dollar began to rise and under the exchange rate regime in operation the baht rose too as the Thai economic policy makers intervened in the market to maintain the pegged rate with the dollar. Unfortunately the rate of inflation in Thailand was higher than the rate of inflation in the US and this resulted in a decline in Thai exports. Thailand had for some years accumulated large current account deficits and, as a result, large quantities of short-term external debt. Speculators began to sell large quantities of the baht in anticipation of a devaluation. The Thai authorities tried to maintain the value of the baht but as their reserves became exhausted they bowed to the inevitable and allowed the baht to float down. Between December 1996 and January 1998 the baht declined in value by 52.02 per cent. The exchange rate speculation then spread to other economies in South East Asia. The Malaysian ringgit fell by 45.98 per cent over the same period and Indonesia's rupiah by 74.48 per cent. South Korea was one of the most successful of the 'tiger economies'. In 1997 it was in fact the eleventh largest economy in world. Nevertheless, its currency (the won)

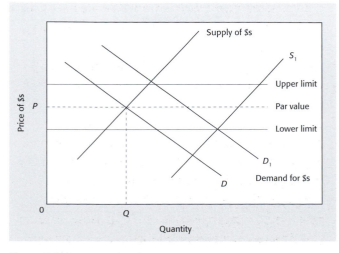

Figure 6.8 A managed exchange rate system

fell by 54.2 per cent and this resulted in the IMF lending the South Korean government a total of $57 billion, its largest ever rescue package. The fallout even spread to Japan with the yen falling to an eight year low against the US dollar. The currency speculation then spread to other regions. In August 1998 and at the beginning of 1999 crises occurred in Russia and then Brazil. The Russian government had maintained a pegged exchange rate between the rouble and the dollar, but, as the speculators turned their attention to the rouble, the Russian authorities were forced to abandon their support for the rouble and it declined in value by 50 per cent in ten days. Brazil's currency, the real, depreciated by 22 per cent in two days. The world economy was on the point of collapse, but complete disaster was averted because the central banks of the US and Europe took action to restore confidence in world financial markets. In addition, the health of the US economy ensured that the threatened economies of South East Asia could restore their economies through sales of exports to US consumers.

Summary

In this section we have recognised that:

- All types of economy are concerned about problems of inflation, balance of payments disequilibrium and fluctuations in their exchange rates.

- These problems have particular relevance and significance for developing economies.

- Inflation is caused by monetary, cost and demand factors.

- If unchecked, inflation affects the domestic and external well-being of a country.

- Disequilibrium in the balance of payments of an economy is caused by a high propensity to import, a lack of confidence in an economy and an expansion in the domestic economy of a country.

- This disequilibrium can have an adverse effect on the domestic economy and lead to a fall in the foreign exchange rate compared with major currencies.

- There are three main types of exchange rate – nominal, real and trade weighted.

- Exchange rates are crudely determined by the demand and supply of a foreign currency in international markets – under certain circumstances, the change in exchange rates may not occur or is managed between certain specified limits.

- Exchange rates can depreciate or appreciate as a consequence of changes in demand or supply for a currency.

- Changing exchange rates affect import and export spending and the balance of payments of a country.

Key words

Definitions of Key words can be found in the Glossary.

appreciation (of exchange rates)
cost-push inflation
demand-pull inflation
depreciation (of exchange rates)
fixed exchange rates
floating exchange rates
foreign exchange
hyperinflation
inflation
managed float
menu costs of inflation
pegged exchange rate system
Quantity Theory of Money
trade weighted exchange rate

7 Policies to correct balance of payments disequilibria

On completion of this section you will know:

➤ how governments can take steps to correct persistent deficits and surpluses in their balance of payments

➤ why their reaction is dependent upon the exchange rate regime under which they are operating

➤ the likely side effects on the domestic economy of the policies they might choose

Introduction

When managed exchange rate systems are in operation, intervention in the foreign exchange market to maintain the rate must take place on a daily basis. In addition governments will need to take remedial action to correct the balance of payments deficit which gave rise to the downward pressure on the exchange rate in the first place. This is because the automatic adjustment mechanism, which occurs in a freely floating exchange rate system, is absent when exchange rates are pegged. The exchange rate will not automatically decline to restore competitiveness. So, without adjustment to export and import prices brought about by exchange rate changes, the balance of payments deficit may well persist. Given that a country's reserves are not limitless, measures must be taken to remove the deficit or the reserves will eventually run out and the country will find it impossible to keep the exchange rate pegged at the agreed value. Policies to remove the balance of payments deficit can be categorised as follows.

Expenditure switching policies

An expenditure switching policy is any action taken by a government which is designed to persuade purchasers of goods and services both at home and abroad to purchase more of that country's goods and services and less of the goods and services produced by others. Effectively this would include any policies designed to persuade domestic purchasers to purchase home-produced goods and services rather than imports. It would also include any policies designed to persuade foreign purchasers to buy more exports from your economy. These policies are not designed to reduce the total amount of spending in a country but to re-direct or 'switch' spending to your country's products rather than those produced in another country. The impact should be a fall in import expenditure and a rise in export earnings. The former will lead to a fall in the supply of a country's currency on the foreign exchange market and the latter will lead to a rise in the demand for the country's currency on the market. Both will lead to upward pressure on the exchange rate.

Expenditure-switching policies include the following measures:

◆ tariffs,
◆ quotas,
◆ exchange controls,
◆ export subsidies.

These have been described in section 4. Along with embargoes and voluntary export restraints, all have the disadvantage that they interfere with market forces and prevent the consumer from benefiting from the effects of specialisation and trade. In addition a government's ability to resort to expenditure switching policies is limited by membership of the WTO (formerly the GATT). As a result they may be forced to resort to expenditure dampening policies.

Expenditure dampening policies

An expenditure 'dampening' policy is any action taken by a government that is designed to reduce the total level of spending in an economy. This will have two principal effects. First, a reduction in spending will mean that there will be fewer purchases of imported goods and services. Secondly, domestic producers will find that their domestic market is 'dampened' and is more difficult to sell in. As a result they may try to make up for the decrease in sales domestically with increases in sales abroad. The overall impact therefore should be a fall in imports and a rise in exports. Expenditure dampening policies include:

◆ *Deflationary fiscal policy*. This means raising taxes and reducing government expenditure. Raising taxes will reduce disposable incomes meaning that less will be available to spend on imports. In addition the reduced government spending will lead to a downward multiplier effect which will depress incomes further. The extent of the reduction in import spending will depend upon the **marginal propensity to import**. This measures the change in import spending as disposable incomes change. A high marginal propensity to import will mean that a fall in disposable incomes will have a great impact upon import spending, and taxes may not have to be raised by much to reduce import spending by the required amount. Alternatively, if the marginal propensity to import is low, it will require a large increase in taxes to bring about the necessary reduction in import spending.

◆ *Deflationary monetary policy*. This means raising interest rates and reducing the money supply. In addition to attracting inflows of foreign capital that will increase the demand for the currency on the foreign exchange market, increases in the rate of interest will reduce the money supply and deflate the economy. This is because the higher interest rate will reduce the demand for loans for consumption and investment and lead to a fall in aggregate monetary demand.

A major disadvantage of a managed exchange rate system is that it creates a deflationary situation when there is downward pressure on the exchange rate as a result of a balance of payments deficit. The deflationary outcome will have the intended effect of reducing spending on imports, but it will also have the additional unintended effect of reducing spending on home produced products. This means that unemployment will rise in the domestic economy.

The maintenance of a pegged rate in times of balance of payments deficit requires exchange market intervention on a daily basis together with expenditure switching and expenditure dampening policies with the resulting negative side effects. If the problem persists then it is clear that the deflationary pressure will cause the economy to operate at less than full capacity, with all the waste in terms of lost output that this implies. Under these circumstances there may be a case for a **devaluation** of the currency. This means that the government announces that it will peg the exchange rate at a new lower value. This has the same effect as a depreciation of the currency. It alters the relative price of imports and exports to restore competitiveness. If the economy continues to suffer from inflation however, devaluation will become increasingly frequent and the benefits of a pegged exchange rate will be lost.

The long-term answer to the difficulties associated with a persistent balance of payments deficit is to improve the quantity and quality of goods and services produced in the economy. As a result governments have increasingly adopted supply side policies to improve the underlying competitiveness of the economy so that persistent deficits do not arise (see section 13). Only in this way can economies enjoy full employment and the full benefits of international trade. A persistent balance of payments surplus can also create difficulties for an

Gold bullion in the vaults at the Bank of England
Source: Bank of England.

economy but under these circumstances the pressure on the government will not be so acute. This is because the government will be selling quantities of its own currency to prevent a rise in the rate. The effect is that the country's reserves of foreign exchange will be rising. Nevertheless if an economy suffers from a persistent surplus it may choose to undertake a **revaluation** of the currency to restore long-term equilibrium to the accounts.

Self-assessment tasks

Study the article below and then tackle the exercises that follow.

America's economic weakness?

	Current account balance ($bn)	As % of GDP
1997	−155	−1.9
1998	−215	−2.5
1999	−324	−3.6
2000	−370	−4.0
2001	−380(est)	−3.8(est)

On the surface, the United States has the strongest economy in the world. While other parts have been in turmoil, investors have been happy to pour their money into the US's booming markets. As a result, the current account deficit has ballooned. In 2001 it stood at an estimated 4 per cent of GDP.

The worry is that foreign investors will be concerned that the US is using their capital to finance low savings and a consumer spending boom rather than boost investment. As a result they will start to shift their money elsewhere – the dollar should therefore fall, boost US exports and slow import growth. A weaker dollar in turn will aggravate fears of inflation and a slow down in economic growth.

1 Refer back to the description of the balance of payments in section 4. Use these terms to explain the current account deficit of the US.

2 As well as currency depreciation, what other policies could the US use to reduce the current account deficit? And with what consequences?

Summary

In this section we have recognised that:

● Governments may find it necessary to use various policies to correct a balance of payments deficit or surplus.

● The use of these policies is necessary where a country has a managed exchange rate.

● Such policies can have short-term detrimental effects upon the domestic economy.

● From a longer-term standpoint, supply side policies can enhance a country's competitiveness.

Key words

Definitions of Key words can be found in the Glossary.

devaluation
expenditure dampening policies
expenditure switching policies
marginal propensity to import
revaluation

Unit 2
Extension (A Level)

8 Basic economic ideas – economic efficiency

On completion of this section you should know:

➤ what economists mean by an efficient or optimum allocation of resources
➤ what is meant by economic efficiency and how this can be looked at in terms of productive and allocative efficiency
➤ the relationship between competition and economic efficiency

Introduction

In section 1 the fundamental economic problem was considered. In essence, this was explained as the difficulty in our world of having limited or scarce resources with which we wish to do an infinite amount of things. In turn, this leads us to having to make economic choices.

Within other earlier sections, the basic concept of **economic efficiency** was seen to stem from this fundamental economic problem. Economic efficiency was said to exist when it could be judged that all of our scarce resources were being used in the 'best' possible way. This means that the greatest possible level of infinite wants is being met with those scarce resources. Thus economic efficiency is a key basic idea of Economics. It is something that is always judged to be desirable. It represents the best possible solution to the economic problem.

The purpose of this section is to develop this important economic concept. In particular, it will consider carefully the two different parts of economic efficiency.

The two parts of economic efficiency

Two things are required if economic efficiency can be said to exist. These are:

- *Products must be made with the least possible scarce resources.* To put it another way, goods and services must be produced at the lowest possible cost. In economics, this is referred to as **productive efficiency**. On its own, it is insufficient to ensure economic efficiency.

- *The products that are most wanted must be produced.* Those goods and services that lead to the greatest possible satisfaction of our infinite wants are those that should be made. In economics, this is called **allocative efficiency**. This is required together with productive efficiency if economic efficiency can be said to exist.

Only when both these sides of efficiency co-exist can it be judged that the best possible use is being made of our scarce resources. This, therefore, constitutes a situation of **optimum resource allocation**.

This idea of economic efficiency can be looked at from a world-wide view. World economic efficiency is achieved if we are using all of the world's resources in the best possible way. Frequently, we hear concerns that, as a global society, we are failing to do this. This point was very clearly made in section 4 where the use of protectionist policies by the US, for example, shows no signs of being curtailed. As such, we must be judged not to be achieving world economic efficiency when this happens. Typical of these concerns are the views expressed in the newspaper article about the world timber market. The suggestion is clearly that our scarce resources are not being used in an optimum way.

Self-assessment tasks

Read the article below and then tackle the exercises that follow.

Breaking the Logjam

Increasing demand for timber is a major threat to forests world-wide. Only one-fifth of the world's original forest cover is intact today. Yet United Nations data show that global wood consumption increased by 40 per cent between 1970 and 1996, and continues to grow.

Inhabitants of the US, Japan, and Western Europe consume on average about ten times as much per person as the average citizen of a developing country, even accounting for the fact that many more of the latter use wood for fuel.

There are now suggestions for consideration at the World Trade Organisation (WTO) that global trade in wood products should be further promoted. A new report by the World Resources Institute and the Centre for International Environmental Law concludes that these proposals could put yet more pressure on forests in Amazonia, the Congo Basin, south-east Asia, and the northern Boreal region. These forests are the home to most of the world's terrestrial biological diversity, and to hundreds of unique, traditional cultures.

The wealthy nations leading the charge for the timber trade – including the US, Canada, New Zealand and Indonesia – have paid scant attention to the potential negative environmental and social side effects of their actions. Perhaps this is because large, powerful forest products companies in these countries stand to benefit directly from the plan.

Rainforest River, Amazon/Peru. Manu National Park
Source: Anuke Bartschi, Still Pictures.

Source: Nigel Sizer, *Guardian*, 1 December 1999 (adapted).

1 Explain why economic efficiency is a fundamental economic concept.
2 Consider the ways in which, according to the article, there would not be economic efficiency if the world timber trade were to be allowed to expand.

Productive efficiency

It has been established that for economic efficiency to exist products must be made using the least possible resources or generating the lowest possible cost of production. This is productive efficiency.

Productive efficiency can be illustrated through considering a firm's cost curves. This is shown in figure 8.1.

Here, we can see that there are two parts to lowest cost production. First, production must take place on the lowest possible average cost curve (AC^3). Secondly, production needs to occur at the lowest point on that lowest cost curve (point x on the diagram). This second condition is known as 'technical' efficiency. The lowest point on a firm's average cost curve is, therefore, a point of technical efficiency.

Productive efficiency might further be understood through the production possibility curve which was introduced in section 1. This shows the maximum production points for combinations of any two products (for example, capital goods and consumer goods produced in an economy). Given this, it must be true that productive efficiency can only exist when an economy is producing right on the boundary of its production possibility frontier as in figure 8.2.

The problem with point X is that more products could be made with the resources available. In other words, the goods are not being produced using the least possible resources. There is productive inefficiency. At point Y, it is not possible to produce any more given the scarce resources that are available to an economy. The minimum possible resources are being used to make the products. This is thus a point of productive efficiency.

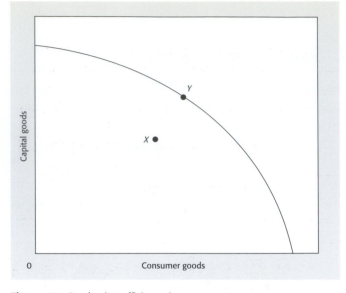

Figure 8.2 Productive efficiency in an economy

Competition can be seen to lead to productive efficiency. In general terms, this is the case as firms are constrained to produce at the lowest possible cost in a competitive market. Firms have the incentive of profit to make their products at the lowest possible cost: the lower the cost, the greater the possible profit. Alternatively, a failure to produce at the lowest possible cost in a competitive market will lead to possible bankruptcy for a firm. As rivals will produce at lowest cost, the price of the firm that has failed to minimise costs will be too high and thus there will be low demand.

More specifically, it can be seen that perfect competition leads to the necessary conditions for productive efficiency (see section 9 for details of this market structure). This can be seen in figure 8.3.

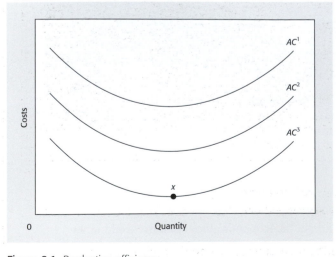

Figure 8.1 Productive efficiency

Figure 8.3 Productive efficiency and perfect competition

The point of long-run equilibrium for a perfectly competitive firm is given by price *p* and output *q*. At this point, it can be seen that the firm is producing at the lowest point on its average cost curve. This implies that there is technical efficiency. Given that the competition in this market will also constrain firms to be producing on their lowest possible average cost curve, then this point is productively efficient.

An attempt to produce at the lowest possible cost can be seen through Marks and Spencer shutting all of their shops in continental Europe (see self-assessment task).

Self-assessment tasks

Read the article 'Marks and Sparks shuts up shop in Europe' and then tackle the exercises that follow.

Marks and Sparks shuts up shop in Europe

Marks & Spencer, the beleaguered retailing giant, is to axe nearly 4,400 jobs as it pulls out of continental Europe and closes its loss-making UK mail order business.

In another desperate attempt to reverse the dramatic decline in its fortunes, M&S announced the closure of 38 unprofitable European stores yesterday and said it would put its American businesses up for sale, including Brooks Brothers, the preppy men's retailer, and the New England supermarket chain Kings. It will also franchise its Hong Kong business.

Although the latest restructuring is the most far-reaching to be unveiled by M & S, it is the sixth attempt by two successive management teams to turn round the company since its problems first emerged in late 1998.

Around 3,350 jobs will go as the company closes its European stores, including the Paris flagship on Boulevard Haussmann, which has been selling scones, crumpets and Indian ready-made meals to the French since 1975.

Another 690 jobs are to be lost in Britain as M & S closes its four-year-old clothing and home mail order business. A further 350 will disappear from its head office in Baker Street, London.

M & S estimated that the closures would boost its flagging profits by £50 million a year. City analysts expect the company to make around £450 million profit before tax and hefty exceptional charges for the year ending this month, substantially lower than the record £1.2 billion pre-tax profit announced three years ago.

Luc Vandevelde, the Belgian food retailer who was appointed as the company's chairman and chief executive in February last year, said that the 'painful changes' were necessary in order to concentrate on its troubled UK business.

Yesterday's announcement comes as UK trading continues to deteriorate sharply at what was once the country's favourite retailer, with M & S revealing that same-store sales of clothing, footwear and gifts fell by almost seven per cent for the nine weeks to March 24.

Source: PA Photos.

Source: *Daily Telegraph*, 30 March 2001 (adapted).

1 What is productive efficiency and what conditions are necessary for it to exist?

2 Why does productive efficiency exist in a perfectly competitive market and why does it not exist in the retail market described in the article?

3 How might the actions being taken by Marks and Spencer lead to it becoming more productively efficient?

Allocative efficiency

It is not enough for products to be produced at the lowest possible cost. The right products must also be produced if there is to be economic efficiency. Allocative efficiency is all to do with allocating the right amount of scarce resources to the production of the right products. It is to do with producing the combination of products that will yield the greatest possible level of satisfaction of consumer wants.

Specifically, the point of allocative efficiency can be deemed to exist when the price of a product is equal to its marginal cost of production. In this situation, the price paid by the consumer will represent the true economic cost of producing the last unit of the product. This should ensure that precisely the right amount of the product is produced. This idea can be illustrated through the following simple example:

Quantity	1 2 3 4 5 6 7
Price ($)	5 5 5 5 5 5 5
Marginal cost ($)	2 3 4 5 6 7 8

For this product, an output of one unit would not be productively efficient. Here, the cost of producing the product is less than the value put on it by the consumer (as represented by the price that the consumer is willing to pay for that product). The product should certainly be produced, but there is scope for further worthwhile production from this point. This is also true when two or three units of the product are made. On the other hand, an output of seven units of the product should not be produced. Here, the seventh unit costs $8 to produce, but is only valued at $5 by the consumer. The same problem exists with output levels of five and six. Thus, there is only one ideal output level (that is, one output level that will yield allocative efficiency) and that is an output of four units where price is equal to marginal cost.

It should be noted that, unlike productive efficiency, it is not possible to illustrate allocative efficiency on the production possibility frontier. Any point on the frontier could potentially be such a point. The exact location will depend upon consumer preferences and these are not indicated on this model.

A competitive market can lead to allocative efficiency. In such a market, firms are constrained to produce those products that consumers most desire relative to their cost of production. As with productive efficiency, there are two motivations. The desire to make the greatest possible profit will drive firms to produce such products. They will lead to the highest possible demand and hence revenue and profit. Alternatively, firms in competitive markets will be forced to produce those products most demanded by consumers as other firms will certainly do so. A failure to produce such products in this sort of market will lead to bankruptcy.

An alternative way to consider how a competitive market will achieve allocative efficiency is through the perfectly competitive diagram as shown in figure 8.3. It can be seen that the point of equilibrium in this diagram (price p and output q) is a position at which price is equal to marginal cost. This is the technical requirement to give allocative efficiency as explained above.

The suggestion is thus made that in fully (or perfectly) competitive markets there will be economic efficiency. Both productive and allocative efficiency will exist.

Self-assessment tasks

1 Explain what type of efficiency each of the following might lead towards:
   - A firm uses a new machine that costs less than its old one but produces more.
   - A company swaps production to a different product that sells at the same price but is in greater demand.
   - A car plant makes 1,000 workers redundant because their jobs can now be done by robots that cost less over a period of time than paying workers' wages.
   - Following privatisation, firms in an industry have to change what they produce in order to make a profit.

2 The use of the internet has allowed consumers to purchase products from all over the world in a way that was never previously possible. It has been seen that this has greatly increased the level of competition faced by firms in different markets as they now have to compete directly in a global market. Discuss the ways in which this development could lead to greater economic efficiency in world markets.

Summary

In this section we have recognised that:

● Efficiency is a fundamental concept in Economics relating to how well scarce resources are allocated.

● There are two parts to economic efficiency. Productive efficiency is achieved when firms produce at the lowest possible point on their lowest cost curve. Allocative efficiency is when the price of a product is equal to its marginal cost of production. Both these forms of efficiency must exist if there is to be economic efficiency.

● Competition can lead to both productive and allocative efficiency. A perfectly competitive market is the only one where this is achieved.

Key words

Definitions of Key words can be found in the Glossary.

allocative efficiency
economic efficiency

optimum resource
   allocation
productive efficiency

9 The price system and the theory of the firm

On completion of this section you should know:

➤ what is meant by diminishing marginal utility and how this can be used to derive demand curves

➤ how to analyse the income and substitution effects of a price change

➤ what is meant by the principle of diminishing returns

➤ the difference between the short run and the long run

➤ why the demand for labour is known as a derived demand

➤ how a firm's demand for labour can be derived from the marginal revenue product for labour

➤ what factors affect the supply of labour in the short and long run

➤ that in a competitive market wages are determined by the demand and supply of labour

➤ how, in theory and practice, trade unions and the government can influence wage determination

➤ what is meant by transfer earnings and economic rent in the labour market

➤ the characteristics of the long-run production function

➤ what economists mean by costs and how various cost concepts can be derived and applied

➤ how economies of scale can produce long-run cost advantages for firms, and how these may accrue within and external to a business

➤ how firms grow and why small firms survive in markets

➤ what is meant by marginal, average and total revenue and how this relates to a firm's demand curve

➤ the difference between the firm and the industry from the economist's perspective

➤ what is meant by the profit maximisation objective of firms and why in certain circumstances firms may pursue other objectives

➤ the characteristics of the market structures of perfect competition, monopoly, monopolistic competition and oligipoly

➤ how barriers to entry can affect the equilibrium position of firms in these market structures in the short and long run

➤ why the concept of a contestable market is of particular relevance in most economies at the present time

➤ how firms behave in practice, from both price and non-price standpoints

➤ what criteria are used and applied by economists to assess the efficiency of firms in different market structures

Utility and marginal utility

Economists have long been interested in the way that consumers behave. Aspects of demand theory were introduced in section 2; here we shall look behind the demand curve and explore why it really is the case that consumers buy more of a good when its price falls.

The starting point is the notion of **utility**. This idea dates back to the nineteenth century and is a term used to record the level of happiness or satisfaction that someone receives from the consumption of a good. It is assumed that this satisfaction can be measured, in the same way that the actual units consumed can be calculated. Two important measures are:

◆ total utility – the overall satisfaction that is derived from the consumption of all units of a good over a given time period;

◆ **marginal utility** – the additional utility derived from the consumption of one more unit of a particular good.

The marginal utility gained from the consumption of a product tends to fall as consumption increases. For example, if you buy an ice cream you will get a lot of satisfaction from its consumption, especially in hot weather. If you consume a second one, you will still get some satisfaction but this is likely to be less than from the first ice cream. A third ice cream will yield even less satisfaction. This aspect of consumer behaviour is referred to as the principle of **diminishing marginal utility**. As consumption increases further, there may actually come a point where marginal utility is negative, indicating dissatisfaction or disutility.

In considering the consumer's equilibrium, it is necessary to remember that Economics assumes that consumers have limited incomes, behave in a rational manner and seek to maximise their total utility. A consumer is said to be in equilibrium, assuming a given level of income, when it is not possible to switch any expenditure from, say, product A to product B to increase total utility. This is referred to as the **equi-marginal principle** and can be represented

$$\frac{MU_A}{P_A} = \frac{MU_B}{P_B} = \frac{MU_C}{P_C} \quad \cdots \quad = \frac{MU_N}{P_N}$$

where	MU	=	marginal utility
	P	=	the price
	A, B, C and N	=	individual products

It is possible to use marginal utility to derive an individual demand curve. The fundamental principle of demand is that an increase in the price of a good will lead to a reduction in its demand. Using the above principle, this can now be proved. The value of the expression $\frac{MU_A}{P_A}$ will now fall as the price of A has increased. So, the marginal utility of A per $ spent will now be *less* than on any other goods. The consumer will therefore increase total utility by spending less on good A and more on all other goods. This will in turn reduce

the value of their marginal utility. In other words, the consumer only maximises total utility by buying less of good A. The conclusion is that the demand curve for a good is downward sloping.

Self-assessment tasks

1 The table below shows the total utility gained from the consumption of lemonade in a week.

Quantity consumed (bottles)	Total utility
0	0
1	20
2	35
3	45
4	53
5	58
6	54
7	48

(a) Calculate the marginal utility.
(b) Sketch the total utility and marginal utility curves (put utility on the vertical axis, quantity on the horizontal axis).

2 If the price of lemonade increases from $1 to $2 per bottle, how might it affect consumption? Explain your answer using the data above.

Budget lines

As shown in section 2, all consumers are constrained in what they are able to buy because of their income and the prices of goods they wish to buy. These two important underpinning principles of consumer behaviour are brought together in the idea of a **budget line**. This shows numerically all the possible combinations of two products that a consumer can purchase with a given income and fixed prices.

Suppose someone has $200 to spend on two products, A and B. Assume the price of A is $20 and the price of B is $10. Table 9.1 shows the possible combinations that can be purchased. Each of the combinations would cost $200 in total. Figure 9.1(a) shows the budget line for this situation. Any point along this line will produce an outcome where consumption is maximised for this level of income.

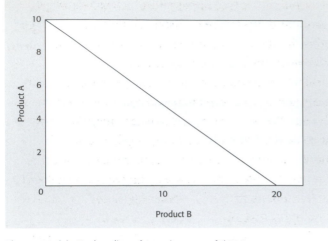

Figure 9.1(a) Budget lines for an income of $200

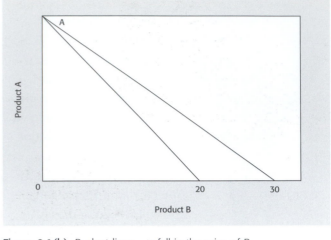

Figure 9.1(b) Budget lines – a fall in the price of B

Quantity of A ($20 each)	Quantity of B ($10 each)
10	0
9	2
8	4
7	6
6	8
5	10
4	12
3	14
2	16
1	18
0	20

Table 9.1 Combinations of A and B with a budget of $200

If there is a change in the price of one good, with income remaining unchanged, then the budget line will pivot. For example, if the price of product B falls then more of this product can be purchased at all levels of income. The budget line will shift outwards, from its pivot at point A. This is shown in figure 9.1(b). So, if the price of B falls by a third to $6.67, then 30 of good B can now be purchased with an income of $200.

As the price of B has fallen relative to that of A, which is unchanged, consumers will substitute B for A. This is known as the **substitution effect** of a price change. It is always the case that the rational consumer will substitute towards the product which has become relatively cheaper. With the fall in the price of B, the

consumer actually has more money to spend on other products, B included. The real income has therefore increased, which may mean that a consumer may now actually purchase more of product B. This is called the **income effect** of a price change.

Self-assessment tasks

1 Re-draw figure 9.1(a) to show how it would change:
   ◆ if the price of B increased, leaving the price of A unchanged,
   ◆ if the price of A decreased, leaving the price of B unchanged.
2 In your own words, describe the substitution and income effects of:
   ◆ an increase in the price of a normal good,
   ◆ a decrease in the price of an inferior good.

Principles of production and the production function
Introduction
At the beginning of section 1 we identified four factors of production. These were land, labour, capital and enterprise. In all cases, the demand for these factors of production comes from a producer, who wishes to use them to make various goods or products. The producer is normally a firm or business whose demand for factors of production is derived from the needs of its operations. Let us take the case of a clothing manufacturer to elaborate this important point.

Ellesse trainer

Reebok trainer

Nike trainer

Collection of trainers produced in the developing economies of South East Asia, not in the home country of their corporate producer

Clothing is a typical example of a business where labour and capital are in direct competition with each other. If labour costs are relatively cheap, as is the case in developing and emerging economies, then the production process is likely to take place using much more labour than capital. In most developed economies, though, the reverse is true. High-tech machines can often be used to replace labour, largely because it is more cost effective to do so. So, in this case, the same amount of output is produced using more capital and far less labour than if it were taking place in a developing economy.

Firms therefore have to choose between alternative production methods. Returning to the case of the clothing manufacturer, figure 9.2 shows three different methods of production, each of which combines different levels of labour and capital to make items of clothing. Line A shows a method whereby labour and capital are used in equal proportions; line B shows a production method which uses twice as much capital as labour and line C shows the output resulting from twice as much labour as capital being used. On these lines, points X, Y and Z show the respective amounts of labour and capital that are needed to produce 100 units of clothing. If we join these points then it gives us what is known as an isoquant, a curve which joins points which give us a particular level of output. This isoquant can of course be extended for other combinations of labour and capital not shown on figure 9.2.

As a consequence of globalisation, many clothing items are now produced in the developing economies of South East Asia, north Africa and central Europe. Designer labels, such as Nike, Reebok, Ellesse and Kappa, are no longer produced in the home country of their corporate producer. Producers in these countries need all of the factors of production in order to make their products for sale in markets which are mainly in developed economies. Their task is to combine the factors of production in an effective way to be efficient, competitive and profitable in the world market. In particular, the most important decision they have to make concerns the relative mixture of labour and capital. The task for the firm therefore is to find the least cost or most efficient combination of labour and capital for the production of a given quantity of output.

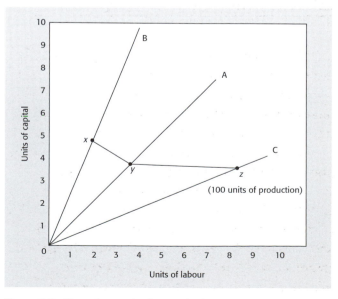

Figure 9.2 Alternative production methods

137

Clothing factory in India
Source: Ron Giling, Still Pictures.

The production function

To simplify our analysis, let us assume that the size of a clothing factory is fixed and that the only way in which the units of clothing produced can be varied is through varying the input of labour. This is referred to as the **short run**. Table 9.2 shows how the quantity of clothing produced depends on the number of workers employed. For example, if there are no workers in the factory, there is no output; with one worker, output is 100 units.

When there are two workers, the total output is 180 units and so on.

Figure 9.3 is a graph of the first two columns of data in table 9.2. It shows the relationship between the quantity of factor inputs (labour/workers) and the *total product* or quantity of output (clothing). It is called the *production function*. Column 3 of table 9.2 shows the *marginal product*, the increase in output that occurs

Number of workers	Output of clothing	Marginal product	Average product
0	0		0
		100	
1	100		100
		80	
2	180		90
		60	
3	240		80
		20	
4	280		70
		15	
5	295		59
		11	
6	306		51

Table 9.2 Production data

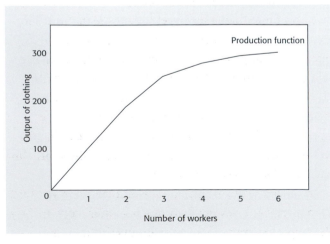

Figure 9.3 A production function

from an additional unit of input (labour in this case). The data in this column show that, when the number of workers goes from one to two, output increases by 80 units; when it goes from two to three workers, the marginal product is 60 units. As the number of workers increases the marginal product declines. This property is referred to as **diminishing returns**.

The final column of table 9.2 shows another important variable, **average product**. This is calculated by dividing the total product (output produced) by the number of workers employed. It is a simple measure of labour productivity, that is how much output is produced by each worker.

Self-assessment tasks

1 Using data from table 9.2, draw graphs which show:
   ◆ the marginal product of labour,
   ◆ the average product of labour.
2 What do you notice about the shape of these two graphs?
3 What implications do these graphs have for a clothing firm planning how much to produce?

From short run to long run

As stated above, the short run is a period of time in Economics when at least one of the factors of production is fixed. The factor that takes the longest to change is capital; the factor that tends to be easiest to change is labour as we have already seen. Students often ask the question, 'How long is the short run?'. This is not an easy question to answer, as it tends to differ for different industries. In the clothing industry it is likely to be no more than a few weeks, the time that is taken to install new capital equipment and to get this operational to produce clothing. In other industries, it will be much longer. A country building a new hydro-electric power station will, for example, take much longer to plan, install and make such a new facility operational. Ten years may well be a realistic estimate in this case. This time is still referred to as the short run since capital is fixed over this time.

In the long run, all factors of production are variable. This therefore gives the firm much greater scope to vary the respective mix of its factor inputs so that it is producing at the most efficient level. So, if capital

becomes relatively cheaper than labour or if a new production process is invented and this increases productivity, firms can reorganise the way in which they produce. Firms must therefore know the cost of the factors of production they use and see this in relation to the marginal physical output which accrues. The right combination of factors can be arrived at as their price varies. Firms should aim to be in a position where

$$\frac{\text{Marginal product}}{\text{factor A}} = \frac{\text{Marginal product}}{\text{factor B}} = \frac{\text{Marginal product}}{\text{factor C}}$$
$$\frac{\text{factor A}}{\text{Price of factor A}} = \frac{\text{factor B}}{\text{Price of factor B}} = \frac{\text{factor C}}{\text{Price of factor C}}$$

and so on for all factors of production they use. For them to be able to do this all factors of production must be variable.

If we go back to the principles introduced in figure 9.2, it is possible to derive the long-run production function for a firm by initially constructing an isoquant map. This shows the different combinations of labour and capital that can be used to produce various level of output. This is shown in figure 9.4.

Let us again assume that this is for a clothing manufacturer. Part (a) of this figure consists of a collection of isoquants for output levels 100, 200, 300, 400 and 500 units of production. From this it is possible to read off the respective combinations of labour and capital that could produce these output levels. Remember that as yet this is only looking at output from a physical standpoint.

If you look at the diagram carefully you will see that as production increases from 100 to 200, relatively less capital and labour is required per unit of output. This is referred to as *increasing returns to scale*. As production expands further, increasing amounts of capital and labour are needed to produce 100 more units and so move up to the next isoquant. In contrast, this indicates *decreasing returns to scale*.

In the long run, both labour and capital can be varied and, as stated above, the actual mix will depend upon their prices. Figure 9.4(b) shows what are known as isocosts, lines of constant relative costs for the factors of production. On this figure, therefore, each of the isocosts shown has an identical slope. In deciding how to produce, the firm will be looking for the most economically efficient or least cost process. This can be obtained by bringing together the isoquants and isocosts, so linking the physical and economic sides of

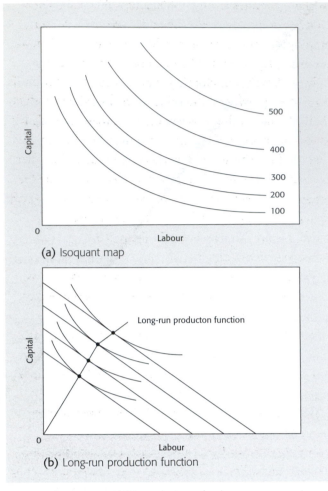

(a) Isoquant map

(b) Long-run production function

Figure 9.4 Isoquants and isocosts

The labour market
Introduction

When you leave school or college (hopefully with a CIE Advanced Level in Economics), the wage or salary you get paid will be determined largely by what type of job you take. If you get a post as a clerk, you are likely to get more pay than if you are a street cleaner. Equally, if you go on to become a teacher, you will get paid more than a clerk. In turn, the manager of a multinational company will get paid more than a teacher. So, why is it that some workers get paid more than others? And why is it that some people with exceptional talent, for example Brian Lara, Tiger Woods or Michael Jackson, are highly paid. The answer to these questions, like many such questions in Economics, is that it all depends on supply and demand. To understand why some people get paid more than others, economists have looked at the labour market and sought to put forward various principles based on the characteristics of this market.

Brian Lara
Source: Popperfoto Reuters.

the production process. The point where the isocost is tangential to an isoquant represents the best combination of factors for the firm to employ. Hence, on figure 9.4(b), the expansion path or long-run production function of the firm can be shown by joining together all of the various tangential points.

It is important to recognise that the above analysis is highly theoretical. In practice:

◆ It is often very difficult for firms to determine their isoquants – they often do not have the data or the experience to be able to derive them.

◆ It is also assumed that in the long run it is quite possible to switch factors of production. This may not always be as easy as the theory might indicate.

◆ Some employers may be reluctant to switch labour and capital – they may feel that they have a social obligation to their workforce and will therefore not alter their production plans with a change in relative factor prices.

Demand for labour

Many of the principles introduced in section 2 can be applied to the labour market. There is though one fundamentally different point, namely the demand for labour is a **derived demand**. By this, we mean that the firm's demand for labour is due to its decision to produce certain goods or services. Labour is therefore demanded not for its own sake but because it is essential for the production of goods or services. Returning to our earlier examples, clerks are employed by a firm because they are necessary for a firm to carry out its business. The streets need cleaning, therefore street cleaners are needed. Children need education so teachers are required. This may seem obvious – it does though underpin the whole basis of labour economics. Brian Lara and Michael Jackson have exceptional talents – the demand for their services is very high indeed and commands a high return.

The analysis that follows is based upon two important assumptions:

◆ The firm which wishes to hire labour is operating in a competitive market; there are in particular many buyers and sellers of labour, and no single firm or worker can affect the wage which is paid.

◆ The firm is a profit-maximiser; its demand and supply of labour are based on it maximising the difference between total revenue and total costs.

Do not worry too much about these assumptions at this stage as their importance will become much clearer during the rest of this section.

The marginal revenue product of labour

So far in our analysis of the demand for labour we have only been concerned with physical inputs and outputs. This is somewhat unrealistic because, in reality, the profit-maximising firm is concerned with how much this output is worth to the firm. We must therefore take into account the cost of employing labour – the wage rate. Let us assume that this is $600 per month and, using data from table 9.2, let us assume that a unit of clothing sells for $10.

When the firm hires the first worker, this worker generates $1,000 of revenue for the firm; this in turn represents $400 of profit. The amount of revenue generated by an additional worker is referred to as the marginal revenue product of labour. Adding a further

worker generates another $800 and $200 profit. There comes a point when, after the third worker has been employed, a further worker adds more to costs than to revenue (it still costs $600 to employ the worker but only $400 worth of clothing is produced). So, above this level of employment, the value of the marginal product that is being produced is less than the wage. This clearly makes no sense to the firm. It can therefore be deduced that the firm should hire workers up to the point where the value of the marginal product of labour equals the wage that is being paid. *The demand curve for labour can therefore be represented by the value of the marginal product curve.* This is shown in figure 9.5.

So, in general terms:

◆ a firm should continue to hire labour as long as the additional worker adds more to revenue than he or she adds to the firm's costs;

◆ the market wage is determined by the marginal revenue product of labour;

◆ the marginal revenue product curve for labour is the firm's demand curve for labour;

◆ if the wage rate rises or falls then fewer or more workers will be employed.

It follows from this analysis that the wages paid to workers are a direct reflection of their marginal revenue product. So, a street cleaner has a lower marginal revenue product than a clerk, who in turn has a lower marginal revenue product than a teacher and so on. It also follows that it is actually possible to measure marginal revenue productivity. This is a very big assumption to make. In a manufacturing firm it may be possible to do this, but in many occupations this is not

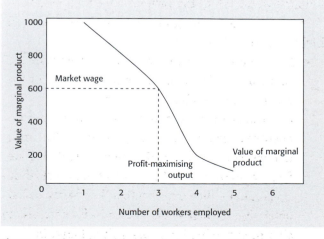

Figure 9.5 The value of the marginal product of labour

Final assembly area – Nissan Sunderland, UK
Source: Nissan.

possible. How, for example, can we measure the marginal revenue of a teacher? The answer is 'with great difficulty'. We therefore need to look at the other side of the labour market, that involving the supply of labour, to give a proper explanation of how wages are actually determined. This will now be considered.

Supply of labour

The labour supply or supply of labour refers to the total number of hours that labour is able and willing to supply at a particular wage rate. In general terms the principles of supply introduced in section 2 apply here. With the supply of labour though it is important to remember that we are dealing with people and their willingness to participate (or otherwise) in the labour market depending upon the rate or price that they are offered for their services. It is useful therefore to consider labour supply at three levels: that of the individual worker, that of a firm or industry and that of the economy as a whole. Different factors affect supply depending upon which of these levels we are dealing with. Let us look briefly at each in turn.

The individual's labour supply

As with any supply, price (or wage in this case) has an important bearing on the decision of any individual worker to enter the labour market. If the wage is too low for example, someone may determine that it is not worth the effort of going to work and decide to stay at home. Not many people are in this position – most of us need to work to live. Economic theory assumes that there is a positive relationship between labour supply and the wage rate. So, as the wage rate increases, more people are willing to offer their services to employers. This is shown diagramatically by the labour supply curve, which is upward sloping in the main (see figure 9.6). Beyond a certain point, though, individuals will take the view that they prefer leisure to work. This point is indicated on figure 9.6 by the backward-sloping curve from point X. Before this point, an individual worker is more willing to supply his labour as the wage rate increases. It must be stressed that this point depends on the individual's attitude to work and leisure – just where point X is on any individual's supply curve will vary.

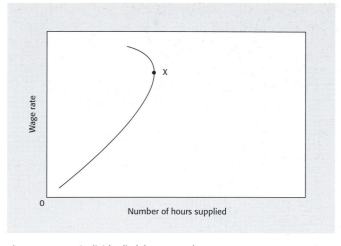

Figure 9.6 An individual's labour supply curve

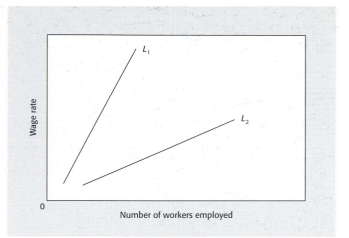

Figure 9.7 The supply curve of labour to a firm or industry

A further factor that can affect an individual's supply of labour is the income tax rate. In all countries this tends to be progressive. Low-wage workers pay little or no tax. As wages rise, more of the increase is paid in tax to the government. In the UK, for example, the standard rate of income tax in 2001 was 22 per cent, with a maximum rate of 40 per cent for high-income earners. In many other countries this higher rate is above 40 per cent. The downside could be that a high tax rate stifles the incentive to work. Governments must therefore be very careful to not do this as it will adversely affect economic prospects if key workers are not encouraged to work because of the high tax rates.

Labour supply to a firm or industry

This supply curve consists of the sum of the individual supply curves of all workers employed in a firm or industry. It is usually upward sloping throughout (see figure 9.7). As with the individual, the number of workers wanting to supply their labour increases with the wage rate that is offered. The slope of this supply curve is measured by the elasticity of supply of labour – the extent to which labour supply responds to a change in the wage rate. Figure 9.7 shows two different supply curves, one inelastic (L_1) and the other elastic with respect to the wages being paid.

There are various reasons for this difference. An obvious one is the skills required to carry out a particular occupation. In general, the more skills required, the more inelastic will be the supply of labour. This also applies to the amount of education and training that are required to carry out a particular job.

Anyone who teaches has to spend at least four years acquiring the necessary qualifications. Supply to such an occupation will be more inelastic than to, say, road sweeping, where no skills and little or no education and training are needed.

The supply curve L_2 in figure 9.7 is therefore likely to be that for an industry where wages are low and where there is a plentiful supply of labour with no particular skills or training.

In a competitive labour market, the wage rates offered in all other industries or occupations will be important in determining the supply of labour to a particular industry. In developing economies, an obvious example could be the difference in wages in agriculture compared with wages in emerging manufacturing industries or food-processing industries which usually pay more to their workers.

The long-run supply of labour

This is of particular significance to the economy as a whole. There are important contrasts here between developed and developing economies, involving wider economic factors including:

◆ *The age structure of the population.* In many developed economies, the total population is relatively stable. This is more or less true of the UK and France; in the case of Italy, the population is actually declining quite markedly. With life expectancy increasing, there are relatively fewer people of working age and this affects the long-run supply of labour. In such cases, therefore, the long-run supply curve of labour is shifting to the left. In

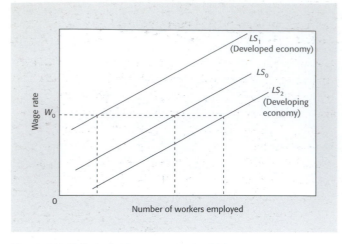

Figure 9.8 Shifts in the long-run supply of labour

contrast, in most developing economies, there is an increase in the overall supply of labour as there are an increasing number of people joining the labour market. Here, the long-run supply curve for labour shifts to the right, indicating that more workers are willing to supply their labour at a given wage rate. These contrasting situations are shown in figure 9.8.

♦ *The labour participation rate.* This is the term used to determine the proportion of the population of working age actually in employment. In many developed economies, workers often choose to leave the labour market, by taking 'early retirement', before the normal age for retirement, so reducing the labour participation rate. At the lower end of the age range, with more students electing for higher education, the labour participation rate is also falling slightly. The combined effect of these has been for a slight reduction in the labour participation rate, so shifting the long-run labour supply curve to the left.

♦ *The tax and benefits levels.* As was shown in figure 9.6 for the individual, there comes a point where the work–leisure trade-off affects labour supply. This also affects the supply of labour for the economy as a whole, particularly in developed economies. Governments therefore have to be very careful in their taxation and social security policies to ensure that the long-run supply of labour is not adversely affected through a reduction in the willingness of people to work. In the UK, as previously stated, the top rate of income tax is now

40 per cent – 15 years ago it was much more progressive, with marginal tax rates as high as 80 per cent of the increase in income for the highest paid. In such circumstances, there is clearly a huge disincentive for someone to stay in the labour market. The level of unemployment and social security payments can also affect the long-run supply of labour in a similar way. Through their supply-side policies therefore governments seek to provide incentives for certain types of labour to remain active in the labour market (see section 13).

♦ *Immigration and emigration.* These too affect the long-run supply of labour in an economy. Where there are labour shortages, as was the case in the UK during the late 1950s and early 1960s, immigration from Commonwealth countries, often to relatively low pay industries and the public services, increased the supply of labour. Emigration from these countries in turn relieved pressures in their labour markets. At the present time, the UK faces labour shortages in nursing, teaching and 'high-tech' industries. Selective immigration from many developing economies is being used to reduce such shortages (see case study opposite).

Wage determination under free market forces

So far, we have established two important features of the workings of the labour market. These are:
♦ the wage paid to labour equals the value of the marginal product of labour;
♦ the willingness of labour to supply their services to the labour market is dependent upon the wage rate that is being offered.

In some respects, it might seem surprising that the wage can do both of these things at the same time. There is no surprise – it is all tied up with how wages are actually determined in a competitive labour market.

The price of labour, the wage, is no different to any other price in so far as it depends on demand and supply. So, as we ascertained in section 2, the wage and quantity of labour adjust to balance demand and supply. This is shown in figure 9.9. As the demand curve reflects the value of the marginal product of labour, in equilibrium, workers receive the value of their

Three Russians teach the three R's

The UK has a serious shortage of teachers, particularly in London. Controversially, Gloucester Primary School in Peckham advertised vacancies in newspapers in St. Petersburg and today, three female Russian teachers have arrived in London to take up their posts.

The Government keeps no record of the number of foreign teachers currently in London – most on what are officially working holidays – but estimates put the number as high as 10,000.

The scale of the influx, as our schools struggle to cope with the mounting recruitment crisis, is indicated by the rise in the far smaller number granted work permits to remain permanently in Britain. That has doubled in 12 months.

In the year to last April, the then Department for Education and Employment processed 734 work permits for teachers arriving in Britain seeking work.

That accelerated later in the year, with 830 overseas staff receiving work permits between April and the end of October.

The flow is likely to increase, following the Government's decision this year to expedite applications for work permits from foreign teachers, giving them high priority.

Overseas recruitment began in earnest in the late Eighties, as cutbacks in teacher training colleges began to have an impact on our schools. It has accelerated in recent years as economic recovery has tightened the domestic labour market and many domestic graduates opted for other careers. The cost of living in London – particularly spiralling house prices – has increased the demand for overseas teachers.

The first to arrive in any numbers were from Australia and New Zealand. More recently, hundreds have come from South Africa and Canada.

London education authorities, including Newham and Croydon, have joined the recruitment drive.

In April, the Government doubled the time limit that foreign teachers on holiday visas could work in British schools from two to four years, and removed a rule preventing them working in the same school for more than four months at a time.

Overseas teachers brought to Britain by recruitment agencies earn slightly more than £100 a day working in London.

Those aiming to stay longer can convert their own qualifications to UK Qualified Teacher Status within a year, through on-the-job training which attracts a salary of more than £12,000. Pay for qualified teachers in London starts at £20,000.

Recruitment agencies are now targeting India, China and Jamaica.

Source: *Evening Standard*, 5 July 2001.

contribution to the production of goods and services. Each firm therefore purchases labour until the value of the marginal product equals the wage. So, the wage paid in the market must equal the value of the marginal product of labour once it has brought demand and supply into equilibrium. The market therefore *clears* at the equilibrium wage.

Like any market though the labour market is dynamic – any change in the demand or the supply of labour will change the equilibrium wage. The value of the marginal product of labour will also change by the same amount, as, by definition, it must always equal the wage rate.

Let us now analyse how a change in the demand for labour and a change in the supply of labour affect the market equilibrium.

Returning to the earlier example of clothing, an increase in the income of consumers in developed economies will shift the demand curve for clothing to the right, indicating that more will be demanded at any price. In turn, this affects the demand for labour producing the clothing – this is shown in figure 9.10 by a shift to the right of the labour demand curve. The

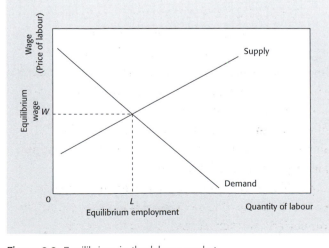

Figure 9.9 Equilibrium in the labour market

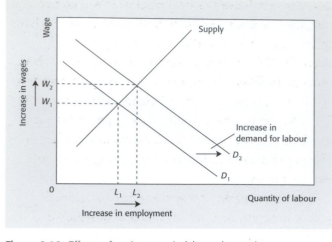

Figure 9.10 Effects of an increase in labour demand

outcome is that the equilibrium wage rises from W_1 to W_2, and employment increases from L_1 to L_2. As before, the change in the wage rate reflects a change in the value of the marginal product of labour.

A change in the labour supply will also affect the market equilibrium. Suppose that there is an increase in immigration which increases the number of workers who are able to produce clothing. When this happens, the labour supply curve shifts to the right. This surplus labour has a downward effect on wages, making it more profitable for firms producing clothing to hire more labour. As the number of workers increases, then so their marginal product falls, as does the value of their marginal product. The outcome in this case is that wages are reduced for all workers, although the level of employment rises. This is shown in figure 9.11.

The role of trade unions and government in wage determination

So far in our analysis of how wages are determined we have assumed that the respective forces of demand and supply operate freely with no intervention. In many respects this is an unreal assumption as in many labour markets, the demand and supply of labour are affected by the actions of trade unions and the government. Such interventions produce what are sometimes referred to as **imperfections in the labour market**.

Trade unions are organisations that seek to represent labour in their place of work. They were set up and continue to exist because individually, labour has very little power to influence conditions of employment, including wages. Through **collective bargaining** with employers, they act on behalf of their members to:

◆ increase the wages of their members,
◆ improve working conditions,
◆ maintain pay differentials between skilled and unskilled workers,
◆ fight job losses,
◆ provide a safe working environment,
◆ secure additional working benefits,
◆ prevent unfair dismissals.

Traditionally, trade unions have been strong in manufacturing and less important in the service sector. As the structure of the UK economy has changed, so total membership has fallen to just 7m workers in 2000, less than one in three of the working population. Many of these trade union members are employed in the public sector. Consequently the power of the trade union movement is not as strong as it was when membership was over 10m in 1985.

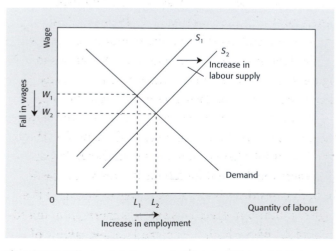

Figure 9.11 Effects of an increase in labour supply

Economic analysis suggests that, in a competitive labour market, a powerful trade union is able to secure wages for its members above the equilibrium wage rate explained in figure 9.9. The basis for this claim is shown in figure 9.12. At the equilibrium wage, the quantity of labour employed is L. If a strong trade union can force up wages to say W_u, which is above the equilibrium, the number of workers who are offered jobs by employers falls to L_u. At this wage though the number of people who would *like* to work is higher. This is shown by L_c. Consequently there is a shortfall between those who actually want to work and those who can actually work, due to the influence of the trade union. This is shown on figure 9.12 as the difference between L_c and L_u.

Empirically, it is really quite difficult to prove whether or not this theory actually applies in labour markets. A much quoted example is that of actors and actresses in the UK and USA where there are very strong unions which restrict the numbers able to work in films, television and theatres. The wages of their members are supposedly supported in this way. Other examples are likely to be in labour markets where a trade union has a monopoly over workers with a particular type of skill. Increasingly though the closed-shop policies of trade unions such as the above have been made illegal, so restricting their powers to act in this way. The case of the print unions in the UK was another typical example. However, new technology has removed their power to secure exceptionally high wages for their workers.

With ever-increasing globalisation, trade unions who try to behave in this way are playing a dangerous game with employers. The fear is that because of high labour costs and restrictive practices employers will go out of business or transfer production to countries which have lower wage levels. This threat has been particularly severe for UK car manufacturers – production has been switched to other EU countries, such as Spain, and also to non-EU countries, such as Poland, Hungary and the Czech Republic, where labour costs can be as little as one-fifth of those in the UK. Consequently, trade unions have very little real influence over the wages paid to their members.

The labour market has seen explicit government intervention through the introduction of national minimum wages. In the UK, after considerable deliberation, the government's Low Pay Commission recommended a national minimum wage of £3.60 per hour from early 1999 for all workers above the age of 21. The main aim of a minimum wage such as this is to reduce poverty and the exploitation of workers who have little or no bargaining power with their employers. In the UK, many women employed in shops, small businesses and low-skill jobs, such as home working and cleaning, were being paid very low wages and, in the eyes of the government, were being exploited. The introduction of the minimum wage was of particular significance for them.

Whether there should be a minimum wage is controversial. Some of the aims have been given above. Additionally, it was argued that the amount of state benefits being paid to low-income families would be reduced with the introduction of a minimum wage. There might also be a small increase in tax revenue. Opponents were not convinced by these arguments, believing that jobs would be lost and that other low-pay workers would seek an increase to maintain their differential with the lowest paid. Cost-push inflation could well result, so affecting the economy as a whole.

The economics of a minimum wage are shown in figure 9.13. The effect on an industry is particularly dependent upon the elasticities of demand and supply for labour in that industry. Part (a) of this figure shows the effects where there is an inelastic demand for labour. The loss of jobs here is much less than shown in part (b) where the demand for labour is more wage elastic. In both cases there is an excess supply of labour at the higher minimum wage. This excess is more pronounced in part (b) where both the demand for and supply of labour are relatively elastic. It can also be seen that the

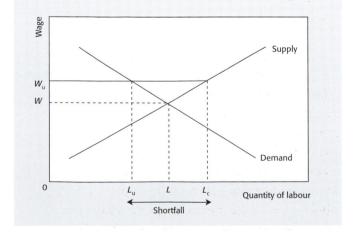

Figure 9.12 The effect of a strong trade union in a competitive labour market

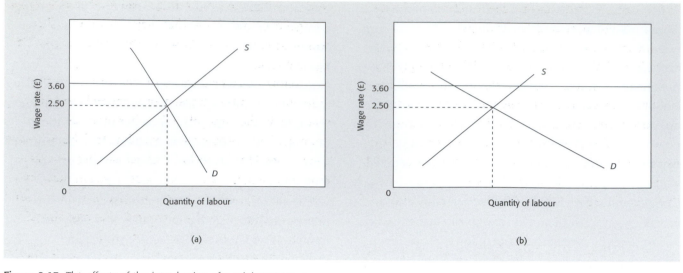

Figure 9.13 The effects of the introduction of a minimum wage

higher the minimum wage is set above the competitive equilibrium (£2.50 in the case of figure 9.13), the greater will be the excess supply of labour willing to work at the national minimum wage.

Monopsony in the labour market

A **monopsony** occurs in the labour market when there is a single or dominant buyer of labour. In such a situation this monopoly buyer is able to determine the price which is paid for the services of the workers that are employed. Unlike other examples we have looked at, in this situation we are now dealing with an imperfect rather than competitive market.

Figure 9.14 shows how the monopsonist can affect the market equilibrium. The monopsonist will hire workers by equating the marginal cost paid to employ a worker with the marginal revenue product gained from this employment. This is the profit-maximising position. The

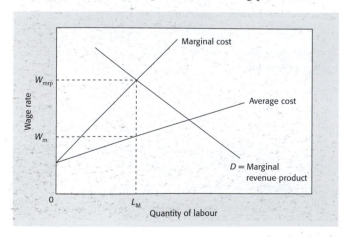

Figure 9.14 A monopsony buyer of labour

wage that the monopsonist pays to hire labour is W_m. This is actually below the wage that should be paid if he was paying the full value of their marginal revenue product, that is W_{mrp}. The level of employment is L_m.

In this situation the power of the employer in the labour market is of over-riding importance and the employer can set a low wage because of this buying power. Monopsonists often exist in local labour market situations, for example where there is just one major employer in a town or where workers may be employed in an extractive industry located well away from where they may normally live. In this way the employer dominates the labour market, setting down wages and all other conditions of employment.

Transfer earnings and economic rent in the labour market

In our introduction to the labour market we posed the question:

Why is it that some people with exceptional talent, for example Brian Lara, Tiger Woods or Michael Jackson, are highly paid?

The answer to this question can in part be given in the same way as to that as to why a teacher is paid more than a street cleaner – supply and demand. To fully answer why these earnings differences occur economists find it useful to split earnings down into two elements. These are:

- **transfer earnings** – this is the minimum payment necessary to keep labour in its present use;

◆ **economic rent** – any payment to labour which is over and above transfer earnings.

Both are shown on figure 9.15(a). Transfer earnings are indicated by the area under the labour supply curve. As we have seen this is upward sloping. Although the equilibrium wage is *W*, at wage rates below this, there are workers who are willing to offer their services to employers. In fact, at any wage rate from zero upwards, workers will join the labour market, until at wage *W*, *L* labour supply is available. In all cases up to *W*, the wage that a worker receives is their best alternative. For those

workers willing to work for less than *W*, then any wages they get over and above what they will accept is their economic rent. This is shown by the triangular area on figure 9.15(a).

It follows, therefore, that different workers receive different amounts of transfer earnings and economic rent even in the same job. Take a bus driver as an example. Some people are very willing to drive buses for a low wage. These have low transfer earnings and large economic rent. Others though will be just induced by the equilibrium wage paid to bus drivers. In such cases they have little or no economic rent, the wage almost entirely consisting of transfer payments.

The case of superstars such as Brian Lara, Tiger Woods and Michael Jackson can be explained using figure 9.15(b). Such people have a scarce and, in some respects, unique talent. Their labour supply curve is completely inelastic and their earnings consist entirely of economic rent. In contrast, workers who have a completely elastic supply, such as many unskilled workers and others in menial jobs, have no economic rent at all; their earnings consist entirely of transfer earnings. Employers can hire an infinite supply of labour at the market wage, *W*. This situation is shown in part (c) of figure 9.15.

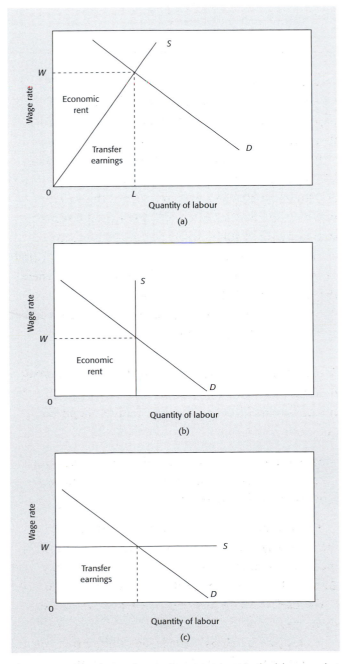

Michael Jackson
Source: Popperfoto Reuters.

Figure 9.15 Transfer earnings and economic rent in the labour market

Other labour market imperfections

The basis of a competitive labour market is that workers are free to move in relation to demand. So, if there are vacancies in one geographical area or in one occupation, unemployed labour will be mobile and fill these vacancies. The mobility of labour is shown in figure 9.16, where in theory, labour will migrate to the South from the North in order to meet the former's demand for labour.

The reality of the labour market is that this seemingly simple operation does not occur as economic theory might expect. In reality, much labour is immobile and not able to flow geographically or occupationally for the following reasons:

- *Geographical* **immobility of labour**. Many people are reluctant to move away from friends and relatives and their local area even when unemployed. The cost of moving, in financial and personal terms, may also be prohibitive. In the UK for example, the cost of housing in areas with job vacancies usually prohibits workers from moving from the lower-cost areas where they live. A lack of information also tends to restrict geographical mobility.

- *Occupational immobility of labour*. This refers to a situation where labour is restricted in the type of job that can be taken up. For example, a street cleaner cannot fill a vacancy for a teacher; a teacher though is likely to be able to clean streets. This issue becomes much more difficult in specialist occupations where extensive training is needed to complete a particular job. A good example is that of dentists, who have to study for a minimum of five years in order to be able to practise. An unemployed worker could clearly not take on such a position.

Another particular issue in labour markets is that of **wage differentials**, namely the differences in wage rates for different groups of workers. The following differentials can be recognised:

- *Between different occupations*. Non-manual jobs tend to pay more than manual posts, due to the high levels of skill that are required. The greater the skill the higher the marginal revenue productivity of labour.

- *Between different industries*. Industries with a strong trade union, as shown earlier, are likely to pay more than those with a weak trade union. Capital-intensive industries usually pay more than labour-intensive industries as worker productivity is likely to be higher. Industries where there are risks, such as the chemical industry, are likely to pay higher wages than many other types of manufacturing.

- *Between males and females*. In all countries the average pay for women is below that for men. In part this is due to many women working part time and not full time, but it is also due to many more women being employed in occupations, such as nursing and secretarial work, where pay levels are often very low.

- *Between regions in the same country*. This is certainly true in the UK where the average pay of workers in peripheral regions, such as Scotland and the north of England, is less than in one of the main cities, such as London or Bristol.

Self-assessment task

Think about the labour market in your country:

(a) What information might you obtain to determine whether labour is mobile, both geographically and occupationally?

(b) What policies does your government use to improve labour mobility?

(c) Explain the main wage differentials that apply. What information might you obtain in order to provide evidence for these differentials?

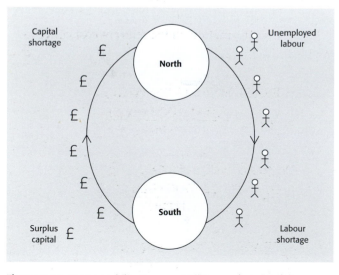

Figure 9.16 Factor mobility in a competitive market

Theory of the firm

The firm's costs of production

The remainder of this section will concentrate on the firm. Although we have already referred to the firm we have not as yet defined it. Essentially a firm is used by economists as a unit of decision making which has particular objectives such as **profit maximisation**, the avoidance of risk-taking and achieving its own long-term growth. At its lowest level the firm may be a sole trader with a small factory or a corner shop. The term is also used for the national or multinational corporation with many plants and business establishments. In economic theory all firms are headed by an entrepreneur (see section 1).

An entrepreneur must consider all the costs of the factors of production involved in the final output. These are the private costs directly incurred by the owners. Production may create costs for other people but these are not necessarily taken into account by the firm (see section 3). The firm is simply the economic organisation that transforms factor inputs into goods and services for the market.

An accountant's view of a firm's costs is that they are incurred when the firm makes a recognised expenditure. They are production expenses paid out at a particular time and price. **Profits** are what are left when the expenses are deducted from the firm's income or sales revenue.

The economist's view of costs is wider than this. The accounting view does not fully recognise the private cost of economic activity. As well as money paid out to factors, there must be an allowance for anything owned by the entrepreneur and used in the production process. This factor cost must be imputed or estimated and included with the other costs. In addition, the concept of opportunity cost is relevant. As seen in section 1, opportunity cost involves the sacrifice of the closest alternative and is the value of what has been given up. The entrepreneur may have capital that could have been used at no risk elsewhere and would have earned an income. There will be a minimum level of profit that the entrepreneur will expect, reflecting what his capital and labour would have earned elsewhere. This is the concept of **normal profit**. Economists regard this element of the entrepreneur's reward as a cost of production, because without it there would be nothing produced by the firm. Profit, to an economist, is:

Total revenue (unit price multiplied by number of units sold) minus total cost (including normal profit).

If this is positive then it is **abnormal profit**. It is the prospect of making abnormal profit which motivates the entrepreneur to take the business risks in supplying goods and services to the market. In order to understand cost structures in business, economists split them into different categories and use specific cost concepts.

Short-run costs

Fixed costs These are the costs that are completely independent of output. Total fixed cost data when drawn on a graph would appear as a horizontal straight line. At zero output, any costs that a firm has must be fixed. Some firms operate in a situation where the fixed cost represents a large proportion of the total. In this case it would be wise to produce a large output in order to reduce unit costs.

Variable costs These include all the costs that are directly related to the level of output, the usual ones being labour and raw material or component costs. Sometimes a cost has elements of both, for example, a firm's electricity bill may consist of the heating and lighting cost of the premises and the power to operate production machinery. Electricity could therefore be considered to be a semi-fixed and semi-variable cost:

TOTAL COST (TC) EQUALS FIXED COST (FC) PLUS VARIABLE COST (VC).

From this information all the relevant cost concepts can be derived.

$$\text{AVERAGE FIXED COST (AFC)} = \frac{\text{TOTAL FIXED COST}}{\text{OUTPUT}}$$

$$\text{AVERAGE VARIABLE COST (AVC)} = \frac{\text{TOTAL VARIABLE COST}}{\text{OUTPUT}}$$

$$\text{AVERAGE TOTAL COST (ATC)} = \frac{\text{TOTAL COST}}{\text{OUTPUT}}$$

Marginal cost is the addition to the total cost when making one extra unit and is therefore a variable cost.

The most important cost curve for the firm will be the ATC, showing the cost per unit of any chosen output. For most firms the decision to increase output will raise the total cost, that is the marginal cost will be positive as extra inputs are used. Firms will only be keen to do this when the expected sales revenue will outweigh the extra cost. Rising marginal cost is also a reflection of the principle of diminishing returns (see above). As more of the variable factors are added to the fixed ones, the contribution of each extra worker to the total output will begin to fall. These diminishing marginal returns cause the marginal and average variable cost to rise, as shown on figure 9.17.

The shape of the short-run ATC is the result of the interaction between the average fixed cost and the average variable cost. AFC + AVC = ATC. As the firm's output rises the average fixed cost will fall because the total fixed cost is being spread over an increasing number of units. However, at the same time, average variable cost will be rising because of diminishing returns to the variable factor. Eventually this will outweigh the effect of falling AFC, causing ATC to rise. This gives the classic 'U' shape to the ATC. On a graph of cost data, the MC will always cross AVC and ATC at their lowest point. In this situation, the most efficient output for the firm will be where the unit cost is lowest. This is known as the optimum output. It is where the firm is productively efficient in the short run, but the most efficient output is not necessarily the most profitable (see section 8 for details). For a firm wishing

to maximise its profits, its chosen output will depend on the relationship between its revenue and its costs.

Costs in the short and the long run As we have already stated, the short run for the firm is a period of time when it cannot alter its fixed inputs. The level of production can only be changed by altering the variable inputs, such as labour. The time taken to alter fixed factors differs, depending on how easy it is to get new capital installed.

In the **long run**, the firm can alter *all* of its inputs, using greater quantities of land, capital and labour, operating on a bigger scale. All the factors are now variable.

In the very long run, technological change can alter the way the entire production process is organised, even the nature of the products themselves. In the case of airlines, the introduction of the jumbo jet suddenly raised the passenger miles per unit of inputs by 50 per cent. In a society with rapid technological progress this will be shrinking the time period between the short run and the long run and suddenly shifting the firm's product curves up and its cost curves down. There are now examples in consumer electronics where whole processes and products have become obsolete in a matter of months as a result of more powerful microchips increasing the volume and speed of the flow of information.

Costs in the long run It is possible that a firm can find a way of lowering its cost structure over time. One way might be by increasing the amount of capital used relative to labour in the production process, with a consequent increase in factor productivity.

The long-run average cost curve shows the least cost combination of producing any particular quantity. Moving from its short-run equilibrium shown in figure 9.18(a), part (b) of this figure shows a firm experiencing falling ATC over time. This would enable it to lower the price without sacrificing profit. Products, such as electronic watches, personal computers and CD players, are examples where prices have fallen through competition and changing technology.

Economies of scale Where an expansion of output leads to a reduction in the unit costs, the benefits are referred to as **economies of scale**. **Internal economies of scale** are the benefits that accrue to a firm as a result

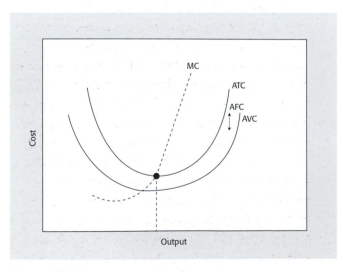

Figure 9.17 Short-run cost relationships

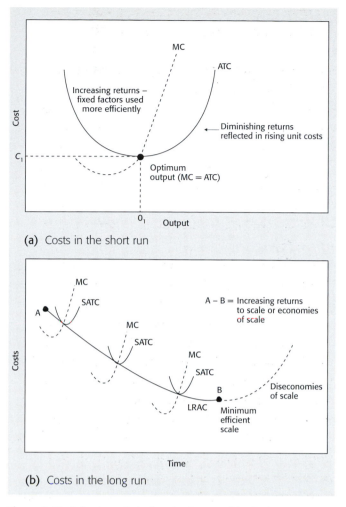

(a) Costs in the short run

(b) Costs in the long run

Figure 9.18 A firm's costs in the short run and in the long run

If one takes the production of a box structure, and doubles the scale, its production costs will double. If it is being used to carry something, then the operating costs may not increase in proportion. The capacity of the box will have increased eightfold, generating a much larger potential revenue. The trick is to make sure that the extra capacity is fully used.

Making full use of capacity is also important on a production line. Car production is the result of various assembly lines. The number of finished vehicles per hour is limited by the pace of the slowest sub-process. Firms producing on a large scale can increase the number of slow-moving lines to keep pace with the fastest, so that no resources are standing idle and the flow of finished products is higher. One of the problems of the British motor industry was its small-scale output limited by low sales. UK firms produced at higher unit cost than competitors and this is one of the motives behind take-overs and mergers over the years, to get a bigger market share and benefit from economies of scale.

- **Marketing economies** This is where large firms can achieve savings in unit costs from advertising or packaging. The usual one is the benefit of lower prices by buying in bulk from suppliers. Large supermarket chains are very good examples of firms that gain in this way.

- **Financial economies** Large firms will find both the access to borrowed funds easier, and the costs lower, than smaller firms will. This is because the perceived risk of lending to large-scale operators is lower.

- **Managerial economies** Firms producing on a large scale may be able to reorganise their structure in order to get a more efficient management of resources. They may also attract the best management talent through higher salaries. Overall this will lead to falling long-run costs of managing the business.

- **Risk-bearing economies** These might explain why, as firms get larger, they become more diversified. It is a way of spreading business risks. A diversified conglomerate can cover any losses in one activity with the profits from another, an option not open to smaller firms. Risks can be further reduced, by co-operating with rivals on large capital projects.

The last example above may be an illustration of an **external economy of scale** since firms can benefit from

of its own decision to produce a larger output. They occur because the firm's output is rising proportionally faster than the inputs, hence the firm is getting increasing returns to scale. If the increase in output is proportional to the increase in inputs, the firm will get constant returns to scale and the LRAC will be horizontal. If the output is less than proportional, the firm will see diminishing returns to scale or **diseconomies of scale**.

The key advantage a firm obtaining economies of scale gains is a reduction in the cost per unit produced, i.e. a fall in the ATC. The nature of the possible economies depends on the nature of the economic activity. Some of the following may apply in a particular industry.

- **Technical economies** This refers to the advantages gained directly in the production process. Some production techniques only become viable beyond a certain level of output. Economies of increased dimension occur in a number of business applications.

savings in research and development costs. This particular economy of scale is a benefit received by all the firms in the industry as a direct consequence of the growth of the industry and may be one reason for the trend towards the concentration of rival firms in the same geographical area. The advantages may include the availability of a pool of skilled labour or a convenient supply of components from specialist producers who have grown up to make the items for all the firms. They may all benefit from greater access to knowledge and research and the better transport infrastructure that will result from general expansion in the economic activities.

Firms where the fixed costs are a very high proportion of total cost have an incentive to increase their output as much as possible, because the marginal cost will be very low. ATC will continue to fall and profits will rise. These low costs may act as a barrier to the entry of competitors and this would be an example of a **natural monopoly** where competing firms are less efficient than the huge firm with a dominant market share.

It must be recognised that there are limits to economies of scale. A firm can expand its output too much with the result that unit costs start to rise. This may be the beginning of what are known as diseconomies of scale. The most likely source of these lies in the problems of co-ordinating large organisations and the effect size has on morale and motivation. In the same way as internal diseconomies of scale are possible, the excessive concentration of economic activities in a narrow geographical location can also have disadvantages. External diseconomies may exhibit themselves in the form of:

- traffic congestion which increases distribution costs,
- land shortages and therefore rising fixed costs,
- shortages of skilled labour and therefore rising variable costs.

A firm that is producing at its optimum output in the short run and the lowest unit cost in the long run (sometimes called the minimum efficient scale), has maximised its efficiency. Industries where the minimum efficient scale is low will have a big population of firms. Where it is high, competition will tend to be between a few large players.

The advantages of size in the form of economies of scale suggest that there will be a tendency for firms to get bigger over time. Why then do some markets feature a large number of small firms?

Self-assessment tasks

1 The following items are a selection of business costs. Indicate whether each one is likely to be fixed, variable or a mixture of both in the short run:
   - the rent of a factory,
   - taxes paid on business premises,
   - workers' pay,
   - electricity bill,
   - raw materials,
   - advertising expenditure,
   - interest on loans,
   - management salaries,
   - transport costs,
   - depreciation on fixed capital.

2 Study the diagram below and then answer the questions that follow.

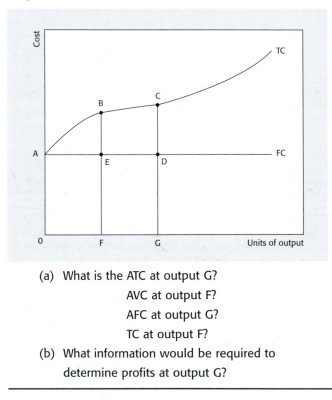

   (a) What is the ATC at output G?
       AVC at output F?
       AFC at output G?
       TC at output F?
   (b) What information would be required to determine profits at output G?

Reasons for the survival of small firms

At least 90 per cent of the business units in Britain are very small firms employing less than ten people. Manufacturing firms tend to be bigger and here the definition of small firms is those employing less than 100 people. The reasons why so many exist in a world where the economic power lies with big businesses include:

- There are economic activities where the size of the market demand is too small to support large firms.

- The business may involve specialist skills possessed by very few people.
- Where the product is a service, for example solicitors, accountants, hairdressers, dentists and small shops, the firm will be small in order to offer the customers personal attention for which they will pay a higher price.
- Small firms can fill in the market niches left by the big ones.
- Small firms may simply be the big firms of tomorrow. Although the number of small firms is high, it is misleading because of the fact that they have a very high 'death rate'.
- There are particular obstacles to the growth of small firms. Probably the largest of these is access to borrowed capital because of the perceived risk on the part of banks.
- The entrepreneur may not want the firm to get bigger because extra profit is not the only objective and growth might involve a loss of control over the running of the business.
- Economic recession and rising unemployment can trigger an increase in the number of business startups as former employees try to become self-employed.

- Small businesses may receive financial help under government enterprise schemes because of their employment and growth potential.
- The disintegration of large firms in an attempt to cut costs and focus on the more profitable core activities creates new business opportunities for small ones.
- It is sometimes cheaper for large firms to contract out some of the peripheral tasks, such as design, data processing and marketing, to specialist small firms. Manufacturing firms may buy in components from small suppliers producing for a range of companies, because it is cheaper than the large firm trying to supply small quantities itself.
- The increased access to technology through personal computers and mobile phones has reduced the optimum size of business units and made them more efficient and therefore competitive with the large ones.
- In the field of computing and technology, it is often the small firms which pioneer new products. This innovation is illustrated by the volume of computer software produced by people who previously worked for large organisations.

Small and medium-sized enterprises

As the structure of the UK economy has changed, largely as a consequence of deindustrialisation, an ever-increasing emphasis has been placed on the role of small and medium-sized enterprises (SMEs). By definition these firms employ less than 250 people (less than 50 in the case of small firms) and have a turnover of less than £11m per annum. In 1999, there were 3.7m such firms, making them *the* typical business unit. As the figure below shows, only 0.2 per cent of firms were large.

SMEs usually sell a limited range of products in a single market or in a limited range of markets. They are particularly prevalent in activities such as IT, food processing, retailing, financial services and a wide range of personal and household services. This makes diversification difficult – the SMEs that grow are invariably those that can diversify. Many SMEs which operate in niche markets have smaller markets and therefore their scope to diversify is further reduced.

Many SMEs are price takers; they follow the prices set by large firms. They invariably face strong competition from such firms who can benefit from economies of scale and so produce at prices well below those of SMEs.

The economic importance of SMEs to the UK economy is substantial in so far as:

- they create jobs;
- they are innovative and create new markets;
- they are very important in regenerating economic activity in many inner-city areas;
- there is always the possibility that they could grow into large firms.

Equally, it should be recognised that SMEs are vulnerable; many are not able to survive due to competitive market forces.

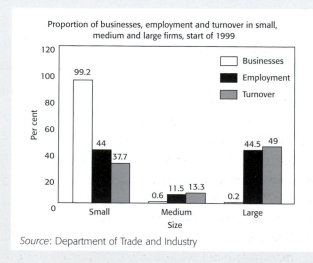

Proportion of businesses, employment and turnover in small, medium and large firms, start of 1999

Source: Department of Trade and Industry

The growth of firms

Although the number of large firms is small, it is true that they dominate both national and international trade. Business growth is strongly linked with the pursuit of profit but the motives behind a firm's growth may be:

♦ *The desire to get a reduction in ATC over time through the experience of economies of scale.* This allows firms to compete more effectively with rivals because they can afford to cut prices without sacrificing profits.

♦ *To get a bigger market share, which would boost sales revenue and therefore profits.* This is sometimes referred to as the monopoly motive but it could be a defensive strategy to maintain market share in anticipation of action by rivals. In the global economy there is a strong argument that only big firms can compete in markets where multinationals are present.

♦ *To diversify the product range.* A multi-product firm has the advantage of being able to spread business risks. If one branch of their activity is stagnating or going into decline, there will still be the revenue from others to keep the firm afloat. Firms often see new business opportunities in related areas. This is at the heart of successful entrepreneurship. Sometimes they can use the same production facilities as for their original activity, keeping the costs down. These benefits are called economies of scope.

♦ *To capture the resources of another business.* Sometimes, firms may realise that resources are being underutilised in another firm and that the real value of the firm is currently above its accounting valuation. The resulting takeovers and mergers can lead to the firm being brought back into profit or being broken up. This is because the sum of the parts sold separately is greater than the current valuation of the whole enterprise. It is sometimes called asset stripping and the cash may be ploughed back into improving the core business.

How do firms grow?

Firms grow in various ways. These include:

Internal growth This is where a firm decides to retain some of the profit rather than pay it out to the owners.

It is ploughed back in the form of new investment in order to increase the productive capacity. This is most likely to occur in capital-intensive activities where the market is expanding. The timing will be influenced by the stage of the business cycle, most investment occurring when the national economy is approaching a boom.

External growth This is where the business expands by joining with others via takeovers or mergers. The objective in a takeover bid is to buy sufficient shares from the owners of the firm to get 51 per cent of the total and therefore have control of the business. A merger often has the same result, a new larger legal entity but the name implies less of a struggle and that both parties have agreed to the action. Mergers may be more numerous when there is a downturn in the economy or where there is a shrinking market and firms are left with excess productive capacity.

In reality both types of growth can be going on at the same time. External growth may be a quicker and cheaper route for firms than internal growth, especially when there is high fixed cost, for example, it may be cheaper for one oil company to buy the assets of another than to expand existing operations, unless there are large recoverable reserves.

The growth of firms can occur through **integration** and this may involve growth in several different directions as figure 9.19 shows. Each of these offers specific advantages. The principal motives for **horizontal integration** are likely to be to get economies

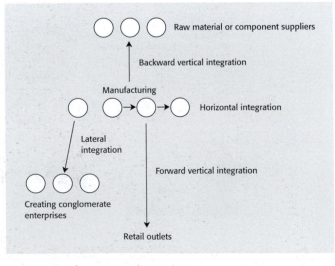

Figure 9.19 The routes to integration

Self-assessment tasks

1 Read the case study below and then tackle the exercises that follow.

Competition Up In The Air

The large airline companies are having to cope with a situation of scarcity, not of aircraft but the lack of takeoff and landing slots at major international airports. This is one reason for their interest in a new generation of very large aircraft or superjumbos.

Aircraft production is clearly an effective duopoly. The European Airbus group is hoping for definite orders for 60 of its new planes which may carry over 500 passengers at a time. They estimate that it will cost at least $15 billion simply to get the first one in the air. At the same time, the American Boeing group is testing its prototype double decker superjumbo. The irony is that there is a surplus of aircraft in the market as a whole. These new planes will only make economic sense if they fly at full capacity all the time. The aircraft will offer operators the prospect of economies of scale and the design is going to be one that minimises fuel costs.

Competition between the airline operators is fierce. The industry is not an oligopoly when all the firms are counted ,but the trend is towards greater concentration, and data on market shares may reveal that the big firms dominate the market. Each firm is trying to strengthen its position through brand loyalty, offering frequent flyer discounts and improving the quality of the provision for business class travellers where demand might be less price elastic. Profits are higher on the long distance routes and new entrants on the European routes have increased competition by offering a lower price no frills service. Some firms may have to use the long haul profits to cover losses on the short routes.

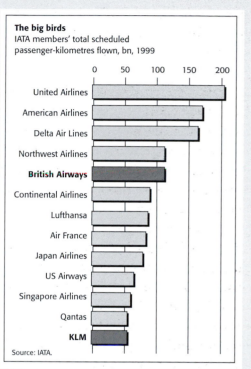

The big birds
IATA members' total scheduled passenger-kilometres flown, bn, 1999

United Airlines	
American Airlines	
Delta Air Lines	
Northwest Airlines	
British Airways	
Continental Airlines	
Lufthansa	
Air France	
Japan Airlines	
US Airways	
Singapore Airlines	
Qantas	
KLM	

Source: IATA.

(a) Why will aircraft production never have many firms competing for sales?

(b) Explain why the airline operators are so interested in the new products.

(c) What is the economic significance of low price elasticity in business travel?

(d) What do you predict will be the motives behind any horizontal integration of airline companies?

(e) With reference to both costs and revenue, how might the airline companies be able to increase their overall profits?

2   Read the case study below and then tackle the exercises that follow.

The Car Industry: competitive or co-operative?

There are 26 firms of different sizes producing cars for the European market but the top 6 have 79% of the total market sales. Most of the others are small in global terms but Fiat, Toyota, Daimler, Chrysler, and Honda are substantial players in world markets. The big firms would all like to produce cars for a global market but the problem is that variations in consumer tastes make it necessary to produce specific models for particular markets. As yet there is no such thing as a world car. Not all of the major car companies have been successful in terms of profit because the industry shows signs of overcapacity and is vulnerable to economic downturns. They all want a higher volume of sales because this will allow them to obtain technical economies of scale and these can increase a firm's competitive edge. The market is clearly competitive but several firms see the creation of alliances with other firms as the quickest way to achieve growth in sales revenue and profits. General Motors has linked up with Fiat and yet both are bidding to take over Daewoo, the Korean car producer. This illustrates that oligopolists may compete in certain areas but it may be in their best interests to co-operate in others. Co-operation involves firms using some common modules, such as engines and floors, and working together on research and development. Having standardised components allows the assembly lines to produce a range of models, allowing them to quickly alter the mix if demand changes. The economic problem is how to cut the cost of production whilst increasing the range of models offered to the consumer. In a recent report, the Competition Commission in Britain analysed the nature of competition between the big players. It concluded that the main companies appeared to set their list prices at about the same level for equivalent models. They compete through other means, such as marketing, quality, product specifications and temporary offers.

In the world market, General Motors' alliances will give them 23% of car sales whilst the Ford group will have 20%. The fastest growing markets are predicted to be in China, Mexico, Brazil, India, Thailand, Poland and Russia in the next few years. Both groups will be hoping to break the Japanese monopoly of the south-east Asian market. Price will be a major factor in this competition and all the firms will be looking for production platforms in countries that offer the combination of high productivity and low wage costs. In rich western countries the car firms may focus on the market segment where prices can be raised in order to increase the profit margin. Product innovation will continue to be a big part of competition. The trick will be to find the kind of vehicle that will be popular in each country whilst differentiating it from similar models offered by their rivals.

Rover – the last UK-owned car manufacturer struggling to survive in a global market

(a) What effect will overcapacity have on the market price of cars?

(b) Explain the nature of the economies of scale that the car firms might hope to achieve.

(c) Apart from economies of scale, suggest six ways in which a car firm can try to reduce its average costs.

(d) Explain how non-price competition might be used to boost sales in the European market. Why might price competition be more important in the predicted growth markets?

(e) What is the danger of cutting the price of a car to increase sales?

(f) Why might there be further horizontal integration in this industry in the future?

3 Read the article below and then answer the questions that follow.

Faced with expiring patents and slowing growth, pharmaceutical firms have turned to mergers as a way to generate the large profit increases their investors have come to expect.

This week saw the biggest merger yet. On January 17th Britain's Glaxo Wellcome and SmithKline Beecham said they were creating a firm with £15 billion ($25 billion) of sales and a market value of nearly £105 billion. With a portfolio spanning treatments for asthma, depression and diabetes, the combined firm will have an industry-leading 7.3% market share.

Any day now Pfizer will announce it is buying Warner-Lambert, an American rival, to form the world's second-largest firm with 6.7% of the market.

New technologies, such as the Internet, will help small drug firms, by drastically reducing their advertising and sales budgets. Today's mergers bring opportunities to smaller firms, in the form of spin-off drugs which are not worth a larger company's effort to market, because there are too few potential patients.

Source: The Economist, 22 January 2000.

(a) What economic explanation can be offered for the British merger?

(b) What benefit might consumers get from the creation of larger companies?

(c) How will the increased horizontal integration affect small companies?

---

of scale and a larger market share. **Vertical integration** offers firms the chance to capture the profit margins at the other stages of production. Backward growth can increase the security of supply and give the firm more control over quality of raw materials or components.

Lateral integration is the beginning of diversification where the company goes into an activity quite closely related to its existing one. In reality there are some firms that launch into completely new areas that have nothing to do with current production.

International growth Firms may take this route to expand either by exporting from a domestic base, setting up licence agreements or joint ventures with foreign firms or setting up directly in other countries. The reasons may include:

◆ saturation of their domestic market caused by too much competition;
◆ domestic recession;
◆ the prospect of economies of scale;
◆ identification of growth markets;
◆ access to materials, technology, patents or new management techniques;
◆ the risk spreading;
◆ low labour costs.

Setting up direct production may also avoid import barriers and reduce some of the difficulties of exporting.

A multinational company is one that owns or controls production facilities in many countries and derives a substantial part of its total revenue from non-domestic sources. Its decisions are made in a global context, even though it has a domestic base. The objective is to maximise its profits by switching investment to areas that offer the highest return on capital employed. This strategy sometimes involves rationalising production and writing off investment in particular locations. Multinational conglomerates can become so large that they are difficult to manage. The decision then is sometimes to break it up, selling off the least profitable parts and concentrating on its core activities.

The firm's revenue

In the theory of the firm, there are only two possible revenue relationships. In a competitive market, each firm has to accept the ruling market price. Its demand curve is horizontal at this level. Any firm in any other market will face a downward-sloping demand curve for its product. If the firm chooses to increase its output, the extra sales will depress the price. To look at it another way, the sales will only increase if the price is reduced from its present level. An increase in price would lead to a fall in the volume of sales. The following definitions are used by economists when looking at a firm's revenue:

Total revenue (TR) is price multiplied
by quantity
Average revenue (AR) is total revenue
divided by output

The firm's demand curve therefore is the average
revenue line or the price line.

The **marginal revenue** (MR) is the addition to the
total revenue resulting from the sales of one extra unit.
Because the firm can only sell more by reducing the
price, it follows that the value for MR will always be
lower than AR. Figure 9.20, derived from the
accompanying data, shows that when the price
moves from 9 to 8, the MR is 7. The addition to TR is
gradually falling as the price falls until when five units
are sold MR = 0. At this point total revenue is
maximised.

**The relationship between price elasticity of demand
and revenue** In the above example the firm would be
facing a straight line demand curve. Even so, the
consumers' reaction to a price change varies at different
prices due to the way in which the price elasticity of
demand (PED) varies along the demand curve.

As the price falls in steps from $10, sales increase
more than proportionally, giving PED a value greater
than 1, until the output of 5 when total revenue is
unchanged. This gives a PED value of 1. Beyond this
output PED has a value less than 1 and the result is that
further price cuts will reduce total revenue.

A relationship between elasticity and marginal
revenue can also be seen. In the elastic part of the
demand curve where PED > 1, the marginal revenue is
positive and total revenue will be increasing. When the
PED = 1, MR will be zero and total revenue will be
maximised. When PED < 1, MR will be negative,
reducing the total revenue.

The most important thing about the concept of
price elasticity from the firm's point of view is that it
determines what happens to total revenue when the
price is altered. It would make sense for any firm
operating in the elastic part of the demand curve to
reduce price and boost total revenue. Conversely, in the
inelastic part, the firm should raise its price if it wants
to see higher revenue. In this example revenue is
maximised at five units of output with a price of 5.

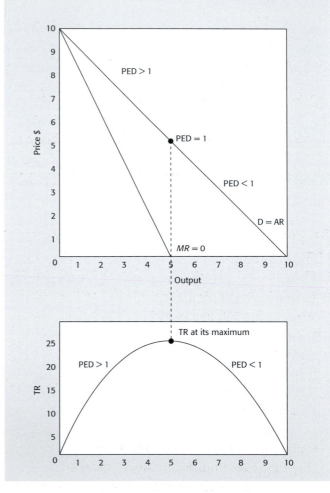

Revenue data

Price (P)	Units sold (Q)	TR (P x Q)	MR
10	0	0	
			9
9	1	9	
			7
8	2	16	
			5
7	3	21	
			3
6	4	24	
			1
5	5	25	
			−1
4	6	24	
			−3
3	7	21	
			−5
2	8	16	
			−7
1	9	9	

Figure 9.20 The relationship between average revenue, marginal
revenue and total revenue

With knowledge of the firm's cost structure and
revenue situation, and the firm's objectives, we are
now in a position to make some predictions about
the output the firm will choose to put on the market.

Self-assessment task

Wok, Stock and Barrel is a small family run engineering company with a production capacity of 9,000 units per year. Market research suggests that the market will take up all of this output at a price of $8. The firms cost structure is as follows:

> direct labour $1.50 per unit,
>
> raw materials $0.50 per unit,
>
> other variable costs $1.00 per unit,
>
> the total fixed costs are $27,000 a year.

(a) Calculate:
   - AFC,
   - AVC,
   - ATC,
   - AR.

(b) If the factory produced its capacity output, what would the firm's abnormal profit be?

(c) Suppose that consumer tastes change away from the product and the firm has to reduce the price to $6 in order to get rid of unsold stock. What situation is the firm now in?

The firm and the industry

A firm As referred to earlier, a firm is a business organisation that buys or hires factors of production in order to produce goods and services that can be sold at a profit. The types might include:

- sole traders or one person businesses,
- partnerships,
- co-operatives,
- private companies,
- public limited companies,
- state-owned firms,
- multinational or transnational firms.

They can range from small simple organisations to ones that are almost too complex to control, and where there is some conflict of interests between the members. The characteristics and behaviour of the firm depend on the type of economic activity and the nature of competition. The factor mix in firms varies enormously, with some firms in the service sector being highly labour intensive. This contrasts with some manufacturing that is capital intensive. The decisions that firms take will vary according to the cost and availability of factors of production in different economic systems. There has been a trend in the rich western economies to make large parts of manufacturing more capital intensive, to the point where some major activities, such as car manufacturing, can largely be done by robots and computer-controlled machinery. Another trend has been increased concentration of ownership in the hands of large multinational conglomerates.

An industry In a competitive market structure, the industry is simply the sum of all the firms making the same product. This is the total market supply.

In other markets, the industry is taken to be the total number of firms producing within the same product group, i.e. things which are close substitutes for each other. It is sometimes difficult to draw the line between different industries; for example are motor cars and motor cycles in the same product group? In reality many multi-product firms operate in more than one industry at the same time. A multinational conglomerate can be in several industries right across the global economy.

The industry is therefore a collection of business organisations which supply similar products to the market. When a firm's market share is discussed it tends to be in terms of the sales of the firm divided by the total sales of the entire industry. The terms 'industry' and 'market' are interchangeable in this context.

The firm's objectives

Profit maximisation The standard assumption made by economists is that firms will seek to maximise their profits, that is maximise the gap between the firm's total revenue and total cost (including normal profit). A firm making the minimum level of normal profit is said to be producing the break-even output. Firms will want to make abnormal profit as a reward for managing the resources and taking business risks.

If the firm produces up to the point where the cost of making the last unit is just covered by the revenue from selling it, then the profit margin will have fallen to 0 and total profits will be at their greatest. In figure 9.21, a firm producing an output to the left of Q is sacrificing potential profit. It can raise total profit by increasing its output, because each marginal unit sold adds more to

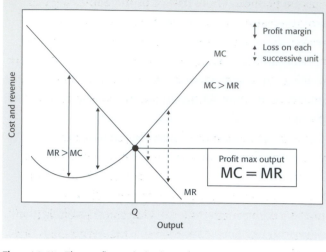

Figure 9.21 The profit maximisation rule

revenue than it does to costs. A firm producing to the right of *Q* is making a loss on each successive unit, which will lower the total profit. It would be better off cutting the output back to *Q* where MC = MR and the area of abnormal profit will be at its highest.

There may be several reasons why firms do not operate at the profit maximisation output:

1 In practice it may be difficult to identify this output. The firm may simply work out the average total cost and add on a profit margin in order to determine the selling price. This cost-plus pricing technique may not result in maximum profit.

2 Short-term profit maximising may not be in the long-term interest of the company since:
   - firms with large market shares may wish to avoid the attention of government watchdog bodies, such as the Competition Commission in Britain;
   - large abnormal profit may attract new entrants into the industry;
   - high profits may damage the relationship between the firm and its stakeholders, such as the consumers and the company workforce;
   - profit maximisation may not appeal to the management, who may have different objectives;
   - high profits might trigger action by the firm's rivals and it could become a target for a take-over bid.

Alternative objectives to profit maximisation

Dissatisfaction with the simple assumption of profit maximisation has led to a number of alternative assumptions that have been labelled as managerial or behavioural theories.

Sales revenue maximisation A firm may be prepared to accept a lower price and produce above the profit-maximising output in order to increase its market share in a growing market. This is a penetration pricing policy. A firm choosing to maximise its sales revenue would raise output beyond MC = MR until MR had fallen to zero. Extra sales after this would contribute nothing to total revenue, therefore it is at its maximum. There may still be abnormal profit if total revenue is higher than total cost. The reason why sales revenue maximisation might be chosen in a large firm is that management salaries might be linked to the value of sales. Shareholders might be more interested in profit. The solution to this conflict of interests is to offer management some shares as a bonus or link their salaries to profits.

Sales maximisation This option maximises the volume of sales rather than the sales revenue. In this option the firm would increase output up to the break-even output where the total revenue just covered the total cost. A higher output implies loss-making behaviour. The only situation where this would be possible is where the firm could use the profit from some other activities to cover these losses using the principle of cross subsidisation. It could be that in a state-owned firm, there are social objectives lying behind price and output decisions. The company might be instructed to keep prices down, to cover their ATC, or to make sufficient profit to be self-financing when it comes to new investment.

A firm in the private sector would not go beyond the break-even output in order to expand sales unless it is part of a diversified grouping where cross subsidisation is being practised. Deliberately cutting the price to reduce profit might be a strategy to deter new entrants into the market. If they still appear, a price war may be a tactic to squeeze them out.

Satisficing profits This behaviour would occur when a firm is determined to make a reasonable level of profits, sufficient to satisfy the shareholders but also to keep the other stakeholding groups happy, for example the workforce and of course the consumers. The firm is seen as a coalition of interest groups, each with its own objectives which may change over time. Workers will expect pay rises and improvements in working conditions which may raise costs. Consumers may expect to see prices falling, particularly if there are rival producers. This is a long way from the simple profit-maximising theory as firms may choose to sacrifice some potential short-term profits to satisfy these expectations.

Where the firm's shareholders are divorced from control of the firm, there may be a conflict of interests. The management's motives may be concerned with growth rather than profit. They may place a lot of importance on comfortable working conditions, job security, status and fringe benefits, such as company cars, private health care and pension rights. Time and money spent on these issues can raise costs. If the firm has close rivals, it may make management more cautious because the risk of failure will threaten their job security and career advancement prospects. Firms may have charitable or environmental objectives which

must be financed at the cost of profit. Satisficing can also be a feature of firms that have enjoyed a high market share over a long period of time. Complacency can lead to firms losing their focus on the cost structure or failing to devote resources to either product or process innovation. Either situation can lead to a loss of profits.

One must be careful of sweeping statements concerning firms' short-run behaviour and recognise the difference in objectives that can exist in different countries. Extra long-run profits may follow from short-term sacrifices. As a working assumption, it is still valid to see profit maximisation as the major long-term objective of privately owned firms operating in a free market system. The search for abnormal profit will be a major factor in explaining firms' behaviour throughout the world.

Self-assessment task

Read the following short case study which looks at some of the objectives of the firm, and then tackle the exercises that follow.

Chefaid plc

A row has broken out in the boardroom of Chefaid plc, the kitchenware company, over the firm's prospects and future direction. The marketing director announced a record level of sales for the last quarter and suggested that there should be a 10 per cent target for the growth of sales revenue over the coming year. It was suggested to him that this was unwise. The firm's latest product, an exclusive set of kitchen tools, has yet to break even. The sales record owes a lot to the current popularity of cookery programmes on TV; there is a danger that the sales boom is a flash in the pan.

The managing director was more interested in the firm's profitability. He was under pressure to declare higher future dividends and to get the funds to finance the planned new factory. He believed that a profit-maximisation strategy was the best way forward. The production director warned the meeting

that cost pressures were building up and that industrial relations with the workforce were fragile because of the beginning of talks about wages and new working conditions. Management in general had been delighted with the new share option scheme and the bonus linked to sales performance.

It was suggested that the prospects for growth in general were good, because of the increase in consumer confidence, and the firm's market share had benefitted from the closure of two large rivals during the recession. It was argued that the market structure was becoming less competitive and this might give an opportunity for price rises. The company must not lose sight of its long-term drive to raise profitability by reducing unit costs. This sparked further disagreement over the firm's sponsorship commitments, its promotions budget and its charitable contributions.

(a) What do economists understand by the phrase 'the market structure is becoming less competitive'?

(b) What will be the best output for the firm if the profit-maximising strategy wins the day?

(c) What are the risks associated with this strategy?

(d) What output would maximise turnover?

(e) What does the phrase 'fail to break even' mean? What advice would you give to improve the performance of the new product?

(f) Explain why the management may not favour profit maximisation.

(g) To what extent does the case study show that businesses have a range of objectives?

(h) Discuss the idea that each business decision to reach an objective has risks attached to it.

Market structures

The term 'market structure' describes the way in which goods and services are supplied by firms in a particular market. In economic theory, a range of models has been developed within what is called the spectrum of competition. These models are shown in figure 9.22. The extreme or limiting models may only exist in theory but give a framework for understanding real world competition. The following stages can help to identify a market structure within this spectrum of competition:

- By counting the number of firms. The bigger the total, the closer to perfect competition the market stucture will be.
- A better guide will be to use sales **concentration ratios** to see the combined market share of the biggest 3, 5 or 7 firms in the industry as a percentage of total industry sales. The bigger the percentage, the closer the industry will be to the oligopoly and monopoly models.
- By considering how easy or difficult it is for new firms to set up and how easy it is for firms to exit the industry. These barriers are indicative of market structures on the right-hand side of the spectrum.
- By considering the importance of economies of scale to the firms. The more important they are the closer the industry will be to an oligopoly structure.

Figure 9.23 provides an elaboration of the above – understanding this figure is very important for the rest of this section.

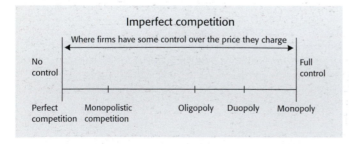

Figure 9.22 The spectrum of competition

Perfect competition

Perfect competition is a theoretical extreme in the spectrum of competition. The main point of studying this model is that it can act as a benchmark for real-world competition. The performance of actual firms can be judged against the most efficient model possible.

Some of the characteristics are shared by the next most competitive model, which somewhat confusingly to students is known as monopolistic competition.

Perfect competition has the following characteristics:

1 There is a large number of buyers and sellers who have perfect knowledge of market conditions and the price.
2 No individual firm has any influence on the market price. Firms are described as being price takers. The ruling price is determined by the forces of market demand and the aggregate output of all the firms.
3 The products are homogeneous. They are all of the same quality and are identical in the eyes of the consumer.
4 There is complete freedom of entry into and exit from the market.
5 Each firm will be seeking to maximise its profits.

The only industry which comes anywhere near this theoretical model is agriculture. The problem in searching for an example is in finding products that are homogeneous. Perfect competition has a lot of appeal as a yardstick because if it were to operate, there would be consumer sovereignty and efficient production with no possibility of exploitation.

In perfect competition, the firm cannot do anything that will influence the market price. Each individual firm makes such a small contribution to the industry output that no alteration in its own output can significantly affect the total supply. The firm can choose to produce any quantity it likes and will be able to sell all of it at the ruling price. The demand curve facing the firm is therefore perfectly elastic at this price. In this situation if the firm sells an extra unit of output it will get the same price as the one before. The marginal revenue is therefore equal to the price or the average revenue. In figure 9.24, all the firm's revenue information is in the line

$$D = \mathrm{AR} = \mathrm{MR}$$

Choosing the output would be the only decision that the firm has to make. This will be done by considering the relevant costs of production. Given the assumption that the firm wants to maximise profits, the chosen output will be where $\mathrm{MC} = \mathrm{MR}$.

The firm's total revenue would be the price multiplied by the output sold. If the total cost of producing this output is lower than the total revenue,

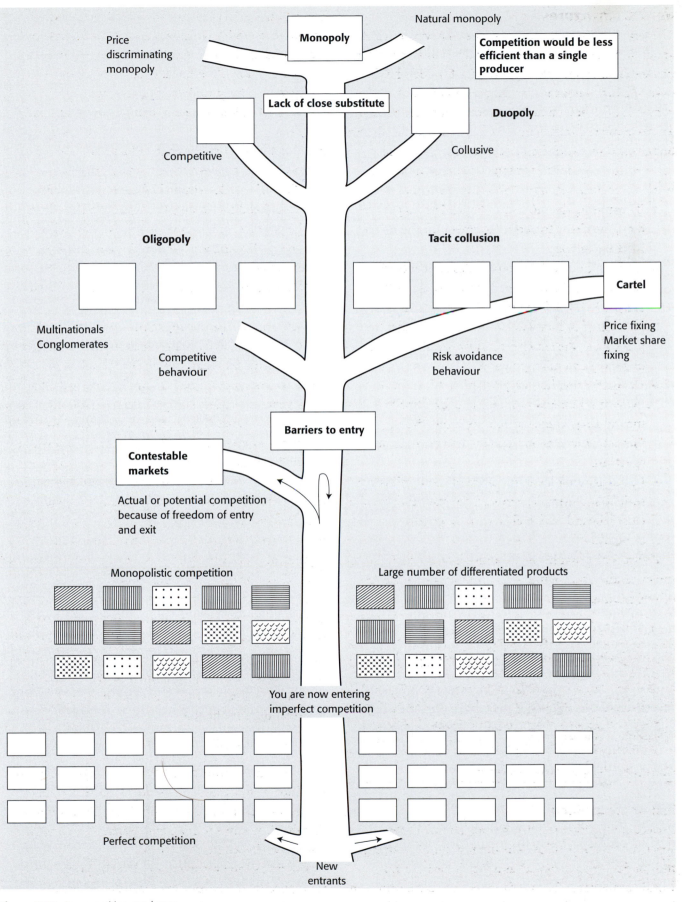

Monopoly

Natural monopoly

Price discriminating monopoly

Competition would be less efficient than a single producer

Lack of close substitute

Duopoly

Competitive

Collusive

Oligopoly

Tacit collusion

Multinationals Conglomerates

Competitive behaviour

Risk avoidance behaviour

Cartel

Price fixing Market share fixing

Barriers to entry

Contestable markets

Actual or potential competition because of freedom of entry and exit

Monopolistic competition

Large number of differentiated products

You are now entering imperfect competition

Perfect competition

New entrants

Figure 9.23 A competition road map

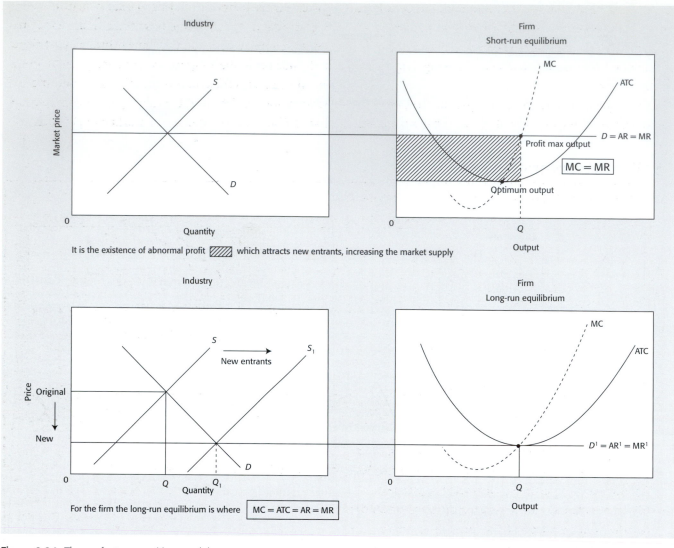

Figure 9.24 The perfect competition model

then the firm will be making an abnormal profit. If TC = TR, then the firm would break even and be making a normal profit. It is possible that the costs could be higher than the revenue, in which case the firm would be about to exit the industry. This may not be immediate, a firm can continue in production making short-term losses, as long as the price covers the AVC, that is the cost of paying the wage bill and buying the materials for production. This is the shut-down price. The firm would be making a loss equivalent to the amount of fixed costs. In this situation the firm's only hope is that the market price will rise to increase its revenue or that it can take action to reduce its costs of production. Firms where the revenue is lower than costs will be leaving the industry. If a lot of them do, the effect will be a reduction in the overall market supply which will raise the market price giving the rest an

opportunity to continue producing and at least make normal profit. In the long run, firms will only supply the market if they can cover all their costs and make a normal profit. The minimum supply for the firm will be the optimum output. In perfect competition, firms will only make different amounts of profit from each other if they have different cost structures. Their behaviour is strictly limited and the only way to boost profit would be to increase productivity and lower average total cost.

Abnormal profit will only be a feature of perfect competition in the short run. This is because its existence will act as an economic incentive for the entry of new firms. The absence of barriers means that the total supply in the market will rise. The effect of this on the existing firms is that the market price will fall and the abnormal profit will diminish. When the abnormal profit goes, the entry of new firms dries up, and the existing ones will simply be covering costs. It is the competitive force of large numbers of new entrants that destroys abnormal profit.

The long-run equilibrium is therefore where the only firms left are the most efficient ones, making a normal profit.

In this model, there is no action that the firm can take to prosper at the expense of rivals. It has no market power. Firms' behaviour in this market structure is easy to understand. The appeal of this model is that abnormal profit is competed away and the only firms that participate in the market in the long run are completely productively and allocatively efficient. It is the efficient economic performance which would occur in perfect competition that can be used to criticise real-world competition.

Self-assessment tasks

1 Study the diagrams below and tackle the exercises that follow.

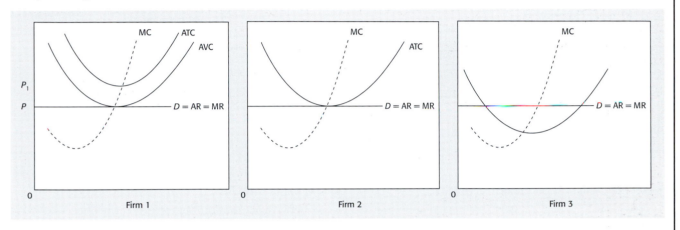

(a) Describe the situation of each firm regarding profit.

(b) If market demand increased and the price rose to P_1, how would it affect each of them?

(c) According to the theory what will happen next?

(d) What output does a firm in perfect competition choose?

(e) How can an individual firm increase its profits?

2 Read the article below and then tackle the exercises that follow.

Shedding light on competition

In Guangdong, people do not hide their light under a bushel. 'Guizhen: Lighting Capital of China', proclaims the sign beside the highway into the village (more of a town), which two decades ago was an unpaved track. Factory after factory, every one of them advertising light fittings, lines the road. In town, hundreds of shopfronts display their variations on a theme: street lights, chandeliers, bedside lights, halogen lights, lights of any sort, from the modern to the eternally tasteless. Guizhen has 60,000 registered inhabitants, says the party secretary, Mr Wu, frantically talking on his cellphone, and though there are officially 1,000 lighting factories, 'there are also 600 or so underground ones . . . they all count.'

One resident in every 40 men, women and children, then, is a factory owner, and that does not take into account the wholesalers and shop owners. On top of that there are some 40,000 migrant workers. It is an intensely competitive industry. The Guizhen factories on average change their designs every fortnight. The specialist designers of light fittings have to come up with three new ideas a day. In return, they are paid 600,000 yuan ($72,000) a year, many times the salary of China's prime minister.

Since the first factory opened in 1986, little-known Guizhen has captured 46% of China's total domestic lighting market. One in every two light fittings you see in China has been trucked out past that bragging highway sign.

Source: *Economist* survey of China, 8 April 2000 (adapted).

(a) Is this an example of perfect competition or monopolistic competition? Justify your choice.

(b) Why is product innovation so highly rewarded?

(c) What is the economic significance of the migrant workers in this industry?

Monopolistic competition

This is the market structure closest to the model of perfect competition because of the large number of competing suppliers.

Monopolistic competition has the following characteristics:

1 There is a large number of buyers and sellers.

2 There are few barriers to entry into the market and it is easy for firms to recoup their capital expenditure on exit from the market.

3 Consumers face a wide choice of differentiated products. Each firm has a slight degree of monopoly power in that it controls its own brand.

4 Firms have some influence on the market price and are therefore price makers.

5 Each firm will seek to maximise profits.

Each firm is competing with a large number of similar producers. In this situation the demand curve facing the individual firm will be downward sloping but relatively price elastic because of the presence of substitutes. It might be an option for firms to reduce their price in order to increase total revenue. As in perfect competition, the firms can make abnormal profit in the short run but the key restraint on their

power is the free entry of rivals. In the long run, the prediction is that the profit-maximising firms will only be able to achieve a normal profit covering all the production costs and the opportunity cost of capital.

The clue to the behaviour of firms in this market structure lies in the concept of product differentiation. The development of a strong brand image must be seen as an act of investment on the part of the individual firm. This highlights the important role that advertising and promotions play in this market structure. Successful advertising will not only shift the firm's demand curve to the right at the expense of the rivals but will also reduce the price elasticity if the consumers feel there are no close substitutes. This is what is meant by brand loyalty – people will not easily shift back to rival products. There are problems associated with advertising because it will be a competitive tool taken up by all the firms. In this case one could argue that the advantage will be temporary and that advertising will simply add to the firm's costs and bring little benefit to its demand curve. If advertising is not equally effective, the successful firms might take advantage of their greater market share and brand loyalty to charge a higher price. It would increase its sales revenue by doing this in the portion of the demand curve where price elasticity of demand has a value less than 1.

It is easy to see how each firm can try and strengthen its market power in the short run. The constraint on firms is that there is freedom of entry into the market, which will threaten the existence of abnormal profit in the long run. By a combination of marketing and product innovation, the individual firms may be able to postpone the long-run equilibrium, if the total market is growing.

At the heart of this model of competition is the fact that there are a large number of competitors using a combination of price and non-price competition to try and increase their market power. If there are few barriers to entry then their success will only be temporary. There are many typical examples of this market structure in operation. For example, local hairdresser's shops, take-away food stores and travel agents exhibit the characteristics of this market structure.

Figure 9.25 shows the equilibrium price and output in monopolistic competition. In the short run, the profit-maximising firm will be seen to make abnormal

It is easy to open a local store but not so easy to stay in business

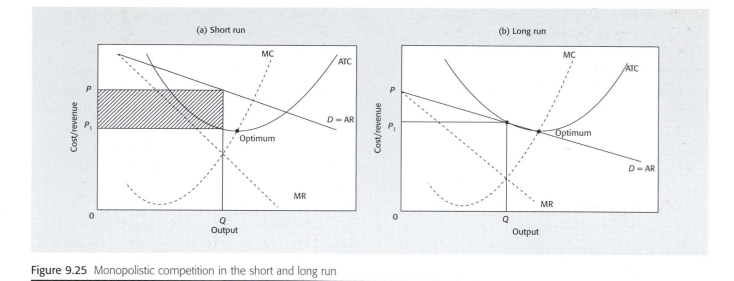

Figure 9.25 Monopolistic competition in the short and long run

profits. In time these will be competed away by the entry of new firms which will shift the original firm's demand curve to the left. The process will continue until the only firms in the industry are making normal profit. A key point though is that in both the short and the long run the firm is inefficient. It is below the optimum point, giving a situation of excess capacity.

Barriers to entry

In the spectrum of competition, it is the existence of **barriers to entry** of new firms into an industry that differentiates oligopoly and monopoly from the others.

Barriers are a mixture of obstacles that deter or prevent new firms from entering a market to compete with the existing firms. They give firms a degree of market power in that decisions can be made by existing firms without the risk of their market share or the price being challenged from outside. The construction and maintenance of these barriers can become part of the firm's behaviour. Below are some of the main barriers that can be identified:

◆ In some countries, it may be impossible for new firms to enter an industry because the economic activity is state owned or the good is produced under licence from the government. This is a legal monopoly created to achieve social and political objectives. The economic justification might lie in the concept of a natural monopoly, where it is more efficient to have a single producer than to have competing firms. In countries where the state-owned resources have been privatised and the

market has been deregulated, the economic justification has been that the injection of competition will bring economic and social benefits. Some economists though believe that there is no such thing as a natural monopoly.

◆ The high fixed cost or setup cost in activities such as electricity generation, aircraft and car production and pharmaceuticals may deter potential entrants. The barrier here is access to capital. Only very large firms will be able to fund the necessary investment. Research and development costs will represent a high proportion of total costs and it will require high sales over a long period of time before the activity becomes profitable.

◆ If these costs cannot be recovered in the case of the firm shutting down, because the resources are specialised and are not easily transferrable to other uses, they are regarded as sunk costs and act as a *barrier to exit* from the industry because the capital investment will be lost. It is therefore the risk of entering and the high cost of failure that deters potential entrants.

◆ Advertising and brand names with a high degree of consumer loyalty may prove a difficult obstacle to overcome. This explains why firms regard their expenditure on advertising and promotions as an act of investment. Existing firms can make entry more difficult through brand proliferation, giving the customers an apparent abundance of choice and closing market niches. Successful advertising cannot only shift a firm's demand curve to the right but it can also reduce its price elasticity of demand. This gives the firm greater market power because consumers do not see the rival firm's product as a close substitute.

◆ Economies of scale can be a barrier because the existing large producers are able to produce at a lower average cost than those just starting up. They also give the large firm an opportunity to cut its price in order to eliminate any high-cost producers. This is the concept of predatory or destroyer pricing which can be used to eliminate any new firms that do enter the industry.

◆ The production process or the products of a firm may be protected by a legal monopoly in the form of a patent, whereby competitors cannot copy without the permission of the owner. The idea is to guarantee a reward to entrepreneurs with original ideas for a reasonable period of time. The barrier here is really access to either technology or information.

◆ Some existing firms may have a monopoly access to raw materials, components or retail outlets, which will make it difficult for new entrants. Vertically integrated manufacturing businesses will be protected by the fact that their rivals' costs will be higher.

◆ In activities such as computer manufacturing and consumer electronics, the pace of product innovation is so rapid that the existing firms will be working on the next generation of products whilst launching the current range. Unless the new entrants have original ideas or can exploit a new market segment, they are destined to fail.

◆ It may be possible for existing firms to hide the existence of abnormal profit by what is called entry limit pricing. This involves deliberately setting a low price and temporarily abandoning profit maximisation. It may be in the interest of all the players to do this and it therefore becomes a form of collusion.

◆ Collaboration between existing producers to develop new products may act as a barrier in that the resources necessary to compete are beyond the means of single producers.

◆ Market conditions, such as a fall in demand resulting from economic recession, can leave producers with surplus production capacity and this will deter entry.

The concept of barriers to entry is central to understanding where the models of oligopoly and monopoly begin within the spectrum of competition.

Where the barriers are strong, the market is likely to be dominated by a few large producers. New firms will only enter if they think that the economic returns will be greater than the cost of breaking the barriers.

Oligopoly

Oligopoly is defined as a market situation where the total output is concentrated in the hands of a few firms. It is possibly the most realistic economic model but ironically the theory does not provide the definite predictions regarding the price and output of the firm that exist in every other model. An effective oligopoly can exist in an apparently competitive industry if a handful of firms dominate the market. Duopoly, where the market is shared between two big players, can be seen as an extreme form of oligopoly.

An oligopoly has the following characteristics:

1 The market is dominated by between two and up to about ten firms.
2 Their decisions are interdependent. Firms must decide their market strategy to compete with close rivals, but they must also try and anticipate their rivals' reactions and think what the next step should be in the light of this response.
3 There are significant barriers to entry.
4 The products may be homogeneous or differentiated.
5 The uncertainty and risks associated with price competition may lead to price rigidity.
6 Firms may or may not choose to maximise profits.

The difficulty in studying oligopoly is that the behaviour can follow two very different routes. There are examples of aggressive competition in some industries whilst in others there is a suggestion of co-operation and even collusion.

Oligopolists are price makers but one of the dangers of using this weapon is that the firm can get drawn into a price war. An oligopolist would only start a price war if its costs of production were significantly lower than its rivals. A price war may be the natural outcome of economic events, such as overcapacity in the industry or the appearance of new firms. Where the firms are highly diversified, a firm may be prepared to sacrifice profits by cutting the price, in an attempt to increase market share. Profits from some of its activities may be used to cover short-term losses on others.

Although they each have market power in the form of influence over the price they charge, the uncertainty surrounding the outcome of competitive tactics means that firms may prefer **non-price competition**. The observation that prices tend to be similar between oligopolists and are stable with time might be explained by the kinked demand curve theory (see figure 9.26).

The diagram illustrates a situation where one firm suspects that it faces a relatively elastic demand curve below the existing price. The temptation would be to cut the price in an attempt to increase total revenue. The outcome depends on the rivals' response. If they also cut their price, then the firm will sell relatively little extra output. It could be worse off than it was before the price cut. It can also be shown that the firm could lose out if it chose to raise the price. Whatever the elasticity was, if the price increase is not copied by the rivals, then the firm will lose a disproportionate amount of sales because the product will look overpriced against rivals. The firm would be better off concentrating on non-price competition to increase revenue. This may include the following:

◆ Advertising and promotions.
◆ Product innovation. This is the attempt to further differentiate the products in the eyes of the consumers.
◆ Brand proliferation. This is where the firm produces lots of brands to saturate the market and to leave no gaps for rivals.
◆ Market segmentation. Producers may decide that there are sub-markets where the consumers have different characteristics and needs. These market niches will be catered for through product innovation.
◆ Process innovation. This is usually seen as a way of reducing average costs, allowing the firm to cut the price without sacrificing profits.

One way for a firm to grow rapidly would be to take over one of its rivals. As seen earlier, this so-called horizontal integration may in fact be the cheapest way of getting growth in sales if the competing oligopolists are a similar size. If a takeover or merger is likely to be resisted, a firm wanting to get rapid growth may prefer to look elsewhere. This leads to a prediction that diversification becomes a feature of businesses in an oligopolistic market. This could explain the growth of conglomerate enterprises which start to look for profits by producing in different countries and eventually become multinational enterprises.

The difficulty of choosing competitive strategies and of predicting the response of rivals may change the objectives of the firm. Profit-maximising strategies may be replaced by satisficing (see above). The firm's management becomes more cautious, preferring to make just enough profit to keep the shareholders happy. The focus shifts towards maintaining market share.

Co-operation and collusion between oligopolists

There are situations where big firms find that it is in their interest to co-operate with rivals. One of the best examples is where the research and development costs are high as a proportion of total costs and where the pace of technical change is very rapid. It is in the interests of all the firms to pool their knowledge and agree on technical standards, perhaps taking part in joint ventures.

Collusion is altogether different. It is an anti-competitive action by producers. Informal or tacit collusion usually takes the form of **price leadership**, where firms automatically follow the lead of one of the group. The objective is to maximise the profits of the whole group by acting as a single monopolist. This illegal activity is difficult to prove since there is no written evidence. A formal **price agreement** or output agreement is known as a **cartel** arrangement. The big problem that the participants have is that there is an incentive for individual members to cheat on the agreement.

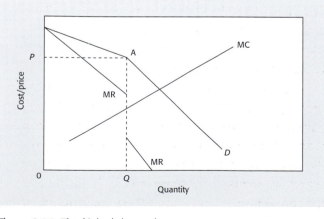

Figure 9.26 The kinked demand curve

Collusion of any kind will work best when:

◆ there is a small number of participants;
◆ a strong element of trust exists between them;
◆ they have similar cost structures;
◆ there is a clear leader;
◆ the agreement can be policed;
◆ there is no danger from new entrants;
◆ the market conditions are stable;
◆ the government will not intervene.

Collusion is more likely to be tacit where the behaviour of each firm is the result of an unwritten rather than formal agreement. One of the simplest forms is a follow-the-leader agreement, where each firm will only adjust its price following a move by the dominant firm. There are other price leadership models, such as using a typical firm as the yardstick for price. This will only change if a rise in costs affects the profit margin. The principle is the same: each firm will act in the same way in the interests of the group as a whole.

In practice it is difficult to identify either tacit or formal agreements. This is because price similarities can be the result of either aggressive pricing in a competitive oligopoly or the outcome of a collusive agreement.

Monopoly

In theory, a **monopoly** is where a single firm controls the entire output of the industry. It is at the complete opposite end of the spectrum to perfect competition. In practice a monopoly situation can arise when a firm has a dominant position in the market in terms of its market share. A complex monopoly is where several firms have combined sales that add up to more than 25 per cent of the total market.

A monopoly will be protected from competition by the barriers to entry explained earlier. The word 'monopoly' conjures up an image of giant powerful firms. However, local monopoly can exist where a relatively small firm dominates a local market either because it is too costly for others to enter or the prospect of profit is not high enough. Even when monopolists are large, the extent of power must not be exaggerated. Sometimes a domestic monopoly can be suddenly broken by new competition from imported goods and services.

A single firm monopolist in theory would face the downward-sloping market demand curve. In this situation it can decide on the price to charge or the quantity to supply, but not both. There may be situations where the monopolist is unable to make abnormal profit in spite of having market power. One such example would be where the fixed costs are so high that the necessary price would be outside the range that the consumers could afford. It may be that all the monopolist can hope for is that the revenue covers the production costs.

Figure 9.27 shows the equilibrium output of a monopolist. A profit-maximising monopolist would choose the output where MC = MR. This output will be somewhere over the price range where demand is price elastic and will be sold at the price consumers will pay. If the total revenue is higher than the production costs, it will make abnormal profit. This will be a permanent feature. In monopoly, there is no distinction between the short run and the long run because of the barriers that prevent the entry of competitors. There is no economic incentive for the monopolist to move away from the profit-maximising output Q.

The monopolist's profits could be increased in certain circumstances by a practice known as **price discrimination**. Price discrimination occurs where the monopolist chooses to split the output up and sell it at different prices to different customers. It is only true price discrimination if the quality of the product is identical in all market segments. The monopolist is making use of the fact that some consumers would have been prepared to pay more than the single price (see figure 9.28). At this price they would be enjoying some consumer surplus. The monopolist's aim is to charge what the consumers will pay and turn the consumer surplus into producer surplus in the form of abnormal profit.

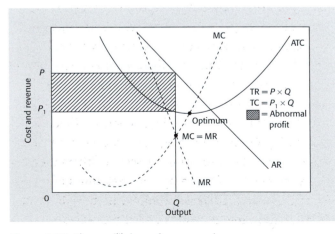

Figure 9.27 The equilibrium of a monopoly

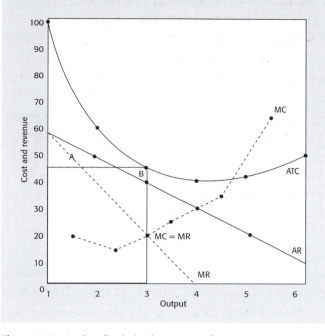

Figure 9.28 A price discriminating monopolist

It may be possible for a monopolist to use price discrimination to produce at a profit when competitive firms or a monopoly charging a single price could not cover costs. Figure 9.28 shows that at the single price profit maximisation output, the total revenue would be $3 \times 40 = 120$ and the total cost would be $3 \times 45 = 135$, giving a loss of 15. If the output was sold separately for what consumers would pay for each individual unit, the revenue would be $60 + 50 + 40 = 150$, giving an abnormal profit of 15. The monopolist has effectively tapped into the consumer surplus and turned it into producer surplus or profit. If triangle A in the diagram is the same size as triangle B, which is the shortfall in cost, the firm will break even, but if it is larger then it makes abnormal profit. As long as the consumers are prepared to pay the higher price, there is no consumer exploitation. The competitive market price would generate losses and therefore there would be zero output in the long run. Price discrimination can only exist in particular circumstances and there are situations where it can be justified on economic grounds. If different groups of customers are being charged different prices because the cost of providing the service differs then it is quite acceptable. For example, at peak times of demand a firm might have to employ more staff. Price discrimination might in fact be used as a way of spreading out demand. This would account for out-of-season holiday tariffs and the lower price for off-peak telephone calls. Spreading out demand may improve efficiency, giving a further benefit to consumers. Price discrimination could be used to generate revenue on parts of a service, such as a rail network, so that the operator can cover losses on the least popular routes. Transport provides several examples of travellers being split into definite categories and charged different prices. There may be social motives for charging older people and children less than others. Consumer loyalty may be rewarded by discounts. The price of a journey may vary with the time of day or the day of the week.

If a firm wishes to split the market up into different segments and charge different prices, it must have a mechanism for keeping the markets separate. It must avoid the possibility of consumers buying in the cheaper part and the product being resold at a higher price. Price discrimination will only make economic sense if the market segments have different price elasticities of demand. The simple rule would be to charge higher prices where the demand is more price inelastic and lower prices where demand is price elastic.

Comparing monopoly with perfect competition

Figure 9.29 shows the equilibrium price and output of a monopoly charging a single price in a market free of government intervention and the situation that would occur in a perfectly competitive industry.

The classic case against monopoly is that its conduct and performance is undesirable when compared with that of firms in more competitive markets. The following observations can be made from the diagram comparing the equilibrium in both perfect competition and monopoly:

- the price in monopoly will be higher than it would be in perfect competition;
- the monopoly output is lower;
- the monopolist is making short- and long-run abnormal profits;
- the firm in perfect competition is productively efficient, producing the optimum output;
- it is also allocatively efficient, producing where price = MC;
- the monopolist captures consumer surplus and turns it into abnormal profit;

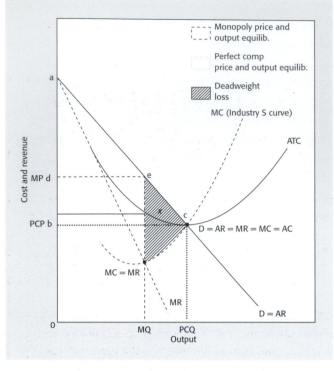

Figure 9.29 A comparison of a perfectly competitive industry with a profit-maximising monopolist

- the monopolist is productively inefficient, producing less than the optimum output in the search for extra profit;
- the price charged is well above marginal cost;
- if a perfectly competitive industry was turned into a monopoly there would be a welfare loss of area *x* in addition to greater allocative inefficiency.

The criticisms of real-world monopolies based on a comparison with perfect competition may not be valid because:

1 Perfect competition is a theoretical ideal. Monopoly must be compared with the real world models of monopolistic competition and oligopoly. These are also characterised by productive and allocative inefficiency. In addition they may involve a waste of resources in competitive advertising.

2 Figure 9.29 is drawn under the assumption that the costs in monopoly will be the same as in perfect competition. This ignores the possibility that the monopolist can achieve internal economies of scale which would reduce unit costs. It is possible that a monopolist could charge a lower price than would occur in perfect competition, making consumers better off, even though the monopolist is making abnormal profits.

A positive case can be made for monopoly in certain circumstances. These include:

- A monopolist cannot always make abnormal profit – it depends how high its costs are. There may be situations where the fixed costs are so high relative to the total cost that the market price can just cover the average costs. In this case the monopolist would only make normal profit. This is a case of natural monopoly, where it would make no economic sense to have the product supplied by competing firms.
- The concept of abnormal profit must be considered carefully. One of the criticisms of a competitive market is the uncertainty of profits in the long run. A monopolist however can plan future investment and finance it through what are guaranteed profits. This may offer customers better products and the workforce greater security.
- The investment may take the form of process innovation, implementing new techniques of production with the objective of lowering unit costs.
- Alternatively, the profit could be used to finance product innovation which will add to consumer welfare in the future, either through an improvement in the product's performance or through widening consumer choice.
- If the benefits of economies of scale and greater investment are passed on to consumers, it could be argued that they have gained from the existence of abnormal profit.

One of the criticisms raised against state-owned monopolies is that the absence of competition makes them become less efficient. The essence of the argument is that firms with a guaranteed market can be complacent. Monopolists are said to suffer from *x*-inefficiency, which means that their cost levels are higher than they would be in competitive firms because they do not have the incentive for process innovation. They become less dynamic, doing things in a particular way simply through tradition. In addition, some of their investment may take the form of erecting barriers to maintain the level of abnormal profit by excluding potential rivals. This will add to costs in the short run. This may be true but there is the possibility that these inefficiencies are outweighed by economies of scale which lower the unit costs.

It is clear that monopolies can operate in ways that lead to inefficiency or consumer exploitation. However,

Self-assessment tasks

Read the case study below and then tackle the exercises that follow.

Does OPEC have a monopoly in the supply of oil?

The Organisation of Petroleum Exporting Countries is a cartel set up in 1960 by five countries. The membership has now risen to 11. OPEC is responsible for 40% of the world production of crude oil and 14% of the world's natural gas. However, its exports of oil represent 60% of the oil that is traded internationally, and it has 77% of the world's proven oil reserves. Its declared objective was to secure fair and stable prices for producers, an efficient, economic and regular supply of oil to consuming nations and a fair return on capital for those investing in the oil industry. The cartel was in a very strong position. It had a geographic monopoly because the distribution of world oil deposits is uneven. The demand for oil has been rising on trend and has been an essential raw material with a low price elasticity of demand because of the lack of a close substitute. In this situation, any reduction in supply will increase the market price without much reduction in the volume traded. The revenue of the OPEC members will certainly increase. OPEC cut production in 1973/4 and 1979 in what have been described as oil crises. In the 1980s, oil prices fell because supply was greater than demand. The only thing that will weaken OPEC's economic power is if new suppliers outside of the cartel appear or consumers take action that will reduce consumption. Technology may provide alternatives to oil in the future. The monopoly will weaken further if there is disagreement over the target price or the production quotas allocated to each member country.

OPEC denies that it is acting as a single monopoly, cutting output in order to charge high prices to consumers and points out that western governments make more money from the tax on oil than the producing countries receive in revenues from selling the oil. At the retailing end of the industry, the supply is in the hands of an oligopoly of oil companies who deny that they are charging too much, insisting that the profit margin is low because of fierce competition. Profits are only high because of the large turnover. Some analysts predict that there will be further horizontal integration between oil companies that are already vertically integrated. The oil industry will continue to be dominated by a few big players mainly because of the high fixed cost and risks associated with exploration and drilling.

1 Is OPEC a monopoly or an example of collusive oligopoly? Justify your answer.
2 Explain the economic logic behind OPEC's decision to reduce output.
3 What factors may reduce the demand for OPEC oil over time?
4 How can the oil companies boost their profits if they have little control over the market price?

one can make a positive case for monopoly. This explains why the investigation of monopoly practices is difficult and each case must be judged on its own merits. It is dangerous to assume that monopoly is always harmful; the performance of a monopolist may be little different from that of firms in oligopoly.

Contestable markets

So far, in dealing with market structures, the models shown in figure 9.22 have been analysed. A **contestable market** is not listed here although it features prominently on the competition road map (figure 9.23). Why is this? The reason is that the concept of a contestable market does not fit neatly into the structure which has been developed by economists to study the conduct and performance of firms and the industry. By definition, a *perfectly* contestable market is one in which there are no costs of entry and exit. So, only perfect competition matches this ideal; monopolistic competition, with few relatively costless barriers to entry and exit, can match it to some extent, as can oligopoly in certain situations.

Allies sought in dogfight to rule skies

When the chief executives of British Midland and Singapore Airlines sat huddled next to each other in a Singapore rickshaw earlier this month, it marked a significant development in global aviation. The duo were making a colourful entrance at the Shangri-La Hotel to celebrate their membership of the world's largest and ever-growing airline grouping, Star Alliance (see below). Together with the bosses of Star's other member carriers, it was easy to see why such images would send the jitters through rival alliances, including One World, led by British Airways.

British Midland is the second biggest airline at Heathrow, while Singapore Airlines is the world's most profitable carrier and a key strategic player in South East Asia. Fellow Star members, American Airlines and Lufthansa, operate trans-Atlantic and German flights from Heathrow. As a consequence, the alliance has an increasingly tight grip on the world's busiest international airport. Overall it controls 24 per cent of all available slots at Heathrow, British Airways' hub. British Midland controls two-thirds of these slots.

Heathrow has always been a battleground for airlines desperate to hold on to their precious slots. The airport though is itself becoming an even more valuable asset in the alliance scenario as it competes more vigorously with the likes of Frankfurt (Lufthansa), Schipol (KLM), Charles de Gaulle (Air France) and Vienna (Austrian Airlines). Because of slot constraints, alliances help airlines to operate services through their partners without committing their own aircraft, thus reducing costs.

British Airways (BA) has proved unable to use its dominant position at Heathrow, where it hold 38 per cent of all slots, to its full potential. It has tried to merge with American Airlines and more recently with KLM, but on both occasions the marriage has had to be aborted. BA's new chief executive Rod Eddington, named only yesterday, will be keenly aware of the lack of progress as he steps into his new job. Rival alliance Star is becoming a very competitive force on his home patch.

Star Alliance

Air Canada	Air New Zealand
All Nipon Airways	Ansett Australia
Austrian Airlines	British Midland
Lauda Air	Lufthansa
Mexicana Air	SAS – Scandinavian Airlines
Singapore Airlines	Thai Airways
Tyrolean Airways	Varig
United Airlines	

Heathrow Airport. A fifth terminal might be profitable but would have a negative impact on the local environment
Source: BAA.

Source: Updesh Kapur, *The Times*, 26 April 2000 (adapted).

A contestable market is not so much a market structure as a means by which governments have sought to regulate industry and the provision of services. It has had particular significance in the UK since 1979, when the principle of contestability became central to the tremendous structural changes that have been made especially to the service sector of the economy.

The important features of a contestable market are:

- *Free entry*. This implies that new and existing market providers will have the same cost structure as in a perfectly competitive market.
- *The number and size of firms are irrelevant*. If a contestable market has only a few large firms, any cost differences should be a reflection of a decision by a particular firm to charge a given price.
- *Normal profits only can be earned in the long run*. If firms are making supernormal profits then this is the signal for others to enter the market. This could be on a 'hit and run' basis – a firm sees an opportunity, enters the market, collects the gains and leaves at no cost.
- *The threat of potential entrants into the market is over-riding*. Oligopolists and even a monopolist are obliged to offer consumers the benefits that they would receive in a more competitive market structure. Otherwise, new firms will enter from the pool of potential entrants.

- All firms are subject to the same regulations and government control irrespective of size.
- Mechanisms must be in place to prevent the use of unfair pricing by established firms to stop new entrants from entering the market.
- Cross-subsidisation is eliminated since firms cannot make normal profits if they sell any of their services below cost.

The application of contestability to the airline market is particularly interesting, since prior to deregulation routes were strictly regulated by governments and there was little competition. The 'open skies' policy of a deregulated market has led to lower fares and a greater choice of airline for passengers. This has particularly been the case in the US domestic market and in Europe, where new low-cost airlines such as easyJet and Ryanair have entered the market and challenged the established national carriers. A further outcome has been the response of these carriers to form alliances (see the case study).

There are other examples of contestable markets in the UK including:

- local bus services and rail services,
- the provision of public services such as electricity, gas and water supplies,
- telecommunications, particularly through the choice of network suppliers.

Self-assessment tasks

Read the article and then tackle the exercises that follow.

German railways – private lines

Bit by bit, private firms are taking business from Germany's state railway company

The station in Kiel is no advertisement for rail travel: like most buildings that are being refurbished, it is an ordeal for both the eyes and the ears. The trains are more welcoming. Head south to Neumünster, or west to Husum and Bad St Peter-Ording, on the North Sea, and you will sit in new, spruce vehicles. As you gaze through their windows, you can listen to music piped to your seat (but bring your own headphones). If you do not have time to buy a ticket before your journey, never mind: get one from a machine on board.

These trains are owned by Nord-Ost-see-Bahn (NOB), which last November took over services on 177km (110 miles) of track from Deutsche Bahn, Germany's state-owned railway company. NOB, which has a ten-year franchise, is a product of a reform in 1994 that handled responsibility for local trains, plus an annual dollop of federal money, to the 16 *Länder* (states). Mainly, the *Länder* buy services through negotiated contracts lasting a few years, although there is a trend towards competitive tenders. DB Regio, part of Deutsche Bahn, still has over 90% of the market. However, some outsiders have fought their way in. Some are owned by the *Länder* themselves; one is part-owned by SNCF, France's state rail monopoly.

The biggest private operator, Connex, a subsidiary of Vivendi Universal, a French conglomerate, owns six regional passenger railways, including NOB. Connex also runs a big commuter network in south-east England, where passengers often complain about delays, cancellations and dirty trains. Dubious reputation? Not in Germany, where its subsidiaries are seen as plucky, efficient underdogs snapping at the big, bad Bahn.

Schleswig-Holstein, the state of which Kiel is the capital, is in the vanguard of change. It has already run tenders for 23% of its services (measured by train-kilometres). Deutsche Bahn's local market share has fallen from 90% to 75% since 1995. The next step, says Bernhard Wewers, head of LVS, the company that oversees local transport in the state, is for local politicians to decide whether to open bigger lines to tender. If they do, and if Deutsche Bahn does badly, its market share could fall below 50%.

The aim, says Mr Wewers, is to cut the state's costs, while improving services and so coaxing people out of their cars and into trains. When the state first asked Deutsche Bahn for cheaper services, he says, 'they told us we were silly.' Yet across Germany, he reckons, competition has cut costs by 10–20%. Rolling stock has to meet certain criteria: hence NOB's smart trains, and similar ones used by DB Regio between Kiel and Flensburg, on the Danish border. New stations have been opened. All this has helped push passenger numbers up by 18% since 1995.

This leaves one crucial question: how can new entrants provide a better service than cash-strapped Deutsche Bahn and still make money? Lower overheads are a plus, says NOB's Mr Bergemann; and people are usually better motivated in a small private business than in a big state corporation. In a small operation, he says, problems can be dealt with speedily and by the people in charge. He makes the point, in a small way, when a train pulls into Neumünster: he strolls through the carriage, picking up discarded newspapers.

Source: The Economist, 16 June 2001.

1 Briefly describe how the railway market in Germany has become competitive.

2 What benefits has contestability brought to:
   ◆ rail passengers?
   ◆ the regional government?

3 Comment upon the extent to which this market really is contestable.

Conclusions – the conduct and performance of firms

The conduct or behaviour of firms has been discussed in each of the four main market structures. The ways firms carry out their businesses will be determined by their objectives and the actual market conditions in which they are carrying out their business. As we made clear from the outset, a firm's market power, and hence its conduct, is directly linked to the ease or difficulty of entry into the market.

In setting their prices, only in perfect competition are firms truly price takers. Any firm that moves away from a policy of charging more or less than the prevailing market price will have to leave the industry in the long run. In all other market structures, firms are price makers to some extent, although there may be some **price competition**. Consequently, non-price competition, where firms compete in terms of product promotion through branding, packaging or advertising, is relevant in monopolistic competition and oligopoly. A monopolist though has complete control over the prices that are charged.

Other aspects of pricing were discussed in the cases of oligopoly and monopoly. Price leadership was stated as being prevalent in oligopoly. Here, a market leader may be the price leader. This firm sets prices and others follow. The rigidity of prices in this market was illustrated by the kinked demand curve (figure 9.26), a clear recognition of the mutual interdependence of firms.

So, in imperfect competition, firms compete with others on a mixture of price and non-price competition. It is only when there are very close substitutes that their conduct becomes less predictable. In this way, firms are interdependent. The extent to which they feel they can take risks with regard to their rivals' responses can lead to a change in a firm's pattern of behaviour. The outcome is often one of collusion.

The perfect competition model is an ideal. All other market structures fail to match it in terms of efficiency and performance. Monopolistic competition, for example, is said to have excess capacity with firms operating at less than the optimum level of output. The prices charged will be higher than what they could charge if they were bigger.

The models of competition make an assumption that, whatever the market structure, each firm will seek to maximise its profits all of the time. In reality this is clearly not the case. There is a particularly strong argument for relaxing this assumption when investigating how oligopolists operate. Alternative motives therefore often make it difficult to really predict the conduct of firms in respect of price and output.

Summary

In this section we have recognised that:

- The principle of diminishing marginal utility can be used to explain the shape and derivation of the demand curve.

- A consumer will choose a combination of goods where the value of the marginal utility divided by the price of the good is equal for all goods.

- A price change for a good can be divided into a substitution effect and an income effect.

- In the short run at least one factor of production is fixed; all factors are variable in the long run.

- The short-run production function shows how the quantity produced varies with changes to the input of a variable factor of production, normally labour.

- The demand for all factors of production is a derived demand; in the case of labour, the firm's demand curve can be derived from the value of the marginal revenue product.

- The supply of labour to a firm depends upon the wage rate; the shape of the supply curve for labour depends upon the responsiveness of labour supply to a change in the wage rate.

- The wage rate in a market is like any other price and is determined by supply and demand; labour markets can be influenced by the actions of trade unions and the government.

- Transfer earnings and economic rent can be used to explain why some workers are paid more than others for their services.

- Economists split a firm's costs of production into fixed and variable costs; marginal and average costs are particularly useful in explaining how costs vary with a firm's output.

- In the long run, as output expands, the benefits from falling average costs are known as economies of scale; these benefits can accrue both within and from outside of a particular firm.

- Although economic power rests with large firms, small firms are more typical and are able to survive for many reasons.

- The normal objective of a firm is profit maximisation; other objectives may also be relevant in some types of business activity.

- The structure of markets can be explained by various characteristics including the strength of barriers to entry, the number and size of firms, the nature of the product and the availability of information.

- Economists recognise various models of economic structure, namely perfect competition, monopoly, monopolistic competition and oligopoly; these models are useful for making comparisons with real market structures.

- Many real-world markets are increasingly contestable in their structure.

- Firms compete in various ways depending upon the market structure in which they operate.

- The main models of market structure themselves can be compared in terms of their relative output, profits and efficiency.

Key words

Definitions of Key words can be found in the Glossary.

abnormal profit
average cost
average fixed cost
average product
average revenue
average variable cost
barriers to entry
budget line
cartels
closed shop
collective bargaining
concentration ratio
contestable markets
derived demand
diminishing marginal
    utility
diminishing returns
diseconomies of scale
economic rent
economies of scale
equi-marginal utility
external economies of
    scale
financial economies of
    scale
fixed costs
horizontal integration
immobility of labour
imperfect competition
imperfections in the
    labour market
income effect
integration
internal economies of
    scale
long run
marginal cost
marginal physical product

marginal revenue
marginal revenue product
marginal utility
marketing economies
mobility of labour
monopolistic competition
monopoly
monopsony
natural monopoly
non-price competition
normal profit
occupational mobility
oligopoly
perfect competition
price agreements
price competition
price discrimination
price leadership
profit
profit maximisation
risk bearing economies of
    scale
sales maximisation
sales revenue
    maximisation
satisficing
short run
substitution effect
supernormal profit
technical economies of
    scale
trade unions
transfer earnings
utility
variable costs
variable proportions
vertical integration
wage differentials

10 Government intervention in the price system

Introduction

In section 3 it was suggested that there may be times when markets do not function well. Three particular reasons were identified:

1 *The existence of externalities*
   ◆ Both negative and positive externalities can cause a market to fail to work effectively.
   ◆ Negative externalities exist when the social cost of an activity exceeds the private cost. There is an external cost that is not paid by those directly involved in the transaction. This leads to over-production of the product involved as the true cost does not directly have to be paid by the producers and consumers of this product.
   ◆ Positive externalities exist when the social benefit of an activity exceeds the private benefit. The full benefit to all of society is not gained by those directly involved in an activity. This means that the product is under-produced as demand will not be as great as it should be.

2 *Public goods*
   ◆ Public goods possess the twin characteristics of non-excludability and non-rivalry. Once the good (such as a lighthouse) is produced for one person, it is impossible to stop others from benefiting. Equally, as more and more people consume the product, the benefit is not diminished to existing consumers.
   ◆ Public goods may not be produced in free markets due to the problem of 'free-riding'. No-one is prepared to purchase the product as there is a strong incentive to wait for someone else to do so and then to enjoy the benefit without incurring any cost. If everyone behaves in this way then the product is not produced.

3 *Merit goods*
   ◆ Merit goods can be defined either as products that generate positive externalities or as products that generate greater benefits to individuals than those individuals realise. Health care could be seen as a clear example.
   ◆ Merit goods are likely to be underproduced in a market as the full benefits are not recognised. The demand for the product is thus less than it ideally should be.

The purpose of the rest of this section is to build upon this earlier analysis and to consider some further ways in which markets can be seen not to function well or to *fail*.

When markets do not work well they are seen to fail. Market failure can now be defined in a more precise manner. It exists when *the operation of a market does not lead to economic efficiency*. A free market may fail to deliver either productive efficiency or allocative efficiency (or both). Resources are thus not being used in the best way possible in that market. The market has failed.

The problem of monopolies

One important way in which markets can be seen to fail is when a market is dominated by a single supplier. There is a monopoly. Typical of the concerns about monopolies are the points made about the British milk industry in the self-assessment tasks.

Self-assessment tasks

Read the article below and then tackle the exercises that follow.

Minister orders competition reforms over milk prices

Ministers ordered a big shake-up of the dairy industry after a Competition Commission report yesterday said consumers pay too much for milk. The Commission found that Milk Marque, the co-operative owned by farmers which is Britain's largest milk supplier, had exploited its monopoly powers to raise the price of raw milk.

In a statement sending shock waves through the dairy farming industry Stephen Byers, Trade and Industry Secretary, demanded changes to Milk Marque's conditions of sale. He announced that Milk Marque will need the permission of the Director General of Fair Trading before any further expansion to processing facilities to make cheese, yoghurts and other dairy products.

The Competition Commission concluded that any increase in processing by the co-operative 'may be expected to operate against the public interest by enhancing its ability to exploit its monopoly power'.

Milk Marque had a 49.6 per cent share of milk supplies after it replaced the defunct Milk Marketing Board for England and Wales in 1994. It now has 39 per cent. Under British rules, a business with more than 25 per cent of a market can be considered an unwelcome monopoly, but in Europe the cut-off is 40 per cent.

Source: David Brown, *Daily Telegraph*, 7 July 1999 (adapted).

1   Explain why a company, such as Milk Marque, could be considered to be a monopoly even though it only supplies 39 per cent of the market.

2   Discuss the ways in which Milk Marque might be seen to 'exploit its monopoly power' in this industry.

A monopoly technically exists where there is just one firm in the industry. However, an industry can be deemed to be a monopoly when it is dominated by one firm. There are two reasons why monopolies might reasonably be expected to develop:

◆ *Economies of scale* Where there are significant economies of scale present in an industry, firms will have to be very large in order to effectively exploit those economies. If demand is limited, there may be room for only one firm in the industry. This is the case of a natural monopoly.

◆ *The profit motive* It is assumed in Economics that firms aim to maximise profits. A very effective way of maximising profits is to destroy competitors. Given this, a free market may see moves towards monopoly markets.

The problem with this possible tendency towards monopoly markets is that there are economic reasons to expect such markets to be inefficient: they are unlikely to be either productively or allocatively efficient. In other words, there tends to be market failure in monopoly markets.

A useful way to understand the problems of monopolies is to try to compare the possible production point of an industry if it were a monopoly as opposed to being a competitive industry. Figure 10.1 is an adaptation of figure 9.29.

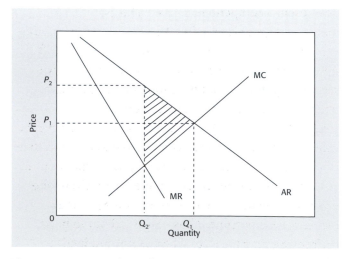

Figure 10.1 A comparison of monopoly and a competitive market

In a fully competitive market (a state of perfect competition), price is determined by the interaction of supply and demand. The equilibrium price and quantity will be where the supply schedule intersects the demand schedule. This information can be seen on the diagram. The average revenue schedule (AR) is the same as the demand schedule. In a perfectly competitive industry, the marginal cost schedule (MC) is the same thing as the supply schedule. Thus the equilibrium price in the perfectly competitive industry is P_1 and the quantity is Q_1.

The situation is different in a monopoly market. Here, the firm has the power to set the price for the whole industry. Given this, the profit-maximising monopolist will choose to set the price at the point where marginal cost is equal to marginal revenue as this is the point of profit maximisation. On the diagram, this is indicated by the price of P_2 and the quantity Q_2. This suggests that price will be higher and quantity lower in a monopoly market than in a competitive market.

The problem is not simply that price is higher under monopoly. The essence of the problem is that price is above marginal cost (as is clear on the diagram). This means that there is not allocative efficiency. Price is higher than the cost of producing the last unit of production and thus demand and production are too low. There are insufficient scarce resources directed to the production of this product. There is inefficiency.

In addition to allocative inefficiency, there may also be productive inefficiency in monopoly markets. It is possible that the cost schedule indicated on the diagram may rise if the market is a monopoly compared to its position in a competitive market. This is due to *x*-inefficiency (see also section 9). This is a phrase used by economists to describe the tendency of costs to drift upwards in monopolies. The reason for this is easy to see. Monopolists do not have the same competitive pressures operating upon them as do firms in competitive markets. Whilst a monopolist may have the incentive of profits to keep costs as low as possible, there is not the same threat of bankruptcy. A monopolist can 'get away with' higher costs as there are no rivals who will take away the trade if costs and thus prices are higher than is possible. Thus costs tend not to be at their lowest possible level. There is not productive efficiency.

The profit-maximising point is where marginal cost is equal to marginal revenue. It can be seen that this point is *not* the minimum point on the average cost schedule and thus that there is not technical efficiency.

The conclusion of this section is clear: monopoly markets tend to fail. They do not lead to resources being used in an optimum way and thus there is economic inefficiency.

Self-assessment tasks

1 Explain why there is not allocative efficiency in a monopoly market.

2 Give some possible specific examples of x-inefficiency for a monopolist.

3 Explain why prices are likely to be higher in a monopoly market than in a competitive market.

Deadweight loss

Market failure can be understood also through an economic concept termed **deadweight loss**. This term refers to the loss of economic welfare due to the fact that potentially desirable production and consumption does not take place. There is thus not as much producer and consumer surplus as there would be if all such desirable trades took place. This loss of surplus is called 'deadweight loss'.

Deadweight loss can be seen to occur in a monopoly market when comparing that market with a competitive market. This is illustrated in figure 10.1. The competitive outcome is given in this diagram by price P_1 and output Q_1. This represents the optimum production and consumption position. Just the right amount of resources is being used to provide this product. This is in contrast to the monopoly outcome given by price P_2 and quantity Q_2. Here, there is underproduction and underconsumption. Too few resources are used in the production of this good because the price is too high. A measure of the resulting loss of economic welfare is given by the shaded triangle in the diagram. This indicates the loss of net consumer and producer surplus due to the monopoly. It is the deadweight loss due to the monopoly.

Deadweight loss can also be seen to operate when a government imposes an indirect tax on a product. This is illustrated in figure 10.2.

The price and quantity of the product are given by the intersection of supply and demand before the tax is imposed. This gives a price of P_1 and a quantity of Q_1. The imposition of the tax is the equivalent of an increase in the costs of production and thus it shifts the supply schedule to the left (S to S_1). This leads to a higher price, P_2, and a lower quantity, Q_2. This means a deadweight loss for the same reason as in a monopoly market. Desirable production and consumption are discouraged because of the higher price. The resulting overall loss of economic welfare is shown by the shaded triangle. It gives a measure of the amount of deadweight loss due to the imposition of the tax. From a wider

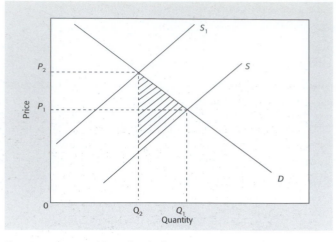

Figure 10.2 Imposition of an indirect tax

perspective, excessive taxes can undermine British competitiveness, as the article in the self-assessment indicates.

Self-assessment tasks

1 Read the article below and then tackle the exercises that follow.

Jam today, road pricing tomorrow?

Singapore invented it, Norway copied it, Stockholm spent 20 years and $1 billion before thinking again, whilst Hong Kong retreated at the last moment in the face of a popular revolt but is determined to try again. It is against this international context that earlier this year the UK government published a highly controversial consultation document which made the most positive statement yet that road pricing would be coming to Britain in an attempt to get to grips with the country's ever-increasing problems of urban traffic congestion. In true British fashion though the commitment is really no more than one to fund further research and to select a handful of towns and cities to try out pilot road pricing schemes.

The bottom line is that politicians are terrified of road pricing; indeed they prefer not to be seen to be interfering with the ability of the country's 25 million drivers to be able to use their vehicles when they want, where they want and at no additional cost above the massive levels of taxation that they are already pouring into the Exchequer from fuel duties, taxes on new vehicles and an annual road fund tax. The scale of the problems which the UK is facing is so serious that it cannot be ignored.

At the same time there is a remarkable consensus amongst economists that road pricing is the only way in which the country's congestion problems can be resolved. It is seen as a sensible way of dealing with the problem of a scarce resource, road space, which is inefficiently used and as a consequence, generates substantial costs to the community. Road pricing is not only the answer to congested city roads – it is a fair and logical outcome to a classic example of *market failure*.

Returning to Singapore, for many years now the government has imposed high customs duties on imported cars and set stiff registration fees and high annual road taxes. In addition it requires anybody buying a new car to get a permit, currently priced at between $27,000 and $49,000, well above the average annual income per head. If this were not enough, for the past 20 years, to enter a restricted city zone, drivers must pay a $2 flat rate charge in the morning peak period, falling to $1.30 at off-peak times. When the peak charge was extended to the rush hour in 1989, it further reduced traffic.

From Spring 1998, a new automatic 'pay-as-you-go' system replaced the above rather crude system. Using the latest micro-chip technology, charging is automatic (smart cards will be pre-loaded up to $150) and is based on the actual contribution to congestion made by

individual car users. To the economist this is in many respects a 'dream ticket' – it matches in full the well-known 'polluter pays' principle so strenuously advocated in text books yet so very rarely applied in practice.

But will it work in Britain? This is highly problematic, not least because, unlike Singapore, we do not have a world-class public transport system to provide a realistic alternative for urban travellers. If we are serious about resolving our transport problem we must be as radical as the objections we face. And for a start, we could learn a lot from Singapore.

Source: *The Economist*, 6 December 1997; C.G. Bamford, 'Road Pricing – Now or Never', *Economics Today*, March 2000 (adapted).

(a) Explain why traffic congestion is a classic example of market failure.

(b) How in theory should a government deal with the problem of traffic congestion?

2 Suppose you have been invited to the UK to make a presentation to politicians and planners on how the experience of Singapore in dealing with its congestion problems might assist the UK in reducing its urban transport problems. Briefly draft this presentation under the following headings:

◆ the main benefits of road pricing in Singapore,

◆ the data you would need in being able to measure these benefits,

◆ why the experience of Singapore may not be entirely relevant for the UK or your own country.

Self-assessment tasks

Read the article below and then tackle the exercises that follow.

Bosses tell Brown to stop meddling with tax system

Leaders of Britain's top companies told Tony Blair yesterday that the Chancellor was making the tax system too complicated.

Since becoming Chancellor, Mr Brown has produced a welter of reliefs to encourage entrepreneurs, but has increased the complexity of the tax system, particularly capital gains tax, and introduced an energy tax. Mr Blair's breakfast talks with more than 20 chairmen and chief executives of industrial and banking groups at his country residence coincided with an accusation in a leading business magazine that Labour was blunting Britain's competitive edge with too much regulation.

Forbes International labelled Mr Blair 'Red Tape Tony' and claimed that he was turning Britain into a high tax country. The accusations were embarrassing for Mr Blair, who has sought to demonstrate that Labour is 'business friendly' and is making Britain an attractive base for multi-national companies.

Source: George Jones, *Daily Telegraph*, 17 February 2001 (adapted).

1 Explain how the imposition of an indirect tax on a product can create a deadweight loss.

2 According to the newspaper article, discuss how the British government is being accused of discouraging desirable business.

Government intervention
Introduction

In section 3 it was seen that when the market did not appear to work well (there was obviously market failure present) then the government intervened in order to try to improve the situation. Specifically, the following forms of government intervention were identified:

1 *Maximum prices*

   ◆ If a price were seen to be too high, then the government might impose a maximum price.

   ◆ A maximum price could be imposed on a monopoly market in order to moderate the price. This is a policy used in some countries, such as the United Kingdom, by regulatory bodies for monopolies.

   ◆ A maximum price might also be used if there were concerns that consumers could not afford an important product, such as housing.

   ◆ The effect of a maximum price could be to create shortages as is could lead to demand exceeding supply.

2 *Price stabilisation*

   ◆ Some markets are susceptible to undesirable swings in the market price of the product. This is particularly true of the agricultural market.

   ◆ Prices may be stabilised by the government to protect the real incomes of both consumers and producers.

   ◆ In agriculture, the use of buffer stocks represents a way by which prices could be stabilised.

3 *Taxes and subsidies*

   ◆ Taxes can be used to discourage the production of a product. Subsidies encourage production.

   ◆ Taxes may be placed on products that generate negative externalities and would normally tend to be overproduced.

   ◆ Subsidies might be paid to producers of goods and services that have positive externalities and are merit goods. Such products, such as health care and education, would be underproduced by the free market.

4 *Direct provision*

   ◆ The government may decide to provide some products itself.

   ◆ The main economic justification for the government of goods and services is that they would not be produced otherwise. This can be seen to be the case with public goods.

The purpose of much of the remainder of this section is to consider further why governments intervene in markets and some extra policies that may be available for such intervention.

Objectives of government microeconomic policy

It is possible to identify two possible economic justifications for the government to intervene in the operation of free markets.

1 *Efficiency*

   ◆ Governments may intervene in markets in order to try to restore economic efficiency. If markets are seen to be failing, for the sorts of reasons indicated in the first part of the section, then the government may try to move the market to a more efficient position through the use of various different policies. Both productive and allocative efficiency could be improved through the introduction of appropriate government policies.

2 *Equity*

   ◆ A further concern over the operation of free markets is to do with **equity**. Even if markets may be judged to be efficient, they may not be judged to be *equitable*.

Equity is to do with 'fairness'. The outcome of a free market may be judged to be 'unfair'. This can be seen in the comparison that is sometimes used between so-called 'political democracy' and 'economic democracy'. A free market is sometimes likened to an economic democracy. Consumers are the voters and money represents the votes. Those products that are 'elected' are those that receive most money votes. Thus, free markets produce allocative efficiency as they ensure that those products most in demand are those that are produced. There is, however, one important difference between these two democracies. The underlying principle of the political democracy is that of 'one–person–one–vote'. This is clearly not true of the economic democracy. Here, the number of votes varies greatly between individuals. Some have very few, if any, while others have very large numbers of votes. Some would judge this to be inequitable and an undesirable aspect of market economies.

This area of economics is not without difficulty. One person's judgement of what may be 'equitable' is not necessarily the same as another person's view. This is 'normative' economics: there are clear value judgements to be made between what is 'right' and 'wrong'. The role of the economist is usually seen as identifying the inequality and allowing others (such as politicians) to judge its desirability.

Self-assessment tasks

Read the article below and then tackle the exercises that follow.

Africa's 'Marshall Plan'

A plan to rescue Africa from poverty and instability will be unveiled tomorrow by President Mbeki at the World Economic Forum in Davos, Switzerland. Dubbed the 'African Marshall Plan', it is hailed as Africa's first home-grown growth initiative designed to break dependence on foreign aid and end the cycle of economic decline.

Drawn up by South Africa, Nigeria and Algeria, the initiative seeks a substantial short-term increase in development aid, including large-scale debt write-offs. This would help reduce the loss of scarce capital, much of which goes on debt repayments.

Increased development assistance would be focused on improving infrastructure, health care and education programmes. In exchange, African leaders are pledged to break with the past track record of economic mismanagement and corruption.

Source: Michael Dynes, *The Times*, 27 January 2001.

1 Explain the two reasons why governments may use microeconomic policy to change the outcomes of the free market.
2 Discuss whether a situation of people owning several houses while other people are homeless requires government intervention.
3 Explain how the suggested 'Marshall Plan for Africa' might reduce world inequity.

If the outcome of the market economy is deemed to be unacceptably inequitable then governments can use policies to try to reduce the inequity. This could be

within a country or it could be international in scale. The article from *The Times* suggests one such international scheme.

Government regulation

One further form of intervention available to governments in addition to those considered in section 3 is that of regulation. Regulation is the use of legal intervention to force consumers and producers to behave in certain ways. It is the use of government legislation in order to produce a more desirable economic outcome than that achieved by the free market.

Economists generally do not favour the use of government regulation. It is seen as a 'blunt' instrument. It forces consumers and producers to do (or not to do) certain things rather than to provide incentives. It can be seen as working against the market rather than with the market. However, governments may judge that regulation is sometimes required if a more desirable outcome is to be achieved.

Government regulation may be used in order to control the behaviour of monopolies. There are several forms of regulation that can be used for this:

◆ *Legislation that outlaws the formation of monopolies* This is usually referred to as merger policy. It takes the view that the formation of a monopoly in a market may be undesirable and thus, under some circumstances, mergers that would create a monopoly would not be allowed to occur.

◆ *Legislation that forbids certain types of monopoly behaviour* An example might be 'predatory pricing'. This is the practice of a powerful producer deliberately setting its price below the cost of production. It does this in order to try to destroy competition. Either a current firm is to be driven out of business or a potential new firm is dissuaded from entering the market. It thus maintains or strengthens the monopolist's position and can lead to inefficiency.

◆ *Laws that insist on certain standards of provision* These try to ensure that there is a guaranteed quality of product provided in monopoly markets.

◆ *Regulations that insist on certain levels of competition in an industry*. A range of possibilities exists here. This has been a policy often used in the telecommunications industry, such as that described in the article from *Business Day*.

Self-assessment tasks

Read the article below and then tackle the exercises that follow.

Telkom says it favours rivalry

Telkom [South Africa's monopoly provider of telecommunications services] has come out in favour of competition being phased into the local telephone market at infrastructure level, saying it will fuel growth in the telecommunications sector and the economy.

This comes ahead of a national meeting to be held by the communications department in Johannesburg next weekend. The meeting aims to create consensus among parties involved in the industry on a new telecoms policy as SA moves to liberalise its phone market.

The government plans to publish a draft policy on the new market structure. This will deal with, among other issues, competition, convergence, consumer delivery and new technologies. Analysts expect the policy to facilitate either one or two big new competitors to Telkom for several years, and then a gradual opening up of the market.

Source: Robyn Chalmers, *Business Day (South Africa)*, 25 January 2001 (adapted).

1 Explain why monopolies may give rise to market failure.

2 Discuss how the policy outlined in the article on South African telecommunications might increase efficiency in this market.

Self-assessment tasks

Read the article below and then tackle the exercises that follow.

EU orders fishing ban to save last of the cod

An emergency ban on all deep-sea fishing in more than 40,000 square miles of the North Sea was ordered yesterday in a desperate effort to save cod stocks from total collapse.

The European Union ban prohibits trawling for deep-sea fish in all the main spawning grounds of North Sea cod for the duration of the spawning season, which ends on April 30.

The ban means yet more hardship for British fishermen, whose North Sea cod quota was nearly halved last month. Experts gave a warning that without such drastic action there would soon be no cod left to fish.

'We are in a crisis. The current cod stock in the North Sea is in danger of collapse. That means there may not be any more cod to fish', a European Commission spokeswoman said. 'The whole purpose is to allow as many young cod to survive this year as possible.'

The scale of the disaster facing North Sea cod is underlined by the figures: in 1972, 300,000 tonnes of cod were taken from the North Sea but in 1999 fishermen only managed to catch 60 per cent of the total EU quota of 81,000 tonnes.

During the same year 48 million juvenile cod were caught, and just 6.4 million older fish.

Commercial fishing, Denmark. North Sea
Souce: Mark Edwards/Still Pictures.

Source: Martin Fletcher, *The Times*, 25 January 2001.

1 Explain why fish stocks could run out if the industry operates with no form of government intervention.

2 Discuss the different forms of government intervention that could be used to prevent fish stocks from being over-fished.

Government regulations can be used in other areas to try to overcome market failures. An important possibility is their use to try to tackle environmental problems. A common approach suggested by economists is to use taxes to tackle negative externalities that lead to excessive environmental costs and to give subsidies to encourage environmentally friendly production techniques. However, a more direct approach is simply to legislate and outlaw certain behaviours that create environmental damage.

Laws may be passed by governments that disallow certain types of pollution. Any producers found to contravene such laws are prosecuted and thus pollution is reduced. Laws are seen as necessary in some situations to stop the excessive depletion of natural resources. There is no marginal cost for the using up of scarce resources such as pasture by cattle herders. However, there is a cost imposed on others if the pasture becomes over-grazed. Thus regulations are needed. A similar situation can be seen with the over-fishing of fish stocks. Without regulation fishing stocks may become dangerously depleted (see self-assessment task).

Government policies to redistribute income and wealth

If there are concerns that the free market leads to inequity then there are policies that the government can try to use to reduce inequality in wealth and income. There are three main types of policies that are available:

1 *Monetary benefits*
   A simple way to redistribute income is to pay benefits to those on low incomes. Money is raised through the tax system and then paid to low income individuals and families in order to increase their disposable income. There are two types of such benefits:

   ◆ *Means-tested.* These benefits are only paid to those on low incomes. They are targeted directly at those who are seen to be most in need. An example would be unemployment benefit. However, they are not always claimed by those for whom they are designed. They can also create a disincentive to work (see section 9). If such benefits are reduced through an individual earning more, then there is an

incentive not to earn more. This is the so-called **poverty trap**.

   ◆ *Universal benefits.* These are paid out to everyone in certain categories regardless of their wealth and income. Examples include universal state pensions and child benefit. Such benefits overcome the two problems associated with means-tested benefits. However, they imply paying out money to many who do not need it and therefore tend to be expensive to operate.

2 *The tax system*
   The tax system can be used in order to reduce inequalities in income and wealth. This is specifically through the use of **progressive taxes**. Progressive taxes lead to those earning higher incomes being taxed a higher percentage of their income than those on lower incomes. Thus income differentials are reduced. Most **income tax** systems are progressive in nature. The average rate of tax rises as people earn higher incomes. Taxes on products which are bought usually tend to be **regressive**.

   Taxes can also be imposed upon wealth in order to reduce wealth inequalities. One example might be inheritance tax. Individuals who inherit more than a certain amount of wealth may have to pay some of the value of that wealth in tax to the government.

   The article from the *Daily Telegraph* suggests the British government may be attempting to use the tax system in this redistributive way as well as using the benefit system.

3 *Direct provision of goods and services*
   A further way of reducing inequalities in society is for the government to provide certain important services free of charge to the user. Such services are financed through the tax system. If such services are used equally by all citizens, then those on lowest incomes gain most as a percentage of their income. Inequality is thus lowered.

   The two most significant examples of such free provision in many contemporary societies are health care and education. These markets are characterised by various market failures. However, these failures do not, according to standard economic theory, justify free provision to the consumer. The justification must

Self-assessment tasks

Read the article below and then tackle the exercises that follow.

Brown aims tax relief at poor families

Gordon Brown's pre-election Budget next month will herald a significant shift in favour of means-tested benefits aimed at low-income families with children and help for mothers who choose to remain at home.

The Chancellor confirmed yesterday that he will use his last big announcement to the Commons before polling day to accelerate the pace of tax redistribution in favour of the poor, in particular those with children. The Budget, expected on March 6, is also expected to set out Mr Brown's ambitions for Labour's second term, including an extra tax subsidy for parents in the first year of a child's life, and help for mothers who choose to stay at home rather than return to work.

From April an extra £1 billion to increase Child Benefit to £15.50 a week for the first child, coupled with the start of the new Children's Tax Credit, would 'put the needs of families with children first', Mr Brown said.

Source: Benedict Brogan, *Daily Telegraph*, 6 February 2001.

1 Explain how each of the following could redistribute either income or wealth:
   ◆ unemployment benefit,
   ◆ a progressive income tax,
   ◆ housing benefit,
   ◆ capital gains tax,
   ◆ child benefit,
   ◆ provision of free school education by the government.

2 Referring to the article, explain how the British Chancellor of the Exchequer is trying to redistribute income towards those on lower incomes.

thus be on the grounds of equity. The view is that everyone should have access to a certain level of health care and education regardless of wealth and income. Thus, these services are provided universally free: they are the material equivalent of monetary universal benefits.

The effectiveness of government policy

In principle, government policies to reduce market failures make economic sense. They increase the level of economic efficiency in markets and thus must be judged to be economically desirable. However, in practice, all may not work out as planned. Governments may themselves fail. There are reasons why government intervention may in fact create further inefficiencies and thus not improve the use of scarce resources in a society.

There are three main reasons why there may be government failure:

1 *Problems of information*

Once the government starts to intervene in the running of markets, it needs information. The correct policies can only be introduced if governments have the correct information. The problem is that governments may have inaccurate information. In that case, they may introduce policies that lead to greater economic inefficiency. Some examples of this problem could be the following:

◆ A lack of information about the true value of a negative externality. It is often very difficult to give an accurate figure for the value of a negative externality such as pollution. It is difficult both to put an accurate figure to all of the costs imposed and to trace the source of the pollution itself. The problem with this is that it then becomes very difficult to impose the correct value of a tax that attempts to reduce production to an efficient level. The wrong level of tax will lead to the wrong level of production.

◆ A lack of information about the level of consumer demand for a product. If the government is providing a product free of charge to the consumer then some estimation of the level of consumer demand is required. This could be the case with a public good, such as a lighthouse or a national defence system. Such products may not be provided by the market system and thus the government provides them. However, the government must try to provide the right amount of such products. If it does not estimate the level of demand accurately then the wrong amount of the product will be produced and thus there is inefficiency.

2 *Problems of incentives*

A further problem arises with government intervention in the economy due to the creation of undesirable incentives. These can create inefficiencies. Some examples of the ways in which this can happen are as follows:

◆ The imposition of taxes can distort incentives. The most obvious example of this is the possible impact of an income tax upon the incentive to work. High **marginal rates of taxation** can create disincentives for people to work harder and gain more income. If this happens then scarce resources are not being used to their best effect and there is inefficiency. A similar point can be recalled from the earlier discussion of the deadweight loss of a tax. The disincentive to consume and produce created by the tax led to the wrong amount of a product being produced.

◆ Politicians may be motivated by political power rather than economic imperatives. Politicians are often seen as being motivated principally by the desire to remain in government. If this is so then economic policies may be designed by governments to try to retain power rather than to try to ensure maximum efficiency in the economy. Thus, an unpopular tax on a product that produces negative externalities, such as car use that creates pollution and environmental damage, may be avoided due to the government's fears that it could lead to a loss of votes.

◆ Those running public services may have inappropriate incentives. Once products are provided by the government then the profit motive of the private sector is largely removed.

After the Second World War, the British government attempted to compete in the international arms race, and produced a wide range of advanced weapons systems including long range ballistic missiles such as 'Blue Streak'. However, economic weakness eventually forced the government to abandon many of these projects, particularly the development of large rockets. In order to prevent a complete monopoly in space technology by the United States of America and the Soviet Union, a number of European governments supported the formation of a European space research agency, and work commenced on the development of a European satellite launch vehicle. Initially the British Blue Streak was used as the first stage of a three-stage rocket, the upper stages being produced by the European partners. Due to systems failures, the test firings met with limited success, and in most cases complete failure. The French government persisted strongly with the work, however, and eventually the highly successful European 'Ariane' series of launch vehicles was developed. This success coincided with a major boom in the requirement for large numbers of commercial satellites, mainly for communications purposes. Ariane is now a major force in the international satellite launch business, and the financial and social benefits deriving from this important industry have been considerable. Although driven primarily by France, the project would have been too expensive for any individual European country to finance alone.

Source: Dick Barnard, with kind permission.

How does the government put a value on the loss of an oil-soaked sea gull?
Source: Paul Glendell, Still Pictures.

The question then remains as to what may motivate those in charge of providing public services. There is no entirely clear answer to this question. At its worst, it could become a total lack of incentive to produce the product well or attempts to defraud the system.

3 *Problems of distribution*
Government intervention in the running of the economy is often justified by the need to reduce inequity. However, it is possible that government intervention might sometimes increase inequity. This is simply understood by recognising that the imposition of any tax will have a distributional effect. Thus, a tax on energy use that aims to reduce harmful emissions of greenhouse gases will have different effects on different groups of people. If the tax is on the use of domestic fuel then older members of society may feel the greatest effect as they use proportionately more domestic fuel for heating than others in society. This could be seen as unfair and increasing inequity in society.

Self-assessment tasks

Read the article below and then tackle the exercises that follow.

Public sector fraud is costing Britain £108m

Fraud in town halls and the National Health Service has risen to record levels, with greater numbers of General Practitioners, opticians and pharmacists attempting to fiddle the system, according to figures published by the Audit Commission today.

Fraud amounting to more than £108m was uncovered in the past year. Councils in England and Wales detected £104m in illegal payments, up 18 per cent on 1997–98, while fraud in the NHS doubled to £4.7m. For the first time corrupt GPs have been highlighted in the statistics with more doctors than ever making false claims for prescriptions, vaccinations and night visits. The figures relate only to fraud which has been identified as having occurred; the suspected amount of undiscovered fraud is far higher.

Source: Paul Waugh, *The Independent*, 1 December 1999 (adapted).

1 Explain why each of the following represent examples of government failure:
   - an underestimation of the full benefit to society of public transport that means only a small subsidy is being provided by the government;
   - the building of a new road that has unclear benefits in an area where the government fears that it could lose votes at the next election;
   - a high tax on health care that forms a significant part of many poorer people's budgets;
   - a high level of unemployment benefit that means that people can sometimes earn more by not entering paid employment.

2 Discuss the ways in which the government failure described in the article could be minimised.

Privatisation

In a simple sense, **privatisation** refers to a change in ownership of an activity from the public sector to the private sector. In many instances, as in the UK, privatisation has returned activities that had been nationalised to new private owners. In a modern sense, privatisation means more than this and is now recognised to include:

◆ The *direct sale* of government-owned and operated activities to the private sector. The nature of the sale can be diverse and includes offering shares to the public, management and worker buyouts, the direct sale to new owners and, in some cases, a partial sale with the government retaining some share in the new business.

◆ *Deregulation* through the removal of barriers to entry which had protected the public sector from outside competition. Through this action, a contestable market can be created (see section 9 for details).

◆ *Franchising*. This can give a new private sector owner the right to operate a particular service or activity for a given length of time. In some cases, the franchise might be an exclusive one; in other cases, some competition may be experienced.

◆ *Contracting out* of services previously provided in-house by public sector organisations. Normally, this involves activities that are deemed not to be core to those organisations. In some cases, contracting out allows public sector-based organisations to openly compete with private sector businesses for a particular contract.

By any yardstick, privatisation in the UK economy since 1979 (when a right-wing Conservative government led by Mrs Thatcher was elected) has been substantial. In 1979, the nationalised industries accounted for about 9 per cent of GDP and 7 per cent of employment. By 2000, these statistics were just 2 per cent in each case. Table 10.1 shows the extent of privatisation in this period.

As table 10.1 shows, the principal privatisations have been in the fuel and power and transport sectors. Both were nationalised in the late 1940s, and under government ownership both relied heavily on various forms of subsidy to cover their losses. Under public ownership, it was also recognised that the government was unable to fund the extensive investment programmes needed to enable them to compete in a rapidly changing UK economy. The table also shows how the government has withdrawn its support from a wide range of manufacturing activities. In many cases,

Fuel and power

National electricity generation and regional supply

National gas production and regional supply

Coal production

Nuclear power production

Transport

Railways, passengers and freight

Local and national bus services

Some major airports

British Airways, the national airline

Some road freight services

Some ferry services and ports

Other

Water supply

Telephones and telecommunications

Various manufacturing companies including British Steel, British Aerospace, British Petroleum, British Sugar Corporation, Rover Group, British Shipbuilders.

Table 10.1 Privatisation in the UK economy

this support had been essential in order to keep 'lame duck' companies solvent and safeguard employment.

Why privatise?

Taking the UK economy as a particular example it is possible to recognise various reasons for the extensive privatisation shown in table 10.1. Some are economic, others much more concerned with political motivation. For example:

◆ In the early phase of privatisation, there is little argument that there was a deliberate commitment *to reduce government involvement in the economy*. A return to market forces was seen as necessary for many nationalised industries to achieve an efficient allocation of resources. Public ownership was believed to be a serious obstacle to these industries meeting their particular objectives.

◆ There was also a deliberate policy *to widen share ownership* amongst the population and amongst the employees of the privatised companies. In this way, people who previously had no opportunity to own shares could purchase small quantities of shares in businesses where they were consumers.

A privatised nuclear power station in Britain
Source: Electricity Association.

From an employees standpoint, share ownership was seen as a way of enhancing motivation and improving labour relations in a company.

◆ Privatisation can generate *benefits for consumers* in the form of lower prices, wider choice and a better quality product or service. *x*-inefficiency would be likely to be reduced as firms become more aware of the need to control costs to stay in business (see section 9). Consumers and shareholders therefore become pivotal in the affairs of privatised companies. Under state ownership they often took second place to the needs of the producers.

◆ The sale of nationalised industries has *generated substantial income* for the UK government over a long period of time. This has been estimated to be £70–80 bn over the past twenty years. As a consequence, governments have been able to reduce the size of the Public Sector Borrowing Requirement (PSBR) and in some years, operate with annual budget surpluses due to the influx of receipts from private sector sales. This income generation has been very important in helping the economy to cope with deficits on the trading account of the balance of payments (see section 4).

◆ It is further believed that privatised companies can be successful in raising capital, lowering prices and cutting out waste. In other words they are *more efficient*, with managers able to operate in a market-led way, without the restriction of trying to satisfy government objectives for their companies. Managerial freedom and a highly motivated workforce become the means by which economic efficiency is realised (see section 8).

One of the most successful recent privatisations in the UK has been the sale of the nationalised rail freight business to the English, Welsh and Scottish Railway (EWS). Seemingly in terminal decline under government ownership, and unable to compete effectively with road freight, EWS has enjoyed considerable success since 1995 (see case study). For example:

◆ goods moved by rail had increased 30 per cent by the end of 1999;

◆ EWS had invested heavily in 200 new freight locomotives and had begun a massive investment in freight wagons;

◆ new customers, who had previously used only road freight, were switching some business to rail.

Rail freight gathering steam

Road haulage is the undisputed king of the UK freight business, but goods trains are starting to rumble out of the sidings to recover a share of the market.

In the Fifties, road and rail took an almost equal share of the business. But in the past 40 years, massive growth in the movement of consumer goods, greater investment in roads than railways and the ability to deliver door-to-door have led to the dominance of lorries over trains.

The low cost of road transport has encouraged centralised warehousing, with more goods being carried greater distances.

Railtrack and English, Welsh and Scottish Railway, which operates 90% of rail freight services, has seen an increase in goods carried over the past year, and EWS predicts that business will triple over the next decade.

The Freight Trade Association says that at its conference last month, companies that currently rely on road transport showed a keen interest in rail freight.

'There is concern about traffic congestion, which increases costs,' the association says. 'Provided investment is put into the rail infrastructure, these companies see it as a definite option.'

In a report on freight to the rail regulator, National Economic Research Associates argues that, unlike railways, road haulage is subsidised substantially because it contributes less to society in tax than it costs in terms of pollution, accidents and damage to infrastructure.

Market researcher Key Note predicts that growing concern about traffic congestion and the environment will result in increased costs for road freight.

The environment department is preparing a White Paper on transport strategy and pressure group Transport 2000 is lobbying for a tax on lorries based on their capacity and the distance travelled.

'At present, lorries are empty on 25% of their journeys. A tax levied per mile, not dependent on weight but on capacity, would discourage this,' says Transport 2000.

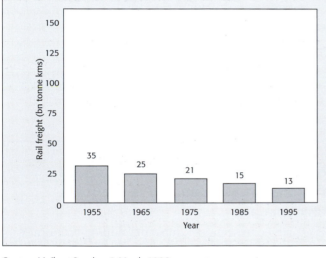

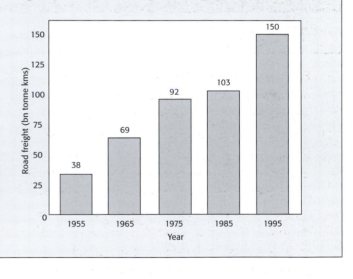

Source: Mail on Sunday, 8 March 1998.

The case against privatisation

The experience of the UK economy especially has been that privatisation does not necessarily always produce the full range of benefits stated above. Let us briefly consider some of these arguments:

- In some situations, a private sector monopoly has replaced a public sector monopoly. The outcome therefore remains the same, namely a lack of competition. This has occurred in the UK in many of the privatisations shown in table 10.1, often on a regional rather than national market basis. Good

examples are in water supply, rail passenger services and local bus operations. In such circumstances, firms can practise many of the practices of monopoly stated in section 9.

- Some economists argue that where there are natural monopolies, then these are best left to the public sector. Water, gas and railways are good examples where the unnecessary duplication of services is wasteful, inefficient and not in the best interests of consumers.

◆ The sale of nationalised industries clearly generates substantial revenue for the government. This income though is a 'one off stream', not to be repeated. Where governments may need further flows of funds, then privatisation sales may not be a future option for them.

◆ A regular complaint about privatisation is that there are often negative externalities associated with the change in ownership. One of the best examples is that of unemployment – many jobs have been lost in all sorts of activities once a private sector owner takes over a former public sector activity.

◆ Privatisation has to be accompanied by the setting up of regulators to ensure that competition is fair and that consumers are not being exploited through high prices and excessive profits for the new owners.

So, all in all, the decision on whether to privatise may not be as straightforward as it may seem. In general though it has been the prevailing view in many economies that the benefits usually outweigh the likely costs. It is for this reason that privatisation is also on the agenda of former centrally planned economies as they move towards market liberalisation and the generation of more competition. This section will conclude with an analysis of this.

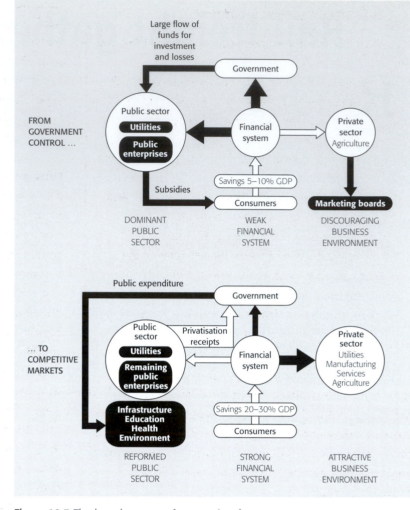

Figure 10.3 The broad process of economic reform
Source: World Bank, 1995 (adapted).

Self-assessment task

For your own country, take each of these activities:

◆ water supply,
◆ rail transport,
◆ telephone services.

(a) Establish whether these activities are operated by the government or private sector businesses.

(b) If government owned, how might the private sector help to improve the economic efficiency of these activities?

(c) Why in your country might the government not wish to pursue a policy of privatisation?

Problems of transition when central planning in an economy is reduced
Basic principles

As explained in section 1, most developing economies have a strong foundation based on the model of a centrally planned economy. Over the past ten or fifteen years most have recognised the benefits for the economy whereby less activity is controlled by the government and where competitive markets and privatisation have an increasing role to play. Internationally, this approach is consistent with that of the World Bank which, as part of its policy to promote development, encourages such economic reforms.

Figure 10.3 shows two diagrams which represent the general position of a centrally planned economy before reform and the situation once changes have been introduced. The labels at the bottom of each diagram generally summarise the state of affairs. The direction

Self-assessment task

Assume that an economy undergoes the process of reform shown in figure 10.3:

(a) ◆ Give an example of an organisation which will disappear with a move to competitive markets.

◆ Give an additional source of revenue for the government.

◆ Give a source of expenditure for the government which is no longer appropriate.

(b) Briefly describe how the roles of government and the private sector will change after the implementation of economic reforms.

(c) Explain the significance for the economy of the increase in savings as a percentage of GDP.

(d) Discuss the extent to which it is appropriate for your country to adopt the market-based system shown in the lower part of the diagram.

and relative size of the arrows are important – these show the relationships between the different sectors and the strength of their importance. In promoting economic development and in the allocation of funding, the World Bank seeks to ensure that recipient countries are implementing the processes of economic reform shown in this figure.

The transition to a market economy: reforms and problems

The task of transforming a centrally planned economy into a market economy is enormous. Not only must the foundations of a fully functioning market economy be put in place but the government needs to react to the inevitable problems during transition. If these issues are not complex enough, governments must conduct this transformation lacking any prior experience on which they can draw. Although the major reforms can be identified, there is little guidance on the speed or the sequence in which the reforms should be implemented. Some countries have chosen to follow the 'shock therapy' approach recommended by some economists. This approach involves extensive privatisation, strict monetary and fiscal policies to reduce inflation and the forces of supply and demand to determining internal market prices and the external exchange rate. Others have chosen to adopt the 'gradual' approach to

transition, arguing that consumers and producers needed time to adapt to the new economic system and that, to maintain public support for the reforms, the pain of transition needed to be softened. The transition to the market is arguably the largest economic experiment conducted in the twentieth century.

The reforms which are needed on the road to the market economy include:

Price liberalisation

The key to microeconomic reform is to allow prices to be determined by supply and demand. By freeing prices from state control, former centrally planned economies should enjoy benefits in the long term. Figure 10.4 shows the efficiency gains which are likely from such price liberalisation. In a command economy, prices bore no relationship to demand and supply. This is represented by a price (P_c) below the market equilibrium (P_m). At this price consumers demand a quantity of Q_2 but the supply is fixed by planners at S_p, with the result that excess demand of $Q_2 - Q_1$ manifests itself as lengthy queues. Price liberalisation causes the price to 'jump' to P_m, encouraging an increase in supply to Q_e in the long run. Producers are better off by the area $P_cP_m$eb (the increase in producer surplus) and consumers are better off by the area $P_mP_c + Q$ae (the increase in consumer surplus). This change in consumer surplus arises because the effective price of the good under the command system was $P_c + Q$ as the price to consumers is raised by the time spent queuing. Similar

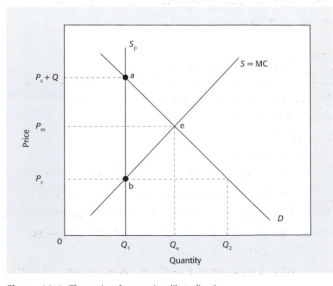

Figure 10.4 The gains from price liberalisation

gains are possible by allowing domestic prices to reflect world prices more closely.

Removal of subsidies

In order to fully realise the gains from price liberalisation the government must also remove the various subsidies to state-owned enterprises (SOEs) which kept prices low. As these subsidies are removed prices will 'jump' even further. Some governments, most notably the Russian government, delayed the introduction of such price reforms for fear of the effect of price rises on the real wages of workers. Sensitive prices, such as food, housing and energy, were not fully liberalised. Another fear was that, if prices were liberalised before competition was introduced, the former SOEs might take advantage of their monopoly power and raise prices even further. Some countries, therefore, delay price liberalisation.

Privatisation

To create a fully functional market economy, SOEs need to be turned into profit-motivated, private sector firms. The privatisation of small-scale SOEs has created few problems – shops, restaurants and bars have largely been handed over to their former managers or, where they could be identified, their former owners. Where those who manage the firm are also its owners and free to make profit, changes can be rapid. Such small-scale privatisation has been the visible sign of transition for many consumers, with a rapid change in the appearance of the 'high street' in terms of window displays and the range of goods and services on offer. Outside the major cities, the typical Central and Eastern European 'restaurant', for example may still exist, but the growth in fast food outlets and trendy bars is apparent nevertheless. Small-scale privatisation has been an important source of employment generation, much needed as large-scale SOEs shed labour in the quest for greater efficiency.

Large-scale privatisation has been much more of a problem. The key to such privatisation is to ensure that firms respond to the new market signals by seeking opportunities to reduce losses and improve profitability. Incentives need to be put in place so that firms become profit maximisers. In market economies these incentives exist in what is called the market for 'corporate control'. Briefly, firms are owned by shareholders who appoint managers to look after their interests. If shareholders feel that managers are not maximising profits, they can either replace the managers or sell their shares on the stock market. The role of the stock market is crucial. As shareholders sell their shares, prices fall and firms become subject to takeover. Managers are kept on their toes by the threat of takeover and businesses are restructured by the new owners after a takeover. However, during the transition phase active share markets are absent or are only partially developed, causing some governments to delay the privatisation process.

Those governments that have privatised large-scale SOEs have had to think carefully about how to privatise. A number of different ways have been attempted:

◆ auctioning them to the highest bidder for cash;
◆ issuing privatisation vouchers to the general public and then auctioning the SOEs in return for the vouchers;
◆ allowing existing managers, workers and/or foreign companies to buy the SOE;
◆ handing over the SOE to managers and/or workers for free.

Private ownership, of whatever kind, is not enough on its own to guarantee success. There is also a need to improve management techniques, especially in the areas of stock and quality control, financial management and marketing. Existing managers, of course, lack such skills and it may take some time for them to be acquired, which has convinced some governments of the need to delay the privatisation process whilst the necessary 'restructuring' takes place. Others have 'imported' the

One of the new range of cars from Skoda. After a liaison with Volkswagen the Skoda image changed from one of scorn to well-engineered reliability

required management techniques by selling (wholly or partially) SOEs to foreign multinational companies, such as the sale by the Czech government of Skoda to the German car giant Volkswagen and the sale of Hungary's largest supermarket chain to Tesco, the UK's biggest grocery retailer. In other words, the type of privatisation during transition is as, if not more, important than the scale of privatisation.

Trade liberalisation

Liberalising prices does not make much sense without trade liberalisation. Since a lot of industry is monopolised by SOEs, liberalising trade can create the competition which might otherwise not exist. However, for trade to be liberalised it is necessary for the currency to be convertible into other currencies, at least for transactions involving goods and services (so-called current account convertibility). As we saw in section 4, international trade brings important benefits. By allowing resources to be allocated on the basis of comparative advantage, economic efficiency is improved and there is a spur to greater dynamism in the long run.

In theory, trade liberalisation can be achieved fairly quickly by removing the state monopoly on trade and all tariffs, quotas and non-tariff barriers to trade, and by allowing the currency to be convertible. Some temporary protection of domestic industries might, however, be justified, given the inefficient state of many SOEs, the need for the government to raise revenue in the early phase of the transition process and the need to stop the 'monetary overhang' being translated into a big surge in the demand for imports and a consequent deficit on the current account of the balance of payments. But tariffs on imports will cause problems for those industries trying to export because they will increase the cost of their imported inputs.

The transition economies of Central Europe have been in a fortunate position with regard to trade. Geographically close to the European Union, they have been able to find alternative markets for their exports after the collapse of Comecon, unlike Eastern European states and the economies of the CIS. In addition, they have gained tariff-free access to the EU in the form of various Europe Agreements, which have, in some instances, paved the way for potential full membership. Consequently, their pattern of trade has undergone a

major change and they are becoming more closely integrated with the economies of Western Europe.

Currency convertibility means that the government has to take some view on what sort of exchange rate regime it is going to adopt (see section 6). Freely floating exchange rates cause problems as the exchange rate will have a tendency to depreciate and this will add to the uncertainty already caused by the transition from one economic system to another. Fixed exchange rate regimes are likely to be difficult for transition economies to support, since they lack the necessary foreign exchange reserves. However, if the exchange rate is fixed at a low enough rate and against the 'right' currency, there is every chance that not much speculation will take place and this will minimise the amount of intervention needed to support the currency. For this reason, most transition economies have opted for a fixed exchange rate regime.

Reform of the financial sector

As we have seen, many of the reforms required as part of the transition process require a fully functioning financial sector. The elements of a typical reform package should include:

1 establishing a central bank to control the money supply and interest rates independently of government and to act as a lender of last resort to the commercial banks;
2 creating banking institutions for collecting savings and channelling these savings to former SOEs so that they can invest and re-structure themselves;
3 setting up a framework to supervise and regulate the activities of the financial sector;
4 creating a market in which governments can sell bonds to finance any excess of expenditure over taxation receipts.

Given the nature of the financial system inherited from the years of planning, these reforms are a major task for the governments and one that is likely to take many years to complete. The experience of financial sector reform has been very mixed. In Hungary, for example, the government refused to bail-out banks which had made poor lending decisions, and started to sell them to foreign investors. In addition, there were tough bankruptcy laws ensuring that banks could recover their bad loans. The result was that, by 1996, almost 50 per cent of Hungarian banks were foreign-owned and their bad debts small. In the Czech Republic, in comparison, almost 50 per cent of loans made by banks are unrecoverable. Here banks remained in state ownership and they were encouraged by the government to finance many of the privatisations of SOEs, creating a conflict of interest. Instead of calling in the bad loans, Czech banks (essentially the owners of the former SOEs) gave them more and more loans. The legal framework tends to favour those who are in debt rather than giving power to the banks to recover their money. Consequently the Czech government has been forced to bail out the banks for fear of a collapse in the financial system and has belatedly begun the process of privatising the banking system.

In pursuing a programme of economic reform, former centrally planned economies have experienced mixed success. The extent and pace of introducing reforms are obviously relevant, as is the degree to which monetary and external stability is achieved. Three further factors should also be recognised. These are:

- the ability to attract aid to underpin the economic reform process;
- the ability to attract foreign direct investment from the USA, EU member states and Japan;
- the extent to which there is political stability and a political commitment to persist with the process of economic reform shown in figure 10.3.

Summary

In this section we have recognised that:

- The operation of markets sometimes does not lead to economic efficiency.

- Monopoly power can create market failure. Monopolies can lead to both allocative and productive inefficiency.

- Deadweight loss is a measure of the welfare loss due to monopolies and the imposition of an indirect tax.

- Governments often intervene in markets in an effort to overcome market failures.

- Government microeconomic policy has two main purposes: to overcome market failures and to reduce inequity.

- Government regulations can be used to try to overcome some market failures.

- Governments may use taxes and benefits to try to reduce inequalities of wealth and income in society.

- When governments intervene in markets they may themselves introduce further inefficiencies. These are called government failures.

- Governments may privatise an industry for various reasons including efficiency.

- There are many problems of transition when an economy progresses from a centrally planned to a market system.

Key words

Definitions of Key words can be found in the Glossary.

deadweight loss	poverty trap
distribution of income	privatisation
equity	progressive taxation
income tax	regressive taxation
marginal tax rates	

11 Theory and measurement in the macro-economy

On completion of this section you should know:

➤ how national income statistics can be used as measures of growth and living standards
➤ the difference between money and real GDP
➤ what is meant by the GDP deflator
➤ why economic growth rates can be used to compare living standards over time and between countries
➤ that there are other indicators of living standards and economic development
➤ the difference between broad and narrow measures of the money supply
➤ about the nature of the budget
➤ the causes and effects of deficit financing
➤ what is meant by the circular flow of income
➤ the key views of Keynesians and Monetarists on how the macro-economy works
➤ how to define aggregate expenditure
➤ the main influences on the components of aggregate expenditure
➤ how national income is determined
➤ how inflationary and deflationary gaps can be analysed
➤ the difference between the equilibrium level of income and the full employment level of income
➤ what is meant by the multiplier effect
➤ the difference between autonomous and induced investment
➤ what is meant by the accelerator
➤ how to define aggregate demand and aggregate supply
➤ the interaction between aggregate demand and supply
➤ why and how the money supply can increase
➤ how commercial banks can create credit
➤ that there are different views on the Quantity Theory of Money
➤ how to analyse different theories on interest rate determination

Introduction

In drawing up their policies, governments and their advisors draw on data about the current and forecasted performance of the economy and upon economic theory. Over time more aspects of the economy have come to be measured and there have been changes in the schools of economic thought promoted by professional economists. In this section we will explore some of the key measures used by governments and consider differences between Keynesian and monetarist economic analysis.

National income statistics
Use of national income statistics

Governments measure the total output of the country in order to assess the performance of the economy. An economy is usually considered to be doing well if its output is growing at a high and sustainable rate.

Governments use a variety of measures of the country's output. These are collectively known as **national income** statistics. This is because the total output of the country is equal to total income (and total expenditure).

The most widely used measure of national income is known as **Gross Domestic Product** (GDP). Gross means total, domestic refers to the home economy and product means output. So, for example, Pakistan's GDP is a measure of the total output by the factors of production based in Pakistan. GDP is calculated by adding up consumers' spending, government spending on goods and services, total investment, changes in stocks and the difference between exports and imports.

From GDP, a number of other measures of national income can be found. GDP plus **net property income from abroad** gives **Gross National Product** (GNP). Net property income from abroad is the income which the country's residents earn on their physical assets (such as factories and leisure parks) owned abroad and foreign financial assets (such as shares and bank loans) minus the returns on assets held in the country but owned by foreigners. So GNP gives a measure of the income of the country's residents.

GNP minus capital consumption gives **Net National Product** (NNP). This can also be referred to as national income. Capital consumption can also be called depreciation or replacement investment as it covers investment undertaken to replace worn out and out-of-date capital. GDP minus capital consumption gives **Net Domestic Product** (NDP). So gross measures include all investment whilst net measures only include investment which *adds* to the capital stock.

GDP is first measured at market prices, that is, the prices charged for goods and services in shops. However, all the measures are recorded in terms of both market prices and factor cost. The latter is the value of output excluding indirect taxes and subsidies. So, to convert a measure from market prices to factor costs, indirect taxes are deducted and subsidies are added.

The ways of measuring GDP

There are three ways of calculating GDP. These are the output, income and expenditure methods. They should give the same total because they all measure the flow of income produced in an economy. Figure 11.1 illustrates the **circular flow of income** in a simplified model of the economy.

The value of output is equal to the incomes which it generates, that is wages, rent, profit and interest. If it is assumed that all incomes are spent, expenditure will, by definition, equal income.

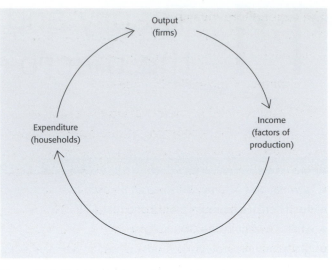

Figure 11.1 The circular flow of income in a simple economy

The output measure

The output method measures the value of output produced by industries including, for example, the output of the manufacturing, construction, distributive, hotel and catering and agricultural industries.

In using this measure it is important to avoid counting the same output twice. For example, if the value of cars sold by car manufacturers is added to the value of output of tyre firms, double counting will occur. Value added is the difference between the sales revenue received and the cost of raw materials used. It is equal to the payments made to the factors of production in return for producing the good or service. So that if a TV manufacturing firm buys components costing £60,000 and uses them to make TVs which it sells for £130,000, it has added £70,000 to output. It is this £70,000 which will be included in the measure of output.

The income measure

The value of output produced is based on the costs involved in producing that output. These costs include wages, rent, interest and profits. All these payments represent income paid to factors of production. For instance, workers receive wages and entrepreneurs receive profits. In using this measure it is important to include only payments received in return for providing a good or service. So transfer payments, which are transfers of income from taxpayers to groups of individuals for welfare payments, are not included.

The expenditure measure

As stated above, the total amount spent in a year should equal total output and also total income:

Output = Income = Expenditure

What is produced in a year will either be sold or added to stocks. So, if additions to stocks are added to expenditure on goods and services, a measure is obtained which will equal output and income. In using this method it is necessary to add expenditure on exports and deduct expenditure on imports. This is because the sale of exports represents the country's output and creates income in the country, whereas expenditure on imports is spending on goods and services made in foreign countries and creates income for people in those countries. It is also necessary to deduct indirect taxes and add subsidies in order to get a value which corresponds to the income generated in the production of the output.

Self-assessment task

Which of the following should be included in measuring GDP by the income method?

- government subsidies to farmers,
- the pay of civil servants,
- the pay of nurses,
- supernormal profits,
- state pensions.

Money and real GDP

Money (or nominal) GDP is GDP measured in terms of the prices operating in the year in which the output is produced. It is sometimes referred to as GDP at current prices and is a measure which has not been adjusted for inflation.

Money GDP may give a misleading impression of how well a country is performing. This is because the value of money GDP may rise not because more goods and services are being produced but merely because prices have risen. For example, if 100 million products are produced at an average price of $5, GDP will be $500 million. If in the next year the same output of 100 million products is produced but the average price rises to $6, money GDP will rise to $600 million. So to get a truer picture of what is happening to output, economists convert money into real GDP. They do this

by measuring GDP at constant prices, that is, at the prices operating in a selected base year. By doing this they remove the distorting effect of inflation. For example, in 2001 a country's GDP is $800 billion and the price index is 100. Then in 2002, money GDP rises to $864 billion and the price index is 105.

Real GDP is money GDP $\times \dfrac{\text{price index in base year}}{\text{price index in current year}}$

So: $\$864\text{bn} \times \dfrac{100}{105} = \$822.86\text{bn}$

The price index used to convert money into real GDP is the **GDP deflator**, which measures the prices of products produced rather than consumed in a country. So it includes the prices of capital as well as consumer products and includes the prices of exports but excludes the prices of imports.

Self-assessment task

In 2002 a country's GDP is $1,000bn. In 2003 nominal GDP rises to $1,092bn and the price index increases by 4 per cent. Calculate:

(a) real GDP;

(b) the percentage increase in real GDP.

Comparison of economic growth over time and between countries

Changes in real GDP are used to calculate economic growth rates. So, for example, if the real GDP of Zimbabwe grows from Z$50bn in 2001 to Z$52bn, the economic growth rate for 2002 is 4 per cent. Table 11.1 shows the economic growth rate of a range of countries during the year 2000.

In comparing economic growth rates over time and between countries, care has to be taken over a number of issues. One of these is that the official real GDP figures may understate the true change in output. This is because of the existence of, and changes in, what is called the hidden, informal or shadow economy. These terms refer to undeclared economic activity. People may not declare to the authorities the incomes they earn for two main reasons. One is that they are seeking to evade paying tax. For example, a plumber may receive payment for undertaking jobs in his spare time and not declare the income he receives to the tax authorities. So some of the services he produces will not be included in

Country	Real GDP (% change 2000) %	Country	%
Argentina	0.0	Japan	1.4
Brazil	4.0	Malaysia	8.7
Chile	5.6	Mexico	7.2
China	8.0	Philippines	3.9
Colombia	3.0	Poland	4.5
Czech Republic	2.7	Russia	7.0
Egypt	5.2	Singapore	9.9
France	3.0	South Africa	3.0
Germany	2.8	South Korea	9.2
Hungary	5.3	Turkey	6.0
India	6.1	UK	3.0
Indonesia	4.5	USA	5.2
Israel	5.1	Venezuela	3.1

Table 11.1 Comparison of economic growth rates in a selected number of countries
Source: The Economist, 27 January 2001.

GDP. Another reason for not declaring economic activity is that the activity is itself illegal, for example smuggling goods.

Some idea of the size of the shadow economy can be found by measuring any gap between GDP as measured by the expenditure and income methods. This is because people will be spending income they have not declared!

If the size of the hidden economy is relatively constant, the rate of economic growth may be calculated reasonably accurately. However, even a stable-sized hidden economy can make international comparisons of economic growth rates difficult. This is because the size of the hidden economy varies between economies. It is influenced by the marginal rates of taxation, the penalties imposed for illegal activity and tax evasion, the risk of being caught and social attitudes towards, for example, different illegal activities. Figure 11.2 shows a comparison between the size of the hidden economy in a number of industrial countries. Greece had the highest percentage of unmeasured economic activity, 29 per cent, and Switzerland the lowest, 8 per cent. The size of the hidden economy grew between

1989 and 1999 in each of the countries shown. In most developing economies this statistic is likely to be high.

Official GDP figures may also not provide an accurate measure of output and changes in output because of low levels of literacy, non-marketed goods and services and the difficulties of measuring government spending.

In countries with low levels of literacy, it will be difficult for government officials to gather information about *all* economic activity. Some people will be unable to fill out tax forms and others will fill them out inaccurately. So estimates will have to made for some output. This is a particular problem in Pakistan, which has a male illiteracy rate of 42 per cent and a female illiteracy rate of 71 per cent.

Estimates also have to be made for non-marketed goods and services. The GDP figures only include marketed goods and services, that is goods and services which are bought and sold and so have a price attached to them. Goods and services which are produced and which are either not traded or which are exchanged without money changing hands go unrecorded. For example, domestic services provided by homeowners, painting and repairs undertaken by homeowners and voluntary work are not included in the official figures. The proportion of goods and services which people produce for themselves and the amount of voluntary work undertaken vary over time and between countries.

It is also difficult to value the output of government goods and services which are not sold, such as defence. In the past in the UK the output was valued at cost, normally

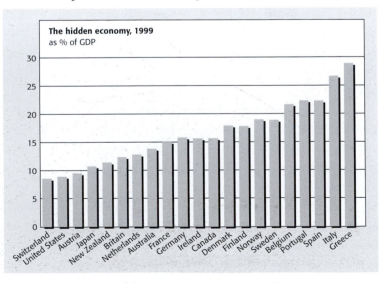

Figure 11.2 The hidden economy in selected developed economies
Source: Dr Friedrich Schneider, University of Linz.

in terms of the value of inputs. This gave a somewhat distorted view of what was happening to output. For instance, if productivity increased in the fire service, fewer firemen and women might have been needed. This would have reduced the cost of providing the fire service. Output as officially recorded would have fallen, although the level of service provided might have been unchanged or may even have increased. To overcome this problem, in 1998 the Office for National Statistics (ONS) in the UK developed a system for measuring government outputs of services other than through the value of inputs. This method covers education, health and social security – around 50 per cent of the public sector – and uses a variety of key performance indicators (such as student numbers for education and claimant numbers for social security) in order to estimate output.

The nature of economic growth

In comparing economic growth rates it is also important to consider the nature of economic growth. A very high rate of economic growth may initially appear to be very impressive. However, this may not be sustainable in either the short run or long run.

For a few months a country's output may increase by a rate greater than the rise in the productive potential of the economy (trend growth) because, in response to high demand, machinery may be worked flat out and workers may be persuaded to work long hours of overtime. However, this cannot be sustained since a time will come when machines have to be repaired and when workers will want to reduce the number of hours overtime they work.

High growth, achieved by depleting natural resources and creating pollution, will also not be sustainable in the long run. Raising fish catches, chopping down more areas of tropical rainforests and rapidly increasing manufacturing output may appear attractive ways of raising economic growth. However, such methods may reduce future generations' ability to achieve economic growth if fish stocks are reduced, new trees are not planted or the environment destroyed by pollution, which also reduces the fertility of the land and the health of the labour force.

Trees killed by acid rain. One tree is resistant to acidity
Source: Mark Edwards, Still Pictures.

Self-assessment tasks

Read the article below and then tackle the exercises that follow.

> # Nature is taking a hammering from the law breakers
>
> Nature is taking a hammering from the law breakers. To damage the environment in the process of industrialising a country and making its people wealthy – as occurred in Europe, America and parts of Asia – is bad enough; to do so before achieving prosperity is even worse.
>
> That is the risk faced by Ghana today. With the economy still struggling to maintain consistent growth, Ghana's environment – and several industries that could contribute to future economic success, including logging and tourism – are threatened by deforestation, desertification and pollution. 'We have serious environmental problems', says Lee Ocran, deputy minister for environment, science and technology.
>
> Ghana's forests, which once covered much of the south and centre of the country with mahogany and other valuable trees will need a ruthlessly efficient protection programme if they are to survive for more than a decade.
>
> At the turn of the twentieth century, Ghana had 8.2m hectares of forest, falling to half that amount by 1950 – according to the ministry – 1.4m ha today, although environmentalists say the true figure is well under 1m ha.
>
> It is estimated that the sustainable yield of the remaining forest is about 1m cubic metres of timber a year, but farmers, illegal timber merchants and the big logging companies whose trucks can be seen on the roads to Takoradi port are thought to be extracting 2.3m–3m cubic metres annually. The installed capacity of the saw-milling industry is even higher.'

Source: Victor Mallet, *Financial Times*, 29 November 2000.

1 Explain what is meant by sustainable economic growth.
2 What evidence is provided in the extract to suggest that Ghana's economic growth is not sustainable?

Comparison of living standards over time

Real GDP per head figures have traditionally been used as one of the main indicators of living standards. If a country's real GDP per head is higher this year than last year, it is generally expected that the country's inhabitants will be enjoying higher living standards. This is indeed often the case but it is not always so.

Real GDP per head is found by dividing total real GDP by the country's population to give an average. However, real GDP is not actually evenly distributed. It is possible that, whilst real GDP per head rises, some people may not experience rises in income and some may even suffer reductions in their income. For instance, in the mid 1990s the Indian economy grew at 7.5 per cent a year but the proportion of Indians living in poverty dropped just 1 per cent to 34 per cent.

The change in real GDP figures may also not reflect the true change in the quantity of goods and services that consumers can enjoy if the level of undeclared economic activity changes over time. A rise in the hidden economy may mean that people are experiencing a higher standard of living than first appears to be the case (see above).

To assess changes in living standards, consideration has to be given not only to the changes in the quantity of products produced but also to changes in the *type* of products produced and the ways in which they are made. Indeed a rise in real GDP does not guarantee a rise in living standards. During a war, output may rise because more weapons are being produced but not many people will say that the quality of their lives is improving. The recruitment of more police to cope with more crime will again increase real GDP but will be unlikely to cause people to feel better off.

The type of products which raise people's living standards are consumer goods and services, such as housing, food and clothing. A shift of resources from consumer products to capital goods will enable more consumer products to be produced and enjoyed in the future. However, in the short run if the economy is operating at the frontier of its production possibility curve such a move will cause people to enjoy fewer consumer products (see section 1).

Even if people are able to enjoy more consumer goods and services it does not necessarily mean that they will be happier. As access to more and higher-quality products rises, the desire for even more and better products may increase at an even faster rate. For example, people who do not have a car are happy when they buy their first car but often within a short space of time they want a better model.

Real GDP measures the quantity of output produced but not the quality. Output could rise but if the quality of what is produced declines, the quality of people's lives is likely to fall. In practice, though, the quality of output tends to rise over time.

Working conditions also tend to improve over time and working hours usually fall. If real GDP per head stays constant from one year to the next but working conditions rise and/or working hours fall people's living standards will rise.

However, whilst workers tend to enjoy improved conditions over time, the quality of the environment in some countries declines as a result of pollution and, for example, deforestation. A decline in environmental conditions will lower living standards but not real GDP. Indeed, if more resources have to be devoted to cleaning up the environment, real GDP will increase whilst living standards decline.

Figure 11.3 shows a comparison of the quality of life in a number of the world's cities. It is based on a survey by William M. Mercer which ranks cities on the basis of 39 criteria of the quality of life, ranging from recreational and transport facilities to crime and education.

Comparison of living standards between countries

The citizens of a country with a higher real GDP per head are likely to enjoy higher living standards than people living in a country with a lower real GDP per head, but again this is not necessarily the case.

Real GDP figures may give a misleading impression of a country's output because of the same problems of measurement as stated earlier in comparing living standards over time.

To compare living standards between countries it is necessary to convert the real GDP per capita into a common currency. To avoid the comparison being distorted by exchange rate changes, economists usually adjust exchange rates to take into account their purchasing power parities. For example, suppose the exchange rate is 6 Malaysian ringgits = $1 and the USA has a real GDP per head of $25,000 whilst Malaysia has a real GDP per head of 6,000 ringgits. From this information it might appear that, when Malaysia's real GDP per head is converted into dollars ($1,000), people in the USA are, on average, 25 times better off than people in Malaysia. However, if $1 can buy more goods and services in the USA than in Malaysia, then using the exchange rate to convert ringgits into dollars will exaggerate Malaysia's output. In terms of ability to buy products (purchasing parities), 12 ringgits may be worth $1. Using this as the basis for converting Malaysia's output into dollars would show that people in the USA are 50 times better off than people in Malaysia.

Even if a country is found to have a higher real GDP per head than another country, using purchasing power parities, it does not necessarily mean that its inhabitants will enjoy higher living standards. For example, Kuwait has a very high real GDP per head but some immigrant workers in the country receive relatively low wages. Where income is very unevenly distributed, only a small number of households may benefit from a high average income.

As with making comparisons over time, in assessing living standards consideration has to be taken of factors not measured in real GDP per head. One difference is in working hours. A study by UBS, a Swiss bank, published in 2000 found that the world's hardest working

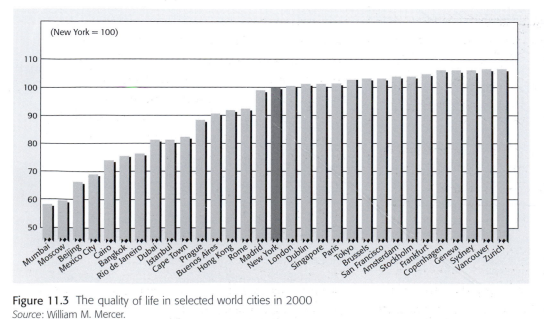

Figure 11.3 The quality of life in selected world cities in 2000
Source: William M. Mercer.

population lives in Santiago, Chile. Measured across a range of professions, the average worker in Santiago worked 2,244 hours a year. Work rates were also high across Asia and Latin America – for example, 2,200 hours in Kuala Lumpar and 2,150 hours in Mexico. Working hours were lower in the USA and Europe with

people in Paris, for instance, only working an average of 1,600 hours. Other factors which are not measured in real GDP per head include working conditions, political freedoms, fear of crime and the quality of the environment. The type and quality of products produced also has to be taken into account.

Self-assessment tasks

Read the article below and then tackle the exercises that follow.

The Economist's Big Mac Index offers a light-hearted guide to whether currencies are at their correct levels, according to the notion of 'purchasing power parity'. Under PPP, exchange rates should adjust to equalise the price of a basket of goods and services across all countries; the Big Mac PPP is the exchange rate at which hamburgers would cost the same in America as in other countries. Dividing the price in shekels of a Big Mac in Israel by the price in dollars of an American Big Mac produces a Big Mac PPP of 5.68 shekels to the dollar. Since the market rate is 4.13, this suggests the shekel is 38% overvalued. At the other extreme, the Philippine peso is almost 60% undervalued; the market rate is 51 to the dollar, against a Big Mac PPP of 21.'

Source: 'Burgernomics, *The Economist*, 13 January 2001 (adapted).

1 Explain what is meant by purchasing power parity.
2 Explain what effect using an undervalued exchange rate for the Philippine peso would have when comparing the GDP of the Philippines with that of the USA.

Other indicators of living standards and economic development

In assessing living standards, economists can use a wide range of indicators including, for example, the number of televisions per household, infant mortality rates and energy use per capita. What they normally do, however, is to use composite indicators. These include a number of indicators of living standards. For example, two American economists William Nordhaus and James Tobin in 1972 developed a new measure of economic welfare. They called this Net Economic Welfare (NEW), although it is now sometimes also referred to as Measurable Economic Welfare (MEW). This measure seeks to give a fuller picture of living standards by adjusting GDP figures to take into account other factors which have an impact on the quality of people's lives.

Factors which improve living standards such as increased leisure hours are added to the GDP figure, whilst factors which reduce living standards, including rising crime and pollution levels, are deducted. Of course, in practice, it is difficult and expensive to measure the value of non-marketed economic 'goods' and 'bads'.

Economic development involves a wider meaning of living standards as it encompasses an improvement in people's welfare, including an increase in their choices and abilities. The most well-known measure of economic development is the United Nations Human Development Index (HDI) which has been published since 1990. The index is a composite one, taking into account real GDP per head (PPP$), life expectancy at birth and educational attainment as measured by adult

	Life expectancy at birth (years)	Adult literacy rate age 15 and above (%)	Combined primary, secondary and tertiary gross enrolment ratio (%)	GDP per capita (PPPUS$)	HDI value	HDI ranking
Canada	79.1	99.0	100	23,582	0.935	1
Norway	78.3	99.0	97	26,342	0.934	2
United States	76.8	99.0	94	29,605	0.929	3
Australia	78.3	99.0	114	22,452	0.929	4
Iceland	79.1	99.0	89	25,110	0.927	5
Sweden	78.7	99.0	102	20,659	0.926	6
Belgium	77.3	99.0	106	23,223	0.925	7
Netherlands	78.0	99.0	99	22,176	0.925	8
Japan	80.0	99.0	85	23,257	0.924	9
UK	77.3	99.0	105	20,336	0.918	10

Table 11.2 Human Development Index 1998
Source: *Human Development Report*, United Nations, Oxford University Press, 2000.

literacy and combined primary, secondary and tertiary enrolment ratio. These are included as it is thought that people's welfare is influenced not only by the goods and services available to them but also by their ability to lead a long and healthy life and to acquire knowledge.

The HDI value for a country shows the distance a country has to make up to reach the maximum value of 1. Table 11.2 shows the top ten countries ranked by their HDI indexes in 1998.

As table 11.3 shows, a country's ranking by HDI does not always match its ranking in terms of real GDP per capita. Indeed, in some cases there are marked

Country	HDI value	GDP per capita (PPPUS$)
Luxembourg	0.908	33,505
Ireland	0.907	21,482
Saudi Arabia	0.747	10,158
Thailand	0.745	5,456
South Africa	0.697	8,488
El Salvador	0.696	4,036

Table 11.3 Examples of countries with similar HDI values but different incomes, 1998
Source: *Human Development Report*, United Nations, Oxford University Press, 2000.

differences. Table 11.3 shows three pairs of countries with similar HDI values but noticeably different GDP per capita figures.

Money supply

Governments measure the **money supply** in their countries to gain information about trends in aggregate demand, the state of financial markets and the need for and effectiveness of monetary policy.

Measuring the money supply is not as easy as it might first appear. This is because it is difficult to decide what to include in any measure of money. Economists define items as money if they carry out the functions of money (see section 1). However, the extent to which items carry out these functions varies and can change over time. As a result, governments use a variety of measures of the money supply which are occasionally altered to reflect developments in the roles carried out by particular items.

The measures of the money supply can be divided into **narrow** and **broad** measures. Narrow measures focus on items which are used primarily as a means of exchange, whereas broad measures include items which are used not only as a means of exchange but also as a store of value.

Self-assessment tasks

Read the article below and then tackle the exercises that follow.

UK is healthier than the US

According to the World Health Organisation (WHO), the US ranks a sickly 24 in a global table of healthy life expectancy. Compared with most other advanced countries, you die earlier and are more prone to disability in the land of the free.

The UK is placed an unremarkable 14 in the table, the first such rankings produced by the WHO, although that falls a long way short of the picture of life in Japan – the healthiest country on earth by some margin.

At the other end of the scale, the rankings reflect graphically the ravages of diseases in much of Africa. All ten lowest-rated countries are in sub-Saharan Africa, and a healthy life expectancy in strife-torn Sierra Leone, at the foot of the table, is put at less than 26 years.

Alan Lopez – co-ordinator of the WHO's epidemiology and burden of disease team, said: 'Healthy life expectancy in some African countries is dropping to levels we haven't seen in advanced countries since medieval times.'

Previous exercises of this kind have been based on death rates. These new rankings, aim to assess the number of years lived at 'full health', with periods of illness weighted by severity and subtracted from overall life expectancy.

On average, people in the healthiest regions lose some 9% of their lives to disability; in the worst-off countries, where disease often strikes young people, people lose 14%.

The US's bleak showing is linked partly to unhealthy habits and to high rates of heart disease, but also to violence and the plight of groups such as the native Americans, rural blacks and the inner-city poor, whose health is said to be 'more characteristic of a poor developing country than a rich industrialised one'.

Average American healthy life expectancy is put at 70.0, below Israel and just above Cyprus and Dominica (both 69.8) and Ireland (69.6).

Christopher Murray, director of WHO's global programme on evidence for health policy, said, 'The position of the US is one of the surprises of the new rating system.

"Basically, you die earlier and spend more time disabled if you're American rather than a member of most other advanced countries."'

Source: David Brindle, *Guardian*, 5 June 2000 (adapted).

Seton Hospital, Austin, Texas

1 Discuss the expected relationship between levels of GDP per head and healthy life expectancy.

2 Comment on the position in the league table of healthy life expectancy of:
- ◆ Sierra Leone,
- ◆ the USA.

In the UK the measure of narrow money is M0. This consists of notes and coins and bankers' deposits with the Bank of England. These deposits are used by banks to settle debts between each other and to draw out cash when needed. M0 is sometimes referred to as the monetary base or high-powered money.

M4 is the UK's broad measure. This includes notes and coins and bank and building society deposits.

The budget

In their budgets, governments usually set out their spending and taxation plans for the next financial year. In the UK the budget is held each March. In recent years the Chancellor of the Exchequer has separated out his announcements about tax changes and spending changes. Details of tax changes are still given in the March Budget, along with a forecast of government spending and taxation. However, spending plans are announced for a three year period in the Autumn statement held in November.

A **balanced budget** would mean that government expenditure equals tax revenue. Some governments seek to balance their budgets over the long run. However, in most years a government is likely to have a budget deficit or surplus. A budget surplus occurs when a government receives more in tax revenue than it spends. In contrast, a budget deficit arises when government expenditure exceeds tax revenue. Indeed, when a government has to borrow to meet a shortfall between spending and revenue, it is said to be engaged in deficit financing.

Self-assessment tasks

Read the article below and then tackle the exercises that follow.

China's budget deficit in 2000 was 180.3bn renminbis (Rmb) ($13.45bn) or just over 2 per cent of its gross domestic product of Rmb 8,319bn. This may not appear particularly alarming but Chinese finance ministers are concerned because of the projected range of future spending demands.

In the next few years China plans to construct a welfare system, first for the 300m people who live in its cities and then for the 900m who live in rural districts. This is at a time when unemployment is rising and the population is ageing rapidly.

The government is also planning to improve the infrastructure in the poor west of the country by financing the construction of a large hydro-electric dam, a new project to transport water and major roadworks.

Gezrouba Dam, China, a huge government-funded project
Source: Hartmut Schwarzbach, Still Pictures

1 Define a budget deficit.
2 Explain why rising unemployment and an ageing population would be expected to increase a budget deficit.
3 Discuss the likely effect of government spending on infrastructure on its budget deficit in the:
   ◆ short run,
   ◆ long run.

The circular flow of income

When governments spend more than they raise in taxation, they add to the circular flow of income. Figure 11.4 shows another version of the circular flow diagram contained in figure 11.1 at the start of this section.

The inner circle shows the real flow of products and factor services and the outer circle the money flow of spending and incomes. This figure is a simplified diagram; it assumes that all income is spent and that households and firms are the only sectors involved in economic activity. In practice, some income is saved, some is taxed and some is spent on imports. Some expenditure is also additional to the spending which comes from the incomes generated by domestic output. These extra items of spending are investment, government spending and spending by foreigners on the country's exports. A diagram can be drawn showing how some income and some expenditure 'leaks' out of the circular flow in the form of saving, taxation and imports whilst other spending is 'injected' into the circular flow in the form of investment, government spending and exports. This is shown in figure 11.5.

Keynesians and monetarists

Keynesians are economists whose ideas and approach are based on the work of the British economist John Maynard Keynes (1883–1946). They believe that if left to market forces there is no guarantee that the economy will achieve a full employment level of GDP. Indeed, they think that the level of GDP can deviate from the

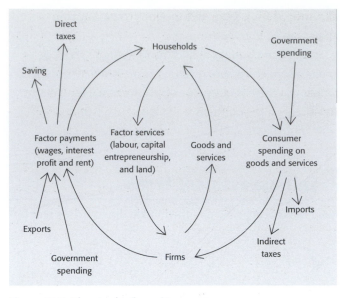

Figure 11.5 The circular flow of income in an open economy

full employment level by a large amount and for long periods. In such cases they favour government intervention to influence the level of economic activity. If there is high unemployment they argue that the government should engage in deficit financing to raise the level of spending in the economy. They believe that a government can assess the appropriate amount of extra spending to inject into the economy in such a situation. For most Keynesians, the avoidance of unemployment is a key priority.

In contrast, for **monetarists**, the control of inflation is seen as the top priority for a government. This group of economists, the most well-known of whom is the American economist Milton Friedman, argue that inflation is the result of an excessive growth of the money supply. So they believe that the main role of a government is to control the money supply. They also maintain that attempts to reduce unemployment by increasing government spending will only succeed in raising inflation in the long run. They think that the economy is inherently stable unless disturbed by erratic changes in the growth of the money supply.

Aggregate expenditure

Aggregate expenditure is the total amount which will be spent at different levels of income in a given time period. This total spending is made up of consumption (C), investment (I), government spending (G) and net exports, that is exports minus imports ($X - M$).

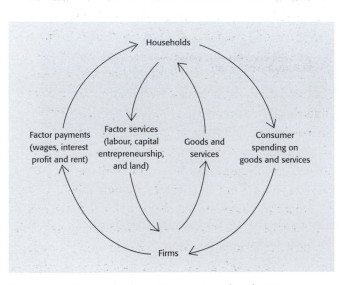

Figure 11.4 The circular flow of income in a closed economy

Consumption Consumption or consumer spending is spending by households on goods and services to satisfy current wants, for example, spending on food, clothes, travel and entertainment. The main influence on consumption is the level of disposable income (income minus direct taxes plus state benefits). When income rises, total spending also usually rises. Rich people spend more than the poor.

However, whilst total spending rises with income, the proportion of disposable income which is spent tends to fall. Economists refer to this proportion as the **average propensity to consume** (apc).

$$\text{apc} = \frac{\text{consumption}}{\text{income}} = \frac{C}{Y}$$

When a person, or country, is poor most if not all disposable income has to be spent to meet current needs. Indeed, consumption may exceed income with people or countries drawing on past savings or borrowing. This situation can be referred to as **dissaving**. However, when income rises some of it can be saved. **Saving** is defined as disposable income minus consumption. The **average propensity to save** (aps) is the proportion of disposable income which is saved and is equivalent to 1 minus apc. As saving rises, the actual amount saved and aps tend to increase. The rich tend to have a lower apc and a higher aps than the poor.

The rich also have a lower **marginal propensity to consume** (mpc) and a higher **marginal propensity to save** (mps) than the poor. The mpc is the proportion of extra income which is spent:

$$\text{mpc} = \frac{\text{change in consumption}}{\text{change in income}} = \frac{\Delta C}{\Delta Y}$$

1 − mpc gives mps which can also be calculated by:

$$\frac{\text{change in saving}}{\text{change in income}} = \frac{\Delta S}{\Delta Y}$$

The relationships between consumption and income and saving and income can also be investigated by using the consumption and saving functions. The consumption function indicates how much will be spent at different levels of income. It is given by the equation: $C = a + bY$, where C is consumption, a is autonomous consumption (that is, the amount spent even when income is 0 and which does not vary with income), b is the marginal propensity to consume and Y is disposable income; bY can also be defined as income-induced consumption, because it is spending which is dependent on income. For example, if $C = \$100 + 0.8Y$ and income is \$1,000, the amount spent will be $\$100 + 0.8 \times \$1,000 = \$900$.

The saving function is, in effect, the reverse of the consumption function and is given by the equation: $S = -a + sY$, where S is saving, s is the marginal propensity to save, Y is income and a is autonomous dissaving (that is, how much of their savings people will draw on when their income is 0; this amount does not change as income changes). The figure sY is induced saving – that is, saving which is determined by the level of income. The saving function can be used to work out how much and what proportion households will save at different income levels. For instance, if $S = -\$200 + 0.2Y$ and income is \$4,000, then:

$$S = -\$200 + 0.2 \times \$4,000 = \$600.$$

The average propensity to save will be $\$600/\$4,000 = 0.15$. This will also mean that apc is $1 - 0.15 = 0.85$.

A number of factors, other than income, influence consumption. These include the distribution of income, the rate of interest, the availability of credit, expectations and wealth. If income becomes more evenly distributed, due to, for instance, an increase in direct tax rates and state benefits, consumption is likely to rise. This is because the rich have a lower mpc than the poor. When they lose income they are unlikely to cut back on their spending significantly, whilst the poor who gain more income will spend most of the extra.

Households will also usually spend more when interest rates are low. This is because the return from saving will be reduced, buying goods on credit will be cheaper and households who have borrowed before to buy, for example, a house, will have more money to spend. If it becomes easier to obtain loans it is likely that total spending will increase. However, people are unlikely to borrow and to raise their spending if they are pessimistic about the future. Indeed, expectations about future economic prospects are thought to be a significant influence on consumption. When people become more optimistic that their future jobs are secure and that their incomes will rise, they are likely to raise their spending. An increase in wealth, which may result, for example, from a rise in the value of houses or the price of shares, will also probably increase consumption.

Investment Investment is spending by firms on capital goods, such as factories, offices, machinery and delivery vehicles. The amount of investment undertaken is influenced by changes in consumer demand, the rate of interest, changes in technology, the cost of capital goods, expectations and government policy.

If consumer demand rises, firms are likely to want to buy more capital equipment to expand their capacity. Similarly, a fall in the rate of interest is likely to stimulate a rise in investment. This is for two key reasons. One is that the cost of investment will fall. Firms which borrow to buy capital goods will find it cheaper and firms which use retained profits will find that the opportunity cost of investment will fall. The second reason is that a lower interest rate is likely to raise consumer demand.

Advances in technology will raise the productivity of capital goods and so will probably stimulate more investment. Similarly, a fall in the price of capital equipment and/or cost of installation of capital goods is likely to raise investment.

As with consumption, expectations can play a key role in determining investment. When firms are optimistic that economic conditions are improving and demand for their products will rise, they will be encouraged to raise their investment. Governments can also seek to increase private sector investment by cutting corporation tax (the tax on company profits) and by providing investment subsidies.

Government spending This covers spending on items such as the wages of teachers in state schools, medicines used in state hospitals and government investment in, for example, new roads and new hospitals. The amount of government spending which is undertaken in any period is influenced by government policy, tax revenue and other factors, including demographic changes. If a government wants to raise economic activity it may decide to raise its spending. Higher government tax revenues will enable a government to spend more, without resorting to borrowing. Pressure for a rise in government spending may come from an increase in the number of children (education) and/or an increase in the number of elderly people (health care and state pensions).

Net exports The level of net exports is influenced by the country's GDP, other countries' GDP, the relative price and quality competitiveness of the country's products and its exchange rate. When a country's GDP rises, demand for imports usually increases. Whereas when incomes rise abroad, demand for the country's exports is likely to increase. A rise in exports may also result from an improvement in the competitiveness of the country's products, due for example to a rise in productivity or improved marketing.

The level of the exchange rate can be a key influence on net exports. If the exchange rate falls in value, the country's exports will become cheaper and imports will become more expensive. If demand for exports and imports is elastic, export revenue will rise whilst import expenditure will fall, causing net exports to fall (see section 6).

Self-assessment tasks

Read the short case study below and then tackle the exercises that follow.

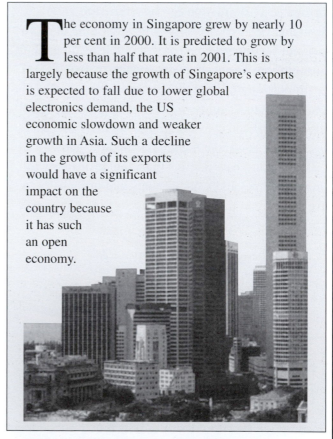

The economy in Singapore grew by nearly 10 per cent in 2000. It is predicted to grow by less than half that rate in 2001. This is largely because the growth of Singapore's exports is expected to fall due to lower global electronics demand, the US economic slowdown and weaker growth in Asia. Such a decline in the growth of its exports would have a significant impact on the country because it has such an open economy.

1 What is meant by an open economy?
2 Explain how 'lower global electronics demand, the US economic slowdown and weaker growth in Asia' would be likely to reduce the growth of exports from Singapore.
3 Discuss two factors which could increase another component of Singapore's aggregate expenditure.

Income determination

The level of income in an economy is determined where aggregate expenditure is equal to output. If aggregate expenditure exceeds current output, firms will seek to produce more. They will employ more factors of production and so will cause GDP to rise. Whereas if aggregate expenditure is below current output, firms will reduce production. So output will change until it matches aggregate expenditure, as shown in figure 11.6.

This diagram is often referred to as a Keynesian 45° diagram. It measures money GDP on the horizontal axis and aggregate expenditure on the vertical axis. The 45° line shows the points at which aggregate expenditure equals national income (GDP). So output is determined where the $C + I + G + (X - M)$ line cuts this 45° line.

If, for example, consumption and investment increase because consumers and entrepreneurs become more optimistic about the future, aggregate expenditure will rise and output will increase from Q to Q_1. Figure 11.7 illustrates this increase in GDP.

Withdrawals and injections

For income to be in equilibrium it is also necessary for **injections** of extra spending into the circular flow of income to equal **withdrawals** (also called **leakages**) from the circular flow. As noted earlier, possible injections into the circular flow are investment, government spending and exports, whilst the possible withdrawals are saving, taxation and imports. Figure 11.8 shows equilibrium income in a two-sector economy (households and firms).

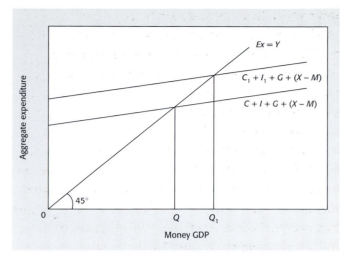

Figure 11.7 Impact of a rise in aggregate expenditure

A rise in investment would in turn cause a rise in GDP. This is as shown in figure 11.9.

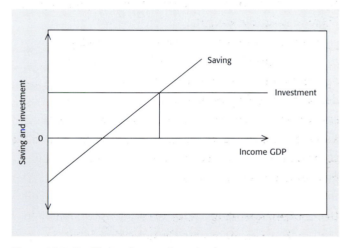

Figure 11.8 Equilibrium income in a simple economy

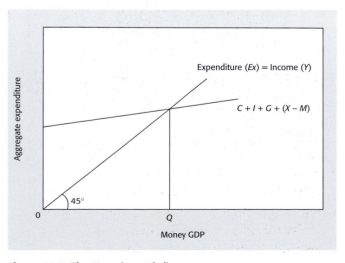

Figure 11.6 The Keynsian 45° diagram

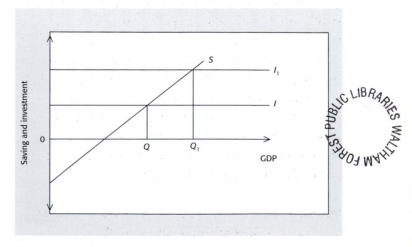

Figure 11.9 A rise in investment in a simple economy

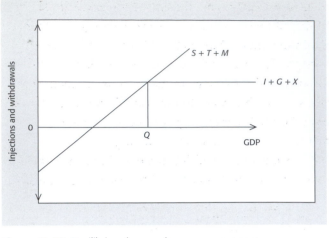

Figure 11.10 Equilibrium income in an open economy

A fall in saving would have a similar effect. Figure 11.10 shows equilibrium income where $I + G + X = S + T + M$ in a four-sector economy (households, firms, the government and the foreign trade sector).

If, for example, tax rates should rise without any change in government spending, GDP will fall as shown in figure 11.11.

A rise in saving will also cause GDP to fall. Indeed, a decision by households to save more can result in them saving less. This is because higher saving can reduce income and hence the ability of households to save. This is referred to as the **paradox of thrift**.

Inflationary and deflationary gaps

In the short run, and Keynesians argue also possibly in the long run, an economy may not achieve full employment. An **inflationary gap** will occur if aggregate expenditure exceeds the potential output of the economy. In such a situation not all demand can be met, as there are not enough resources. As a result the excess demand drives up the price level. Figure 11.12 shows that the economy is in equilibrium at a GDP of Q, which is above the level of output, X, that could be achieved with the full employment of resources. The distance ab represents the inflationary gap.

A government may seek to reduce an inflationary gap by cutting its own spending and/or by raising taxation in order to cut consumption.

Figure 11.13 shows a reduction in government spending moving the economy back to the full employment level.

The equilibrium level of GDP may also be below the full employment level. In this case there is said to be a **deflationary gap**. Figure 11.14 shows that the lack of aggregate expenditure results in an equilibrium level at a GDP of Q, below the full employment level of X. There is a deflationary gap of vw.

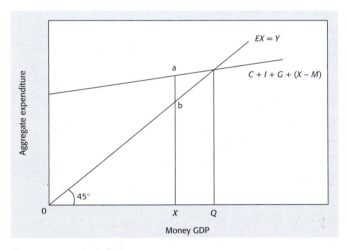

Figure 11.12 An inflationary gap

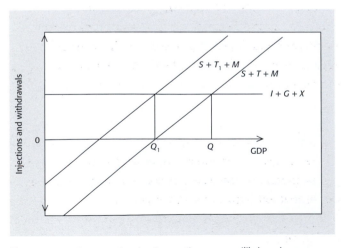

Figure 11.11 Impact of a rise in taxation on equilibrium income

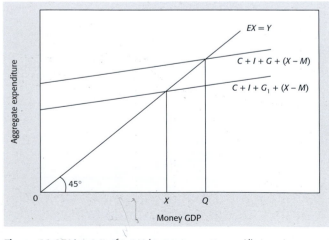

Figure 11.13 Impact of a cut in government spending

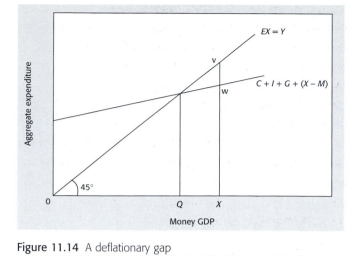

Figure 11.14 A deflationary gap

The Keynesian solution to a deflationary gap is increased government spending financed by borrowing. Figure 11.15 shows an increase in government spending eliminating the deflationary gap.

The multiplier

Figures 11.13 and 11.15 show that a change in government spending (or taxation) results in a change in GDP of greater magnitude. This tendency for a change in aggregate expenditure to result in a greater rise in GDP is known as the **multiplier** effect. This effect occurs because a rise in expenditure will create incomes, some of which will, in turn, be spent and thereby create more incomes. For example, if people spend 80 per cent of any extra income, an increase of government spending of $200m will cause a final rise in GDP of $1,000m. This is because the initial $200m

spent will create higher incomes. People will spend $160m of these incomes thereby generating a further rise in incomes. Of the $160m, $128m will be spent. This process will continue until incomes increase to $1,000m and the change in injections is matched by a change in withdrawals. In the example above, GDP rises until the $200m of extra government spending is matched by an extra $200m of saving.

The value of the multiplier can be found after the change in income has occurred by using the formula:

$$\frac{\text{change in income}}{\text{change in injection}} = \frac{\Delta Y}{\Delta J}$$

In the example above, the multiplier is

$$\frac{\$1,000m}{\$200m} = 5$$

The multiplier can also be estimated in advance of the change by using the formula:

$$\frac{1}{\text{marginal propensity to withdraw}}$$

The multiplier and equilibrium income in two-, three- and four-sector economic models

As we saw with the circular flow, economists often seek to explain their analysis first in a simplified form and then go on to include more variables. This is also the case with the multiplier where economists start with a simple model of the economy which only includes two sectors and then move on to a model which includes three sectors and then finally one which includes all four sectors.

Two-sector economy In a two-sector economy (households and firms) there is only one withdrawal, saving, and one injection, investment. In such an economy the multiplier can be found by using the formula:

$$\frac{1}{\text{mps}}$$

where mps is the marginal propensity to save. Because in this model income is either spent or saved, it can also be calculated by using the formula:

$$\frac{1}{1 - \text{mpc}}$$

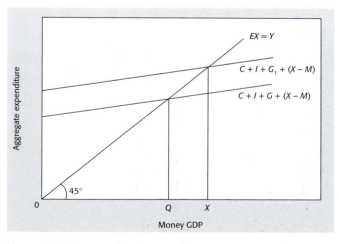

Figure 11.15 Impact of an increase in government spending

Equilibrium income will occur where aggregate expenditure equals output, which in this case is where $C + I = Y$ and injections equal withdrawals, $I = S$.

A two-sector economy is sometimes referred to as a closed economy (that is one which does not engage in international trade) without a government sector.

Three-sector economy The additional sector is the government sector. So the model is still based on a closed economy but there is now an additional sector, the government, and so an extra injection, G, and an extra withdrawal, T (taxation). The multiplier is now:

$$\frac{1}{mps + mrt}$$

where mrt is the marginal rate of taxation (the proportion of extra income which is taxed). Equilibrium income is achieved where aggregate expenditure equals output, $C + I + G = Y$, and injections equal withdrawals, $I + G = S + T$.

Four-sector economy This is the most realistic model as it includes all four possible sectors and is an open economy: households, firms, the government and the foreign trade sector. Again equilibrium income is where aggregate expenditure equals output, but this is now where $C + I + G + (X - M) = Y$, and injections equal withdrawals, which is now where $I + G + X = S + T + M$. The multiplier is now:

$$\frac{1}{mps + mrt + mpm}$$

where mpm is the marginal propensity to import (the proportion of extra income which is spent on imports).

Self-assessment task

In an economy, mps is 0.1, mrt is 0.1 and mpm is 0.2. GDP is $300bn. The government raises its spending by $6bn in a bid to close a deflationary gap of $20bn. Calculate:

◆ the value of the multiplier,
◆ the increase in GDP,
◆ whether the injection of extra government spending is sufficient, too high or too low to close the deflationary gap.

Autonomous and induced investment

Investment can rise or fall by significant amounts and it interacts with changes in income to cause significant changes in economic activity.

Investment which is undertaken independently of changes in income is known as **autonomous investment**. For example, a firm may buy more capital goods because it is more optimistic about the future or because the rate of interest has fallen. In this case, the aggregate expenditure line will shift upwards as shown on figure 11.16. As a result of an increase in investment from I to I_1, GDP rises by a multiple amount, from Q to Q_1.

In contrast to autonomous investment, **induced investment** is illustrated by a movement along the expenditure line. This is because induced investment is investment which is influenced by changes in income. If income and hence demand increases firms will be likely to buy more capital equipment. However, they will only continue to add to their capital stock if GDP continues to rise.

The accelerator

The **accelerator** theory focuses on induced investment and emphasises the volatility of investment. It states that investment depends on the rate of change in income (and hence consumer demand, and that a change in income will cause a greater proportionate change in investment. If a £1 million increase in GDP causes induced investment to rise by £3 million, the accelerator co-efficient is said to be 3.

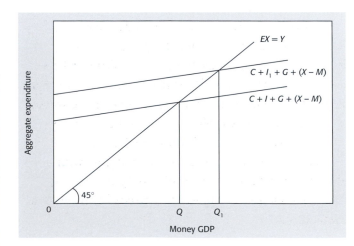

Figure 11.16 An increase in autonomous investment

Year	Consumer demand	No. of machines at start of period	No. of machines required	Replacement investment	Induced investment	Total investment
1	800	8	8	1	0	1
2	1,000	8	10	1	2	3
3	1,600	10	16	1	6	7
4	1,800	16	18	1	2	3
5	1,800	18	18	1	0	1
6	1,700	18	17	0	0	0

Table 11.4 Changes in investment

If GDP is rising but at a constant rate, induced investment will not change. This is because firms can continue to buy the same number of machines each year to expand capacity. However, a change in the rate of growth of income can have a very significant influence on investment. An example may help to show this.

In table 11.4 it is assumed that the firm starts the period with eight machines, that one machine wears out each year and that each machine can produce 100 units of output per year.

The table shows that when demand for consumer goods rises by 25 per cent (from 800 to 1,000) in the second year, demand for capital goods rises by 200 per cent (from 1 to 3). When the rate of growth of demand for consumer goods slows in year 4, demand for capital goods falls. In the last year when demand for consumer goods falls, investment falls to zero with the worn out machine not being replaced, and hence productive capacity is reduced.

However, an increase in demand for consumer goods does not always result in a greater percentage change in demand for capital goods. For instance, firms will not buy more capital goods if they have spare capacity or if they do not expect the rise in consumer demand to last. It may also not be possible for firms to buy as many capital goods as they wish if the capital goods industries are working close to full capacity. In addition, with advances in technology, the capital output ratio may change with fewer machines being needed to produce a given output.

The shape and determinants of aggregate demand

Whilst aggregate expenditure is total spending in an economy's products at different levels of income in a given time period, aggregate demand (AD) is also total spending on an economy's products in a given time period but at different values of the general price level. It also consists of four components: consumption, investment, government spending and net exports. So $AD = C + I + G + (X - M)$. Figure 11.17 shows a typical aggregate demand curve.

It slopes down from left to right because a lower price will:

♦ raise demand for net exports because the country's goods and services will have become more price competitive;

♦ increase the purchasing power of households with savings in the form of bank and building society deposits and other financial assets because their wealth will enable them to buy more;

♦ reduce the rate of interest and so stimulate consumption and investment.

A change in the price level causes a movement along the AD curve. If, however, any of the components of AD change for reasons other than a change in the price level, the AD curve will shift. Figure 11.18 illustrates an

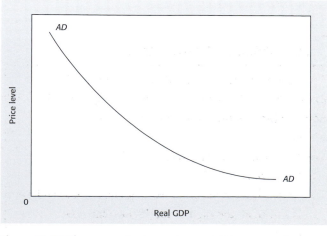

Figure 11.17 The aggregate demand curve

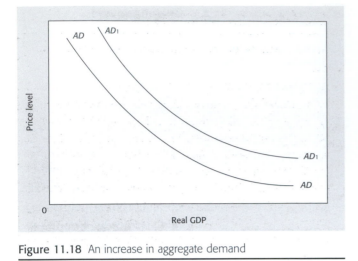

Figure 11.18 An increase in aggregate demand

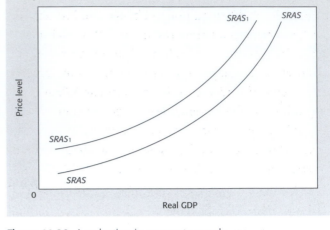

Figure 11.20 A reduction in aggregate supply

increase in aggregate demand. This could occur because of, for example, a rise in expectations about the future, a cut in direct tax, an increase in the money supply, a fall in the exchange rate and a rise in the quality of domestically produced products.

Aggregate supply

Aggregate supply (AS) is the total output that firms in an economy are willing and able to supply at different price levels in a given period of time.

It is possible to distinguish between short-run aggregate supply (SRAS) and long-run aggregate supply (LRAS). Short-run aggregate supply is the output which will be supplied at different price levels in a period of time when the prices of the factors of production remain unchanged. Figure 11.19 illustrates a typical SRAS curve.

It slopes up from left to right. This is because a higher price level will enable firms to meet any extra unit costs in the form of, for example, overtime payments, and to enjoy higher profit margins.

The SRAS curve will shift if productivity or the payments to factors of production change. For example, an increase in wage rates, not matched by an increase in productivity, will shift the SRAS curve to the left, as illustrated in figure 11.20.

Long-run aggregate supply is the output which firms would produce after the price level and factor prices have fully adjusted after any shift in aggregate demand. Keynesians often illustrate the LRAS curve as perfectly elastic at low levels of output, then upward sloping over a range of output and finally perfectly inelastic. This is to emphasise their view that in the long run the economy can operate at any level of output and not necessarily at its full capacity. Figure 11.21 shows that

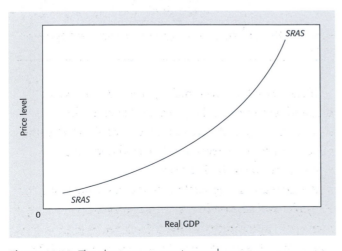

Figure 11.19 The short-run aggregate supply curve

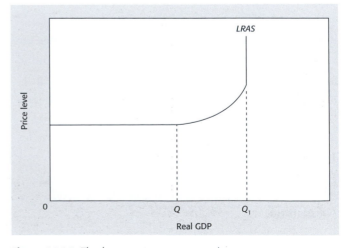

Figure 11.21 The long-run aggregate supply curve

from Q to Q_1, output can be raised without increasing the price level. When output and hence employment are low, firms can attract more resources without raising their prices. As output rises from Q_1 to Q_2, firms begin to experience shortages of resources and bid up wages and the cost of land and capital equipment. When output hits Q_2, the economy reaches the maximum output it can make with existing resources.

New classical economists illustrate the LRAS curve as a vertical line because they believe that, in the long run, the economy will operate at full capacity. This version of the LRAS curve is shown in figure 11.22.

Both Keynesian and new classical economists agree that the factors which will shift the vertical part of the LRAS curve are changes in the quantity and quality of resources as these will affect the productive capacity of the country.

The LRAS curve will shift to the right if there is an increase in the quantity and/or quality of resources. For example, improvements in training will raise the quality of the labour force and an increase in investment will increase the quantity and, possibly, the quality of capital goods. Both of these changes will increase the maximum amount of output the country can produce. Other causes of changes in LRAS include changes in technology, the quality of education and net immigration (see also section 13).

Interaction of aggregate demand and supply

The equilibrium level of output and the price level are determined when aggregate demand and aggregate supply intersect, as shown in figure 11.23.

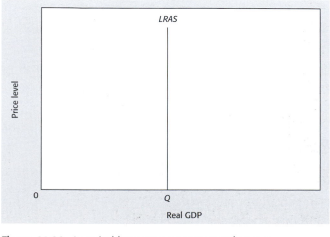

Figure 11.22 A vertical long-run aggregate supply curve

Self-assessment tasks

Read the article below and then tackle the exercises that follow.

In December 2000 Mexico was experiencing a shortage of skilled labour. This had begun to create bottlenecks to increased growth and pushed up wage rates. For example, in Chihuahua, a northern border state, a centre for assembly-for-exports plants, real wages had risen by 32 per cent over the year. The government was seeking to raise productivity, in the short run, by introducing more flexible labour laws and, in the long run, by improving education and training.

1 Using a Keynesian LRAS curve, explain at what position on the curve the Mexican economy was seemingly operating in December 2000?
2 Illustrate, and explain, the effect of:
 ◆ a rise in wage rates on the SRAS curve,
 ◆ improved education and training on the LRAS curve.

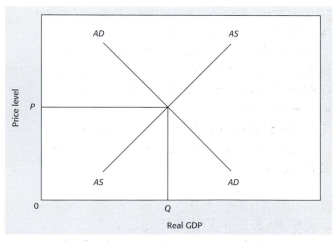

Figure 11.23 The interaction of aggregate demand and aggregate supply

If the price level was initially below P, the excess demand would push the price level back to the equilibrium level. Whereas, if price was above P, some goods and services would not be sold and suppliers would have to cut their prices.

An increase in aggregate demand resulting from, for example, an increase in government spending is likely to increase output and raise the price level, at least in the short run. This outcome is illustrated in figure 11.24.

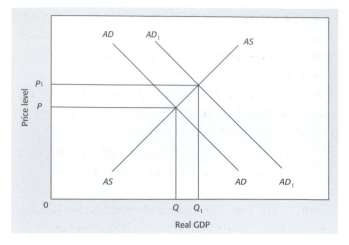

Figure 11.24 The effect on output and the price level of an increase in aggregate demand

An increase in aggregate supply will also be likely to raise output and so lower the price level, as shown in figure 11.25.

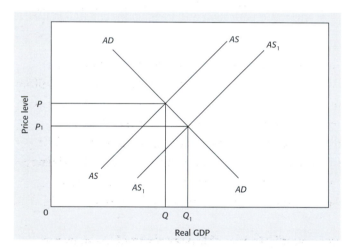

Figure 11.25 The effect on output and the price level of an increase in aggregate supply

Self-assessment task

Identify the effects of the following on aggregate demand, aggregate supply, output and the price level:
  ◆ a reduction in the rate of interest,
  ◆ an increase in government spending on health care,
  ◆ advances in information technology,
  ◆ an increase in the quality of training,
  ◆ a cut in income tax,
  ◆ an increase in wealth.

Sources of the money supply

As noted above, one of the causes of an increase in aggregate demand is an increase in the money supply. There are three main causes of an increase in the money supply:
  ◆ an increase in commercial bank lending;
  ◆ an increase in government spending financed by borrowing from the banking sector;
  ◆ more money entering than leaving the country.

Credit creation **Commercial banks**, also called high street and retail banks, make most of their profits by lending to customers, and when they lend they create money. This is because when a bank gives a loan (also called an advance by bankers), the borrower's account is credited with the amount borrowed. So every loan creates a deposit. Banks are in a powerful position to create money because they can create more deposits than they have cash and other liquid assets (that is, items which can be quickly converted into cash).

From experience, banks have found that only a small proportion of deposits are cashed. When people make payments, especially large payments, they tend to make use of cheques, credit cards and direct debits. These means of payments involve a transfer of money using entries in the records that banks keep of their customers' deposits rather than by paying out cash. So, banks can create more deposits than they have liquid assets.

Nevertheless, they have to be careful when calculating what liquidity ratio (the proportion of liquid assets to total liabilities, that is deposits) to keep. The lower they keep the ratio, the more they can lend. However, they have to be able to meet their customers' demands for cash. If they miscalculate and keep too low a ratio or if people suddenly start to cash more of their deposits, there is a risk of a run on the banking system. Indeed, banking is based on confidence. Customers have to believe there is enough cash and liquid assets to pay out all their deposits even though, in practice, this is not the case.

The credit multiplier By estimating what liquidity ratio to keep, a bank will be able to calculate its credit multiplier. This can also be referred to as a bank or credit creation multiplier, and shows by how much additional liquid assets will enable banks to increase their liabilities. It is given by the formula:

$$\frac{\text{total value of new deposits created}}{\text{value of change in liquid assets}}$$

For example, if total deposits rise by £600m as a result of a new cash deposit of £100m, the **credit multiplier** is £600m/£100m = 6. It is also possible to calculate the credit multiplier by using the formula:

$$\frac{100}{\text{liquidity ratio}}$$

If a bank keeps a liquidity ratio of 10 per cent, the credit multiplier will be 100/10 = 10. Knowing this enables a bank to calculate how much it can lend. It first works out the possible increase in its total liabilities. This is found by multiplying the change in liquid assets by the credit multiplier. So, if the credit multiplier is 10 and liquid assets rise by £40m, total deposits will rise by £40m × 10 = £400m.

To work out the change in loans (advances), the change in liquid assets is deducted from the change in liabilities. This is because the change in liabilities will include deposits given to those putting in the liquid assets. In the example the change in loans will be £400m − £40m = £360m.

In practice, however, a bank may not lend as much as the credit multiplier implies it can. This is because there may be a lack of households and firms wanting to borrow or a lack of creditworthy borrowers.

A bank may also change its liquidity ratio if people alter the proportion of their deposits they cash, if other banks alter their lending policies or if the country's central bank requires banks to keep a set liquidity ratio.

A **central bank** may seek to influence commercial banks' ability to lend. For example it may engage in **open market operations**. These involve the central bank buying or selling government securities to change bank lending. If the central bank wants to reduce bank loans it will sell government securities. The purchasers will pay by drawing on their deposits in commercial banks and so cause the commercial banks' liquid assets to fall.

Self-assessment task

A bank keeps a liquidity ratio of 5 per cent. It receives additional cash deposits of $20,000. Calculate:
- the credit multiplier,
- the potential increase in total liabilities (deposits),
- the potential increase in bank lending.

Deficit financing If the government spends more than it raises in taxation it will have to borrow. If it borrows by selling government securities, including National Savings certificates, to the non-bank private sector (non-bank firms and the general public) it will be using existing money. The purchasers will be likely to draw money out of their bank deposits. So the rise in liquid assets resulting from increased government spending will be matched by an equal fall in liquid assets as money is withdrawn.

However, if a budget deficit is financed by borrowing from commercial banks or the central bank the money supply will increase. When a government borrows from its central bank it spends cheques drawn on the bank. This spending increases commercial banks' liquid assets, which will increase their ability to lend. Commercial banks will also be able to lend more if the government borrows from them by selling them short-term government securities. This is because these securities count as liquid assets and so can be used as the basis for loans.

Total currency flow The **total currency flow** of the balance of payments refers to the total outflow or inflow of money resulting from international transactions as recorded in the current account, financial account, capital account and balancing item (see section 4). If there is net inflow of money into, for example, Malaysia the excess surplus currency will be converted into ringgits, thereby adding to Malaysia's money supply.

The Quantity Theory of Money revisited As shown in section 6, monetarists believe that changes in the money supply can have a significant impact on the price level of a country. They assume that changes in V and T are determined independently of the money supply. So they believe that a change in the money supply will cause an equal proportionate change in the price level. For example, if $M = 100$, $V = 5$, $P = 2$ and $T = 250$, then with a constant V and T, a rise in the money supply of 50 per cent to 150 will cause the price level to rise by 50 per cent to 3.

However, Keynesians dispute the validity of the quantity theory. They argue that a change in the money supply can affect any or all of the other three variables and so it is not possible to predict what will happen when the money supply changes. For example, M could rise by 50 per cent but if T also rises by 50 per cent, P will not change.

Self-assessment tasks

Study the table below and then tackle the exercises that follow.

Country	Narrow money supply (annual % change)	Consumer prices (annual % change)
Australia	9.3	5.8
Britain	4.8	2.9
Canada	14.2	3.2
Japan	4.3	−0.2
Sweden	1.9	1.4
Switzerland	−2.6	1.5
USA	−3.0	3.4

Source: The Economist, 3 February 2001.

1 Distinguish between narrow and broad measures of the money supply.

2 Analyse the relationship between changes in the money supply and inflation rates shown in the data.

3 Discuss whether an increase in the money supply will necessarily cause inflation.

Interest rate determination Monetarists and Keynesians also disagree over how the rate of interest is determined. Most monetarists support the **loanable funds theory**. This states that the rate of interest is determined by the demand and supply of loanable funds, as shown in figure 11.26.

The demand for loanable funds comes from firms wanting to invest, households wanting to (say) buy a car on credit and from the government seeking to fund a budget deficit. Government demand for loanable funds is not very sensitive to a change in the rate of interest but a rise in the rate of interest will lower firms' and households' demand. So the demand for loanable funds curve slopes down from left to right. The supply of loanable funds comes from savings. A higher rate of interest will increase the return from savings and so the supply curve is upward sloping.

An increase in the supply of savings will lower the rate of interest and cause an extension in demand for loanable funds, as illustrated in figure 11.27.

In contrast, Keynesians argue that the rate of interest is determined not by the demand and supply of loanable funds but by the demand and supply of money. It is assumed that the supply of money is determined by the monetary authorities and is fixed in the short run.

Keynes developed the **liquidity preference** theory to explain the demand for money. He identified three main motives why households and firms may decide to hold part of their wealth in a money form. The motive most people will be familiar with is the **transactions motive**. This is the desire to hold money to make everyday purchases and meet everyday payments. How much is held by a household or firm is influenced by the income received and the frequency of the income payments. Generally the more income received and the more infrequently the payments are received, the higher the amount which will be held.

Firms and households also usually hold rather more of their wealth in a money form than they anticipate

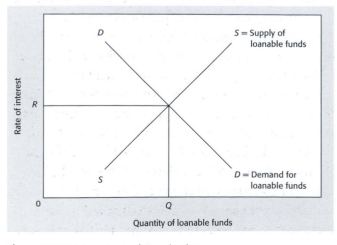

Figure 11.26 Interest rate determination

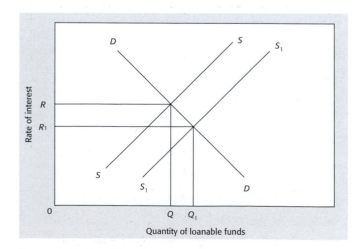

Figure 11.27 The effect of an increase in savings on the rate of interest

they will spend. This is so that they can meet unexpected expenses, and take advantage of unforeseen bargains. The name given to this motive is the **precautionary motive**. Money resources held for the transactions and precautionary motives are sometimes referred to as **active balances** as they are likely to be spent in the near future. They are relatively interest inelastic so that, for example, a rise in the rate of interest will not result in households and firms significantly cutting back on their holdings of money for transactions and precautionary reasons.

In contrast, the third motive for holding money balances, the **speculative motive**, is interest elastic. Households and firms will hold what are sometimes called **idle balances** when they believe that the returns from holding financial assets are low. One financial asset which firms and households may decide to hold is government bonds. These are government securities which represent loans to the government. The price of government bonds and the rate of interest (in percentage terms) move in opposite directions. For example, a government bond with a face value of £500 may carry a fixed interest rate of 5 per cent of its issue price. If the price of the bond rises to £1,000 the interest paid will now represent 2.5 per cent of the price of the bond. Households and firms are likely to hold money when the price of bonds is high and expected to fall. This is because they will not be forgoing much interest and because they will be afraid of making a capital loss. Whereas, the speculative demand for money will be low when the price of bonds is low and the rate of interest high.

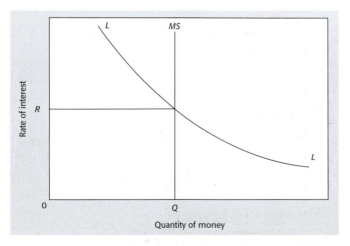

Figure 11.28 The liquidity preference theory of interest rate determination

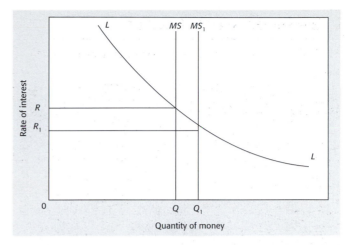

Figure 11.29 An increase in the money supply and a fall in the rate of interest

Figure 11.28 shows the combined transactions, precautionary and speculative motives for holding money in the form of liquidity preference (or demand) for money. The rate of interest is at R since this is where the liquidity preference curve intersects the supply of money curve.

An increase in the money supply will cause a fall in the rate of interest, as illustrated in Figure 11.29.

The rate of interest falls because the rise in the money supply will result in some households and firms having higher money balances than they want to hold. As a result they will use some to buy financial assets. A rise in demand for government bonds will cause the price of bonds to rise and so the rate of interest to fall.

The liquidity trap Although it is expected that an increase in the money supply will cause the rate of interest to fall, Keynes described a situation where it would not be possible to drive down the rate of interest by increasing the money supply. He described this situation as the **liquidity trap** and thought it could occur when the rate of interest is very low and the price of bonds very high. In this case he thought that speculators would expect the price of bonds to fall in the future. So if the money supply was to be increased they would hold all the extra money. They would not buy bonds for fear of making a capital loss and because the return from holding such securities would be low. Figure 11.30 shows that at a rate of interest of R, demand for money becomes perfectly elastic and the increase in the money supply has no effect on the rate of interest.

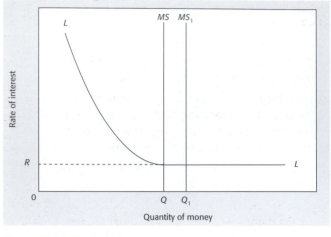

Figure 11.30 The liquidity trap

From blossom trees to Tokyo
Source: Photo by Shingu Fueta.

Self-assessment tasks

Read the article below and then tackle the exercises that follow.

Japan's gesture

When Masaru Hayami was appointed governor of the newly independent Bank of Japan two years ago, he had a reputation for stubborness. Now he has demonstrated that trait with a vengeance.

In recent weeks he has faced a barrage of calls for him to stick with the Bank's ultra-loose monetary policy which has kept overnight rates at about zero by flooding the markets with liquidity. But on Friday Mr. Hayami persuaded the Bank's policy board to raise the overnight money rate to 0.25 per cent. For the first time in 10 years, Japanese interest rates moved up rather than down.

The immediate economic effects of ending the zero interest rate policy instituted in February 1999 may be modest.

As Bank of Japan officials point out, Friday's decision in itself is hardly likely to tip Japan's economy into recession. A rise of 0.25 per cent is small, and still leaves interest rates at remarkably low levels.

Nor will it necessarily translate into an immediate rise in borrowing costs for all companies. Corporate loans are pegged not only to overnight market rates but also to the official discount rate, which remains at 0.5 per cent. Economists estimate that typical corporate lending rates might rise by just 0.1 per cent.

Japan has for many years looked like John Maynard Keynes' description of an economic slump in which businesses become so fearful that there is nothing monetary policy can do to persuade them to spend. Cutting interest rates in those conditions is as useless as 'pushing on a string'. But if cutting rates in Japan had little impact, then raising them may turn out to be considerably more significant.

Source: Gillian Tett and Ed Crooks, *Financial Times*, 14 August 2000 (adapted).

1 Define liquidity.
2 Explain why 'flooding the markets with liquidity' would be expected to keep interest rates low.
3 Discuss the possible effect that the rise in Japanese corporate lending rates may have on investment.
4 Explain why cutting interest rates can be 'as useless as "pushing on a string"'.

Summary

In this section we have recognised that:

- Economic growth is an increase in national output.

- GDP is measured by the output, income and expenditure methods.

- Real GDP is money (nominal) GDP adjusted for inflation.

- In measuring economic growth rates care has to be taken to ensure the quality of the information is good and that the size of the hidden economy and value of non-marketed goods and services are estimated accurately.

- Sustainable economic growth is economic growth which can be sustained over generations.

- An increase in real GDP per head is likely to mean higher living standards but may not do so if, for example, the size of the hidden economy falls, people receive less enjoyment from the products produced, working conditions deteriorate, working hours rise and pollution increases.

- In using economic growth rates to compare living standards between countries, it is advisable to convert exchange rates using purchasing power parities.

- Other indicators of living standards and economic development include healthy life expectancy, the Human Development Index and Measurable Economic Welfare.

- Measures of the money supply include items which carry out the functions of money. Narrow money measures focus on items used as a medium of exchange whereas broad money measures cover items used both as a medium of exchange and store of value.

- Budgets are statements of government spending and taxation plans for the next financial year.

- Deficit financing occurs when a government spends more than it raises in taxation.

- The circular flow of income shows the flow of money and resources around the economy.

- Keynesians believe that output and employment can deviate from the full employment level by substantial amounts and for long periods. In contrast, monetarists believe that the economy is inherently stable and that a government's key role is to ensure that the economy is not moved from the long-run equilibrium by excessive increases in the money supply.

- Aggregate expenditure is total planned spending at different levels of income and is composed of consumption, investment, government spending and net exports.

- Equilibrium national income is achieved where aggregate expenditure equals output.

- An inflationary gap occurs if aggregate expenditure exceeds the full employment level of output, whereas a deflationary gap exists if aggregate expenditure is below the full employment level of output.

- Any change in injections and leakages will have a multiplier effect on GDP.

- Induced investment is undertaken due to increases in GDP, whereas autonomous investment occurs due to changes in other influences such as advances in technology, changes in the cost of capital equipment and changes in expectations.

- The accelerator theory states that investment depends on the rate of change of GDP and that changes in GDP create greater percentage changes in investment.

- Aggregate demand is total spending on goods and services produced in an economy at different price levels.

- The aggregate demand curve is downward sloping.

- Aggregate supply is total output in an economy at different price levels.

- The long-run aggregate supply curve will shift to the right if the quality and/or quantity of resources increases.

- Equilibrium output and the price level are determined where the AD and AS curves intersect.

- The money supply can increase as a result of increases in bank lending, government borrowing and a net inflow of money into the country.

- Commercial banks create money because they lend more money than they have liquid assets.

- Monetarists believe that the quantity theory of money shows that increases in the money supply cause proportionate increases in the price level. In contrast, Keynesians argue that there is no direct, proportionate relationship between changes in the money supply and the price level.

- The loanable funds theory states that the rate of interest is determined by the demand and supply of loanable funds. In the liquidity preference theory, it is the demand and supply of money which determines the rate of interest.

Key words

Definitions of Key words can be found in the Glossary.

accelerator
active balances
aggregate demand
aggregate expenditure
aggregate supply
autonomous investment
average propensity to
    consume/save
balanced budget
broad money
capital output ratio
central bank.
circular flow of income
closed economy
commercial banks
consumption
credit creation
credit multiplier
deflationary gap
dissaving
gross domestic product
gross domestic product
    deflator
gross national product
idle balances
induced investment
inflationary gap
injections
Keynesianism
leakages

liquidity
liquidity preference
liquidity trap
loanable funds theory
marginal propensity to
    consume/save
monetarism
money supply
multiplier
narrow money supply
national income
net domestic product
net national product
net property income
open economy
open market operations
paradox of thrift
precautionary
    motive/demand for
    money
saving
speculative
    motive/demand for
    money
total currency flow
transactions
    motive/demand for
    money
withdrawals

12 Macroeconomic problems

On completion of this section you should know:

➤ the difference between economic growth and economic development

➤ how economies can be classified in terms of their comparative development

➤ how economists measure the characteristics of developing economies

➤ what factors cause economies to grow

➤ why economic growth can have certain costs as well as benefits

➤ how to define unemployment and the problems of its measurement

➤ the main causes of unemployment

➤ the relationship between the internal and external value of money

➤ the relationship between the balance of payments and inflation

➤ the relationship and trade-offs between inflation and unemployment

Economic growth and development

Economic growth

In strictly economic terms, economic growth occurs when an economy achieves an increase in its national income, measured by Gross National Product (GNP), in excess of its rate of population growth. This will lead to an increase in GNP per capita. For many years it was assumed that the existence of poverty in many of the world's poorer economies could be eradicated if these countries managed to sustain economic growth over a period of time. As a result economic growth was seen as synonymous with economic development. If economies grew they would also experience development. It was assumed that increased availability of goods and services

Economic growth predicted this year

The UK economy will enjoy a strong upturn in the final quarter of this year and will strengthen further into 2002, new indicators show.

The leading indicator, compiled by NTC Research from data from different areas of the economy, suggests that the current strength of domestic demand will help the UK weather the current global economic downturn.

In April, the indicator, which predicts trends and turning points in the business cycle nine months in advance, rose to 101.9 from 100.8 in March. Above 100 the index indicates growth, below that implies contraction.

It is the fifth successive increase in the indicator. NTC said: 'The recent rise in the indicator was largely the result of strengthened contributions from consumer confidence, the yield curve, reflecting lower short-term interest rates, and unfilled job centre vacancies.

'Recovering contributions from new housing starts and share prices also helped to push up the indicator. M4 money supply and new car registrations also continued to have a positive influence on the indicator.'

The index, formerly compiled by the Office for National Statistics, has a good track record of accurately predicting trends in the economy.

David Hillier, economist at Barclays Capital, said: 'It ties in with our view that interest rates will only fall another 25 basis points and will have to rise again before the end of the year.'

The upbeat picture on the economy has been mirrored in research from Cross-border Capital, a firm of independent city analysts. Its World Liquidity Index which measures the amount of money in the financial system has picked up sharply since January, gaining 30 points to 52, to breach the growth point of 50. The index leads the real economy by around 12 months.

Source: David Litterick, *Daily Telegraph*, 19 May 2001.

in an economy would lead to a 'trickle down' effect which would have an impact upon all, including the poorer members of society, in terms of jobs and other economic benefits. In reality however, despite the fact that in recent years many developing countries have achieved quite high growth rates, it has been observed that, although economic growth has resulted in benefits for poorer members of society in some countries, in others the levels of living of the mass of the population remained unchanged. In some cases this level may even have deteriorated. As a result a wider perception of economic development is now accepted which is related to, but distinct from, economic growth.

Economic development

In it's 'World Development Report' of 1991 the World Bank offered the following view of development,

> The challenge of development… is to improve the quality of life. Especially in the world's poor countries, a better quality of life generally calls for higher incomes – but it involves much more. It encompasses as ends in themselves better education, higher standards of health and nutrition, less poverty, a cleaner environment, more equality of opportunity, greater individual freedom, and a richer cultural life.

Although this statement acknowledges that economic growth is important it makes it clear that higher income in itself is not sufficient to ensure that there is a rise in the quality of life for the citizens of a country. This is a much broader view of development than one confined purely to increases in GNP. It is one that provides a different focus for those responsible for development policy planning, and moves away from measures designed purely to increase and maintain an economic growth target. Todaro states that development must be seen as a multidimensional process.

> Development…must represent the whole gamut of change by which an entire social system, tuned to the diverse basic needs and desires of individuals and social groups within that system, moves away from a condition of life widely perceived as unsatisfactory toward a situation or condition of life regarded as materially and spiritually better.
>
> (M. P. Todaro, *Economic Development*, 1995)

Homelessness – Mumbai, India. Homeless families bedding down for the night in front of Mahim railway station
Source: Hartmut Schwarzbach, Still Pictures.

According to Todaro and others the movement to a better life can be analysed and measured against three core values:

SUSTENANCE: The ability to meet basic needs

SELF-ESTEEM: To be a person

FREEDOM FROM SERVITUDE: To be able to choose

Indicators of comparative development

Classification according to levels of income The simplest way in which economies can be classified is according to the value of their Gross National Product (GNP) per capita. Every economy can be classified as low income, middle income (subdivided into lower and upper middle), or high income. Low-income and middle-income economies are sometimes known as **developing economies**. Classifying economies in this way is convenient, but as we have seen the level of development of a country goes beyond relative levels of income. It can also be misleading if it is assumed that all countries classed as 'developing' are at the same stage of development. In fact economies grouped together in terms of income may well be at completely different stages of development. Nevertheless, categorising economies according to their levels of income provides a simple and measurable way of grouping economies.

The income groups were categorised as follows in 2000:

LOW INCOME	$755 or less
MIDDLE INCOME	$756 to $2,995 (lower middle)
	$2,996 to $9,265 (upper middle)
HIGH INCOME	$9,266 or above

The thresholds between the categories are updated each year to account for international rates of inflation. As a result the thresholds are constant in real terms over time.

Classification according to levels of indebtedness

Sometimes it is useful to classify developing economies according to the degree of their indebtedness. These categories are: severely (or highly) indebted, moderately indebted and less indebted. The categorisation depends upon a number of measures of international indebtedness, the most important of which is the proportion of GNP which is devoted to servicing the debt. The fact that such a categorisation is used is a reflection of the extent to which international indebtedness is an obstacle to economic development.

The characteristics of developing economies The term 'developing economy' is used to describe a great variety of different countries and there are many differences between them, so in some ways it is wrong to think of them as a distinct group with the same characteristics. Very often the differences which exist between them are related to the geographical area in which the countries are located. This also means that developing countries located in the same region are usually affected by the same types of problem. The development problems of developing countries in Sub-Saharan Africa may, for example, be quite distinct from those of developing countries in Asia. In this sense there is no such thing as a 'typical developing country', and policies to foster economic development may need to be country specific. The policies that are appropriate for one may not be appropriate for all. Nevertheless, for some purposes it is necessary to treat developing countries as a group and it is useful to identify their shared characteristics. Very often the characteristics that they share generate the similar problems that they have to face. The following is a brief description of the shared characteristics of developing economies. Recognising the differences between developing countries while identifying the characteristics that they have in common can be characterised as '*UNITY IN DIVERSITY*'.

Economic structure Economic activity can be placed in the following sectors:-

1 The Primary Sector. This includes agriculture and the extractive industries, such as oil extraction and coal mining.
2 The Secondary Sector. This is all manufacturing industries and the construction sector.
3 The Tertiary Sector. This is also known as the service sector.

Developing countries typically have a high dependency upon the primary sector. In those economies classified as low-income economies, agriculture contributed between 30 per cent and 60 per cent of output in the 1990s. This high dependency on agricultural output makes developing countries vulnerable to the forces of nature. In those economies in which agricultural output is mainly for subsistence a drought can swiftly lead to famine. In those developing economies that are dependent upon agricultural products for their exports the drought can wipe out their foreign currency earnings. In contrast to this, in high-income economies the average figure for agricultural production was only 5 per cent or less of GDP.

Population growth and population structure World population in mid 2000 was estimated to be 6.06 billion and growing by 75 million people each year. More than 95 per cent of this growth is taking place in developing countries.

Many observers suggest that the theories of Malthus can be applied to the current population problems of the developing countries. Writing as long ago as 1798 the Reverend Thomas Malthus offered a quite pessimistic view of population growth. The essence of his view was that a country's population had a tendency to grow in geometric progression over time. However, food supplies had a tendency to increase only in arithmetic progression:

> population grows in geometric progression 1, 2, 4, 8, 16, 32, 64...
> food supplies grow in arithmetic progression 1, 2, 3, 4, 5, 6, 7...

This was because the quantity of land was in relatively fixed supply (the fixed factor), and, as increasing quantities of ever-more readily available labour (the variable factor) were added in production, diminishing returns would set in. The tendency over time therefore was that population increases would outstrip increases in food supplies. This would cause a number of 'checks' to population growth so that the population would fall to a level sustainable by the available food supplies. These checks included famines brought on by the overpopulation, diseases and epidemics caused by malnourishment, and wars as countries, increasingly desperate to feed their growing populations, fight over dwindling resources.

This Malthusian view of population growth can be challenged on a number of grounds. The main weakness is that it fails to recognise the impact of changes in technology upon food production and distribution. Malthus could not have been aware of the huge changes that have occurred in agricultural production, such as mechanisation, the application of more effective fertilisers and insecticides and the introduction of new high yield seeds such as the 'miracle' strains of rice introduced in Japan, Taiwan and South Korea. These changes mean that food supplies have increased to a level capable of supporting a much higher level of world population. Nevertheless, malnourishment and famine remain depressing features of many developing countries. However, these problems are more likely to be caused by a wider range of factors than an overall Malthusian analysis would suggest. These include factors such as the uneven distribution of resources in the world, poor management of agricultural sectors, vulnerability to sudden shocks, such as floods and drought, and an inability to respond to these. As we shall see the crippling impact of international debt in developing countries also creates conditions in which human miseries, including hunger and famines, can flourish.

The fact that developing countries have much higher birth rates than the developed economies does not only lead to greater increases in the total population of developing countries but all the attendant problems which this brings. It also has an impact upon the population structure of these countries. It means that when the age composition of developing countries is considered it is seen that they tend to have a large number of very young people. This creates a high proportion of dependent, non-productive members of the population. They are said to have very high **dependency ratios**. This means that a proportionally small working population has to produce enough goods and services to sustain not only themselves but also a large number of young people who are economically dependent upon them. This will give rise to conditions of poverty and in addition create pressures to force the young into the workforce. The Human Development Report 2000 illuminates the problem of child labour. It estimated that there are now 100 million children who live or work on the streets. Developed countries also tend to have problems with the age structure of their populations. Here the problem is different because the birth rate is so low and below the rate required to

A retiring nation

Italy has far more pensioners than it can afford

Italy's greying population and falling birth rate put the country on course for a debacle over its pension system. One of Italy's leading experts on pensions, Giuliano Cazzola, points to an array of figures that, unless other trends are reversed within a decade or so, will spell doom for the country's pensioners.

Italians now get a state pension at the age of 56, or after 35 years of work, whichever comes first; this is gradually being scaled up to the age of 62, or 37 years in work, by 2006. Those who retire after fewer years in work get smaller pensions. Various governments since 1990 have tinkered with the system, but the savings will take time to come through.

At present, 60% of Italy's welfare pot is gobbled up by pensions, against an EU average of 45%. Until the new arrangements kick in, some public-sector workers can collect a pension – and will go on collecting it – after only 20 years' work. Many of them have two or more state pensions.

The number of pensioners is rising inexorably, partly because the average age of the population is bring pushed up by the low birth rate, partly because people are living longer, and partly because Italians retire ridiculously early. On current trends, Professor Cazzola reckons, by 2030 some 42% of Italians will be pensioners – the highest proportion in Europe. If nothing is done, he says, the average Italian's pension package, now typically amounting to 54% of final salary and indexed for inflation, by 2050 will drop to less than 30%.

The best bet, most experts reckon, is to get more people into private pension schemes to top up their state pensions, and to raise the retirement age still further. So far, only 1.8m out of about 20m workers have joined private schemes. Yet in the run-up to the recent general election, the subject was barely mentioned.

They won't be sitting pretty forever
Source: Stephanie Haze, Corbis.

Source: *The Economist*, 7 July 2001.

---

replace the present population. The result is that the population is actually ageing. In Britain, for example, it is estimated that the number of people aged 40 or below will fall by 2.7 million by the year 2030. In the European Union as a whole by 2050 it is estimated that two-thirds of the population will be over 65 and therefore considered 'not economically active'. Again, dependency ratios are high and this brings problems, but this time because of the high number of old people who are reliant upon the productive proportion of the population for support.

The concept of optimum population The concept of the optimum is useful when considering the idea of overpopulation and underpopulation. The **optimum population** is said to exist when output per head is the greatest, given existing quantities of the other factors of production and the current state of technical knowledge (see figure 12.1). As the population grows it can make better use of the stock of the other factors of production such as land and capital. This is because increasing returns are enjoyed as the population grows. If as the population increases the output per head continues to grow we could consider the country to be underpopulated. As the population continues to grow we would expect the output per head to eventually peak and then decline as decreasing returns are experienced. At this stage the population has gone beyond the optimum and the country is considered to be

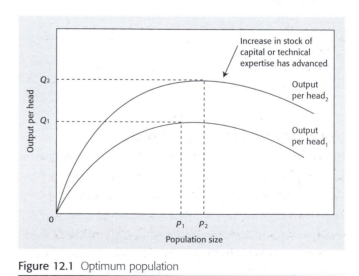

Figure 12.1 Optimum population

overpopulated. In the real world, of course the situation is more dynamic and the state of technical knowledge is constantly improving. The quantity of the other factors also continuously changes so that the optimum population for a country is not a fixed entity. In addition the criteria for assessing under- or overpopulation are purely economic and may be disputed by conservationists.

Income distribution It is a general characteristic of developing countries that income is unevenly distributed. This is partly because income-generating assets, especially land, are owned by the few. As a result there are great extremes of rich and poor. In 1998 for example World Bank figures show that in Peru the poorest 20 per cent of the population had only 4.4 per cent of total household income, while the richest 20 per cent had 51.3 per cent of total household income. In Brazil the inequality is even greater, with the poorest 20 per cent having only 2.5 per cent and the richest 20 per cent having 63.4 per cent of total household income. The transition of Eastern European countries from centrally planned to market economies has, not unsurprisingly, increased inequality. In the Russian Federation and in Ukraine inequality increased so rapidly in the 1990s that the distribution of income is now more unequal than in the rich and established economies of the Organisation for Economic Co-operation and Development (OECD). The great extremes of rich and poor in developing economies means that deprivation is common.

Employment Developing countries tend to suffer from higher levels of unemployment and underemployment than developed countries. Unemployment tends to be high because in countries with surplus populations the supply of labour tends to exceed the supply of the other factors of production. Typically, developing economies suffer from shortages in capital and entrepreneurial skills but in addition there is pressure on the supply of land suitable for the production process.

External trade The foreign trade of many developing countries tends to show a great reliance upon the export of primary produce. When considering manufactured goods as a proportion of an economy's exports, it is clear that generally speaking developing countries depend upon primary products and developed economies depend upon manufactured goods. For example when considering the forty-five countries included in the High Human Development category of the HDI, manufactures made up 80 per cent of merchandise exports in 1997 (see section 11 for details). This average fell to 58 per cent when considering the ninety-four countries categorised as Medium Human Development. Very few countries categorised as Low Human Development had any significant manufacturing exports at all. This is unsurprising since many of the population live at the margins of subsistence.

The significance of these data is that those developing countries that participate in international trade become reliant upon primary exports for foreign currency earnings. This makes them vulnerable in their trading relationships because of the demand and supply conditions in the markets for primary products. The demand for primary products tends to be price inelastic. Similarly, the supply of primary products tends to be price inelastic. The supply of some are also subject to frequent shifts depending for example on the size of the harvest. This means that the market for primary products is subject to frequent and severe fluctuations in price.

These fluctuations in price can de-stabilise the economies of developing countries. In addition, the demand for many primary products especially foodstuffs is income inelastic. This means that as world incomes rise there is little impact upon the demand for primary products as most of the higher incomes are spent on manufactured goods. Over time there is a tendency for the terms of trade of primary goods to decline compared to manufactured goods (see section 4). Therefore those developing countries that are dependent upon primary products are receiving relatively lower prices for their exports of primary products and paying relatively higher prices for imports of manufactured goods. It should be noted, however, that there has been a decline in the number of developing countries that are heavily reliant upon primary products as manufacturing sectors are established in some developing countries. In others, principally in Sub-Saharan Africa, there remains a heavy reliance upon a narrow range of primary exports.

Off to the city

Government eases the rules

It was one of Mao Zedong's many big ideas, and thus far one of his most enduring. In the late 1950s, at the time of the 'great leap forward', China established its *hukou*, or household registration system, which required people to live and work only where they were officially permitted to. For a government intent on running its economy according to a strict central plan, it was well to have people stay where they were told. For China's hundreds of millions of rural dwellers it made leaving their village nearly as difficult as leaving the country.

Over the past 20 years China has moved steadily further from central planning, and workers have moved in huge numbers away from the nation's economically backward countryside to its far more vibrant cities. According to official estimates, China's migrant labour force now numbers somewhere around 100m. The government expects another 46m to come looking for jobs in the cities in the next five years as the number of surplus rural workers swells to 150m.

In light of such numbers, China's announcement on August 16th that it plans to revamp the registration system seems a bit like closing the barn door after the horse has escaped. But if the government carries through with its plan to abolish restrictions on labour mobility, it will in fact make a huge difference to the lives of those migrants.

While that is clearly true, it has also helped avert an outcome that many of China's urban dwellers dread: an unrestrained influx into the cities of people from the countryside. While city people are glad to have enough migrants to handle the jobs they themselves do not want, they fear that too many will put unbearable strain on housing, communications and other resources. Some municipal governments have already tinkered with existing rules to admit only 'desirable' outsiders. The cities of Shenzhen and Zhuhai offer residency to those who can buy property, and Beijing grants documentation to technical workers with senior qualifications.

Now to move in
Source: PA Photos.

Source: *The Economist*, 1 September 2001.

Urbanisation Developing economies still have high proportions of their populations living in rural areas. On average over half of the population of developing countries are classified as rural. Nevertheless developing economies show very rapid rates of rural–urban migration. High-income countries already have the majority of their populations living in urban areas. As a result there is little growth in the urban population of developed countries. The rural–urban migration in developing countries can cause extra pressure on resources in already overcrowded urban areas. There is pressure on the infrastructure, with housing, roads and schools incapable of coping with the extra demand. The 1999/2000 World Development Report for example shows that from 1980 to 1998 the urban population of Bangladesh grew from 11 per cent to 20 per cent but only around 41 per cent of this growing urban population had access to sanitation.

Technology The gap between developed and developing countries in terms of the application of new technology is deep and widening. This covers a wide range of applications including new production techniques, new more efficient means of communication and the electronic storage and retrieval of information. Only 5 per cent of the world's computers are located in developing countries. Although the application of the internet to commerce will increase efficiency, especially in distribution, it will widen the technology gap for those developing countries that lack the technical skills and the infrastructure to participate effectively.

A well-known development economist has summarised the common problems that stem from these common characteristics as follows:

widespread and chronic absolute poverty, high and rising levels of unemployment and underemployment, wide and growing disparities in the distribution of income, low and stagnating levels of agricultural productivity, sizeable and growing imbalances between urban and rural levels of living and economic opportunities, serious and worsening environmental decay, antiquated and inappropriate educational and health systems, severe balance of payments and international debt problems, and substantial and increasing dependence on foreign and often inappropriate technologies, institutions and value systems.

Self-assessment tasks

1 Consider each of the common characteristics of developing countries discussed above. Explain how each affects the ability of an individual in a developing country to achieve the core values of sustenance, self-esteem and freedom from servitude.

2 Discuss why an increase in a country's GNP might not result in an improvement in the well-being of a citizen of that country.

Economic growth and developing economies

Introduction

The production possibility curve as described in Section 1 can be used to explain the important distinction between changes in the *actual* output of goods and services and changes in the *potential* output of goods and services.

A change in the actual output of goods and services could be achieved by the better utilisation of existing factors of production. In figure 12.2 assume the economy is currently producing at point X. This is a point well within the production frontier shown by the

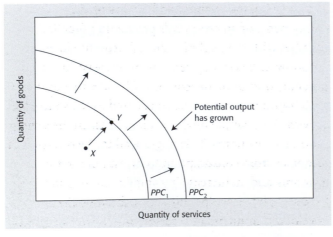

Figure 12.2 An increase in the potential output of an economy

production possibility curve. Production at this point might be caused by a lack of aggregate demand in the economy. The movement from point X to point Y on the curve could be achieved for example by increasing demand through fiscal and/or monetary policy. This would lead to an increase in the output of both goods and services. In turn it would certainly lead to an increase in Gross Domestic Product and be considered as actual economic growth. In the long run, however, further increases in output could only be achieved if the potential output of the economy was to grow. This would be represented by a shift in the production possibility curve itself. In the above diagram the shift of the curve from PPC_1 to PPC_2 represents a growth in the potential output of this economy. In the long run therefore explanations of economic growth need to focus upon those factors which increase the potential output of an economy.

Factors contributing to economic growth

The position of the production possibility curve is determined by an economy's production function (see section 9). This shows the maximum output that can be produced by an economy given the current endowment of factors of production and the current state of technical expertise.

In order to achieve economic growth which can be sustained over time it is necessary to:

◆ *Increase the quantity of resources at the disposal of the economy.* All of the factors of production could potentially be increased. Clearly, given the growth in population in developing countries it would seem that the supply of labour would grow through the natural increase in population. If there is a positive net migration the population will also grow as the number of immigrants exceeds the number of emigrants. An increase in the labour force will not create a great impact upon production possibilities, however, without an increase in the other factors. Capital goods can only be increased if investment takes place. Enterprise can be increased through training and government policies that encourage risk-taking in the economy. Land can only really be increased through conquest. Any land gained through reclamation schemes should really be considered as a type of capital because it needs investment before it becomes available.

◆ *Increase the quality of resources at the disposal of the economy.* Improvements in the quality of resources will increase the productivity of the factor inputs. The quality of labour can be improved through education and training. This is known as *investment in human capital.* This term can also be applied to any development of the factor enterprise. The quality of capital goods is improved through time as technology improves. The quality of capital goods used in developing countries improves as these countries participate in international trade. The quality of land for agricultural use can be improved through the application of fertiliser, and through irrigation and drainage schemes.

The main obstacle to increases in the quantity and quality of resources in developing countries is of course the opportunity cost of diverting resources away from their current use. Although labour may well be in abundance it is difficult to improve its quality. Many young people are deprived of education because of a shortage of schools, teachers and textbooks. Devoting more resources to education means they have to be diverted from some other use. In addition, many children are required to work to support family incomes. Capital goods are created through the process of investment. Because many developing countries are barely above the subsistence level it is impossible for them to divert resources away from current consumption without creating a decline in living standards below that required for survival. The opportunity cost is too high. Very often the only way in which capital goods can be acquired in such circumstances is for the necessary resources to be provided from abroad in the form of loans or aid. As we have seen many developing countries have acquired a large debt problem which has necessitated the transfer of funds in the form of debt repayments from themselves to the richer countries. This again diverts much needed resources away from development projects and poverty alleviation in the developing countries. The provision of development aid might be considered to be the answer to the difficulties of providing sufficient funds for development.

One important factor necessary for growth is to improve the state of technical expertise utilised in the economy. The high rates of growth experienced by the developed countries in the industrial era have been sustained by the application of technological innovations to mass production. This could only be achieved through extensive research and development into new techniques of production.

Again the concept of opportunity cost can be used to illustrate the problems faced by the developing countries. Research and development is expensive and has a high opportunity cost in the developing countries who can ill afford to divert scarce resources into this use. The benefits to the economy will only be experienced in the medium to long term. Today over 90 per cent of the world's research and development expenditure takes place in the countries of the developed world. This allows the developed economies to maintain their dominance of world markets in manufactured goods. In addition the new technology developed in the richer countries has been developed to be applied to rich countries' problems. For example, rich countries tend to use capital-intensive production methods. They try to economise on the use of highly skilled and expensive labour which is in short supply in the rich countries. They also produce for the mass market, so the scale of production is large. The developing countries have large supplies of unskilled labour and often produce for much smaller markets. As we have seen they cannot afford to divert resources to the production of capital goods which are capable of utilising the new technologies. As a result the new technologies cannot be easily transferred from the developed countries to the developing countries. The technology transfer which might be considered necessary to allow the developing countries to progress is seen as inappropriate.

Improving the quantity and quality of the components of an economy's production function, together with the level of technical expertise in an economy, will certainly result in an increase in the potential output of an economy. Changes that lead to such improvements can be considered as the sources of growth. An example might be an increase in the savings ratio in an economy. This might lead to the diversion of resources from consumption to investment in the economy and an increase in capital accumulation. We have seen, however, the difficulties faced by the developing countries in accessing the sources of growth.

We now need to consider the difficulties that result from an over-reliance upon foreign loans.

The impact of indebtedness on economic growth and development

As stated earlier, a further categorisation of developing economies considers the extent of their indebtedness. Some are categorised as heavily indebted poor countries (HIPC). This means that one of two key debt ratios is exceeded. The first ratio is the relationship between the debt service ratio and the GNP. The second is the relationship between the present value of debt service to exports. If either the proportion of debt service exceeds 80 per cent of GNP or the present value of debt service is 220 per cent of exports then the country is considered to be heavily indebted. If either of the two ratios exceeds 60 per cent of the critical level then the country is said to be moderately indebted. The presence of debt on such a scale diverts resources to debt repayment and away from spending on health and education, on infrastructure and poverty relief. Such debt provides a very real obstacle to development.

Jubilee 2000 The London-based organisation Jubilee 2000 was established in 1996. It became a coalition of 100 voluntary groups and ran a high profile four-year campaign to cancel the debts of fifty-two HIPCs. These countries have a total combined debt in the region of $375 billion. In 1998 it cost them $23.4 billion to service this debt. Most of the debt is owed to government departments in OECD countries, the World Bank, the IMF and international aid agencies. The campaign gathered huge support and produced the world's largest petition signed by 24 million people in 166 countries. Despite this the campaign has fallen short of its objective. Campaigners criticise the slow pace of progress on debt reduction and also point out the limited extent of the debt relief so far achieved. Campaigners place blame for their failure upon the World Bank and the IMF, which jointly administer the main debt relief vehicle, the HIPC initiative. So far of the fifty-two HIPCs only twenty-two countries meet the criteria for debt relief set by the World Bank and the IMF. To qualify for debt relief HIPCs must have poverty reduction strategies in place that meet World Bank/IMF criteria. Only one country, Uganda, has satisfied the criteria sufficiently to have its debts cancelled. Twenty-

one other HIPCs gained agreement for debt service levels to be reduced in December 2000. It may be several years however before their poverty reduction strategies satisfy the World bank/IMF sufficiently to have their debts cancelled. In the meantime sixteen of these countries will still be spending more on debt than on health. Mauritania, for example, despite the reduction agreed, will be paying $63 million on servicing its debt and only $51 million on education and $17 million on health. Tanzania will pay out $168 million on debt servicing compared to $87 million on health. In addition to the slow progress, the debt relief so far achieved covers only twenty-two of the fifty-two HIPCs. Their total combined population is 205 million, but the combined population of all the HIPCs is 1,030 million, so that only 20 per cent of those living in an HIPC will benefit from any kind of debt reduction in the near future. Despite such limited successes what the campaign has done is to place debt on the international agenda. The pressure for relief from debt burden for the world's most indebted countries goes on, and a successor to Jubilee 2000, Jubilee Plus, is planned.

Benefits and costs of economic growth
Benefits

The main benefit of economic growth is the increase in goods and services which become available for the country's citizens to enjoy. This raises their material living standards. If you have difficulty in believing this, ask your parents what life was like when they were your age!

Economic growth also makes it easier to help the poor. Without any increase in output and income, the only way in which the living standards of the poor can be raised is by taking income and hence goods and services from higher income groups. Whereas if economic growth occurs at least some of the extra income can be given to the poor in the form of higher benefits, thereby enabling them to enjoy more goods and services.

A stable level of economic growth increases firms' and consumers' confidence. This makes planning easier and encourages investment. Economic growth may also increase a country's international prestige and power. For example, China's rapid growth in the early 1990s increased its status in world politics.

Fate of a collapsing country rides on anti-poverty plan

Zambian finance minister fears the help is not enough

The scene in Prague put Katele Kalumba in a quandary. Inside the congress hall he was part of September's annual meeting of the International Monetary Fund and the World Bank; outside, protesters were laying siege to the building.

'I was not sure whether I should be inside with my fellow finance ministers or outside with the demonstrators,' he said recently.

There may be poorer countries on earth than Zambia, but not many. Landlocked and susceptible to floods and droughts, it is trapped in a cycle of economic underdevelopment. Corruption, too, is a contributor. Eight per cent of the population lives in poverty and one in five are HIV positive.

Zambia's borrowings mean that 25% of its annual budget of $800m (£545m) goes to repay foreign creditors rather than being spent on schools, clinics and roads. Its plight is summed up in one statistic: the country needs to spend $25 (£17) for each person annually on health care; it is actually spending less than $3.

'If Zambia was a company it would have been closed down a long time ago,' Venkatesh Seshamani, economics professor at the University of Zambia, says.

'This is a bankrupt nation.' It is hard to disagree.

In 25 years living standards have dropped by 30%. Evidence of economic failure is everywhere. Lusaka is awash with street children and those struggling to make a few kwachas in the informal economy; villagers have to walk two days down rutted tracks to get to market to buy seed.

In Kayola, 25 miles from the nearest paved road, Barnabas Michelo, a village elder, says: 'Life is tougher than it was 10 years ago.

'We never used to pay user fees in the clinics and hospitals. Now we have to dip into our empty pockets where there is nothing. We don't feel we are independent; we feel we are still in the days of colonisation.'

People have to beg medical fees from other poor people, he says. 'By the time they have raised the money many of them have died.'

The Kayola farmers point to their shoes, made of car-tyre inner tubes. 'Our children sleep on the ground. They have no blankets, only old fertiliser sacks to cover them. We feel near hopelessness. If it were possible we would tear the souls from our bodies.'

Help, of a sort, is coming. Zambia is one of the 22 countries granted debt relief under the Heavily Indebted Poor Country initiative (HIPC) – an IMF and World Bank scheme under which the poorest states get financial help provided the money is spent on an agreed programme to combat poverty.

Until the bank and IMF acted earlier this month, it looked as though Zambia might have to pay more after receiving debt relief than it paid before.

The reason was that it had made no debt repayments for five years, and these arrears were due next year. The solution has been to front-load Zambia's debt relief – that is, concentrate a lot of the relief in the near term.

In four years the payments will start to rise again. In the meantime it will be paying $168m a year to its creditors out of its £800m budget.

The real question is whether Zambia can run its economy better, because while debt relief is a necessary condition for faster growth, it is insufficient in itself. Much will depend on the policies pursued as part of the anti-poverty strategy. Here there is a gap between what Zambia thinks it needs and what the IMF thinks it needs.

Source: Larry Elliott, *The Guardian*, 19 October 2000 (adapted).

Costs

Economic growth may bring with it a number of costs. If the economy is operating at the full employment level there will be an opportunity cost involved in achieving economic growth. To produce more capital goods, in order to increase the country's productive capacity, some resources will have to be moved from producing consumer goods to producing capital goods. So current consumption of goods and services will have to be reduced. However, this will only be a short-run cost since in the long run the increased investment will increase the output of consumer goods and services.

Economic growth may also bring increased stress and anxiety. A growing economy is a dynamic economy that also undergoes structural changes. Workers may have to learn new skills and may have to change their occupation and/or where they live. Some workers may find this difficult to cope with. Economic growth may also be accompanied by increased working hours and

Recycling paper – a sustainable activity

pressure to come up with new ideas and improvements. When Japan was growing rapidly in the 1980s some workers put in very long hours and students felt under considerable pressure to pass examinations.

Economic growth may also be accompanied by the depletion of natural resources and damage to the environment. Higher output may, for example, involve firms using more oil, building on green field sites and creating more pollution. However, this does not have to be the case. Output can be increased in ways which do not damage the environment.

Sustainable economic growth

Very rapid growth may be achieved but this may be at the expense of the living standards of future generations if it results from the reckless use of resources. Countries are now becoming more concerned to achieve **sustainable economic growth**. This occurs when output increases in a way which does not compromise the needs of future generations. Materials such as aluminium, paper and glass can be recycled. More use could be made of renewable energy resources in preference to non-renewable resources, and improvements in technology may both increase output and reduce pollution.

Freight 'cancelling out' warming curbs

International trade growth, with more use of aircraft and lorries, is making a mockery of attempts by world leaders to curb global warming, according to economists.

A report published today reveals uncontrolled growth of greenhouse gas emissions from international freight. According to the report, entitled Collision Course, emissions from the transport sector will cancel out the benefits of reducing green house gas emissions by more efficient use of fossil fuels elsewhere.

The report comes out two days before 160 nations meet in the Hague to negotiate reductions in greenhouse gas emissions, and in the same week that the Chancellor cut fuel duty to buy off lorry drivers.

The report says that greenhouse gas emissions from transport are among the fastest growing contributors to climate change. Road freight and aviation, the most polluting methods of moving freight, are increasing dramatically.

The situation is worse in the EU, where demand for more freight is growing faster than the economy, and railways, inland waterways and coastal shipping are losing out to road transport and air freight. Just-in-time deliveries mean more lorries running empty – in fact, up to 30% of all journeys.

Andrew Simms, co-author of the report, says the world economy is hooked on fossil fuels, an addiction that is taking a heavy toll on the environment. 'Just like normal addicts, our politicians and economists construct elaborate excuses to justify their destructive addiction,' said Mr Simms. 'We have to return to a scale of economic activity that is humanly and environmentally sustainable.'

He added: 'If the projected 70% rise in international freight transport materialises by 2004 the resulting increase in greenhouse gas emissions will make a mockery of both the reduction targets set for industrialised countries and the current exclusion of international freight from climate controls.'

Waste

Kiwifruit Carried by plane from New Zealand to Europe; 5kg of carbon dioxide pumped into the atmosphere for every 1kg of fruit carried.

Asparagus 1kg of asparagus from California uses 4kg of aviation fuel. If grown in Europe, 900 times less energy would be used.

Apples Importing South African apples rather than growing them within 20 miles of the selling point causes 600 times as much nitrogen oxide pollution.

Strawberry yoghurt Delivering full glasses of yoghurt to Germany involved a total journey of 5,000 miles for the ingredients.

Orange juice 80% of orange juice drunk in Europe comes from Brazil. For every tonne consumed at least 25 tonnes of materials are used up. Blackcurrant juice produced in Europe would be just as nutritional.

Source: Paul Brown, *Guardian*, 11 November 2000.

Unemployment

People are unemployed when they are able and willing to work but they cannot find a job. Unemployment can bring with it serious problems both for those who are unemployed and for the country. With some people being out of work, the country's output will be below its potential level, tax revenue will be lower and more state benefits will have to be paid out. The unemployed, in addition to having lower incomes, may experience higher rates of divorce and mental and physical illness and will miss out on training and work experience. There is also increasing evidence of a link between levels of unemployment and crime.

Economists measure not only the level of unemployment but also the rate of unemployment. The level refers to the number of people who are unemployed, whereas the rate of unemployment is the number of people unemployed as a percentage of the number of people in the labour force (that is, the employed and the unemployed).

Full employment is often considered to be achieved when unemployment falls to 2–3 per cent. This may appear to be somewhat surprising as you might have expected it to be 0 per cent unemployed. However, in practice, at any particular time some people may be experiencing a period of unemployment as they move from one job to another job.

The **natural rate of unemployment**, which can also be referred to as the non-accelerating inflation rate of unemployment (Nairu), is largely a monetarist concept. It is the level of unemployment which exists when the aggregate demand for labour equals the aggregate supply of labour at the current wage rate and so there is no upward pressure on the wage rate and the price level. The inflation rate is constant, with the actual inflation rate equalling the expected one.

Whilst monetarists argue that the natural rate of unemployment cannot be reduced, in the long run, by expansionary monetary or fiscal policy, it can change over time. The factors which do determine the natural rate of unemployment are supply side factors. Over time the natural rate of unemployment may fall as a result of:

- an increase in the mobility of labour,
- an improvement in the education and training levels of workers,
- a reduction in trade union restrictive practices,
- a reduction in state unemployment benefits,
- a cut in income tax.

Difficulties in measuring unemployment

There are two main methods most governments use to measure unemployment. One is to measure the number of people in receipt of unemployment-related benefits; this is called the claimant count. It has the advantage that it is relatively cheap and quick to calculate as it is based on information which the government collects as it pays out benefits. However, the figure obtained may not be entirely accurate. This is because it may include some people who are not really unemployed and may omit some people who are genuinely unemployed. Some of those receiving unemployment benefit may not be actively seeking employment (the **voluntary unemployed**) and some may be working and so claiming benefit illegally. On the other hand there may be a number of groups who are actively seeking employment but who do not appear in the official figures. These groups may include the elderly, those below a certain age, those on government training schemes, married women looking to return to work and those who choose not to claim benefits. As this measure is based on those receiving benefits, it changes every time there is a change in the criteria for qualifying for benefit.

The other main measure involves a labour force survey using the International Labour Organisation definition of unemployment. This includes as unemployed all people of working age who, in a specified period, are without work, but who are available for work in the next two weeks and who are seeking paid employment. This measure picks up some of the groups not included in the first measure. It also has the advantage that as it is based on internationally agreed concepts and definitions, it makes international comparisons easier. However, the data are more expensive and time-consuming to collect than the unemployment benefit measure. Also as they are based on a sample survey they are subject to sampling error.

The causes of unemployment

Monetarists believe that even at the natural rate of unemployment, when the labour market is in equilibrium, some people will still be unemployed. These are the people who are not able or willing to work at the current wage rate. This equilibrium unemployment can be divided into two main categories, frictional and structural. **Frictional unemployment** is unemployment which arises when workers are between jobs. One form of frictional unemployment is search unemployment. This arises when workers do not accept the first job or jobs on offer but spend some time looking for a better-paid job and when employers hold out in the hope of recruiting more-productive workers. Casual and **seasonal unemployment** are two other forms of frictional unemployment. Casual unemployment refers to workers who are out of work between periods of employment including, for example, actors, TV scriptwriters and roof repairers. In the case of seasonal unemployment, demand for workers fluctuates according to the time of the year. During periods of the year, people working in, for example, the tourist, building and farming industries may be out of work.

Unemployment can also arise due to changes in the structure of the economy. Over time the pattern of demand and supply will change. Some industries will be expanding and some will be contracting. Because of the immobility of labour, workers may not move smoothly between industries, so structural unemployment may arise. Structural unemployment can be divided into a number of forms. One is **technological unemployment**. In this case people are out of work due to the introduction of labour-saving techniques. In many EU countries a high number of banking staff have lost their jobs in recent years with the introduction of phone and internet banking.

When the declining industries are concentrated in particular areas of the country, the unemployment is sometimes referred to as regional unemployment. Another form of **structural unemployment** is international unemployment. This is when workers lose their jobs because demand switches from their industries to more competitive foreign industries.

Keynesians, however, think that, in addition to these causes of unemployment, people can be without work because of a lack of aggregate demand. This will affect the whole economy and is referred to as **cyclical**, **demand-deficient** or disequilibrium **unemployment**. Figure 12.3 shows the labour market initially in equilibrium at a wage rate of W. Then, as a result of a fall in aggregate demand, firms reduce their output and aggregate demand for labour shifts to AD_1. If workers

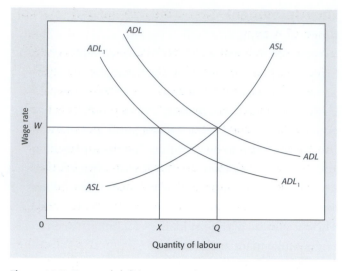

Figure 12.3 Demand-deficient unemployment

resist wage cuts, disequilibrium unemployment of XQ will exist.

Even if wage rates fall, disequilibrium unemployment may persist. This is because a cut in wages would reduce demand for goods and services, which would cause firms to cut back their output further and make more workers redundant.

Self-assessment tasks

Read the short article below and then tackle the exercises that follow.

A report by the UK Department of Trade and Industry and development agencies for Wales and London published in February 2001 predicted that the British call centre industry, an important provider of jobs in many depressed areas, may lose a significant number of jobs to India.

The author of the report, Mike Havard, said, 'India is building some of the highest-quality call centres in the world, supported by state of the art technology and staffed by a skilled, English-speaking workforce. Many of the facilities are better than the best the UK can offer.'

He urged British operators to improve the quality of their service, for example by reducing the time callers have to wait for an operator, if they do not want to lose business.

1 What type of unemployment may some UK workers experience according to the report?

2 Discuss whether an increase in government spending would reduce such unemployment.

The relationship between the internal and external value of money

The internal value of a country's currency and its external value are closely connected. If the value of a country's money falls as a result of a rise in its inflation rate above that of its competitors, demand for its products will fall. As a result demand for the currency will fall as foreigners buy fewer of the country's exports, whilst the supply of the currency on the foreign exchange market will rise as more imports are purchased. The outcome will be a depreciation of the currency, depending on the strength of these effects (see figure 12.4).

A change in the exchange rate will, in turn, affect the internal purchasing power of a country's money. A fall in the exchange rate will raise the price of a country's imports in terms of the home currency. This will directly and indirectly reduce the value of the country's money. Each unit of currency will buy fewer of the now more expensive finished imported products. Purchasing power may also be reduced as a result of the increase in the price of imported raw materials and the reduction in competitive pressure, driving up the prices of domestically produced products. So the internal and external value of the money tend to be directly related.

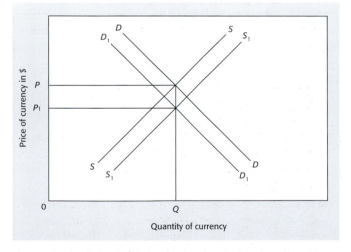

Figure 12.4 Relationship between the demand for foreign currency and the rate of inflation in an economy

Relationship between the balance of payments and inflation

If demand for exports and imports is price elastic, a fall in the exchange rate will result in a rise in export revenue and reduced import expenditure. This will improve a country's balance of payments position. This is sometimes referred to as the Marshall–Lerner

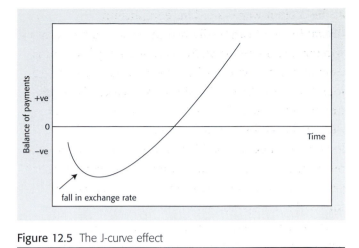

Figure 12.5 The J-curve effect

condition: namely, a fall or devaluation of the exchange rate will improve a balance of payments deficit when the combined price elasticities of demand for exports and imports are greater than 1. However, if inflation rises due to the extra demand generated and the rise in the price of imported finished products and raw materials, the balance of payments position will worsen in the longer run.

The **J-curve effect** is related to the Marshall–Lerner condition. In some countries, a fall in the exchange rate will actually *worsen* the balance of payments deficit before it starts to improve it. The reason for this is that many economies (the UK, some transitional and developing ones, for example) need to import raw materials, supplies and components in order to produce their exports. With the fall in the exchange rate, they must pay more for such items in the short term. Hence, demand for imports is relatively inelastic, although the demand for exports is more elastic. Figure 12.5 shows a diagrammatic representation of this idea.

If a country's inflation rate rises above that of its main competitors, its price competitiveness will fall. Export revenue will decline whilst import expenditure rises and the current account balance will deteriorate.

Relationship between inflation and unemployment

Economists have devoted considerable attention to the relationship between inflation and unemployment. The most famous study on the relationship was carried out by Bill Phillips, a New Zealand economist based at the London School of Economics. He analysed the relationship between changes in money wages (taken as an indicator of inflation) and unemployment in the UK

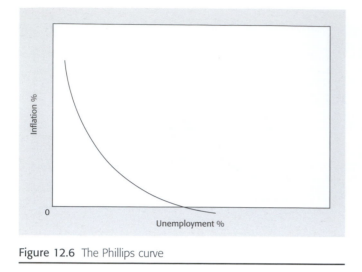

Figure 12.6 The Phillips curve

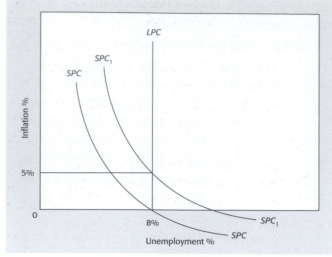

Figure 12.7 The expectations augmented Phillips Curve

over the period 1861–1957. He found an inverse relationship, as shown in figure 12.6.

A fall in unemployment may cause higher inflation due to the extra aggregate demand generated and the possible upward pressure on wages.

This traditional **Phillips curve** suggests that a government can select its optimum combination of inflation and unemployment and can trade off the two. For example, if the current unemployment rate is 8 per cent and its inflation rate is 4 per cent, a government may seek to lower unemployment to 5 per cent by increasing its expenditure whilst accepting this improvement may have to be bought at the cost of higher inflation.

However, this interpretation is questioned by monetarists. They argue that whilst there may be a short-run trade-off, in the long run expansionary fiscal or monetary policies will have no impact on unemployment, but will succeed in raising the inflation rate. To illustrate this view Milton Friedman developed the expectations-augmented Phillips curve (also known as the long-run Phillips curve) as shown by the vertical line in figure 12.7. The position of this line is determined by the natural rate of unemployment.

The diagram shows that an increase in aggregate demand does succeed in reducing unemployment from 8 per cent to 4 per cent but creates inflation of 5 per cent and moves the economy on to a higher short-run Phillips curve. Firms expand their output and more people are attracted into the labour force as a result of the higher wages. However, when firms realise that their costs have risen and their real profits are unchanged,

they will cut back on their output and some workers, recognising that real wages have not risen, will leave the labour force. Unemployment returns to 8 per cent in the long run but inflation of 5 per cent has now been built into the system. Firms and workers will presume that inflation will continue at 5 per cent when deciding on their prices and putting in their wage claims.

Self-assessment tasks

Study the table below and then tackle the exercises that follow.

	USA Unemployment %	Inflation %
1995	5.6	2.3
1996	5.4	2.2
1997	4.9	1.9
1998	4.5	1.1
1999	4.2	1.8
2000	4.0	2.4

Source: Tables, 5, 14 and 15, *National Institute Economic Review*, No.175, January 2001, National Institute of Economic and Social Research.

1 Explain the expected relationship between changes in unemployment and inflation.
2 Analyse whether the data above support this expected relationship.

Summary

In this section we have recognised that:

- There is a difference between economic growth and economic development.

- Comparative income levels and the degree of indebtedness are useful ways of classifying economies.

- Developing economies have certain common characteristics; geographical variations in the characteristics should also be recognised.

- Developing economies in general are facing many problems of population pressure.

- In general, the economic growth experienced by an economy depends on the quantity and quality of factors of production that are available.

- There are various definitions of unemployment and ways of measuring it.

- Economists recognise various causes of unemployment.

- There is a relationship between the internal and external value of a currency and the balance of payments; the J-curve effect should often be recognised.

- The Phillips Curve suggests that unemployment and inflation are inversely related.

Key words

Definitions of Key words can be found in the Glossary.

cyclical unemployment
demand-deficient
  unemployment
dependency ratio
developing economies
frictional unemployment
full employment
J–curve
Marshall-Lerner condition
natural rate of
  unemployment

optimum population
Phillips curve
seasonal unemployment
structural unemployment
sustainable economic
  growth
technological
  unemployment
voluntary unemployment

13 Macroeconomic policies

On completion of this section you should know:

➤ the main objectives of macroeconomic policy

➤ how developing economies use a range of policies to further their economic development

➤ what is meant by fiscal, monetary, exchange rate and supply side policies

➤ how policies can be used to control inflation, stimulate employment and economic growth and correct balance of payments disequilibria

➤ how economists assess the effectiveness of policies

➤ the possible conflicts between policy objectives

➤ why governments seek economic stability to counteract fluctuations in economic activity

Introduction

Governments share the same main objectives of macroeconomic policy regardless of whether they are developed, transitional or developing economies. However, at any particular time, they may have different priorities. In seeking to achieve these macroeconomic objectives, governments can use a range of policies, although each of these policies has its limitations. There can also be conflicts between policy objectives.

The main government macroeconomic policy objectives are:

- full employment,
- low and stable inflation,
- a satisfactory balance of payments position,
- sustainable economic growth,
- avoidance of exchange rate fluctuations.

Governments also seek economic stability because fluctuations in economic activity create uncertainty, discourage investment and reduce long-term growth potential.

Policies for development

As we have seen in section 12, economic development is distinct from economic growth. Economists also refer to 'sustainable development' as a desirable goal of policy so that through this we can meet the growing needs of present generations without compromising the needs of future generations. This implies that some consideration should be given to the environment in our development policies. Policy makers may build into their planning the aim of no net loss of environmental assets. For example any exploitation of timber resources should be matched by re-planting of forests to preserve the overall environmental balance. As we shall see later, environmental considerations are increasingly acknowledged in the development goals of international agencies.

Developments in world trade policy

During the 1930s, the world was gripped by a massive depression with millions unemployed. Governments resorted to protectionist policies to try to safeguard jobs (see section 4, for example). Tariff levels rose and often governments resorted to competitive devaluations of their currencies to reduce imports and boost exports. These policies were often called 'beggar-my-neighbour' policies because they tried to solve domestic problems with policies that could only have a detrimental impact upon other economies. Of course, if all countries engage in 'beggar-my-neighbour' policies, then *none* can win and the problems for all get worse. In fact, during the 1930s the volume of world trade reduced drastically under the impact of protectionist policies. After the Second World War, there was a resolve amongst the world's major trading nations that there should not be a return to the disastrous protectionist policies of the 1930s. As a result, three institutions were established to help to regulate the international economy. These institutions were:

1   *The International Bank for Reconstruction and Development (later renamed The World Bank).* This was established to assist in the reconstruction of the war-damaged economies of Europe and Asia. Once this had been achieved, its focus became the provision of funds to assist projects in the developing economies.

2   *The International Monetary Fund (IMF).* This was established to promote international monetary stability and co-operation. One of its aims is to avoid competitive devaluations through the provision of loans to those countries faced with balance of payments problems.

3   *The General Agreement on Tariffs and Trade (GATT).* This was founded in 1948 with the intention of promoting international trade. It established a series of multilateral trade negotiations between member countries designed to reduce the protectionist measures that remained in place from the 1930s. The negotiations were known as 'rounds' and they resulted in 45,000 tariff concessions covering about one-fifth of world trade. These tariff reductions helped to contribute to high world growth rates averaging 8 per cent in the 1950s and 1960s. By the early 1980s deteriorating world trading conditions led to the Uruguay Round which concluded in 1994. This updated and extended the rules governing international trade. It has been estimated that world merchandise trade will be 755 billion US dollars higher in the year 2005 than it would have been without the package of measures agreed during the 4th Uruguay Round.

In 1995 the functions of GATT were taken over by the World Trade Organisation (WTO). This organisation, based in Geneva, has a potential membership larger than the 128 countries that signed up to GATT. It also has more extensive responsibilities. Whereas GATT supervised trade in goods, the WTO also has responsibility for services and ideas or 'intellectual property'. The WTO is a permanent institution with an annual budget of 80 million US dollars.

Trade and development

As we saw in section 4, in terms of economic theory it is clear that participation in international trade brings benefits to participant countries in respect of economic welfare. In the early nineteenth century David Ricardo developed the Principle of Comparative Advantage to argue that where differences in opportunity cost ratios exist, specialisation and free trade will result in participant economies enjoying living standards beyond those achievable if they pursued a policy of self-sufficiency. Developing this idea further it can be argued that if developing countries pursue policies to encourage the growth of trade not only will living standards rise in the present time period, but also the economy will experience an increase in the pace of its economic development. This view suggests that international trade can act as an engine of growth.

This approach offers a very positive view of the participation of developing countries in international trade. The full benefits can be summarised as follows:

1   International trade improves supply conditions in economies.
    ◆   Economies of scale become possible because the market is much wider.
    ◆   The increased competition encourages domestic entrepreneurs to innovate and look for new techniques of production.
    ◆   Trade leads to the transfer of skills and technology from developed to developing economies.
    ◆   Because international trade raises incomes it provides the means for increased savings and investment. This is especially true because entrepreneurs, who are expected to have a high propensity to save, will enjoy the increases in incomes. As a result it is claimed that international trade increases the supply of capital.
    All of the above will lead to reduced costs and more efficient production and provide a stimulus for growth.

2   In addition to the impact upon the supply side of the economy, participation in international trade will impact upon demand conditions. This is because the expansion of production to cater for the export market will draw formerly unused resources into production. The result will be an expansion of spending power in the home market that will create demand for domestic output.

Although the beneficial effects of international trade upon the growth rates of developing economies have a strong theoretical basis many economists have a far more pessimistic view. This was based upon the pattern of world trade that emerged as economies specialised. Developed economies specialised in manufactured products, while the developing countries specialised in primary products. This meant that the developing countries were at a distinct disadvantage in trading relations:

1 The prices of primary products have declined relative to the prices of manufactured products over time. This is for two reasons:
   ◆ The income elasticity of demand for primary products is low so that as world incomes have risen, there has been little extra demand for primary products and demand has shifted to manufactured goods.
   ◆ Producers of manufactured goods in developed economies have an element of monopoly power which they have used to maintain high prices.

2 In addition the effects of trade have been quite limited in their impact upon the internal economies of developing countries. This is because:
   ◆ Usually the production of primary products took place on plantations and mines that were foreign owned so that profits were remitted abroad. Profits were seldom re-invested in the host country.
   ◆ The techniques of production adopted in the plantations and mines were often inappropriate in terms of the resource endowments of the developing country. As discussed earlier, developing economies have abundant labour but usually capital-intensive methods were used. This typically had to be imported from abroad, as did the skilled labour, and had negative effects upon the balance of payments position of developing economies.

Unsurprisingly, given these features of trading relationships between developing and developed economies many have questioned the value of policies designed to generate export-led growth in developing economies. Trading patterns are seen as essentially exploitative. As a result many developing economies turned to import substitution policies. They tried to prevent imports of manufactured goods from developed countries in order to develop their own manufacturing industries. The overall trend is that developing countries are now generally less dependent upon exports of primary products than they once were. The total number of developing countries in which the export of primary products makes up 80 per cent or more of total exports is now falling. Those countries that remain overly dependent upon primary products, with all the attendant problems that this dependency brings, tend to be concentrated in Africa. Developing countries in other regions tend to have more balanced exports.

Development thinking is now inclined to accept that there is no single policy which is appropriate for all countries at all times. There is a recognition that sweeping policies are often incomplete and development issues are often quite complex. Policies that were appropriate and successful in generating development in some countries at some times are not necessarily appropriate in all countries at all times. In any given country, progress depends on a wide range of factors, the relative importance of which shifts over time. Sustainable development has many objectives of which raising per capita incomes is only one among many. Although governments matter in the development process, there is no simple set of rules which tell governments what to do and which apply in which circumstances.

Globalisation and developing economies: opportunity or threat?

Current issues in development policy need to be considered in the context of the growing globalisation of the world economy. The term **globalisation** is used to describe the increasing interactions between people across national boundaries. These interactions may be economic, but they may also be cultural, social or technological (see figure 13.1). Some of the effects of globalisation are positive, innovative and dynamic but the process can also be negative and disruptive. For example, consumers in most countries enjoy an increased range of goods and services produced worldwide. This will improve choice and raise living standards; however, the import of these goods may threaten the existence of domestic producers and

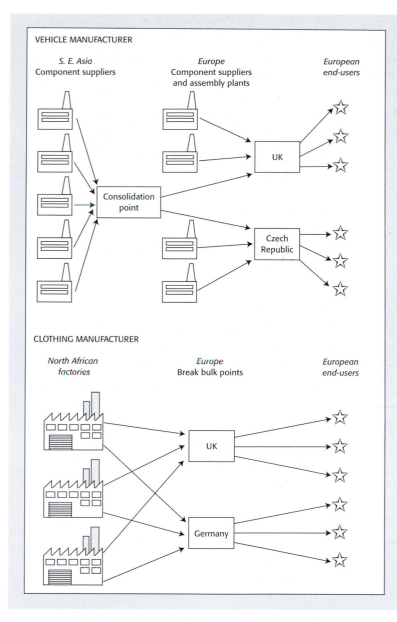

Figure 13.1 Examples of globalisation

needed funds for development but can also create instability as higher returns are chased and there is response to speculative pressures. This was seen in the South East Asian currency crises of the late 1990s (discussed in section 6).

Examination of the statistics makes it clear that the expansion of world trade on such a scale has improved world living standards. The world is certainly more prosperous, with average per capita incomes having trebled in the last fifty years. Using other indicators it is also apparent that improvements have occurred. Child death rates have fallen by half since 1965. In developing countries the combined primary and secondary enrolment ratio has more than doubled over this time period. In addition adult literacy rates have also risen, from 48 per cent in 1970 to 72 per cent in 1997. Despite these improvements globalisation has failed to benefit huge numbers of the world's population. This is because the benefits of increased world trade have not been distributed evenly. Globalisation is concentrating power, which has resulted in raised living standards for those countries that can take advantage of the process, but it increasingly leaves behind those countries that do not participate. The World Development Report 1999 provided many examples of the unevenness of the distribution of gains from the process of globalisation.

◆ Since the 1970s developing countries such as Botswana, China, the Dominican Republic and the Republic of Korea took advantage of the increasing globalisation of the market for goods and services to enjoy an increase in average annual growth rates of exports of 10–13 per cent. At the same time exports from Bulgaria, Niger, Togo and Zambia actually declined.

◆ More than 80 per cent of foreign direct investment in developing countries in the 1990s has gone to just 20 countries.

The impact of globalisation is therefore to emphasise the divide between those developing countries that are benefiting from globalisation and those that are not.

destroy jobs. In the UK, for example, consumers can now choose between a vast array of textile goods imported from all over the world, but textile workers in the UK have lost their jobs. In the 1970s world exports were 17 per cent of world GDP. In the 1990s this had risen to 21 per cent of a much higher GDP. In the tourist industry also many British people now increasingly enjoy holidays sold by long-haul tour operators to far off destinations. At the same time the traditional British seaside holiday is in decline. In addition flows of foreign capital can provide much-

Uganda. Billboard for anti-poverty co-op society
Source: Ron Giling, Still Pictures.

A third way for the Third World?

The Secretary of State for International Development is nothing if not ambitious. Tomorrow, Clare Short is publishing a White Paper on how globalisation can be made to work for the world's poor. She wants everyone to read it – and then say: 'For God's sake get on with it.'

She wants to get on with shaping the current world system to halve the proportion of people living in extreme poverty, to ensure that every child goes to primary school and that the mother of every baby has proper health care – and all by 2015. She is impressed by the way the Asian Tigers have managed to use access to world markets, investment in education, controlled capitalism and energetic government to lever themselves towards Western living standards in less than a generation. The task now, she believes, is to ensure that the countries of South Asia and Africa repeat the Tigers' lead.

Her mission is to save development from those who think it is 'pictures of African children with flies on their faces that moves their heart, they put some money in the charity box and feel depressed.' Instead, she wants to offer a programme 'that is practical and achievable; that removes the cause of their

suffering'. This, she hopes, will generate demands for action and a transformation of how we think about the world's poor.

Her main concern is Africa: conflict-ridden, devastated by Aids and home to the majority of the world's extreme poor. She sees the success of Mozambique and Uganda in winning inward investment and sustaining Asian Tiger-type economic growth rates that allows them to keep ahead of population growth – albeit from a desperately low base – as a model for the rest of the continent.

But although she praises free trade and private inward investment, Short still carries 'the white woman's burden' – the belief that the rich countries must take responsibility. A Western country like Britain has to get stuck in and help, especially in providing health and education and also to stop corrupt governments, she believes. Good governments must uphold rigorous standards in both the private and public sectors – and above all in their 'unreliable' African banks which ship out of Africa proportionally 10 times more savings than happens in Asia.

She is a staunch advocate of increasing the aid budget towards the United Nations target of 0.7 per cent of GDP, and of allowing the recipients to spend it as they choose.

Source: Will Hutton, *The Observer*, 10 December 2000.

Gaps in income between the poorest and richest countries and between people have continued to widen. In 1960 the 20 per cent of the world's population who lived in the richest countries had 30 times as much income as the poorest 20 per cent; in 1997 they had 70 times as much. In South East Asia per capita incomes are more than seven times what they were in 1960, and three times what they were in 1980. In Sub-Saharan Africa however, average per capita incomes are actually lower today than they were in 1970.

We still have an estimated 840 million people who are malnourished, one in seven children of primary school age is out of school and nearly 1.3 billion people do not have access to clean water.

The World Development Report 2000/2001

In September 2000, The World Bank published its World Development Report 2000/2001 entitled 'Attacking Poverty'. In this report the World Bank emphasised the continued existence of widespread poverty in the world. World Bank statistics continue to show that 1.2 billion people in the world live on less than $1 dollar per day and virtually half of the population of the developing world lives on less than $2 dollars per day, in conditions described as extreme poverty. The report pointed the way to alleviating poverty in three areas:

OPPORTUNITY

EMPOWERMENT

SECURITY

Development goals

A joint OECD, United Nations and World Bank conference identified six social goals which were to be the focus of a new international development strategy:
- POVERTY: Reducing by half the proportion of people in extreme poverty by 2015.
- MORTALITY: Reducing by two-thirds the mortality rates for infants and children under five and by three-quarters the mortality rates for mothers by 2015.
- HEALTH: Providing access to reproductive health services for all individuals of appropriate age no later than 2015.
- EDUCATION: Achieving universal primary education in all countries by 2015.
- GENDER: Demonstrating progress toward gender equality and the empowerment of women by eliminating gender disparities in primary and secondary education by 2005.
- ENVIRONMENT: Implementing national strategies for sustainable development by 2005 to ensure that the current loss of environmental resources is reversed globally and nationally by 2015.

It is vital that these strategies are implemented. The accompanying article shows the UK's position on these strategies at the beginning of the twenty-first century.

Fiscal policy

Fiscal policy involves changes in taxation and government spending. A government can deliberately alter tax rates and levels of government spending to influence economic activity. This can be referred to as discretionary fiscal policy and can be used to influence aggregate demand. If a government wants to raise aggregate demand it will increase its spending or cut tax rates. Keynesians favour raising government spending because they believe this will have a bigger multiplier effect (see section 11). This is because the rise in government spending, especially if it is on benefits, is most likely to benefit the poor who have a high marginal propensity to consume. In contrast, a cut in tax rates may benefit mostly the rich who tend to have a low mpc.

A government can also allow **automatic stabilisers** to influence economic activity. Automatic stabilisers are forms of government spending and taxation which change, without any deliberate government action, to offset fluctuations in GDP. For example, during a recession government spending on unemployment benefits automatically rises because there are more unemployed people. Tax revenue from income tax and indirect taxes will also fall automatically as incomes and expenditure decline. Figure 13.2 shows how tax revenue and government expenditure automatically change as GDP changes.

Fiscal policy may also be employed to affect aggregate supply by changing incentives facing firms and individuals. In recent years, governments throughout the world have increasingly been using fiscal policy to increase aggregate supply.

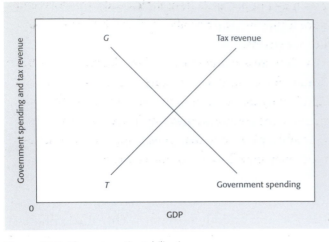

Figure 13.2 The automatic stabilisation process

For fiscal policy to be effective it is important that the government can estimate accurately the impact that changes in government spending and taxation will have on the economy. To do this they have to have a good idea of the value of the multiplier and an awareness of the possible side effects of policy measures. If a government underestimates the value of the multiplier, it may inject too much extra spending and thereby generate inflation and balance of payments problems. Fiscal policy instruments may also have undesirable side effects. For example, a government may raise more tax in order to reduce aggregate demand. However, this may also have disincentive effects and so reduce aggregate supply (see section 9).

Some instruments of fiscal policy also suffer from significant time lags. Whilst changes in indirect taxes are relatively easy to change, alterations in direct taxes and government spending take longer to implement and to work their way through the economy.

It can be difficult to raise taxation and lower government spending because of the political unpopularity of such measures and because of, in the case of government spending, the long-term nature of some forms of government spending. For example, once a decision has been announced that the pay of government employees will be increased it would be difficult to reverse it, and will commit the government to higher spending for some time.

Monetary policy

Monetary policy covers government changes in either the supply of money or interest rates. These policies are usually implemented by the Central Bank of the country

or area. In recent years, in a number of countries, changes in interest rates have been the main policy used to control inflation and, more recently, to influence economic activity.

An increase in the rate of interest, for example, will tend to reduce aggregate demand. This is because saving will be encouraged, borrowing discouraged and the spending power of households, who are borrowers, will be reduced. This downward pressure on spending is likely to reduce inflationary pressure but it may have an adverse effect on the balance of payments. This is because a higher rate of interest will attract hot money flows into the country which will raise the value of the currency and cause export prices to rise and import prices to fall.

It has been found difficult to control the money supply. In the past governments have sought to limit the growth of a range of money supply measures, without great success.

The use of interest rates is also not without problems. As with some fiscal policy instruments, there is a time lag between changing interest rates and the change taking effect. Some economists have estimated that it can take as long as eighteen months for interest rate changes to work their way through the economy.

Self-assessment tasks

Read the short article below and then tackle the exercises that follow.

In January 2001 the Zimbabwean government cut interest rates. The move was welcomed by business leaders. However, economists expressed concern that the lower rate of interest would increase pressure on the exchange rate, making devaluations inevitable, and would raise inflationary pressure. Inflation, which averaged 56 per cent in 2000, is forecast by the government to rise to 70 per cent in 2001. The IMF has warned that unless the Zimbabwean government tightens its fiscal and monetary policies then its support will be cut off.

1 Discuss why the Zimbabwean government may have decided to cut interest rates.

2 Explain why a lower interest rate may:
   ◆ make 'devaluation inevitable',
   ◆ increase inflation.

Interest rates are a powerful instrument but they are also a blunt and uncertain one. When the rate of interest is changed all households and firms are likely to be affected, some of which are more likely to cope with such a change. For example, a rise in the rate of interest may hit the poor more than the rich as they are more likely to be net borrowers. Firms and households may also not respond in the way the government expects. If the economy is entering a recession, lowering interest rates may not persuade households and firms to spend more if they are worried about their job prospects and future markets.

With increasing mobility of financial capital, it can be difficult for a country to operate an interest rate that is significantly different from its competitors. If, for example, the country reduces its interest rates to a level noticeably lower than that in its competitor countries, hot money may flow out of the country.

Self-assessment tasks

Read the article below and then tackle the exercises that follow:

Interest rate cut to zero as Japanese tighten their belt

Japan returned to zero interest rates yesterday in a desperate move to stave off recession and a deflationary spiral.

The decision came as President George W Bush and the Japanese Prime Minister, Yoshiro Mori, met in Washington to compare notes on the economic downturn.

Recent dramatic stock market falls around the world have been triggered by worries about an American slowdown and fears over Japan's fragile financial sector.

Mr Mori said he believed that the interest rate cut would have a 'positive effect' on the Japanese economy and called for America to take measures to increase growth.

The Japanese return to zero interest rates comes only seven months after it abandoned the policy. The Bank of Japan was responding to intense political pressure to steady plunging share prices amid worrying signs that Japan's economy is failing to pull out of a 10-year slump.

There are fears that the interest rate cut can do little to help the world's second largest economy. The rate was already a phenomenally low 0.15 per cent, leaving the bank with little leverage compared with America and Britain, where rates are far higher.

Economists fear that the change will not deal with Japan's fundamental problems. Many Japanese have already deserted the banking system. Rather than spending the cash they withdraw, most are keeping money at home, generating a boom in the sale of home safes.

Sceptics about the benefits of lowering interest rates include Masaru Hayami, the governor of the bank. He argued that the economy would recover only if firms restructured and banks were forced to write off their huge bad loans.

For much of the past 10 years, the ruling Liberal Democratic Party's response to recession has been to throw money at vast public works projects of little economic value.

In an economy characterised by falling prices, many consumers have learnt to wait for goods to get cheaper. Others fear the future so much that they would rather hoard their cash for a rainy day than spend it now.

Japan's 10 years of stagnation is sometimes called a 'golden recession' because its adverse effects have not been immediately apparent. Tokyo's shopping districts are packed at the weekends with expensively dressed young people.

But such impressions obscure real change and genuine hardship. Unemployment and bankruptcies have led to homeless people becoming a feature of urban life in Japan. Some make a living from collecting discard adult *manga* comics and reselling them at a discount. The fact that Japanese now buy the second-hand magazines is itself remarkable. In an image-conscious society, people would once have been embarrassed to be seen buying a used comic.

Source: Daily Telegraph, 20 March 2001 (adapted).

1 Why are interest rates normally well above 0 per cent?

2 Using material in the article and your knowledge of Economics, explain the effects of 0 per cent interest rates on:
   ◆ consumers,
   ◆ businesses,
   ◆ the banking system.

3 What other policies could Japan try to get out of this so-called 'golden recession'?

Exchange rate policy

Exchange rate policy covers government decisions on whether to influence the value of its currency, whether to operate a fixed, pegged or floating exchange rate and whether to link its exchange rate to that of other countries (see section 6).

A government can influence the value of its currency by changing its interest rate and/or buying and selling its currency. Raising the value of the currency will increase its purchasing power and put downward pressure on inflation. However, it may also harm its balance of payments position and reduce economic activity. In contrast, reducing the value of the currency may increase employment and growth, help the balance of payments position but increase inflationary pressure.

Operating a floating exchange rate helps market forces to determine its value but may create some uncertainty. A fixed exchange rate removes uncertainty but to maintain it a government may have to introduce policies which harm its other objectives. For example, if there is downward pressure on the exchange rate, the government may raise taxes to discourage spending and thereby reduce expenditure on imports. Such a measure may lower economic growth and increase employment.

Twelve of the current members of the EU (but not the UK for the time being) have eliminated separate exchange rates between each other by adopting a single currency, the euro. Among the advantages claimed for such a move is reduced transaction costs (firms and households saving money and time from not having to change currencies), reduced exchange rate uncertainty and increased transparency (as it is easier to compare prices in the member countries). However, these countries have given up the ability to set their own interest rates and increase their price competitiveness by devaluing.

A number of Latin American countries including Ecuador and El Salvador have dropped their currencies in favour of using the US dollar. They hope that this move will bring greater stability to their countries.

In deciding on its exchange rate policy a government may face a number of restrictions. As noted above it may be a member of a single currency or may have adopted another country's currency.

If a country is operating an independent exchange rate policy and decides to have a fixed exchange rate, it can be difficult to decide on the rate. It should be at the long-run equilibrium level but this is hard to assess. If

the government, for example, over-estimates the value it may run out of resources in seeking to maintain it or may have to raise interest rates to an unacceptable level. If it operates a floating exchange rate, speculation may result in significant fluctuations in its value. Changing an exchange rate to achieve a macroeconomic objective may not always work because its effects can be offset by other factors. For example, lowering the exchange rate to improve the balance of payments position will not work if demand for exports and imports is interest inelastic or if the quality of the country's products falls.

Self-assessment tasks

Read the short article below and then tackle the exercises that follow.

> Argentina linked its currency, the peso, to the dollar in the mid 1990s. So as the dollar rose in value so did the peso. It is estimated that the peso experienced a 15 per cent real appreciation between 1996 and 1999. This reduced Argentina's price competitiveness which, added to high real rates of interest, pushed the country into recession in 1999. This in turn increased the country's fiscal deficit.

1   Define appreciation of a currency.
2   Explain why an appreciation may result in a reduction in a country's price competitiveness.
3   Discuss why Argentina experienced a recession in 1999.
4   Explain why a recession would be expected to create a fiscal deficit.

Supply-side policies

Supply-side policies are policies designed to increase aggregate supply by improving the workings of product and factor markets. Among supply-side policies are increasing incentives to work, education and training, trade union reform, privatisation and deregulation.

More people may be encouraged to enter the labour force by cutting income tax and welfare benefits. This will increase the return from working and reduce the return from not working.

Improving education and training will raise workers' productivity and increase their flexibility and mobility. Trade union reform may also increase workers' flexibility and mobility and cut down on the number of days lost through strikes.

Many countries in recent years have adopted privatisation programmes in the belief that firms operate more efficiently under private ownership (see section 10). A number have also deregulated a number of their industries. This involves removing barriers to entry.

Supply-side policies have become very popular in recent years and there is evidence that labour market reforms have increased the responsiveness of labour markets and reduced unemployment. However, the effectiveness of some labour market reforms and some of the other measures is more uncertain. For example, cutting income tax may encourage some people to work fewer hours if they are currently content with their earnings, and lowering welfare benefits will not succeed in reducing unemployment if there are no jobs available. Privatisation may also not result in an increase in efficiency if the privatised industries act as a monopoly and do not take into account external costs and benefits.

Supply-side policies tend to be long term and uncertain in their measurable outcome as they require structural changes to be made to increase aggregate supply in the economy. They therefore have little relevance from the point of view of short-term economic management.

Policies to control inflation

The policies adopted to control inflation will be influenced by the size of the inflation rate, whether it is accelerating and what is thought to be causing it.

In the short run a government may seek to lower demand-pull inflation by implementing deflationary fiscal and/or monetary policy. Raising income taxes, reducing social benefits and cutting government spending are politically unpopular but have often been used. In many countries in recent years, however, the main measure used has been to increase interest rates. Unfortunately all of these policies have the unpopular side effect of reducing output and increasing unemployment.

The only effective long-run policy of reducing inflationary pressures is to use supply-side policies. These should avoid the problems mentioned above.

Policies to stimulate employment

It might seem easy to reduce unemployment. All the government needs to do is to create more jobs and produce greater output. In terms of the AD/AS model it

Self-assessment tasks

Read the article below and then answer the questions that follow.

On the loose

For the taxpayers of continental Europe, this year's budget season is bringing some pleasant surprises. Across the 12-nation euro-zone, governments are cutting income and corporate taxes and making an effort to broaden and simplify national tax bases.

Fundamentally, the tax-cutting trend reflects the new conditions in which the euro-zone countries find themselves, having adopted the euro and fixed the exchange rate irrevocably against each other in January 1999. 'Without the option of currency devaluation and given the increasingly global nature of world trade, there is now a greater incentive to find other means of improving competitiveness', says Robert Prior-Wandesforde of HSBC's Economics and Investment Strategy division. 'One such way is to cut taxes in order to aid existing businesses and encourage investment from overseas.'

For no country is this more true than Ireland, where the top rate of corporation tax is 24 per cent, the lowest in the euro-zone, and foreign investment has poured in. Conversely, high taxes have often deterred foreign companies from investing in Germany, in spite of the skilled workforce, modern infrastructure and other attractions. Overall, the euro-zone's tax burden – the ratio of government tax receipts to GDP – stood at 44 per cent last year, compared with 40 per cent in the UK, 30 per cent in the US and 28 per cent in Japan.

Another reason why tax cuts are in vogue is that, for the first time in years, governments feel they can afford them. Stronger economic growth this year has yielded larger than expected budgetary revenues, while falling jobless rates have reduced spending on unemployment benefits.

Source: Tony Barber, *Financial Times*, 29 September 2000.

1 Explain how tax cuts can 'aid existing business and encourage investment from overseas'.
2 Discuss two supply-side policies which can be used to improve competitiveness.
3 Define 'tax burden'.
4 Explain why economic growth enables countries to cut tax rates.

means shifting either the AD curve to the right or the AS curve to the right or both simultaneously.

In the short run, fiscal and monetary policies can operate to increase aggregate demand and so reduce unemployment. The possible adverse effects are that inflation may rise and balance of payments problems may occur. If interest rates are lowered, for example, this could reduce the value of the exchange rate, allowing export prices to fall but leading to higher import prices, in turn feeding domestic inflation. In the long run, supply-side policies targeted at the labour force may prove more effective. This is likely to be particularly true in the case of long-term unemployment where policies designed to improve the skills, confidence and experience of the unemployed are likely to make it easier for such people to obtain work.

Policies to stimulate economic growth

Economic growth is an objective in all modern economies, as through growth, living standards can improve as more goods and services become available to the population. To achieve this is difficult and the effects of policies to promote growth are by no means certain. One thing that economists do agree, though, is that for a country to be able to continue to produce more goods and services there must be an increase in the quality and quantity of the factors of production. Such an increase will increase the productive potential of the economy as shown by an outward shift of the production possibility curve (see section 12).

One of the most important ways to foster economic growth is to increase labour productivity. In other words, the amount of goods and services produced per worker must increase. This can be achieved by making the capital stock more efficient, either by replacing old outdated machinery and buildings by improved new ones or expanding the stock with new efficient capital. Alternatively, it can be achieved by making the labour force more efficient through education and training.

A significant way to increase productive potential is by making use of improved technology. This can be achieved by using better equipment and improved organisation and management.

Chicago – its growth and prosperity are indicative of growth in the US economy in the late 1990s

The US economy grew very rapidly in the period 1995 to 2000, largely as a result of taking advantage of improvements in information technology and significant improvements in productivity.

How best governments can achieve growth is a complex matter and subject to some disagreement amongst economists. If the economy is producing below capacity, **reflationary measures** to increase aggregate demand will raise output, although, as mentioned, in the long run aggregate supply will have to be increased.

Increases in investment have the advantage of increasing both aggregate demand and aggregate supply. However, there are disagreements among economists about how governments can best promote investment. Monetarists argue that this has to be done through removing restrictions on firms and thereby freeing up market forces. In contrast, Keynesians believe that government intervention is necessary to ensure the high levels of investment needed to sustain long-term economic growth.

Policies to correct balance of payments disequilibria

Policies to correct a balance of payments deficit can be divided into expenditure-reducing and expenditure-switching measures (see section 7). Expenditure-reducing measures seek to reduce imports and increase exports by lowering aggregate demand. Deflationary fiscal and monetary policies will be likely to reduce consumption and investment. If, for example, the Jamaican government raises income tax, Jamaican consumers will buy less French cheese and fewer UK cars, less sports clothing from China and Taiwan and will go for fewer holidays in Dominica. Jamaican firms will cut back on purchases from the USA. Imports of raw materials should also fall as there will be less domestic output being produced. Such deflationary policies are unpopular; they can raise unemployment and reduce living standards, at least in the short run.

Expenditure-switching measures, in contrast, seek to move demand away from foreign towards domestic products. There are a range of such measures including tariffs, **exchange control** and devaluation. If a government lowers the exchange rate, export prices will fall and import prices will rise. In the short run, such a measure may initially make the trade balance worse.

Demand for exports and imports may be inelastic in the short run. In the long run if demand for exports and imports becomes elastic as purchasers become aware of the price changes and contracts expire, the trade balance will improve (see section 12).

However, there is a danger that the price competitive advantage gained through devaluation can be eroded through higher inflation and low productivity. Indeed in the long run, the most effective policies are supply-side policies which seek to improve the efficiency and competitiveness of the economy. These imply making factories, offices and farms more efficient, cutting costs, improving the quality and design of products, putting more effort into marketing and after-sales service, and so on. This is a long and slow process, carried out against the background of a global economy where all other countries are following the same set of procedures.

Conflicts between policy objectives

Policy objectives may, on occasions, be considered to clash. Traditionally it has been thought that the objectives of economic growth and full employment will benefit from increases in aggregate demand, whilst to achieve control of inflation and a balance of payments equilibrium it may be necessary to reduce aggregate demand.

When governments pursue one objective, the policy measures they use may have an adverse effect, at least in the short run, on other objectives. In 1999 in the UK, the Bank of England raised the rate of interest to keep inflation close to the government's target. However, this pushed up the value of the pound which made it more difficult for UK firms to sell their products at home and overseas. It may also have discouraged some firms from investing and thereby may have reduced the economic growth rate.

The improved performance of the US and UK economies in the second half of the 1990s has led some economists to argue that the structure of economies is changing, making it easier for countries to achieve all their objectives simultaneously. This view is based on the belief that advances in information technology are raising productivity and creating new products and jobs. These advances combined with increased international competition are also keeping down rises

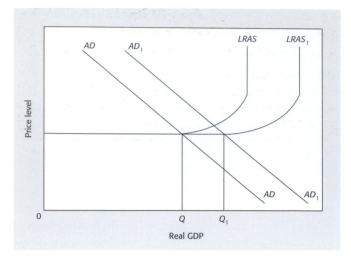

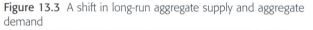

Figure 13.3 A shift in long-run aggregate supply and aggregate demand

in the price level. So with the long-run aggregate supply curve shifting to the right in line with increases in aggregate demand, as shown in figure 13.3, economic growth and higher employment can be achieved as well as low inflation.

Some doubts were expressed about this optimistic view of the 'new economy' in 2001 when economic growth slowed dramatically in the USA. However, supporters of the 'new economy' argue that this is only a temporary decline in economic growth rates caused by over expansion. Time will tell!

Self-assessment tasks

Read the article below and then tackle the exercises that follow:

India's central bank governor sees his policy juggling act as being the best

Not many central bankers lie awake at night worrying about the price of onions. But for Bimal Jalan, the veteran policy maker who is governor of the Reserve Bank of India, the control of inflation has some unique challenges.

Many central banks round the world are converging on a single model of targeting one variable, namely consumer price inflation, using one instrument – short-term interest rates.

Exchange rates, long-term interest rates, economic growth and money supply have been relegated to secondary concerns. The Bank of England which has

provided a working example, boasts that its model has been adopted in countries as diverse as South Africa, Poland and Brazil.

But not in India. The RBI still tries simultaneously to deliver low inflation, a stable rupee and high economic growth.

Recently this eclectic approach was criticised by a RBI advisory group.

'The RBI does not have much accountability as it juggles with the almost impossible task of fulfilling contradictory objectives', it concluded, suggesting India move closer towards international best practice.

Source: Alan Beattie, *Financial Times*, 24 November 2000.

1 Explain how changes in interest rates can influence inflation.

2 Discuss whether control of inflation and the promotion of economic growth are contradictory objectives.

Summary

In this section we have recognised that:

- The main objectives of macroeconomic policy are full employment, low and stable inflation, a satisfactory balance of payments position, sustainable economic growth and avoidance of exchange rate fluctuations.

- For developing economies, policies of trade, aid and industrialisation can aid their development.

- External debt still remains a massive obstacle for many in pursuing their development objectives.

- Fiscal policy, which involves the use of taxation and government spending, has an important bearing on the level of aggregate demand in the economy. It can also affect aggregate supply.

- Monetary policy involves the manipulation of the supply of money or interest rates in the economy.

- Exchange rate policies are concerned with whether to influence the exchange rate and the choice of the type of exchange rate system to operate.

- Supply-side policies are longer term in their effects than fiscal and monetary measures. They are designed to affect the total output of the economy.

- Unemployment may be reduced in the short run by increasing aggregate demand, but to reduce long-term unemployment the skills, confidence and experience of the unemployed may have to be increased.

- In the short run a government may seek to reduce inflation by implementing deflationary fiscal and/or monetary policies, but in the long run the only effective way is to use supply-side policies.

- To achieve sustained economic growth it is necessary to increase long-run aggregate supply.

- To correct a balance of payments deficit a government can employ expenditure-reducing or expenditure-switching measures. One expenditure-switching measure is devaluation. For devaluation to succeed in improving the trade position, the price elasticity of demand for exports and imports must exceed 1.

- Policy objectives may conflict. Increases in aggregate demand are likely to raise economic growth and employment but may cause balance of payments difficulties and create inflationary pressure. However, the new economy suggests that the structure of some economies has changed, making it easier for them to achieve high economic growth, low unemployment and low inflation simultaneously.

Key words

Definitions of Key words can be found in the Glossary.

automatic stabilisers	globalisation
deficit financing	monetary policy
exchange controls	reflationary measures
fiscal policy	supply-side policies

Preparing for examinations

On completion of this section you should be able to:

⇒ Know how to plan your work and how to use your study time effectively before an examination

⇒ Know what sort of examination questions to expect and how to apply a simple method to understand what they mean

⇒ Know what CIE Economics examiners are looking for when marking your examination script

⇒ Know the most common errors students make in Economics examinations

Introduction

In many respects this is the most important section in the book. To make a sporting comparison, the examination is your FA Cup Final, your Wimbledon tie break or your Superbowl decider. If you approach it in an appropriate way, it should be the means by which you realise the grade you were expecting, consistent with helping you achieve a result based on the effort you have put into your work. For some students, though, this is not the case. It can be like missing a penalty in the last minute or serving a double fault at match point. When this happens it is very unfortunate and examiners do not derive pleasure in witnessing it. For many students who are in this situation it is *not* that:

> they have failed to complete the work for the paper;
>
> they have not understood the main concepts involved.

The principal cause of under performance or even failure can be bad examination technique. Experience has shown over and over again that some students make basic errors in their Economics examinations. The consequence of these errors is that they can make at least a grade difference in the final assessment or, in some cases, the difference between a pass grade and an unclassified result.

These common faults are explained at the end of this section. But before you get to this, it is important that you know what you need to do to succeed in CIE Economics. The seeds for success are sown well before you enter the examination room. The key to success is preparation! A well-used and highly relevant phrase for you to remember is:

'A FAILURE TO PREPARE IS A PREPARATION TO FAIL'

For many years, this was on the office wall of Howard Wilkinson, the former Leeds United Manager, and one of the longest-serving football club managers in the UK. Why not put it on your wall? But, if you do, remember to practise what it says.

How to plan your work and study effectively

Get into the study habit and plan ahead

As a student, study is something you do from the first day of your course. The process of study involves the gradual accumulation of knowledge and should also include its regular review. Revision is not something you should do just before an examination. *Make study a habit. Make revision a habit.*

Each of us has our own preferences for when and where to study in an effective manner. Some people are most receptive to study in mornings; others prefer to work late and 'burn the midnight oil'. Think about what is best for yourself and do it.

At school or college, *use your time effectively*, particularly if you are in a situation where you have only to attend for time-tabled classes. Think about how much additional time there is at your disposal; by all means have a social life, but reserve regular periods for your own private study *and do it*. In other words, build breaks into your study time – not the other way around. So, get into a routine of regular study. Have a set time and place to work, and stick to it.

Adapted from an original drawing by Emily Bamford

A second important aspect of time management is that of *planning*. As a student, this is something you should try to do. It is particularly important where you are taking papers on a staged basis, as time is limited between the start of teaching and you taking the first examination. So, here are a few simple things you should do:

Read through your class notes on a *daily* basis; follow this by reading about the subject matter in this text. You will also find it useful to use some of the other texts on the recommended reading list, particularly to obtain other examples and applications of economic concepts.

Make a *weekly* plan of what you have to do and what you have actually done. Tick off items as you complete them. Table 1 shows an example of a simple planner you might like to use.

Above all, *think and plan ahead*. Find out when mock examinations are to be held; know precisely when your actual examinations will be taking place.

And remember what was said earlier: 'A failure to prepare is a preparation to fail.'

Week commencing 16 October	Lesson topic	Homework due	Study tasks
Monday			Homework for 19 October completed
Tuesday	Price elasticity of demand – definition, calculations, meaning		N R
Wednesday			
Thursday	Business relevance of price elasticity of demand. Other elasticities – income and cross elasticities	Essay on how prices are determined	N
Friday			
Saturday			
Sunday			Assessment task from section 2 completed
Outstanding work for next week	Read up about topics from Thursday's lesson. Look at past papers for other questions on elasticities of demand.		

Table 1 A daily and weekly study planner pro-forma
Notes: N – notes checked through
R – topic read up in text books

A few hints on how to study effectively

Each of us has a preferred study environment where we can work in an effective and efficient way. For most of us it is likely to be a bedroom or a school library where the distractions going on around us can at least be shut off for an hour or two. The best time for study may also vary – much will depend upon your family circumstances and how you can arrange to study in relation to these and other commitments on your time. Whatever the best time, the following advice should help you.

Put yourself in a position where you can *concentrate on your work*. This is most unlikely to happen if there is your favourite television programme being broadcast in the same room. The *attention span* of most people is 40–60 minutes. After such a period, have a drink and a rest, maybe watch a short television programme before studying for a further period.

When reading, *make notes* on what you have read and incorporate these into your class notes on a particular topic. You will also find it useful to do the self-assessment exercises in this book and work through sample examination questions on a topic. Writing and working in this way greatly enhances your understanding of a topic. *Do not just read material on its own* – the problem with this approach to study is that you will very quickly forget what you have read. The big advantage also of making notes is that they will be there for future revision when you need them.

Once you have completed the study of a particular topic, condense your notes down onto a *revision card*, which you will find invaluable for use shortly before examinations. An example of such notes is shown in figure 1.

So, it is not so much how long you study but how effective you are in your studying. Make sure you use your time effectively so that you *feel in control of your own learning experience*.

And remember: 'A failure to prepare is a preparation to fail.'

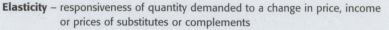

Elasticity – responsiveness of quantity demanded to a change in price, income or prices of substitutes or complements

$$PED = \frac{\% \text{ in qty demanded}}{\% \text{ in price}}$$

elastic   >1 ⎤
inelastic   <1 ⎬ applies to all measures
unitary   =1 ⎦

$$YED = \frac{\% \text{ in qty demanded}}{\% \text{ in income}}$$

+ve – normal goods
–ve – inferior goods

$$XED = \frac{\% \text{ in qty demanded, good A}}{\% \text{ in price, good B}}$$

+ve – substitutes
–ve – complements

Use and applications: prediction of effects of price changes on demand
    forecast effects of a change in income on demand
    pricing strategies for firms in competition or producing complements

Examples: low PED   – petrol, peak rail fares
    normal goods – many consumer goods, holidays
    inferior goods – cheap margarine, black and white TVs
    substitutes   – pork and lamb, car travel and rail
    complements – bread and butter, petrol and car travel

Figure 1   Example of revision card

Examination questions
Types of question

The appendix contains some examples of specimen examination questions which have been produced by CIE. There are three main types of question:

multiple choice questions (Paper 1 and Paper 3),
data response questions (Paper 2 and Paper 4),
essay questions, which are structured (Paper 2 and Paper 4), or unstructured (Paper 4).

All questions are of course based on the subject content of the core and extension syllabuses – the variety of questions are designed to assess in various ways what you know.

(You might find it useful to go back to the Introduction to refresh yourself on some of the points made concerning the 'economists' tool kit'.)

Taking each type in turn:

Multiple choice questions are an important part of the overall pattern of assessment. They are used in examinations to measure the extent to which you understand the content of the whole (as distinct from a part) of the syllabus. Typically, they take the form of a 'stem', followed by four possible answers. You are required to identify which of these is the correct answer – this is sometimes referred to as the 'key'. The nature of these questions is that two of the incorrect answers may be temptingly correct, with one other being clearly wrong. So, beware, these questions are not as easy as they might appear to be! It is perhaps also relevant to say that in some questions, you should select the one that seems to be most appropriate.

When tackling a multiple choice question paper, it is very important that you answer all questions – if you are running out of time, make a guess. You have still a 1 in 4 chance that it will be correct!

Practice is essential. There are various strategies you could try when taking a multiple choice question paper. Here is one:

Go through the paper, answering questions that **you can answer quickly**. Leave any you find difficult, including those which might require a lot of calculations or complicated reasoning in order to arrive at the correct answer.

Now tackle those which have calculations in them or which require you to spend time answering, provided you know what to do.

Finally, look at those questions where you are experiencing difficulty.

As the examination comes to a finish, make a guess at all the questions you have not attempted.

What is really important after a 'mock' examination is for you to find out the correct answers to all the questions and in particular to be sure how and why you got the right answer or why you got the wrong key. This point cannot be stressed too strongly.

Data response questions, as their name indicates, require you to answer a small number of questions drawn from 'data'. This term is used in the widest sense and can include:

numerical data or data in the form of graphs and diagrams;

a paragraph or so of text, followed by a set of data in tabular, graphical or diagramatic form;

an extract from a newspaper, magazine or other publication which contains some limited data.

All CIE questions of this type will be derived from original real-world data sources.

Typically these questions have 5–7 parts. Those set at AS are more likely to require you to demonstrate that you have acquired the basic data handling and interpretation skills given in the introduction to this book. All questions though will follow an 'incline of difficulty', the later questions commanding more marks than the earlier more straightforward questions. These later questions will also require you to analyse, discuss or comment upon economic situations underpinning the dataset. They may take the form of normative statements (see the Introduction).

When you come across a data response question for the first time:

look at the title – this may give you some clues about its content;

read any table headings, labels or footnotes which accompany the data;

see if you can pick out the main patterns in the data, using the 'eye-balling' principle;

if the data contain a chart or diagrams, look to see if you can identify any outstanding features;

check the source, as this may give you a few clues.

Once you have done this you should feel comfortable with the information provided, before putting pen to paper.

The early parts of some data response questions often require you to interpret the data or make some simple deductions from them. These should not take up much time if you have understood what is on the question paper. All data response questions are based on some economic theory or set of economic principles. If this is not clear to you at first, they ought to emerge as you systematically work your way through the questions. So, think back to these concepts as you have studied them – this should help you gain confidence and, hopefully, help you to avoid writing about irrelevant things.

Data response questions require short answers. It is important for you to remember this. In some cases the answer may be no more than a single word, a phrase or possibly a number which you have calculated. In other cases, you might be required to draw a diagram, followed by a sentence or two of explanation. One final point – look at the marks allocated to the question – these should give you an indication as to how long your answer should be. And remember, do not write any more than you have to.

Essay questions require extended writing. They should be written in continuous prose and you should include relevant diagrams. The CIE examination papers contain two types of essay question. These are:

> *Structured*, whereby the individual question is divided into two parts, each with a mark allocation. Usually, the two parts are related; the second part though invariably will require a 'higher order' answer from you (see below).

> *Unstructured*, whereby there is just one question which carries all of the marks that are available (some questions in Paper 4).

In some cases, both types of question maybe preceded by an introductory statement or 'stem' (similar to that in the multiple choice questions). This is designed to give you advice on the economic context which underpins the question or questions that follow.

(**The Introduction gave you some general advice on how to write in an effective way – why not go back and refresh yourself on the main points?**)

Self-assessment task

Spend a few minutes reading the data response question contained in Paper 2 of the appended question papers. When you have done this, ask yourself the following:

(a) What is the key economic concept or concepts in this question?

(b) Is this confirmed by the title? Or is there more information in the data than there might seem to be from the title?

(c) Can you identify any important features in the table of data and in the two figures?

(d) Do you recognise how these features relate to your knowledge of this topic?

Make a few notes on each.

(You may also like to repeat this process for the data response question in Paper 4. You will note that this question is of a slightly different format to that in Paper 2.)

The wording of questions

A lot of care, thought and attention goes into the final production of all CIE examination papers. So, when you sit an examination, it is important to appreciate that the questions which are on the examination paper have been set by an examiner who is requiring you *to answer these questions*. Put another way, examination papers never contain questions such as:

Write all you know about ...

or:

Write as much as you can remember about ...

Unfortunately, this point is not always appreciated by some students.

All examination questions contain two very important instructions. These are called:

> *Directive words* – these words indicate what form the answer should take. For example, it could be in the form of a description, a discussion, an explanation or merely a statement. These words are there for a purpose, namely that they have been used by the examiners to say what they are looking for (in skill terms when you answer a particular question).

> *Content words* – these are much more diverse in nature since they cover the whole of the subject area of the syllabus. Their aim is to make clear to you, the candidate, what is the focus of the question being set, and indeed, what examiners expect you to write about.

Table 2 shows a list of key directive words which are most likely to occur in CIE Economics examination questions. *You should study these carefully and understand what each means.* You will then appreciate that a question which asks:

'Define price elasticity of demand'

is not the same as

'Explain what is meant by price elasticity of demand'

is not the same as

'Discuss the relevance of price elasticity of demand in business'

Directive word	What it means	Where you can expect it to be used
Calculate	Work out using the information provided	Usually in the early parts of data response questions
Define	Give the exact meaning	
Describe	Give a description of	
Give (an account of)	As 'describe'	
Give (an example of)	Give a particular example	
How	In what way or ways	
Illustrate	Give examples/diagram	
Outline	Describe without detail	
State	Make clear	
Summarise	Give main points, without detail	
What	State clearly	
Which	Give a clear example/state what	
Analyse	Set out the main points	In the later parts of data response questions and in part (a) of structured essay questions
Apply	Use in a specific way	
Compare	Give similarities and differences	
Explain	Give clear reasons or make clear	
Account for	Give reasons for	
Consider	Give your thoughts about	
Assess	Show how important something is	In the final part of data response questions and in part (b) of structured essay questions. Also, in unstructured essay questions
Comment upon	Give your reasoned opinions on	
Criticise	Give an opinion, but support it with evidence	
Discuss	Give the important arguments, for and against	
Evaluate	Discuss the importance of, making some attempt to weight your opinions	

Table 2 Key directive words

A simple method for understanding and interpreting examination questions
Short answer data response questions

The appendix to this section gives typical examples of CIE AS and A level examination papers. You will now find some valuable advice on how you can understand what the data response questions on Papers 2 and 4 mean and, therefore, how you are expected to answer them.

Look at Question 1 on Paper 2, 'Inflation in the UK'.

Part (a) is asking some basic data handling skills (see the Introduction for more details).

Part (b) (i) requires further data handling skills, this time comparing the rate of change of two adjacent columns of data. (This is more difficult, but, if you have understood what is meant by 'rate of change' in the Introduction, then it should pose few problems). Part (b) (ii) asks you to think about differences in the rates of change and to explain one supply and one demand factor that might have caused such differences.

For part (c), the question requires you to reflect on your knowledge of Economics so far – it does not actually require you to explicitly use the data provided.

Read part (d) carefully. It contains two of the directive words listed in table 2, and being the last part, is asking the most difficult question of all. It requires you to interpret figure 2 and then explain and comment upon what you have found. Careful thought is needed.

Let us look more specifically at a few of these questions. For example:

(a) (i) As table 2 indicates, 'calculate' means that you have to work out something from the data which has been provided. This calculation is a simple index number, which will give you the increase in the 'all items' for the period shown in the table of data. So:

1987 is the base date, which equals 100

1995 – the 'All items' index is 149.1

So, the increase in price over the whole period is

$$\frac{1995 \text{ index}}{1987 \text{ index}} = \frac{149.1}{100} \quad 100\%$$

$$= 49.1\%$$

(b) (i) As stated earlier, this question requires you to eyeball two columns of data. The 'compare' directive word means that you must look for important differences (especially) or similarities in the 'rate of change' between the two columns over the period as a whole. You should also look in general for how the year-by-year variations compare. (Do not just write out the data as they appear in the table – this will not give you any marks.)

The most obvious difference over the period is clearly shown by the indices for 1995, compared with the base date of 100. The retail price of alcohol and tobacco has increased by almost 70 per cent between 1987 and 1995, whilst consumer durables has increased by just over 16 per cent. So, 'the change in retail prices of consumer durables has been less rapid than the change in retail prices of alcohol and tobacco'. You could then quote the data to support your answer or make reference to the very rapid relative increase in the latter between 1989 and 1992 especially.

To answer part (d) effectively, you need first of all to be clear as to what the data in figure 2 are showing for the G7 countries. Three important points emerge, namely:

Italy has clearly experienced the highest rate of inflation of the G7 countries from September 1994–95.

In Japan, consumer prices have actually fallen by a very small percentage over this period.

France and Germany have inflation rates below the G7 average.

Once you have got these points sorted out, you can then tackle the question which is focussing upon the 'external consequences', that is, the consequences for external trade of the differences you have noted. Looking back to table 2, you must try to give reasons for this state of affairs and also comment upon their significance from an external trade perspective.

Section 6 of the book should help you explain the consequences, such as:

export prices in Italy and the UK will be increasing at a faster rate than in other G7 countries;

this might have an adverse effect on the balance of trade of the UK especially as imports are likely to be relatively cheaper than exports;

Japan's international competitiveness will be enhanced relative to that of the other G7 countries; there may also be implications for investment flows between these countries or from elsewhere in the world;

the exchange rate of Italy and UK especially might depreciate.

You do not need all of these points. Two or possibly three, clearly explained, will give you the marks available. Your answer will be enhanced if you draw on the data and quote a few statistics. To get a really good mark though you must also 'comment upon' what you have found. In other words, try to make a reasoned opinion of what the consequences are. This is best done by again looking at it from an Italian/UK perspective when compared with other G7 members.

Although the process has been spelled out at length, what is involved is really quite simple – if you follow this general advice you should be able to answer data response questions in an effective way.

Essay questions

In some respects, understanding and interpreting essay questions is less complicated *provided you have understood the subject content of the questions*. Figure 2 shows a simple but effective method that you can use to understand this type of question. If you follow the method, you will not only have the basis for a meaningful answer to the question, you will also have a logical structure to follow when you are writing it.

Look at Q2 (a) in Section B of Paper 2. This question reads:

'Explain the link between opportunity cost and the production possibility curve.'

Note that the directive word 'explain' occurs again here. (It is very widely used in Economics examinations!) As table 2 showed, 'explain' means 'give clear reasons or make clear'. The content words in the question are two of the concepts which were included in section 1, namely 'opportunity cost' and 'the production possibility curve'. The other important instruction in there is 'link', in other words, relate these two particular concepts.

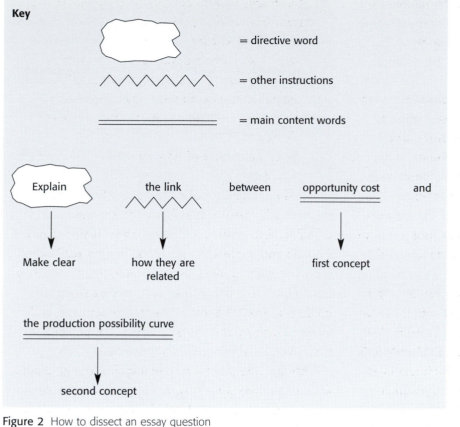

Figure 2 How to dissect an essay question

Figure 2 shows some general symbols you can apply to dissect any essay question. These symbols are then used to show how you can dissect the question given above.

Figure 2 will also help you to plan your answer. An obvious structure would be:

    briefly define what is meant by opportunity cost and give a few simple examples;

    briefly say what a production possibility curve is and include a simple diagram;

    explain the link between the two – the simplest way to do this is to look at examples of trade-offs as an economy switches production from one good to another;

    make sure you use your diagram to aid your explanation referring to it in your written answer.

How to impress CIE economics examiners

Let us start with a few typical comments that CIE examiners will write on some of the examination answers they read:

'Does not answer the question'
'Too vague'
'Misses point of question'
'No application'
'Commentary not made'
'Ignores second aspect of question'

These comments clearly indicate that the candidates have not done what was expected from them in the question. So, the first way to impress any examiner reading your examination scripts is:

To answer the question

In other words, produce an answer as directed by the question. The information above, in particular the simple method for dissecting various examination questions, should help you to write your answer in a clear, well-structured manner as directed by the question. This point cannot be emphasised too much!

There are various other ways in which you might impress an examiner. For example:

Diagrams These are very important and a relevant means of economic explanation. Many of the topics you come across in Economics can be illustrated by a diagram or by means of an explanation supported by a diagram. You have only to glance at the sections in this book to see this. So, a relevant correctly drawn diagram, used effectively in your answer, will impress an examiner reading your examination script. An example of good technique is shown in figure 3.

The diagram shows how the price of theatre tickets will be affected by the introduction of a subsidy. As this diagram indicates, the subsidy will lead to an increase in supply, shifting the supply curve downwards and to the right. The price which theatre goers will have to pay falls from P_1 to P_2 – it does not fall to P_3, as part of the subsidy (that shown between P_3 and P_2) will be retained by the theatre owners to offset the higher costs incurred as a result of the increase in the number of theatre visits demanded.

Current issues and problems. One of the reasons for studying Economics is to help you understand some of the things that are taking place around you. So, when you get the opportunity, do so! For example, if you are answering a question on the negative externalities associated with environmental pollution, you might refer to a local case which is known to you or something you have seen in a newspaper or magazine. Most of the topics in the syllabus can be supported by additional up-to-date material, not always found in text books.

Refer to things you have read. It follows that there are instances where it would support your answer if you referred to this source material by name, for example an article, an example from a text book or the views of a particular economist.

Common mistakes made in CIE Economics examinations

In addition to a failure to answer the question, the other main mistakes made by candidates are:

1 A failure to allocate writing time in an appropriate way.

2 Confusion over similar terms.

3 Meaningless, wrongly drawn diagrams or diagrams which add nothing to an answer.

Let us conclude this section by looking at each in turn.

1 The time available for Paper 2 of the AS examination is relatively short – 1 hr 30 minutes. You must therefore make sure you allocate your writing time in the examination in a meaningful way.

Table 3 shows how you can do this. The following important principles should be applied:

Roughly speaking, allocate your writing time in direct proportion to the marks available.

Do not exceed the time you have allocated for each part.

If you cannot do a particular question, leave it and move on to the next part. (You can always return to it later on in the examination if time permits.) You will only get marks for the questions you answer – your script, though, will always be marked out of the total marks which are available.

2 A second problem in Economics examinations is that, on occasions, candidates sometimes confuse terms

Paper 2   Time allowed : 1 hour 30 minutes

In principle allocate 45 minutes to each of the two sections.

You will need to spend about 5 minutes in carrying out the five initial familiarisation steps for the data response question (see above) and again about 5 minutes thinking about which essay question you will attempt. This leaves about 40 minutes writing time for each question.

Question 1

	Approx. minutes		
40 mins (writing)	8	(a)	4 marks
	12	(b)	6 marks
	8	(c)	4 marks
	12	(d)	6 marks
			20 marks
		1 mark =	2 mins. writing

Section B

	1 mark = 2 mins. writing
40 mins. (writing)	Look at the mark splits and allocate your time accordingly. Avoid the temptation to spend too much time on part (a).

Table 3 A simple method for allocating writing time in an examination

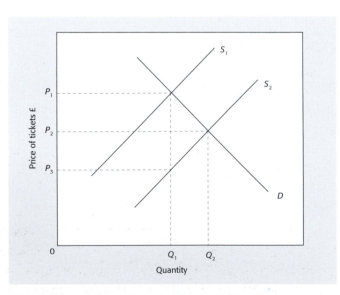

Figure 3 How to use a diagram effectively in your answers
Notes: D – Demand curve for theatre tickets
S$_1$ – Supply curve of theatre tickets
S$_2$ – Supply curve after introduction of subsidy

which are similar (in terms of content) or which have similar names (but mean something different). Table 4 contains a few common examples.

Topic	Often confused with
elastic demand	inelastic demand
allocative efficiency	productive efficiency
prices	costs
merit goods	public goods
direct taxation	indirect taxation
external costs/benefits	social costs/benefits
real income	nominal income
rate of interest	exchange rates
fiscal policy measures	monetary policy measures
aggregate demand	aggregate supply
balance of trade	balance of payments
income	wealth
monopoly	monopolistic competition

Watch out also that you express formulae correctly – in particular elasticity formulae

Table 4 Common errors over terms and topics in the CIE Economics syllabus

3 Finally, a common mistake which candidates often make is in the way in which they use diagrams in their answers. Common errors are:

to label axes incorrectly or not to label them at all;

to make diagrams too small;

to draw lines and curves incorrectly, usually through being wrongly sloping;

to fail to use a diagram in an answer when asked for one to be included;

to include a diagram when one is not needed and where it does not enhance an answer at all.

Self-assessment task

When you have completed studying each of the two units, see if you can do the specimen examination papers which follow on from this section. Do this under examination conditions and in the time allocated.

Remember to think about the matters raised in this section when you are completing this task.

Self-assessment task

Three examples of badly drawn/incorrect diagrams are shown in figure 4. How many improvements can you make to them?

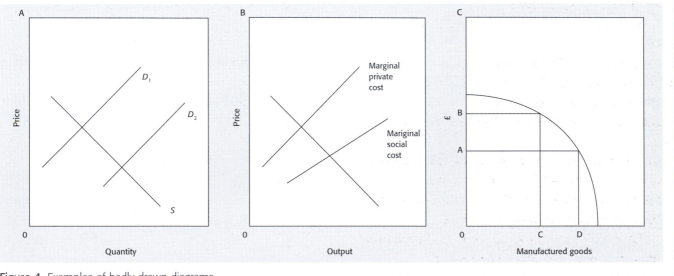

Figure 4 Examples of badly drawn diagrams

Summary

In this concluding section we have established that:

➡ It is very important for you to be well-organised and to be able to plan ahead if you are to succeed in CIE Economics.

➡ Revision should be an ongoing process, not just a last-minute activity you carry out just before a written examination.

➡ CIE's examinations contain a variety of forms of external assessment, with three main types of question.

➡ Candidates who underperform in examinations have usually not been adequately briefed on the type and style of question.

➡ A lack of time and an inability to understand the relevance of directive words are the most common causes of underperformance.

CAMBRIDGE
INTERNATIONAL EXAMINATIONS

CAMBRIDGE INTERNATIONAL EXAMINATIONS
General Certificate of Education Advanced Subsidiary Level
and Advanced Level

ECONOMICS   **8708/1, 9708/1**

PAPER 1 Multiple Choice (Core)

1 hour

Additional materials:

    Multiple choice answer sheet
    Soft clean eraser
    Soft pencil (type B or HB is recommended)

Specimen Paper for syllabus for first examination in
2001 (Advanced Subsidiary Level) and 2002 (Advanced Level)

Time 1 hour

INSTRUCTIONS TO CANDIDATES

Do not open this booklet until you are told to do so.

Write your name, Centre number and candidate number on the answer sheet in the spaces provided unless this has already been done for you.

There are **thirty** questions in this paper. Answer **all** questions. For each question there are four possible answers, **A, B, C** and **D**. Choose the **one** you consider correct and record your choice in **soft pencil** on the separate answer sheet.

Read very carefully the instructions on the answer sheet.

INFORMATION FOR CANDIDATES

Each correct answer will score one mark. A mark will not be deducted for a wrong answer.

Any rough working should be done in this booklet.

This specimen question paper consists of 14 printed pages.

 UNIVERSITY *of* CAMBRIDGE
Local Examinations Syndicate

© CIE 2000
SPECQPV1

[Turn Over

1   A student decides to stay in her room to do some work rather than going to the cinema.

What is the opportunity cost of her decision?

A   the enjoyment she would have derived from a visit to the cinema

B   the improvement in the mark she obtains for her assignment

C   the increase in her electricity bill

D   the money she would have spent in the cinema

2   The diagram shows the production possibilities of an economy that has a rate of capital consumption of 0W.

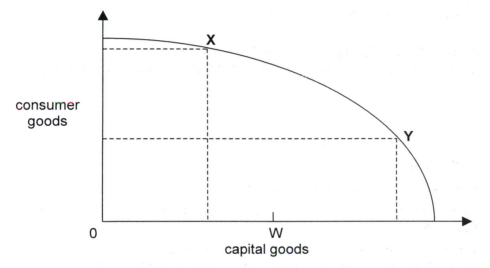

What will be the effect on current and future living standards of a movement from **X** to **Y** on the curve?

	current living standards	future living standards
A	decrease	decrease
B	decrease	increase
C	increase	decrease
D	increase	increase

3 The diagram shows the production possibility curve of an economy which uses two factor inputs, capital and labour, to produce two goods, **X** and **Y**.

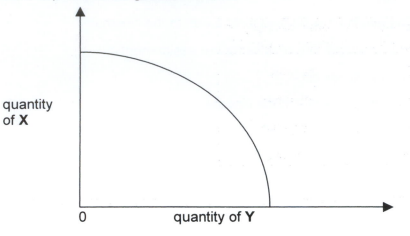

The amounts of capital allocated to both **X** and **Y** are fixed.

What explains why the curve is bowed outwards?

A   decreasing opportunity costs

B   diminishing returns

C   diseconomies of scale

D   economies of scale

4 Which characteristic of money is essential, if it is to be used as a medium of exchange?

A   It must be durable.

B   It must be legal tender.

C   It must be limited in supply.

D   It must have intrinsic value.

5 What would be likely to cause an increased demand by private motorists for petrol?

A   an increase in road toll charges

B   an increase in the price of second-hand cars

C   a reduction in bus fares

D   a reduction in the price of steel

6 Total expenditure on good X rises if its price falls, but decreases if income falls.

What can be concluded from this information?

	price elasticity of demand for good X	income elasticity of demand for good X
A	elastic	negative
B	elastic	positive
C	inelastic	negative
D	inelastic	positive

7 The diagram shows different demand and supply curves within a country for home-produced coal.

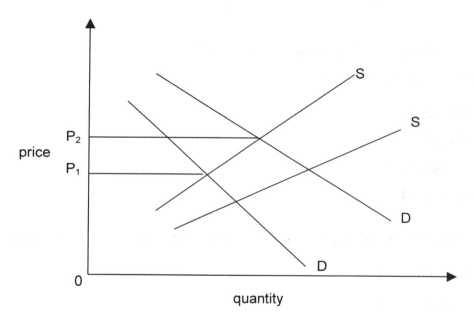

What could explain the fall in the price of coal in the diagram from OP_2 to OP_1?

A a fall in the cost of oil-fired central heating

B an increase in the duty on imported petroleum

C an increase in the industrial demand for coal

D a subsidy for the coal industry

5

8 The points in the scatter diagram indicate the prices and quantities sold of an agricultural commodity in different time periods.

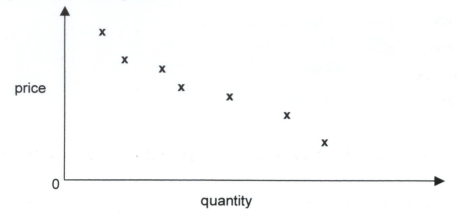

It may be concluded that these points were generated primarily by changes over time in

A advertising.

B consumers' incomes.

C supply.

D the price of a substitute commodity.

9 In the diagram, S_1 and D_1 are the initial supply and demand curves for a product.

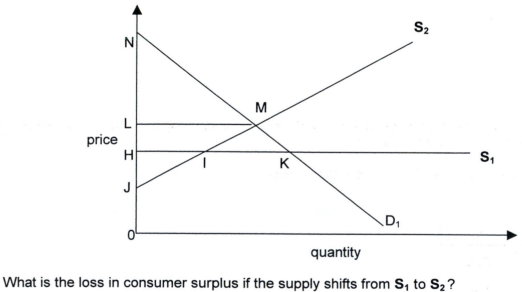

What is the loss in consumer surplus if the supply shifts from S_1 to S_2?

A HIML   **B** HKML   **C** IKM   **D** NLM

10 Which schedule shows the maximum price at which a firm would be able to sell any given level of output?

    A   demand schedule

    B   marginal revenue schedule

    C   production schedule

    D   supply schedule

11 A manufacturer progressively reduces the price of his product in an attempt to increase total revenue.

The table shows the outcome of this policy.

price ($)	total revenue 000's ($)
10	750
9	750
8	750

What is the price elasticity of demand for the product?

    A   perfectly inelastic

    B   relatively inelastic

    C   perfectly elastic

    D   unitary elastic

12 Owing to a fall in the price of cameras, the demand for film has risen by 20%. The cross-elasticity of demand between cameras and films is −2.

Which change in camera prices has brought this about?

	from	to
A	$55	$50
B	$55	$45
C	$50	$45
D	$50	$40

13 The diagrams show four market supply curves.

Which diagram shows the market supply curve where a fall in price would cause an equal proportionate fall in quantity supplied at all levels of output?

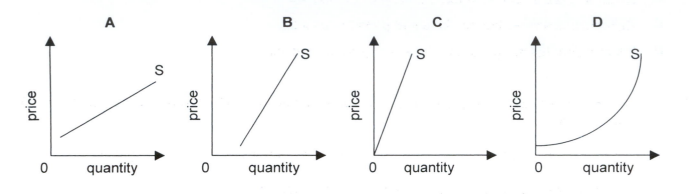

14 The diagram illustrates a market for wheat with a government set maximum price of 0P above the current equilibrium price.

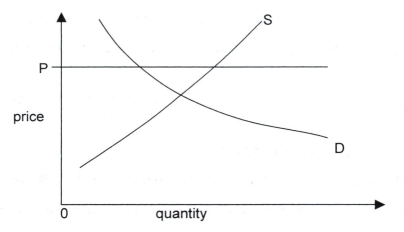

What could cause the set price to have an impact on the market?

A   a bumper wheat harvest

B   a fall in the price of rice

C   an advertising campaign for bread

D   an increase in subsidies to wheat farmers

8708/1 Specimen 2001.   **[Turn over**

15 Why is government action often necessary to persuade firms to provide or contribute towards industrial training?

   A   External benefits are gained by firms that do not provide training.

   B   External costs affect firms that do not provide training.

   C   External economies benefit firms that provide training.

   D   Internal benefits are gained by firms that provide training.

16 A government reduces the speed limit on major roads from 100 kilometres per hour to 70 kilometres per hour.

Which cost should be excluded from a social cost-benefit evaluation of the new regulation?

   A   the increase in average journey times for private motorists

   B   the increase in congestion on minor roads resulting from a diversion of traffic from the major roads

   C   the increase in police manpower required to enforce the new speed limit

   D   the loss to the government resulting from a reduction in revenue from petrol duty

17 Why would it **not** be practicable to supply pure public goods, for example street lighting, through the ordinary market mechanism?

   A   Private monopolies would earn excess profits.

   B   Some households would not be able to afford to make their full contribution towards the cost.

   C   The benefits would not be confined to the buyers, but would automatically be available to non-buyers.

   D   The provision of public goods is essential, and therefore cannot be left to private initiative.

18 A government replaces cash grants paid to students in full-time higher education with a scheme of loans to be repaid by the students from their future incomes earned within the country.

Which of the following is likely to result in the absence of offsetting changes?

   A   a decrease in the opportunity cost of higher education to the student

   B   a decrease in the private rate of return on investment in higher education

   C   a switch in demand by students away from job-related courses

   D   reduced emigration on the part of graduates

19 The table shows a country's trade and inflation figures for 1999, expressed in index number form (1990 = 100).

volume of exports	102.3
volume of imports	101.7
unit value of exports	126.6
unit value of imports	129.4
index of retail prices	127.1

What were the country's terms of trade in 1999?

A   97.8   **B**   99.4   **C**   127.1   **D**   128.0

20 The diagrams show the demand and supply curves for computer chips in country X and country Y, with the prices in the two countries measured in a common currency.

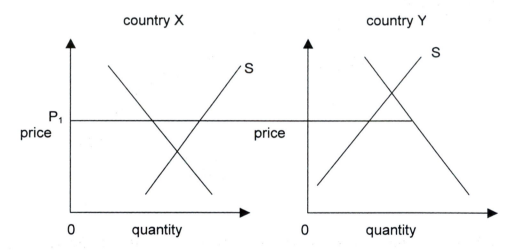

Initially, there is a ban on trade in computer chips. When the ban is lifted, trade in chips between X and Y commences at price OP_1.

There are no transport costs and the exchange rate is fixed.

What is the result of international trade?

A   Country X exports chips and its producers receive a higher price.

B   Country X imports chips and its consumers pay a lower price.

C   Country Y exports chips and its producers receive a lower price.

D   Country Y imports chips and its consumers pay a higher price.

21 A car manufacturer faces a quota on its exports to a large foreign market.

Which strategy would help to increase sales to this market?

A establishing and subsidising a dealer network in the foreign market

B improving the quality of the cars it produces

C reducing the price of exports to that market

D setting up a manufacturing plant in the foreign country

22 The diagram represents the production possibilities of two economies X and Y.

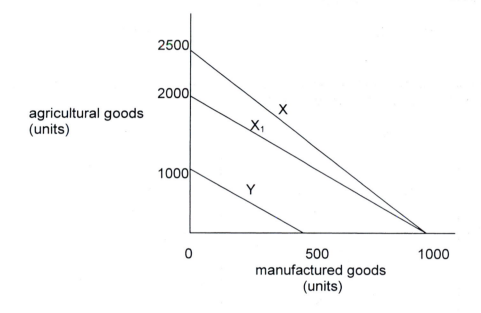

As a result of soil erosion in economy X, the production possibility curve shifts from X to X_1.

According to the law of comparative advantage, what should country Y now do?

A cease to trade with country X

B export agricultural products to country X

C export manufactured products to country X

D import both agricultural and manufactured products from country X

23 Suppose the average consumer's expenditure is divided between bread, meat, milk and vegetables in the ratio 4:3:2:1.

During the course of a year, the price of bread increases by 10%, the price of meat **falls** by 10% and the prices of both milk and vegetables increase by 20%.

What is the increase in the average price level during the year?

  A   6%   **B**   7%   **C**   12.5%   **D**   15%

24 The table shows the values of selected economic variables expressed in the form of index numbers.

	price level	money supply	income velocity of circulation	number of final transactions
year 1	100	100	100	100
year 2		120	100	80

What was the index for the price level in year 2?

  A   100   **B**   120   **C**   150   **D**   180

25 The table shows the index of retail prices for a country **on January 1st** in successive years.

year (Jan 1st)	Retail Price Index
1994	60
1995	80
1996	100
1997	125
1998	160

During the course of which year was the rate of inflation at its highest?

  A   1994   **B**   1995   **C**   1996   **D**   1997

[Turn over

26 In the diagram D_1 and S_1 are the initial demand and supply curves of the pound (£) on the foreign exchange markets.

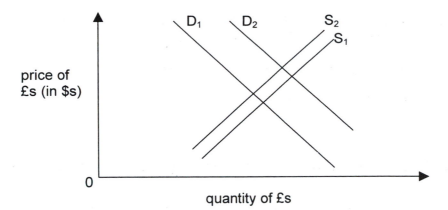

What will cause the demand curve to shift to D_2 and the supply curve to S_2?

A an appreciation of the pound

B an increase in UK interest rates

C a reduction in the level of UK import tariffs

D a reduction in the quality of UK goods

27 A country experiences a rate of wage inflation twice that of its international competitors. At the same time, its currency appreciates because of an inflow of capital funds.

Which of the following is most likely to occur?

A a decrease in profits

B a decrease in money supply

C a decrease in the rate of unemployment

D an increase in the volume of exports

13

28 A Japanese company builds a factory in the UK with the intention of increasing its sales in the European market.

What is likely to be the long-run impact on the UK's visible trade balance and on its invisibles balance?

	visible trade balance	*invisibles balance*
A	worsen	worsen
B	worsen	improve
C	improve	worsen
D	improve	improve

29 The table shows indicators of a country's economic performance over a two year period.

year	exchange rate	volume of exports index	volume of imports index	balance of trade ($)
1	100	100	100	zero
2	100	90	100	+500 million

Which of the following is consistent with the above information?

A There has been a fall in the price of exports.

B There has been an improvement in the terms of trade.

C There has been an increase in the price of imports.

D There has been no change in the level of real income per head.

[Turn over

14

30 In diagram 1, X represents exports, and M represents imports. In diagram 2, r is the level of domestic interest rates.

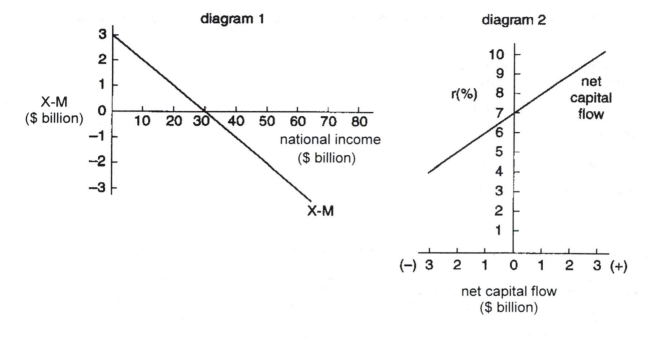

If the country's national income is $50 billion, at which level of domestic interest rates will the country's balance of payments be in equilibrium?

A   5%   B   7%   C   8%   D   9%

CAMBRIDGE
INTERNATIONAL EXAMINATIONS

CAMBRIDGE INTERNATIONAL EXAMINATIONS
General Certificate of Education Advanced Subsidiary Level and Advanced Level

KEY SHEET FOR MULTIPLE CHOICE SPECIMEN QUESTION PAPER

Syllabus for first examination in 2001 (Advanced Subsidiary Level) and 2002 (Advanced Level)

ECONOMICS		
8708/1	Multiple Choice (Core)	(Advanced Subsidiary Level)
9708/1	Multiple Choice (Core)	(Advanced Level)

MAXIMUM MARK: 30

UNIVERSITY *of* CAMBRIDGE
Local Examinations Syndicate

2

ANSWER KEYS

Item	Key	Syllabus Topic	Skill	Item	Key	Syllabus Topic	Skill
1	A	1	1	16	D	3	1
2	B	1	1	17	C	3	1
3	B	1	1	18	B	3	2
4	C	1	1	19	A	4	2
5	D	2	2	20	A	4	2
6	B	2	2	21	D	4	2
7	A	2	2	22	A	4	2
8	C	2	2	23	B	5	2
9	B	2	2	24	C	5/6	2
10	A	2	1	25	A	6	1
11	D	2	2	26	B	6	1
12	C	2	1	27	A	6	2
13	C	2	2	28	C	6	1
14	C	3	2	29	B	4/6	2
15	A	3	1	30	D	7	2

Topics:

1	Basic Economic Ideas (Core)
2	The Price System (Core)
3	Government Intervention in the Price System (Core)
4	International Trade (Core)
5	Measurement in the Macroeconomy (Core)
6	Macroeconomic Problems (Core)
7	Macroeconomic Policies (Core)

Skills:

1	Knowledge and understanding
2	Interpretation and analysis

CAMBRIDGE
INTERNATIONAL EXAMINATIONS

CAMBRIDGE INTERNATIONAL EXAMINATIONS
General Certificate of Education Advanced Subsidiary Level
and Advanced Level

ECONOMICS   **8708/2, 9708/2**
PAPER 2 Data Response and Essay (Core)

1 hour 30 minutes

Additional materials:

Answer paper

**Specimen Paper for syllabus for first examination in
2001 (Advanced Subsidiary Level) and 2002 (Advanced Level)**

Time   1 hour 30 minutes

INSTRUCTIONS TO CANDIDATES

Write your name, Centre number and candidate number in the spaces provided on the answer paper /
answer booklet.

Answer **two** questions.

Write your answers on the separate answer paper provided.

If you use more than one sheet of paper, fasten the sheets together.

Section A

Answer this question.

Section B

Answer any **one** question.

INFORMATION FOR CANDIDATES

The questions in this paper carry equal marks. The number of marks is given in brackets [ ]at the end of
each part question.

You may answer with reference to your own economy or other economies that you have studied where
relevant to the question.

This specimen question paper consists of 4 printed pages.

UNIVERSITY *of* CAMBRIDGE
Local Examinations Syndicate

© CIE 2000
SPECQPV1

[Turn Over

2

Section A
Answer this question.

Question 1

Inflation in the UK

In October 1992, the then Chancellor of the Exchequer set out a new framework for monetary policy by pledging the government to 'the objective of keeping inflation within the range of 1-4 per cent'.

Table 1

General Index of Retail Prices in UK
(January 1987 = 100)

Year	Annual Averages		
	All Items	Alcohol & Tobacco	Consumer Durables
1988	106.9	105.7	103.7
1989	115.2	110.8	107.2
1990	126.1	120.6	111.3
1991	133.5	136.2	114.8
1992	138.5	146.8	115.5
1993	140.7	155.1	115.9
1994	144.1	161.4	115.5
1995	149.1	169.0	116.2

UK Inflation: year-on-year percentage changes in retail prices

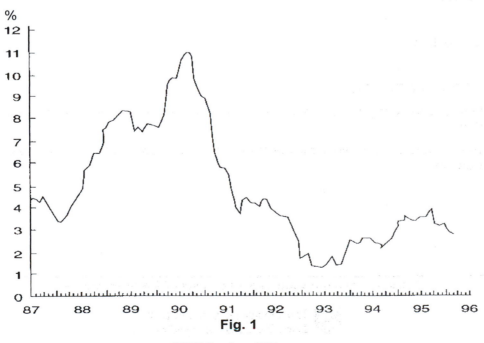

Fig. 1

8708/2 Specimen 2001

3

Change in consumer prices¹: G7 comparison, September 1995

Percentage change over 12 months

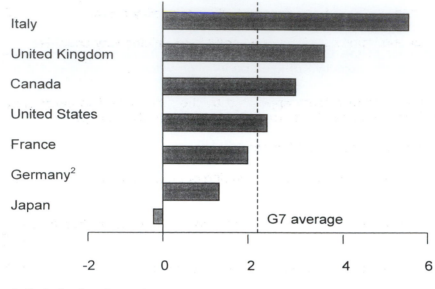

1 Excluding housing costs.
2 Former Federal Republic.

Fig. 2

(a) With reference to Table 1 and Fig. 1:

    (i)   Calculate the increase in the price of 'All Items' between 1987 and 1995.   [1]

    (ii) In which year was the rate of increase in retail prices the highest?   [1]

    (iii) What was the trend in retail prices in the UK between 1990 and 1993?   [2]

(b) With specific reference to Table 1:

    (i)   Compare the rate of change of prices of Consumer Durables with the rate of change in the price of Alcohol and Tobacco.   [2]

    (ii) Explain **one** supply and **one** demand factor which might have caused the differences identified in **1(b)(i)**.   [4]

(c) How might savers and borrowers be affected if the government was successful in keeping inflation within its target range?   [4]

(d) Explain and comment upon the external consequences of the relative rates of inflation shown in Fig. 2.   [6]

[Turn over

4

Section B
Answer any **one** question from this Section.

2   **(a)** Explain the link between opportunity cost and the production possibility curve.   [8]

    (b) Discuss how the concept of opportunity cost may be useful in explaining why countries trade with each other.   [12]

3   You have been asked to work as part of a team appointed by the government to carry out a cost-benefit analysis of the building of an additional runaway at an international airport.

    (a) Explain what is meant by the term *cost-benefit analysis.*   [8]

    (b) Discuss the problems that might be encountered in carrying out this analysis.   [12]

4   **(a)** Explain why governments are sometimes concerned about the level of the exchange rate of their country's currency.   [10]

    (b) Discuss what policies they might adopt to influence the exchange rate.   [10]

CAMBRIDGE
INTERNATIONAL EXAMINATION

CAMBRIDGE INTERNATIONAL EXAMINATIONS
General Certificate of Education Advanced Subsidiary Level and Advanced Level

MARK SCHEME FOR SPECIMEN QUESTION PAPER

Syllabus for first examination in 2001 (Advanced Subsidiary Level) and 2002 (Advanced Level)

ECONOMICS

8708/2 Data Response and Essay (Core) (Advanced Subsidiary Level)

9708/2 Data Response and Essay (Core) (Advanced Level)

MAXIMUM MARK: 40

UNIVERSITY *of* CAMBRIDGE
Local Examinations Syndicate

2

Question 1

(a) (i)   49.1% or points   [1]

   (ii)   1989/90   [1]

  (iii)   Rising (1), at a decreasing rate (1)   [2]

(b) (i)   Consumer durables less rapid (1), numerical support (1)   [2]

   (ii)   Change in demand reason, e.g. income, taste (1) plus change in supply reason, e.g. tax, costs (1), plus application to explain difference   [4]

(c)   Consideration of savers (2) and borrowers (2) such as real values, confidence and interest rate. 1 or 2 depending on quality of explanation of each.   [4]

(d)   Impact may be on exchange rate, trade balance, finance flows. analysis of impact (3), application to data (1), evaluation/judgement (2)   [6]

Question 2

(a)   Definition of two terms, explanation of production possibility curve, presentation of correct diagram (not explicitly required by question but reasonable to be expected in this case), meaning of opportunity cost in terms of production forfeited.

For a thorough explanation   7-8

For good definitions and competent explanation   5-6

For a correct but undeveloped explanation or incomplete definitions   3-4

For an answer that contains inaccuracies and only a few correct points   1-2

(b)   Explanation of comparative advantage, discussion of availability of resources, methods of production, link to opportunity cost

For a thorough explanation and a reasoned discussion   10-12

For a competent explanation with accurate but limited discussion   7-9

For a correct but undeveloped explanation with only brief discussion   4-6

For an answer that contains inaccuracies and only a few correct points   1-3

3

Question 3

(a)   Explanation of the scope of the analysis and its purpose.

For a sound explanation with good illustrations and a clear   6-8
understanding of the principles involved

For a correct but undeveloped explanation   3-5

For an answer that has some basic correct facts but includes   1-2
irrelevancies and errors of theory

(b)   Description of types of information required – benefits and costs
for both consumers and producers, difficulties of collecting
information, giving a monetary value to the findings, discussion of
the meaning of the value given and the likely conclusions that
might be drawn from a cost-benefit analysis. Consideration of
balance of differing aims and the power of various groups involved
and the difficulties of forming an agreed decision even after the
analysis has been undertaken. Political versus economic
considerations.

For a thorough attempt with an ability to query some of the   10-12
assumptions surrounding the collection of information, and a clear
consideration of the problems of interpretation of data

For a competent discussion with limited critical comment   7-9

For a correct but undeveloped comment   5-6

For an answer that contains inaccuracies and only a few correct   1-4
points

4

Question 4

(a) *For a thorough explanation of exchange rate influences on the economy* 7-10

For an accurate but undeveloped explanation 4-6

For an answer that shows some knowledge but does not indicate that the question has been fully grasped, or where the answer is mostly irrelevant 1-3

(b) *For a thorough analysis of how exchange rates might be effectively controlled, with an evaluation of the policies* 8-10

For a competent explanation that does not fully analyse but makes some attempt at evaluation 6-7

For a competent explanation that contains no attempt at evaluation 3-5

For an answer that shows some knowledge but does not indicate that the question has been fully grasped, or where the answer is mostly irrelevant 1-2

CAMBRIDGE
INTERNATIONAL EXAMINATIONS

CAMBRIDGE INTERNATIONAL EXAMINATIONS
General Certificate of Education Advanced Level

ECONOMICS

9708/3

PAPER 3 Multiple Choice (Extension)

1 hour

Additional materials:

Multiple choice answer sheet
Soft clean eraser
Soft pencil (type B or HB is recommended)

Specimen Paper for syllabus for first examination in 2002

Time 1 hour

INSTRUCTIONS TO CANDIDATES

Do not open this booklet until you are told to do so.

Write your name, Centre number and candidate number on the answer sheet in the spaces provided unless this has already been done for you.

There are **thirty** questions in this paper. Answer **all** questions. For each question there are four possible answers, **A, B, C** and **D.** Choose the **one** you consider correct and record your choice in **soft pencil** on the separate answer sheet.

Read very carefully the instructions on the answer sheet.

INFORMATION FOR CANDIDATES

Each correct answer will score one mark. A mark will not be deducted for a wrong answer.

Any rough working should be done in this booklet.

This specimen question paper consists of 14 printed pages.

UNIVERSITY *of* CAMBRIDGE
Local Examinations Syndicate

© CIE 2000
SPECQPV1

[Turn Over

2

1 A firm has two variable factors of production, capital (K) and labour (L), that it employs at fixed prices of P_K and P_L per unit respectively. AP_K, AP_L and MP_K, MP_L refer to the average and marginal products of capital and labour.

Which of the following represents the way in which the firm should utilise capital and labour in order to minimise the cost of producing a given output?

A $\dfrac{AP_K}{P_K} = \dfrac{AP_L}{P_L}$ **B** $\dfrac{MP_K}{MP_L} = \dfrac{AP_L}{AP_L}$ **C** $\dfrac{MP_K}{MP_L} = \dfrac{P_L}{P_K}$ **D** $\dfrac{MP_K}{P_K} = \dfrac{MP_L}{P_L}$

2 A rational consumer allocates his expenditure so as to

A equate the marginal utilities obtained from each good.

B equate the total utilities obtained from each good.

C maximise the marginal utility from each good.

D maximise total utility from his expenditure as a whole.

3 An employer currently employs 200 workers.

The marginal cost of hiring an additional worker is $502.

If the employer's current wage bill is $20 000, by how much will the wage paid per worker need to be increased in order to attract one more worker?

A $1.50 **B** $2.00 **C** $2.50 **D** $3.00

4 An individual works 40 hours per week when the wage rate is $7 per hour. When the wage rate is increased to $9 per hour, the individual works 36 hours per week.

What explains the change in the number of hours worked?

A a negative income elasticity of demand for leisure

B an income effect offsetting a substitution effect

C an income effect reinforcing a substitution effect

D a zero income effect

9708/3 Specimen 2001

5   The diagram shows the demand and supply curves in a labour market.

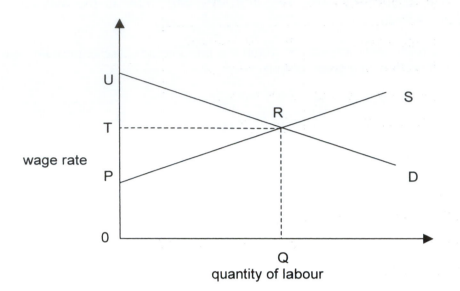

Which areas measure economic rent and transfer earnings, when the market is in equilibrium?

	economic rent	transfer earnings
A	PRU	OQRP
B	PTR	OQRP
C	PTR	UTR
D	PRU	UTR

6   A builder pays $20 000 for a plot of land with planning permission to build up to five houses. If he builds only four houses, the cost of building each house will be $30 000. If he builds five houses the building costs will be $25 000 each.

What is the marginal cost and average total cost when five houses are built?

	marginal cost	average total cost
A	$5 000	$25 000
B	$5 000	$29 000
C	$25 000	$25 000
D	$25 000	$29 000

4

7 As a result of a fall in demand for a product, the price received by a firm falls from $10 to $8. Its output and costs are then as follows :

output/sales	100 units per week
total fixed costs	$500 per week
total variable cost	$400 per week
total costs	$900 per week

What will the firm now do?

A close immediately

B close when its fixed assets need replacing

C continue to operate until its stocks of raw materials are used up

D continue to produce in the long run

8 Given that a particular firm's marginal cost is zero at each level of output, it follows that

A average fixed cost equals average variable costs.

B average total cost equals average fixed costs.

C average total cost equals average variable costs.

D average total cost is constant at each level of output.

9 What would explain why a firm's long-run average cost curve is U-shaped?

A an increase in capacity utilisation as output expands

B changes in technology

C economies and diseconomies of scale

D rising factor prices after a certain level of output

10 The diagrams show the total revenue curves for four different firms.

Which firm is producing under conditions of perfect competition?

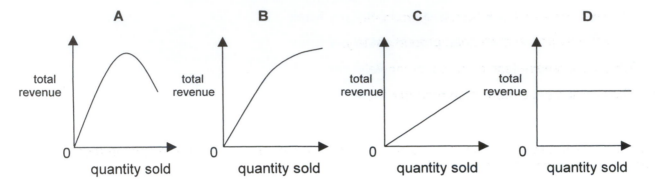

11 The diagram shows the demand curve faced by a firm in a monopolistically competitive industry.

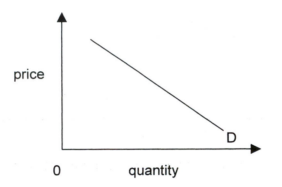

What will be the effect on the position and the slope of the demand curve, if new firms enter the industry?

	position	slope
A	shifts to left	becomes flatter
B	shifts to left	becomes steeper
C	unchanged	becomes flatter
D	unchanged	becomes steeper

12 In an economy with a progressive tax system, there is an increase in before-tax incomes.

What will happen to after-tax incomes?

A They will decrease less than proportionately.

B They will decrease more than proportionately.

C They will increase less than proportionately.

D They will increase more than proportionately.

13 The diagram represents the supply and demand of labour in a market where the government imposes a minimum wage rate of OW.

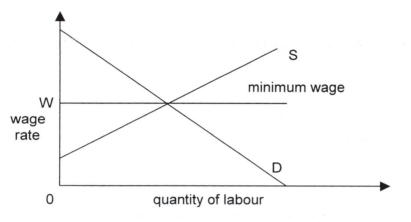

What will happen to the wage rate and to employment, if the supply of labour decreases?

	wage rate	employment
A	increases	decreases
B	increases	unchanged
C	unchanged	decreases
D	unchanged	unchanged

14 The consumption function of an economy with no government sector and no foreign trade is
$C = \$180 + 0.6\,Y$
(where C = aggregate consumption and Y = national income).

If investment expenditure is autonomous and equal to $300, what is the equilibrium level of income?

A $480   **B** $640   **C** $800   **D** $1200

15 In the diagram, a change in the pattern of saving in the economy causes a shift in the consumption function from C_1 to C_2.

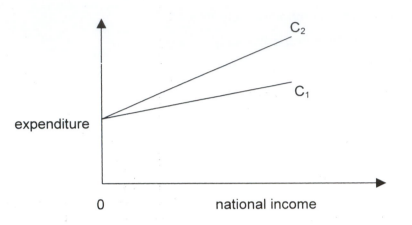

What are the effects of this change on the multiplier and on the marginal propensity to consume?

	multiplier	marginal propensity to consume
A	decreases	increases
B	increases	decreases
C	increases	increases
D	decreases	decreases

8

16 The diagrams show the investment and consumption functions in a closed economy with no government.

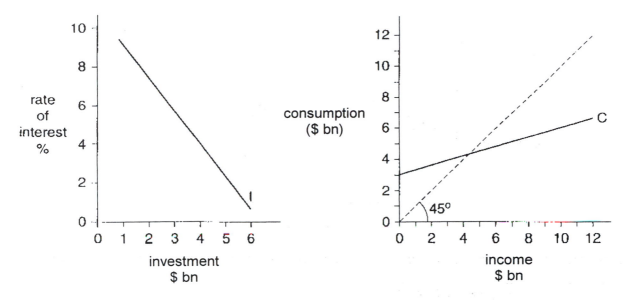

What is the equilibrium level of income if the rate of interest is 4%?

A $3 bn   B $4 bn   C $7 bn   D $10 bn

17 A country has a marginal propensity to import of 0.3 and a marginal propensity to save of 0.1. There are no taxes.

Other things being equal, by how much will a rise of $10 bn in exports increase national income and improve the balance of trade?

	increase in national income	improvement in balance of trade
A	$25 bn	$2.5 bn
B	$25 bn	$7 bn
C	$40 bn	$4 bn
D	$40 bn	$10 bn

18 The following equations relate to an open economy with a government sector.

E = aggregate expenditure on domestically produced goods
C = consumption
I = investment
G = government expenditure
T = taxes
M = imports
X = exports

Which equation is correct?

A E = C + I + G

B E = C + I + G + M − X

C E = C + I + G + X − M

D E = C + I + G − T + M − X

19 In a Keynesian model, why would a $100 million increase in government expenditure on goods and services have a greater impact on aggregate monetary demand than a $100 million **reduction** in tax revenue?

A Consumers spend only part of any extra disposable income.

B Government expenditure does not create wealth.

C The marginal tax rate affects the value of the multiplier.

D The multiplier does not apply to consumer expenditure.

20 What would cause the value of the accelerator to increase?

A a reduction in tax rates

B an increase in the capital-output ratio

C an increase in the saving ratio

D an increase in the marginal propensity to consume

21 In a closed economy with no government, the marginal propensity to consume is 0.9 and the average propensity to consume is 0.8.

What is the value of the multiplier?

A 5 **B** 8 **C** 9 **D** 10

9708/3 Specimen 2001

[Turn over

22 In the diagram Y_E indicates the equilibrium level of income corresponding to different levels of investment.

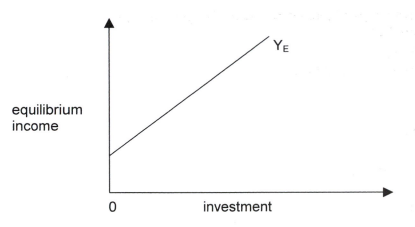

What does the slope of the line Y_E measure?

A   the investment multiplier

B   the marginal propensity to save

C   the rate of growth of investment

D   the rate of growth of national income

23 The diagram shows the saving function in a given economy.

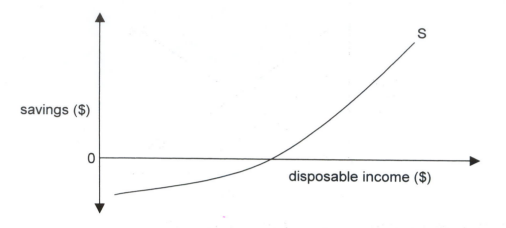

What happens to the marginal propensity to save (MPS) and average propensity to save (APS) as disposable income rises?

	MPS	APS
A	fall	fall
B	fall	rise
C	rise	fall
D	rise	rise

24 What is the average propensity to save?

A   the proportion of an addition to national income that is saved

B   the ratio of saving to national income

C   the ratio of the proportionate change in saving to the proportionate change in national income

D   the relationship between saving and national wealth

25 In the diagram, AD$_1$ and AS$_1$ are an economy's initial aggregate demand and supply curves.

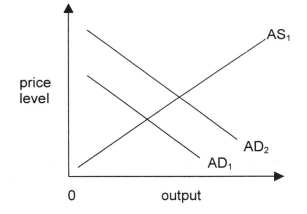

What will cause the aggregate demand curve to shift to AD$_2$?

A   an appreciation of the currency

B   an increase in government spending

C   an increase in interest rates

D   an increase in the price level

26 The diagram shows two different demand curves for holding money balances (LP). The money supply is MS and the initial equilibrium rate of interest is r_1.

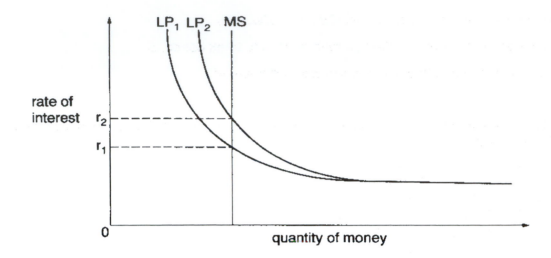

What could have caused a rise in the rate of interest from r_1 to r_2?

A a fall in exports with imports constant

B an increase in savings

C a rise in the price level

D an increase in unemployment

27 Which policy tends to **reduce** both the rate of inflation and a balance of payments deficit?

A an increase in import tariffs

B a reduction in government spending

C a reduction in the level of interest rates

D a rise in the country's currency exchange rate

28 Which of the following is **not** an automatic fiscal stabiliser?

A corporation taxes

B income tax

C state retirement pension

D unemployment benefit

14

29 Other things being equal, what will cause a **reduction** in the stock of money?

A a balance of payments surplus

B an increase in the public's demand for bank advances

C an increase in the public's desired ratio of cash to bank deposits

D an increase in the public sector borrowing requirement

30 What will be the effect of a central bank's purchase of securities on the money supply and on the level of interest rates?

	effect on money supply	effect on interest rates
A	increase	increase
B	increase	reduction
C	reduction	increase
D	reduction	reduction

CAMBRIDGE
INTERNATIONAL EXAMINATIONS

CAMBRIDGE INTERNATIONAL EXAMINATIONS
General Certificate of Education Advanced Level

KEY SHEET FOR MULTIPLE CHOICE
SPECIMEN QUESTION PAPER

Syllabus for first examination in 2002

ECONOMICS	
9708/3 Multiple Choice (Extension) Advanced Level	
MAXIMUM MARK: 30	

UNIVERSITY *of* **CAMBRIDGE**
Local Examinations Syndicate

2

ANSWER KEYS

Item	Key	Syllabus Topic	Skill	Item	Key	Syllabus Topic	Skill
1	D	9	2	16	D	11	2
2	D	9	1	17	A	11	2
3	B	9	1	18	C	11	1
4	B	9	2	19	A	11	2
5	B	9	1	20	B	11	1
6	B	9	1	21	D	11	1
7	B	9	2	22	A	11	1
8	B	9	2	23	D	11	1
9	C	9	1	24	B	11	1
10	C	9	1	25	B	11	1
11	C	9	1	26	C	11	1
12	C	10	2	27	B	13	2
13	A	10	1	28	C	13	1
14	D	11	1	29	C	13	2
15	C	11	2	30	B	13	1

Topics:

8	Basic Economic Ideas (Extension)
9	The Price System and the Theory of the Firm(Extension)
10	Government Intervention in the Price System (Extension)
11	Theory and Measurement in the Macroeconomy (Extension)
12	Macroeconomic Problems (Extension)
13	Macroeconomic Policies (Extension)

Skills:

1	Knowledge and understanding
2	Interpretation and analysis

CAMBRIDGE
INTERNATIONAL EXAMINATIONS

CAMBRIDGE INTERNATIONAL EXAMINATIONS
General Certificate of Education Advanced Level

ECONOMICS

9708/4

PAPER 4 Data Response and Essays (Extension)

2 hours 15 minutes

Additional materials:

Answer paper

Specimen Paper for syllabus for first examination in 2002

Time 2 hours 15 minutes

INSTRUCTIONS TO CANDIDATES

Write your name, Centre number and candidate number in the spaces provided on the answer paper / answer booklet.

Answer **three** questions.

Write your answers on the separate answer paper provided.

If you use more than one sheet of paper, fasten the sheets together.

Section A

Answer this question.

Section B

Answer any **two** questions.

INFORMATION FOR CANDIDATES

The questions in this paper carry equal marks. The number of marks is given in brackets [ ] at the end of each question or part question.

You may answer with reference to your own economy or other economies that you have studied where relevant to the question.

This specimen question paper consists of 4 printed pages.

 UNIVERSITY *of* **CAMBRIDGE**
Local Examinations Syndicate

[Turn Over

2

Section A
Answer this question.

Question 1

Developments in the UK Petrol Retailing Market

Table 1

Who gets how much from a litre of petrol 1 litre of unleaded petrol at 54.7p	
Duty	34.3p
VAT	8.15p
Production cost	8.19p
Retail margin	2.00p
Company margin	2.06p

Table 2

Major Petrol Retailers

Company	type of company	market share %
Esso	P	16
Shell	P	14
BP	P	10
Tesco	S	8.5
Texaco	P	8
Mobil	P	7
Sainsburys	S	6.5
Safeway	S	4
Asda	S	2.5
P = Petrol Company	S = Supermarket	

BP and Mobil link up

Combining BP and Mobil's European fuel and lubricants businesses may be a sound strategy for the oil giants and their shareholders but the outlook for customers and employees is less good.

The plan, which covers 43 countries from Ireland to Russia and Finland to Turkey, means BP will run all of Mobil's petrol stations, which will be re-branded.

For years BP and Mobil wrestled with overcapacity in European oil refining. Their refineries were producing more petrol than they could sell. UK retail petrol sales, for example, have been static at around 8 billion gallons a year.

BP and Mobil stressed that the deal was not a response to Esso's low price campaign, which was launched in July last year.

Nevertheless, there can be no doubt that Esso's brutal attempt to fight its way back up from 16 per cent of the UK market reinforced the case for drastic action. NatWest Securities estimate that the price reductions stimulated by Esso could cut UK petrol retailers' revenue by a staggering £1.4bn this year compared with 1994.

The petrol companies are already facing fierce competition from supermarkets. The BP/Mobil deal is not certain to go ahead because it requires approval from the European Commission.

3

(a) (i) Use Table 1 to calculate the percentage of the price of a litre of unleaded petrol taken in tax. Show your working. [2]

(ii) Explain **two** reasons why the government might have imposed a high level of tax on petrol. [4]

(b) The petrol retailing industry has been described as oligopolistic. What evidence in the data supports this assertion? [4]

(c) Explain **two** possible reasons why supermarkets, which normally sell groceries, have started to sell petrol in recent years. [4]

(d) Discuss the factors the European Commission would be likely to have considered in approving the link between BP and Mobil. [6]

4

Section B
Answer any **two** questions.

2 To what extent are differences in pay explained by differences in productivity? [25]

3 Discuss whether it is necessary to have government intervention in order to achieve an efficient allocation of resources. [25]

4 The Botswana government is moving towards privatisation of state-owned industry as part of its plans to encourage the growth of the economy in the next five years.

    (a) What is meant by 'the growth of the economy'? [12]

    (b) Discuss why a government might consider the policy of privatisation to be beneficial to its economy. [13]

5 **(a)** Explain what is meant by the equilibrium level of national income and describe the multiplier process when national income moves to a new equilibrium. [13]

    (b) How would the outcome of the multiplier process be affected by an increase in the propensity to save? [12]

6 'Many countries have both unemployment and a deficit on their balance of payments. Both of these problems can be cured if the countries produce goods at home whenever they can do so rather than purchase them from abroad.'

Explain this view and examine its economic justification. [25]

7 Discuss what policy measures a government might adopt if the rate of inflation were to become unacceptably high. [25]

Glossary

The CIE syllabus contains a checklist of economic terms and concepts. These are divided into topics included at the Core (Advanced Subsidiary) and Extension (Advanced Level) stages. Terms and concepts introduced at the Core stage may also be examined at the Extension stage.

The checklist has been developed by CIE to provide information to teachers for the effective delivery of the syllabus. When they first occur, terms and concepts in this checklist have been reproduced in bold in the text and aggregated in a box at the end of each chapter.

This glossary provides an alphabetical listing of the most important of these key words – in particular it includes those terms and concepts which are most likely to be used in CIE examination questions and data response material. For the convenience of students, this glossary is divided into Core and Extension sections.

Core stage – economic terms and concepts

absolute advantage – used in the context of international trade to represent a situation where, for a given set of resources, one country can produce more of a particular good than another country.

appreciation – an increase in the value of a currency as measured by the amount of another foreign currency it can buy. Domestic currencies are normally measured against major world currencies, such as the $US, euro or £ sterling.

at market prices – used in measuring national income to denote where information is represented in terms of the prices actually paid by consumers, including any indirect taxes and subsidies.

balance of payments – a record or overall statement of a country's economic transactions with the rest of the world, usually over a year.

balance of trade – the difference between the exports of goods and services and imports of goods and services (visibles). This is a major item in the current account of the balance of payments for all economies.

base date – the period or year whose data are identified as 100 in the construction of an index number.

capital – one of the factors of production; a man-made aid to production, such as industrial machinery, factories and roads.

capital account – part of the balance of payments showing transfers of financial assets between a country and the rest of the world.

change in demand – the outcome of a change in those factors which can be illustrated by a shift in the demand curve. Not to be confused with a …

change in quantity demanded – this term is used to illustrate the outcome of a movement along a demand curve, that is to show the change in quantity demanded when price changes.

comparative advantage – used in the context of international trade to explain why trade can be beneficial even if one country has an absolute advantage in production but where the opportunity costs of production vary compared with another country.

consumer surplus – the difference between the value a consumer places on units consumed and the payment needed to actually make a purchase of a commodity; it is represented by the area under the demand curve and above the price line.

cost–benefit analysis – a technique for assessing the desirability of a particular project, taking into account all of the respective costs and benefits.

cost-push inflation – a situation where inflation is caused by an increase in particular prices or wage rates.

cross elasticity of demand – a numerical measure of the responsiveness of demand for one product following a change in price of a related product; this measure is positive in the case of substitutes and negative for complements.

current account – the most important part of the balance of payments; a record of the trade in goods and services, investment income and current transfers.

deflation – a reduction in economic activity due to a lack of aggregate demand in the economy. Usually indicated through an increase in unemployment and a slowing down in the rate of inflation.

demand-pull inflation – a situation where inflation is caused by an increase in aggregate demand such as an increase in government spending or a reduction in the overall level of taxation in the economy.

demerit goods – any good that has negative externalities associated with it, such as passive smoking or the excessive consumption of alcohol.

depreciation – a decrease in the value of a currency as measured by the amount of another foreign currency it can buy.

devaluation – an explicit decrease in the value of a currency. Similar to depreciation except that depreciation usually occurs gradually through the working of foreign exchange markets.

direct taxation – a tax such as income tax which cannot be passed on to someone else. The real burden of payment falls directly on to the person or firm responsible for paying the tax.

dumping – selling goods in an overseas market at below their cost of production.

economic growth – an increase in the productive potential in an economy which can be illustrated by an outward shift of the production possibility curve.

elastic – a situation where the estimated elasticity of demand value is above 1.

elasticity of demand – the responsiveness of demand to a change in one of the variables affecting demand, such as price, income or the prices of substitutes and compliments.

elasticity of supply – the responsiveness of supply to a change in one of the variables affecting supply, such as price, technological change and the ability of firms to employ more labour.

enterprise – one of the factors of production; it refers to the willingness to take risks in order to achieve business success. This process is managed by an entrepreneur.

equilibrium – a situation in a market where there is no tendency for change under present circumstances.

exports – any goods or services sold to another country.

external benefit – a benefit which accrues to a third party; social benefits exceed private benefits.

externalities – a situation where a third party is affected, negatively or positively, by the decisions or actions which are taken by others.

factor of production – anything that is useful in producing goods and services: land, labour, capital and enterprise are the various factors of production used by economists.

fixed exchange rate – an exchange rate which is pre-determined and cannot be altered.

floating exchange rate – an exchange rate where the rate is determined by the forces of demand and supply in the international currency market.

free trade – a situation where international trade takes place unimpeded by any restrictions; maximises the benefits for the countries involved.

hyperinflation – a very high rate of inflation which results in people losing confidence in money as a medium of exchange.

imports – any goods and services purchased by another country.

incidence of a tax – the extent to which the real burden of a tax is felt by the person or firm paying it.

income elasticity of demand – a numerical measure of the responsiveness of demand following a change in income.

indirect tax – a tax whereby the burden of the tax will be passed on to the consumer from the firm responsible for paying it; value added taxes are a typical example.

inelastic – a situation where the estimated elasticity of demand value is between 0 and ±1.

inflation – a persistent increase in the level of prices in an economy.

interest rate – a payment that has to be made in order to obtain money or a reward for parting with money; in practice there are many interest rates in operation.

investment – the creation of capital goods or of adding to the stock of productive assets in an economy.

invisible balance – the net value of international trade in services as recorded in the current account section of the balance of payments of an economy.

labour – the human resources available in an economy; one of the factors of production.

land – the factor of production which consists of the natural resources available in an economy.

managed floating – an exchange rate system whereby the exchange rate of a currency can vary due to market forces but only between prescribed limits.

market – whenever buyers and sellers get together for the purpose of trade or exchange. Economics recognises many types of market, such as the product market, markets for different types of goods, the labour market, the money market and the foreign exchange market.

merit goods – goods such as health care and education which have positive externalities associated with them and where there is likely to be underconsumption without government intervention.

money – anything which people regularly use to purchase goods and services from each other.

negative externalities – a situation which occurs when there are external costs associated with the production or consumption of a good or service.

non-excludability – a characteristic of public goods whereby it is impossible to stop all from benefiting from the consumption of that good.

non-rivalness – another characteristic of a public good, this time referring to a situation where as more people consume a given good, the benefit to those already consuming is not diminished.

opportunity cost – the amount or cost of any other good or service that could have been obtained instead of a particular good or service; often expressed in terms of the next best alternative.

positive externalities – a situation which occurs when there are external benefits associated with the production or consumption of a good or service.

price elasticity of demand – a numerical measure of the responsiveness of demand to a change in the price of a particular product.

private benefits – the benefits which directly accrue to an individual consumer or firm.

private costs – costs which are directly incurred by the owners of a firm or an individual carrying out a particular activity.

private goods – any good or service which is produced and consumed through the market mechanism and which when used is not available to anyone else. Most consumer goods are private goods.

production possibility curve – a representation of the maximum level of output that an economy can achieve when using its existing resources to the full.

protectionism – processes whereby measures such as quotas and tariffs are applied to safeguard industries or the economy from foreign competition.

public goods – goods which possess the combined characteristics of non-excludability and non-rivalry. Can be provided by the private as well as public sector. Typical examples are roads, national defence, street lights and policing. Consumption is on a collective rather than individual basis.

quotas – a physical restriction on imports into an economy.

revaluation – an explicit increase in the value of a currency relative to others on the foreign exchange market.

social benefits – the total benefits accruing to the community as a whole from a particular action.

social costs – the total costs borne by the community as a whole from a particular action.

specialisation – a situation whereby an economy concentrates on producing certain goods and services, whilst relying on others to provide what it does not produce.

standard of living – a broad measure of the welfare of the population, often measured in terms of consumption per head. GDP per head or real GDP per head is often used by economists to measure it.

subsidy – a payment made by government to producers or consumers to reduce the market price of a good or service.

substitute goods – pairs of goods for which a rise in the price of one increases the demand for the other. Such goods have a positive cross elasticity of demand.

tariffs – a tax imposed by a government on imported goods for protectionist reasons.

terms of trade – a numerical measure of the relationship between export prices and import prices.

trade creation – associated with a customs union and referring to the way in which high-cost domestic production is replaced by more efficient imports from within the customs union.

trade diversion – when joining a customs union, a country may experience trade being moved from a lower cost source outside the customs union to a higher cost supplier within.

unemployment – a broad term used to describe those who are willing and able to work not being able to obtain a job.

visible balance – the net value of international trade in goods as recorded in the current account section of the balance of payments of an economy.

wages – the money which is paid to labour in return for its services.

Extension stage – economic terms and concepts

abnormal profit – profits earned by firms or an industry over and above normal profits; earned by a monopoly in the long run; in other market structures, they are likely to attract new firms to enter an industry, so reverting to normal profits in the long run.

accelerator – a process or model linking investment to changes in output in the economy.

aggregate demand – the total spending on goods and services produced in an economy.

aggregate supply – the total output of an economy.

allocative efficiency – this occurs where the selling price of a product is equal to its marginal cost of production.

automatic stabilisers – changes in fiscal policy unprompted by government which stimulate aggregate demand when an economy is going into recession or which reduce aggregate demand in an expansionary period.

average cost – total costs divided by the quantity produced; it decreases as output increases.

average fixed costs – total fixed costs divided by the quantity produced; it decreases as output increases.

average product – total output divided by the number of workers employed; a measure of productivity.

average revenue – total revenue divided by the quantity that is sold.

average variable cost – total variable costs divided by the quantity produced; it decreases with output but only up to a certain level of output.

barriers to entry – anything that stops new firms entering a particular market; they tend to be more prevalent as the degree of competition in a market decreases.

barriers to exit – anything that prevents firms from leaving a particular market or industry; typically these take the form of a legal or contractual commitment.

cartel – a group of firms which deliberately collude with each other to protect their own interests and well being.

circular flow of income – a simple model of the process by which income flows around an economy.

closed economy – an economy which does not trade or interact with other economies.

concentration ratio – a measure of the extent to which a market is in the hands of a given or particular number of firms; used to measure the degree of oligopoly or monopoly in a market.

consumption – the process by which goods and services are used to satisfy wants.

contestable market – a market structure with few barriers to entry and where there are potential entrants waiting to join if abnormal profits are being earned.

deadweight loss – the reduction in total surplus that results from a market distortion, such as a tax or negative externality.

deflationary gap – the difference between the level of demand in the economy and that needed to achieve a normal level of economic activity, such as full employment.

derived demand – where the demand for a good or service depends upon the final output that is being produced; typical examples are a firm's demand for labour or transport services.

diminishing returns – the consequence of the benefit from an extra unit of input declining as the quantity of input increases; sometimes known as diminishing marginal product.

diseconomies of scale – when long-run average costs start to rise as a consequence of the output of a firm increasing too rapidly.

economic efficiency – where an economy is using scarce resources in the most effective way in order to meet the highest level of wants.

economic rent – a payment made to a factor of production above what is necessary to keep it in its current use.

economies of scale – the benefits to a firm of falling long-run average costs as output expands.

external economies – benefits which accrue to a firm or industry as a consequence of developments directly outside of its control, for example the benefits to be gained through a group of firms being located close together.

fiscal policy – the use of taxation and government spending to influence the economy, involving a change in aggregate demand or, if neutral, a change in the composition of aggregate demand.

fixed costs – costs that are independent of output in the short run.

Gross Domestic Product (GDP) – a measure of total output produced in an economy by activities located in that country.

Gross National Product (GNP) – a measure of total output produced that takes into account the net income of residents from activities carried out abroad as well as in the home economy.

horizontal integration – where two or more enterprises combine activities at the same stage or type of production; for example, transport firms which also own warehouses or food manufacturers producing their own packaging.

immobility of labour – any reason which inhibits the smooth flow of labour in the economy, such as geographical or occupational factors.

increasing returns – a situation where a firm's output is rising proportionately faster than the inputs into the production process.

inflationary gap – a situation where there is excess demand in the economy, above that which is normally needed to ensure full employment.

injections – an autonomous addition to the circular flow of income; examples include government spending, investment and exports.

integration – the process or processes by which individual parts are brought together; can apply in the context of a firm or in the case of economies joining together to form a single economic organisation.

internal economics of scale – the benefits which accrue from within a firm, leading to falling long-run average costs as output expands; typical sources are bulk buying, marketing and technology.

leakages – an autonomous withdrawal from the circular flow of income which does not give rise to a further round of income; typical examples are savings, taxation and imports.

liquidity preference – the factors which determine the amount of money people want to hold.

long run – the time period when the firm can alter all of its factor inputs; all factors of production by definition are variable in the long run.

marginal cost – the addition to total cost when one more unit of output is produced.

marginal physical product – the increase in output that arises from an additional unit of input, for example one more worker.

marginal revenue – the addition to total revenue when one more unit of output is sold.

marginal revenue product – the addition to total revenue as a consequence of employing an additional unit of input, for example one more worker.

market failure – any situation where a free market does not produce the best use of scarce resources; typical examples are where there are externalities present, where there is monopoly power or where it is necessary for public and merit goods to be provided by the government.

monetary policy – the use of interest rates or control of the money supply to influence the level of economic activity.

monopolistic competition – a market structure with a large number of competing sellers and few barriers to entry.

monopoly – a market structure where there is one seller protected by barriers to entry; in practice a monopoly may technically exist where one firm has 25–30 per cent control of a particular market.

monopsony – a market situation where there is only one buyer.

multiplier – a numerical estimate of the relationship between a change in spending and the final change in economic activity; this estimate and the formula by which it is derived can be used to explain the process by which this change takes place.

national income – the total income of residents of a country measured at factor cost, allowing for capital consumption or depreciation.

natural rate of unemployment – the unemployment rate which would prevail in an economy with a constant rate of inflation.

non-price competition – a feature of certain imperfect markets by which firm's compete other than through price cutting; typical examples are branding, customer service and advertising.

normal profit – included in the costs of production of a firm and just sufficient to keep that firm in operation in that industry; a long-run feature of all market structures except for monopoly.

oligopoly – a market structure with only a few firms, each of which has to consider the reaction of competitors when making price changes; it can also apply to a market structure with a small number of large firms and large number of small firms.

open economy – an economy which is involved in trade and interacts with other economies.

perfect competition – a market structure used by economists to compare other theoretical and real world market structures; has the characteristics of a large number of buyers and sellers acting as price takers.

Phillips curve – a curve showing the relationship between the rate of increase of wages and unemployment in an economy; named after its inventor.

price discrimination – a feature of monopoly markets whereby the monopolist seeks to segment the market by charging different prices to different customers for the same product.

privatisation – the sale of publicly owned businesses, assets or services to the private sector; also includes deregulation and contracting out of former public sector activities.

productive efficiency – this occurs where production is at the lowest point on a firm's lowest average cost curve.

profit – the difference between the revenue and costs of a firm.

profit maximisation – assumed to be the usual objective of a firm in economic theory; it occurs at the output where marginal cost is equal to marginal revenue in all market structures.

progressive taxation – a tax where the revenue collected rises more than proportionately to income; income tax is a good example.

reflation – a situation where the government explicitly seeks to increase the level of economic activity through expansionary fiscal and/or monetary policies.

regressive taxation – a tax where the ratio of tax paid to income falls as income rises; the most regressive taxes are those which are a fixed sum or are levied at a fixed rate, for example poll taxes and value added taxes.

saving – the difference between income and consumption.

short run – the time period when a firm is unable to alter factor inputs except for one, for example labour.

supernormal profits – used in the same way as abnormal profits but usually only in the case of perfect competition.

supply-side economics – a general term used to explain how policies affecting the total output of the economy actually operate.

sustainability – the outcome of any policy which has the objective of safeguarding the interests of future generations without compromising the present generation; it is also used in the context of economic growth to denote a situation where a level output can be contained indefinitely without depleting an economy's stock of resources.

transfer earnings – the amount that any factor of production can expect to earn in its best alternative use.

variable costs – costs which are directly related to the level of output of a firm.

vertical integration – where a firm combines two or more stages of production normally operated by separate firms; for example, a farmer growing crops and selling them in his own shop, a petroleum refining company owning its own filling stations or a car manufacturer having its own network of retail sales outlets.

withdrawals – the same as leakages from the circular flow of income.

Answers to selected self-assessment tasks

Below are some suggested answers to a few of the self-assessment tasks contained in the book. These answers are for guidance – you should appreciate that in some cases other answers are possible. Please ask your teacher for assistance.

Section 1
Choices facing an economy (p. 28)

If point *p* was chosen, then gross investment is less than capital consumption. Net investment is therefore negative. The capital stock in this economy will decline and the production possibilities will diminish. The PPC will therefore shift inwards. Although the present standard of living is high the future standard of living will be less.

If point *q* was chosen, gross investment would equal capital consumption. Net investment is therefore zero. The capital stock and production possibilities are unchanged. The PPC maintains its current position. The future standard of living will remain at its present level.

If point *r* is chosen, gross investment would exceed capital consumption. Net investment is therefore positive and production possibilities will increase in the future. The PPC will shift outwards from the origin. This choice has reduced the standard of living at present as fewer consumer goods have been produced; the benefits will be seen in the future as future generations enjoy a higher standard of living with the increased capital stock accumulated in the present time period.

All the above assumes no other factors affect the position of the PPC.

Section 2
The demand curve (p. 38)

1 5,500 PCs
2 $1,930

3 'Ceteris paribus', that is, all other factors, such as income, the price of related products and our attitudes towards PCs, remain the same.

The supply curve (p. 43)

1 2,500 PCs
2 $860
3 'Ceteris paribus', that is, any other supply-influencing factors – such as the costs associated with supplying the product, the size, structure and nature of the industry or government policy – remain unchanged.
4 Advantages – a very simple representation
   Disadvantages – not always easy to accurately read off price and quantity data

Price elasticity of demand (p. 52)

1 Branded products in general, such as Coca Cola, are likely to have a relatively low or inelastic price elasticity of demand. Producers try to build up a brand image in order to protect the status of their products. To some though Coca Cola and Pepsi Cola may be seen as substitutes and therefore an increase in the price of one may cause consumers to switch to the other. The broader group of products will have a more elastic price elasticity of demand (soft drinks and sweet products). Fuel has no close substitutes and is therefore likely to have an inelastic price elasticity of demand.
2 All PED estimates are negative; that is, an increase in price will lead to a fall in demand or vice versa. Mail order ties have the most elastic demand, whilst ties sold from fashion stores have a low inelastic price elasticity of demand. For independent retailers, any reduction in prices is met with an equal increase in demand or vice versa.

Section 3
Methods of government intervention (p. 77)

(a) Regulation: the government has used legislation to limit pollution from vehicles. In this case the government regulates the quantity of pollution produced by a vehicle's exhaust emissions. Regulation is used to correct for a market failure owing to negative externalities.

(b) Regulation: the government has used legislation to fix prices. In this case the government fixes the minimum price of labour or the wage rate. Minimum wage rates may be used to redistribute income or to overcome market failure caused by uneven power in the labour market (employers have more power than low-paid workers).

(c) Financial intervention: higher tax rates on petrol are used to discourage consumption of leaded petrol. In this case the government is keen to stop the production of leaded petrol which causes more pollution than unleaded petrol. Thus this type of financial intervention is used to reduce negative externalities.

(d) Financial intervention: free eye tests are the same as a total subsidy. They are used to encourage pensioners to have their eyes tested on a regular basis. This may be to correct a market failure – pensioners are unable to value the importance of frequent eye tests – or they may be free for equity reasons.

(e) Regulation: the government uses legislation to impose a minimum standard of driving on the community. This is intended to ensure that all drivers show a minimum competence to drive a vehicle. It corrects for two potential market failures: external costs and imperfect information.

(f) Regulation: legislation is imposed to restrict the purchase of lottery tickets by age. Some people argue that young people are unable to correctly value the costs and benefits of addictive products, such as gambling, and thus need protecting against them. Thus the government is protecting young people against market failure due to imperfect information.

(g) Income transfers: job seekers allowance is a form of transfer of income from taxpayers to those seeking work. One reason for this intervention is to protect against loss of income due to unemployment.

However, if the individual has large amounts of savings then it is argued that they do not require as much protection against loss of earnings as they have a source of income on which they can draw.

(h) State production: in this case the state is producing education by providing both the building and the staff to run the schools. Alternatively the government could have used financial intervention by providing the finance for the schools to be built privately and staffed by a private education 'company'. The reasons for intervention of this type in education are varied and will include market failure owing to external benefits from education not being valued by private markets. Market failure might also result from imperfect information because both parents and students are unable to correctly value the private costs and benefits of education. Finally government may intervene to produce education for reasons of fairness or equity, meaning that all children have an equal and fair access to education regardless of their parents' income.

Section 4
Free trade is fair (p. 86)

1 Fair trade is used to describe a situation whereby developing economies are paid a 'fair' price for their products by importers in developed economies. This fair price would be above the prevailing world market price for the products involved, such as coffee, tea, cocoa, bananas and so on.

A small number of manufacturers and charities operate a fair trade policy. This involves products being labelled as 'fair trade' and which are sold to consumers at a price which will provide a stable, longer-term income for the farmers and producers. In some cases, MNCs such as Nestlé, have agreed to pay a reasonable minimum price, in part to secure supplies but also to show social responsibility in their dealings with small producers lacking market power. However, it could be argued that the 'fair trade' label is a marketing device to sell more goods to a seemingly caring consumer. The world price of coffee especially needs to rise substantially if many farmers in Columbia and Tanzania are to stay in production, let alone support their families in a reasonable way.

2 The UK, like all other EU countries, has to operate within the regulations of the EU customs union. For agricultural goods, some preference is given to the products of former colonial countries (Lomé Convention) but in general the EU seeks to protect the interests of its farmers, seemingly to the detriment of the economic welfare of many developing countries.

EU policy is particularly protectionist towards those products which the EU can produce itself, such as certain types of fruit, meat and dairy products. The Common External Tariff tends to be high for these, as it is for many manufactured goods from developing economies. Self-interest, for employment reasons particularly, tends to override the objective of helping developing economies progress through trade development.

Less protectionist measures could, if applied, lead to a much more efficient allocation of resources as advocated through the principle of comparative advantage.

Section 6
Exchange rate changes (p. 119)

1 (a) $400 (an increase of $100)
  (b) £6,000 (a decrease of £2,000)
  (c) The appreciation in value of the £ sterling against the US dollar, has made UK exports relatively more expensive and imports relatively cheaper. The simple deduction is that the volume of UK exports of cashmere sweaters would fall and the import of US cars would increase.

This is an oversimplification because it does not take into account the respective price elasticities of demand. The demand for cashmere sweaters in the UK is likely to be price inelastic – such sweaters are luxury items and their demand is unlikely to be price sensitive. The price elasticity of demand for US cars is likely to be more price elastic, as there are many manufacturers of cars in the EU and rest of the world and price competition is prevalent.

So the change in the volume of demand will depend heavily on the price sensitivity of the product.

Section 7
US balance of payments (p. 125)

(a) The description implies that the balance of trade is in deficit, that the US is importing more goods than it is exporting. The 'booming markets' is indicative that the US is experiencing a consumer spending boom; domestic savings are low.

In contrast, the income account is strongly in surplus. Investment is flowing into the US. The dollar appears to be strong, hence this strong position.

A depreciation of the dollar could be expected to reduce the deficit on the balance of trade but also reduce the flow of foreign investment into the US.

(b) An obvious policy would be to dampen down domestic demand by various fiscal and monetary measures. Direct tax rates on private incomes and company profits could be increased; taxes on imported goods especially could increase, alongside a more general increase in expenditure taxes. The Federal Reserve Bank might also increase interest rates to cut demand. The consequences though may not be politically acceptable – increased unemployment, reduced business confidence and possibly a modest increase in the rate of inflation are electorally unpopular.

Alternative policies, which the US has keenly supported, are those which seek to reduce the volume (and value) of imports. Increased tariffs (see also above), import quotas and other measures designed to make it difficult for exporters to sell to the US market are likely to reduce demand – they are very unpopular in the world trade arena, especially because of their effects on developing economies. US administrations though have seen such policies as being more acceptable politically than those which reduce domestic aggregate demand.

Section 8
Marks and Sparks shuts up shop in Europe (p. 131)

(a) Productive efficiency in the case of a firm occurs where a firm is producing at the lowest point on its lowest average cost curve. Both of these situations must occur at the same time.

For the economy, productive efficiency takes place when it is operating on its production possibility curve. Here, production is maximised for the resources that are available and which are being fully utilised.

(b) In a perfectly competitive market, in the long run, the firm and the industry are producing where average costs are at a minimum. The output is therefore that associated with the lowest point on the AC curve. In all other market structures, there is productive inefficiency, with firms and the industry producing above the minimum AC point.

The retail market is not perfectly competitive – it is either an oligopoly or monopolistically competitive, depending on how the market is defined. Branding is strong; the Marks and Spencer brand has for many years been a market leader, particularly in the clothing and food retail markets. The article indicates that Marks and Spencer's European stores outside the UK are unprofitable. This is commensurate with operating above the minimum point on the AC curve and at a level of sales well below that necessary to maximise profits.

(c) Marks and Spencer are taking the following actions:
- closing unprofitable stores,
- selling off its US interests and franchising its Hong Kong operation,
- closing its mail order operation,
- cutting back on head office staff.

All of these measures are designed to cut costs, at the expense of sales. The outcome should be a smaller, leaner business, hopefully operating much closer to the minimum point of its AC curve in order to remain competitive in a fiercely competitive market.

(Note: parts (b) and (c) could be re-visited after study of section 9.)

Section 9
Demand and supply of labour (p. 146)

1 The demand for labour is a derived demand. A fall in the demand for labour could therefore be due to a fall in demand for the products that are being produced. Typical examples could be typewriters (superseded by word processors), cheap processed foods (superseded by more healthy alternatives) or formal types of clothing (superseded by jeans and casual wear). The effect of the fall in demand is to shift the demand curve for labour to the left. The wage level will fall, as will the quantity of labour which is being demanded.

The demand for labour could also fall through technological change and innovation, with fewer workers being needed to produce the same amount of output.

(Now draw the diagram and see if you can think of some more examples.)

2 The supply of labour available for an industry could fall for various reasons, such as a fall in population, a lack of trained workers, an outward migration or an unwillingness to work in that particular industry. The effect of this fall in supply is to increase the wage rate for those still in employment, but with fewer workers being employed.

(Now draw the diagram and see if you can think of some more examples.)

3 If you have drawn this diagram correctly, you will see that the overall effect is likely to be one of no change in the wage rate but an increase in employment. In other words, the shift of D and the shift of S cancel each other out as far as wages are concerned.

The assumption above is that there are equal shifts in D and S. If this is not the case, then the final outcome will depend on whether the shift in D is greater or less than the shift in S. If the shift in D is greater than the shift in S, the wage will be higher than W_1; alternatively, if the shift in S is greater than the shift in D, the wage will be in equilibrium below W_1.

(You may like to draw diagrams that illustrate the situations described in the last paragraph.)

Mergers in the pharmaceutical industry (p. 159)

(a) According to the article, the Glaxo Wellcome and Smith Kline Beecham merger has come about because of:
- the need to create a large company due to expiring patents on products (which will result in more competition from other producers) and a slowing of growth in the world market for pharmaceutical products;
- the opportunity to market a broader range of pharmaceutical products;

◆ the opportunity to create the world's largest pharmaceutical company.

It could also be argued that the merger will provide an opportunity to benefit from economies of scale and to protect the UK industry from possible US takeover aggression.

(b) Consumers may benefit through:

◆ cost savings due to the benefits to be gained from economies of scale;

◆ a wider product range, covering a much broader range of medical conditions;

◆ longer-term benefits in the form of new products as a result of increased investment in product research and development.

(c) Smaller companies seem to be in a position to benefit. They could have new business opportunities as smaller, more specialist producers of certain types of drug and markets where the size of market is still small and as yet not worthwhile from the giant producer's standpoint. There may also be less pressure on them to spend huge sums of money on marketing and sales promotion – the internet for example could be used to promote sales, so reducing development costs.

OPEC and the supply of oil (p. 175)

(a) Overall, OPEC is technically a monopoly with 40 per cent of world production and 60 per cent control of international sales of oil. Although clearly not 100 per cent, both measures of monopoly power are above the 25 per cent market share regarded as a given dominant market share. It can also be described as collusive oligopoly as it has 11 members who agree to fix production levels in order to strongly influence the world price of crude oil. Regular meetings of OPEC determine production quotas. The strength of the cartel is dependent upon no member 'breaking ranks'.

(b) The logic is simple supply and demand economics. If output (supply) is reduced and demand remains the same (or increases) then the world price of crude oil will increase. As the article indicates, this is a low risk strategy on the part of OPEC as the price elasticity of demand is low (inelastic) and, as yet, there are no close substitutes for oil.

(c) The future demand for OPEC oil could reduce over time because of:

◆ an economic downturn (more short term);

◆ technological advance, which sees oil replaced by a cheaper, more efficient alternative, ideally from a renewable resource;

◆ improved energy conservation, smaller vehicles and other ways of reducing demand;

◆ increased production from a non-OPEC producer or an OPEC producer withdrawing from the cartel.

(d) Although petrol companies have little control over the retail price of petroleum, they can control their costs and the prices which they sell to retail outlets. The high taxes on petrol are normally imposed on the price at which petrol is sold by companies to filling stations. The petroleum companies can also boost profits by controlling retail outlets of petroleum and, as well as fuel, offering a wide range of convenience products for sale at these outlets. Although profit margins may be low, total profit is not because of the huge volume of sales involved.

Section 10
Jam today, jam tomorrow (p. 184–5)

1 (a) Traffic congestion is a classic example of market failure as a result of negative externalities being present. These externalities include additional travel time and costs for motorists using congested urban roads, delays to buses and bus passengers and additional pollution from stationary and slow-moving traffic.

Market failure arises where the market does not allocate resources (such as roadspace) efficiently (by allowing traffic to flow freely). Consequently, social costs exceed private costs.

(d) In theory the government could introduce a tax which would be set at a rate which would equate social costs and private costs. This tax would be paid by users of vehicles in congested urban areas (see figure 10.2). This would be consistent with the 'polluter pays' approach. The example of Singapore referred to in the extract is a relatively sophisticated way of trying to achieve this ideal. A cruder means would take the form of a toll or flat rate entry charge at peak periods.

Section 11
The Singapore economy (p. 214)

1 An open economy is one which carries out transactions with the rest of the world. These normally include trade in goods and services and, in a global context, flows of capital or foreign direct investment into and out of the economy. The term could also be used to describe an economy where there are legal two-way flows of labour.

2 The three reasons given have a downward effect on aggregate demand. Singapore is a major producer of electronic goods, so any downturn in the world economy, particularly where this is due to the US economy slowing down, will reduce demand for this important export. The economic situation in Asia will similarly have an effect on the demand for electronic goods in Singapore's neighbouring countries. A further factor is that in general the demand for certain types of electronic good (such as mobile telephones) is falling as market saturation is being reached, especially in developed economies.

3 As well as exports, Singapore's aggregate expenditure is affected by changes in any of the other components of aggregate demand. For example:

- An increase in government spending would in turn increase aggregate expenditure. This spending could be on transport, housing, health and so on. The likely effects would be to trigger off a series of multiplier effects in the economy.

- An increase in foreign inward investment would also increase aggregate expenditure. This investment could be in the financial services sector for example. Again, it would work its way around the economy through the multiplier process.

Section 12
UK unemployment (p. 242)

(a) Technological unemployment – India is constructing call centres which are technologically more advances than those in the UK.

(b) An increase in government spending would be unlikely to reduce such technological unemployment because its cause is outside the long-term scope and control of the UK government. In the short term, an increase in government spending could provide unemployment benefit. Longer term it is the responsibility of the private sector to assess whether to invest in state of the art call centres and so compete in a positive way with similar providers in India.

Section 13

The Japanese economy (p. 253)

1 Interest rates are normally well above 0 per cent in order to encourage savings. As the article indicates, as no interest is being paid on savings in banks, Japanese people are now holding their cash at home. There seems little point in having money in a bank which is struggling to survive.

2 *Consumers* – there is every incentive to borrow money to spend on consumer goods but, as prices are falling, there seems little point – if they wait, the goods they want could be even cheaper.
Businesses – a 0 per cent interest rate means that the cost of borrowing is irrelevant. In theory, firms should be investing extensively and using the opportunity to restructure.
Banking system – this does not function effectively, with banks not being able to generate an appropriate return on their banking assets. The big increase in private cash holdings will have had a substantial impact on bank liquidity.

3 The article briefly mentions demand-side policies, although it is dismissive of the vast public works expenditure that has been made. Other fiscal measures could include indirect and direct tax reductions, such as measures to get businesses to invest in new capital equipment. The key to ending the recession though must lie with the huge private sector MNCs; investment by them is necessary to get the economy on a better footing. An improvement in business confidence across the global economy, particularly in SE Asia, would also help to kickstart an economy that has been in the doldrums for the past ten years.

Index